ENCYCLOPEDIA OF
SUPREME COURT
QUOTATIONS

ENCYCLOPEDIA OF

SUPREME COURT

QUOTATIONS

CHRISTOPHER A. ANZALONE

EDITOR

M.E.Sharpe
Armonk, New York
London, England

Library of Congress Cataloging-in-Publication Data

Anzalone, Christopher A., 1963-
    Encyclopedia of Supreme Court quotations / Christopher A.
Anzalone.
        p. cm.
    Includes index.
    ISBN 0-7656-0485-X (alk. paper)
    1. United States. Supreme Court—Encyclopedias. 2. Law—United
States Quotations. I. Title.
KF8742.A35A59   2000
347.73' 26—dc21
                                                            99-41504
                                                                CIP

Printed in the United States of America

The paper used in this publication meets the minimum requirements of
American National Standard for Information Sciences
Permanence of Paper for Printed Library Materials,
ANSI Z 39.48-1984.

BM (c)   10   9   8   7   6   5   4   3   2   1

Dedication

This volume is dedicated to three very important people: Karen, my wife, whose good humor gave me the inspiration to read just one more Supreme Court case—day after day, night after night; Patricia, my mother, who was the first to instill in me my love for the law; and Anthony, my father, who was unable to see this effort through to its conclusion, but would undoubtedly be pleased with its logic, perspective, and evenhanded approach.

. . . to do our utmost to make clear and understandable
the reasons for deciding cases as we do.
—*Douglas v. Jeanette 319 U.S. 157 (1943)*
Associate Justice Robert H. Jackson, concurring

It is a joy to take my pen in hand and endeavor to write for
the gracious and civilized society to which free men aspire.
—*U.S. Supreme Court Associate Justice Frank Murphy*
to Henry M. Bates, former dean of the Michigan Law School
(December 25, 1943)

If the Supreme Court is ever composed of imprudent men or bad
citizens, the Union may be plunged into anarchy or civil war.
—*Alexis de Tocqueville*

Contents

Preface   xi

Acknowledgment   xv

   1. The Givers of Law   3

   2. The Enforcers   17

   3. The Least Dangerous Branch   22

   4. The Sacred Parchment   54

   5. Expectations and Deliverance   75

   6. The Good of the Fifty   101

   7. Due Process and Equal Protection   113

   8. Opinions, Dissents, and Recorders   129

   9. In the Beginning   152

 10. Liberty, Freedom, Happiness   167

 11. The Arrest . . . The Trial . . . The Punishment   190

 12. The Global Community   224

 13. Everything Else   235

Appendices

   A. The Constitution of the United States of America   249

   B. Table of Cases with Case Summaries   267

   C. Table of Justices and Decisions by Justices   363

   D. Keyword Index   367

Preface

The symbolic language selected by our nation's leaders—historical and contemporary—has a profound impact on the evolution of our democracy. Benjamin Franklin, Thomas Jefferson, and Alexander Hamilton created the nation. So did Chief Justice John Marshall. Abraham Lincoln fought to preserve a nation in turmoil. So did Justice John Marshall Harlan. Woodrow Wilson and Franklin Delano Roosevelt pushed the nation to its rightful place on the world stage. So did Justice Robert Jackson. Martin Luther King warned us that freedom and liberty could truly be achieved only by acceptance and equality. So did Justices Hugo Black, Thurgood Marshall, and William Brennan. It should be clear that the members of the Supreme Court have had a significant impact on American history. The words of the Court are, in fact, theories of government. Collectively, the passages included in this book, and those that are not, constitute the grand debate about the goals of democracy and its limitations, successes, and failures. Understanding the value of the Supreme Court is crucial to understanding our history. The Supreme Court is but one branch in our federal system. It "competes" with the presidency, the Congress, and the states. The other branches determine what is good. The judiciary, headed by the Court, determines what is right. The purpose of this book, therefore, is to give life to this very powerful, often misunderstood branch of federal government. The Court, its mechanisms for delivering its decrees, and the personalities of the members have been shrouded in mystery. For the most part, this mystery has been created and perpetuated by the Court itself. Its decisions, crafted in arcane, dusty language, are discernible only by the academic and legal elite. Although it is the only branch of government that provides painstakingly detailed and written analysis for most of their edicts, the specialized language ultimately is a disservice. For the government as a whole, as well as its integral components, must be understood first before it can be appreciated, accepted, and revered. This book will, in a nutshell, demonstrate that the Court is a human institution. The Court struggles with its mission. For the scores of steps it takes to force itself and the nation it is charged to protect into the future, there are occasional missteps and lapses, some accidental, others calculated. It has been a small (and fairly homogeneous) community of individuals (110 men, 2 women) who have presided—generally nine at a time—over the nation's top court.

Several criteria were used to select the passages that appear on the pages that follow. Selection, however, was not as difficult as not selecting. Each year the Court decides hundreds of legal controversies. The Court has been in existence for over two hundred years. Decisions generate an opinion of the Court (majority opinion); depending upon agreement of the nine members of the Court, an outcome may also generate a flurry of concurring opinions and dissents—all of which constitute the universe of potential excerpts. The calculus is staggering; we could have easily selected a hundred thousand quotes. Is it not an inspiring notion that the total universe of excerpts is so overwhelming that great efforts were made to pare the number down to a manageable 900? This question in itself should fill the reader and citizen with pride in the Court's place in American history.

For the most part, the only criterion used in the selection process was the quotability of the passage. Inherent beauty, literary quality, profound philosophy—these were the intersecting points determining what to include and what to omit. Arbitrary as this trinity may be, the selections are typically not the rationale of a given decision, rather the obiter dicta generally favored. An intensive effort has been made to avoid excessively legalistic or complex passages. The quotes should be able to stand on their own. I would like to think the selections follow Chief Justice Charles Evans Hughes's posit on "the four corners of good judicial craftsmanship"—accuracy, clarity, conciseness, power.

Like Thomas Jefferson's *Dialogue Between Head and Heart*, there should be dual consequences of each passage. On the visceral side, if there is an instinctive raising of the reader's eyebrow and

a thoughtful "hmm," then inclusion of the quote was appropriate. However, if the reader frowns in disbelief at the passage, then we are equally pleased with our choice. If, on some cerebral plane, the passage stimulates some unfulfilled intellectual appetite and the reader strives to consume the entire decision, then the selection was appropriate.

The reader will not agree with every statement. From the outset, such motivation was never our intention. This volume will be a failure if our readers consider it an exploration of one or two philosophies. It is not a book solely about the federalist or nationalist or states'-rightist or judicial-activist or original-intention perspective. Nor will it trumpet one justice as being any more important than another. (However, it is a simple numbers game. Some Justices have contributed more opinions, concurrences, or dissents than their contemporaries and are thus represented more often.) On the contrary, the aim of selecting passages in totality was to visit various issues from a 360-degree (or at least as many as the Court has offered) perspective. Looking at the Court's opinions, either concurrences or dissents (or, as Chief Justice Charles Evans Hughes is known to have remarked, dissents are "the brooding spirit of the law, to the intelligence of a future day") will allow the reader to gravitate toward certain jurisprudential views and reject others. It is to be hoped that the rejections will not be made blind, but will result from some form of contemplation. In short, the ultimate goal of this volume is to provoke critical thinking about the Nation's history and its possible paths for its future.

The mechanics of the book are as follows. The passages are grouped into thirteen chapters. Chapter 1 is on the legislative branch. Chapter 2 is on the executive branch. Chapter 3 is on the judiciary; here you will find clues to how courts and their judges should and do decide cases. Chapter 4 is about constitutional law. Chapter 5 is about the history and political role of the country. Chapter 6 covers states' rights; here you will find excerpts about the demise and rebirth of the Tenth Amendment. Chapter 7 is based on the Fourteenth Amendment, in particular the use of, and controversy about, the doctrines of due process and equal rights. Chapter 8 is about free speech and free press. Chapter 9 covers freedom of religion. Chapter 10 provides evidence of how the Court conceptualizes other personal freedoms and liberties. Chapter 11 delves into the arena of criminal law and criminal procedure. Chapter 12 explores how international events influence American institutions; for example, you will see some of the Supreme Court's decisions on the military, war, treaties, immigration, and deportation included in this chapter; moreover, insurrections, civil war, and Indian affairs are included. Finally, chapter 13, as its title indicates, is about "Everything Else." Here you will find passages about various substantive legal areas—family law, wills, torts, and so forth.

Each passage, in accordance with standard legal citation, includes the name of the case, primary citation, year, author, and kind of decision (concurring or dissenting—otherwise it is an opinion for the Court). The reader must be cognizant of the fact that the recognized author of the citation may not be the actual author of all of the passage or even of a portion thereof. The simple reality of authoring decisions is that as a political process, it is a collaborative practice. To sustain support, justices often provide passages to the assigned author for inclusion. Additionally, passages may be taken from legal briefs, law review articles, or historical/philosophical statements. Finally, much has been written about the role of law clerks assigned to the justices. The reader must be forewarned that perhaps the selected passage bears the imprimatur of a justice but in fact may have its birth elsewhere.

Four appendices provide a contextual framework for the excerpts. The United States Constitution is provided in full in the first appendix. Its purpose is simply to remind the reader what the quotes are expounding.

The second appendix is a table of cases. Various excerpts from a decision may be included in different chapters. This appendix will allow the reader to experience quickly the 360-degree philosophy of this book. The table of cases also includes a brief history (relevancy and outcome) of each case for those researchers curious about the nature and merit of any specific legal dispute.

The third appendix is an index of Supreme Court justices. Historically, the Court (like the presidency and Congress) has three kinds of members. At the pinnacle are the American legends (John Marshall and Oliver Wendell Holmes Jr., to name just two) who have been leaders in the charting of American democracy, not just the legal system. Justices in the next tier have contributed to the growth and development of the American legal system. The third level belongs to those justices who have contributed little to the understanding or direction of the Constitution. (Excepting Marshall and Holmes, this book draws no conclusions about where a particular justice falls.) This appendix will allow the reader to find quickly all the excerpts of a given justice.

The fourth appendix is a keyword index to assist the researcher in targeting specific concepts and how the Court has pondered them. The terms and phrases that constitute the keyword index also correspond to the keywords that follow each excerpt.

Acknowledgment

I would like to thank the gang at M.E. Sharpe, especially my editor, Peter Coveney, his assistant Esther Clarke, and my production editor, Eileen Maass.

ENCYCLOPEDIA OF

SUPREME COURT
QUOTATIONS

1. The Givers of Law

As the Constitution begins, so too does this volume. Article I is the detailing of legislative powers; Chapter 1 is the constitutional justifications of the legislative branch. The structures, functions, and responsibilities of Congress are the particular focus of this chapter.

Justice Samuel Chase
Turner v. Bank of North America,
4 U.S. 8, 10 (1799)
The notion has frequently been entertained, that the federal courts derive their judicial power immediately from the constitution; but the political truth is, that the disposal of the judicial power, (except in a few specified instances) belongs to congress. If congress has given the power to this Court, we posess [sic] it, not otherwise: and if congress has not given the power to us, or to any other Court, it still remains at the legislative disposal. Besides, congress is not bound and it would, perhaps, be inexpedient, to enlarge the jurisdiction of federal Courts, to every subject, in every form, which the constitution might warrant.
Keywords: *Congress, Federal courts, Judicial authority, Judiciary, Jurisdiction, Legislative authority, Political truth*

Chief Justice John Marshall
United States v. Fisher
6 U.S. 358, 390 (1805)
Where rights are infringed, where fundamental principles are overthrown, where the general system of the laws is departed from, the legislative intention must be expressed with irresistible clearness to induce a court of justice to suppose a design to effect such objects.
Keywords: *Court of justice, Fundamental principles, Legislative intent, Rights*

Chief Justice John Marshall
United States v. Peters,
9 U.S. 115, 136 (1809)
If the legislatures of the several states may, at will, annul the judgments of the courts of the United States, and destroy the rights acquired under those judgments, the constitution itself becomes a solemn mockery; and the nation is deprived of the means of enforcing its laws by the instrumentality of its own tribunals. So fatal a result must be deprecated by all; and the people of Pennsylvania, not less than the citizens of every other state, must feel a deep interest in resisting principles so destructive of the union, and in averting consequences so fatal to themselves.
Keywords: *Citizens, Constitution, Judiciary, Legislative review, Legislatures, Rights, States, Union*

Justice William Johnson
United States v. Hudson,
11 U.S. 32, 34 (1812)
The legislative authority of the union must make an act a crime, affix a punishment to it, and declare the court that

3

shall have jurisdiction of the offence.
Keywords: *Crime, Judicial authority, Jurisdiction, Legislation, Legislative authority, Punishment*

Chief Justice John Marshall
McCulloch v. Maryland,
7 U.S. 316, 421 (1819)
. . . we think the sound construction of the constitution must allow to the national legislature that discretion, with respect to the means by which the powers it confers are to be carried into execution, which will enable that body to perform the high duties assigned to it, in the manner most beneficial to the people. Let the end be legitimate, let it be within the scope of the constitution, and all means which are appropriate, which are plainly adapted to that end, which are not prohibited, but consist with the letter and spirit of the constitution, are constitutional . . .
Keywords: *Constitutional construction, Constitutional spirit, Legislative authority, Legislature, Necessary and Proper Clause*

Justice Bushrod Washington
Houston v. Moore,
18 U.S. 1, 23 (1820)
If, in a specified case, the people have thought proper to bestow certain powers on Congress as the safest depositary of them, and Congress has legislated within the scope of them, the people have reason to complain that the same powers should be exercised at the same time by the State legislatures. To subject them to the operation of two laws upon the same subject, dictated by distinct wills, particu-

larly in a case inflicting pains and penalties, is, to my apprehension, something very much like oppression, if not worse. In short, I am altogether incapable of comprehending how two distinct wills can, at the same time, be exercised in relation to the same subject, to be effectual, and at the same time compatible with each other. If they correspond in every respect, then the latter is idle and inoperative; if they differ, they must, in the nature of things, oppose each other, so far as they do differ. If the one imposes a certain punishment for a certain offence, the presumption is, that this was deemed sufficient, and, under all circumstances, the only proper one. If the other legislature impose a different punishment, in kind or degree, I am at a loss to conceive how they can both consist harmoniously together.
Keywords: *Congress, Congressional authority, Legislation, Oppression, People, Power, Punishment, States*

Justice Bushrod Washington
Ogden v. Saunders,
25 U.S. 213, 270 (1827)
It is but a decent respect due to the wisdom, integrity, and patriotism of the legislative body, by which any law is passed, to presume in favor of its validity, until its violation of the Constitution is proved beyond a reasonable doubt.
Keywords: *Integrity, Judicial review, Legislature, Patriotism, Wisdom*

Justice Samuel Nelson,
Dred Scott v. Sandford,
60 U.S. 393, 464 (1856)
It must be admitted that Congress possesses no power to regulate or abolish

slavery within the States; and that, if this act had attempted any such legislation, it would have been a nullity.

Keywords: *Congress, Congressional authority, Federalism, Judicial review, Slavery, States*

Justice John Catron, concurring
Dred Scott v. Sandford,
60 U.S. 393, 427 (1856)
Congress cannot do indirectly what the Constitution prohibits directly.

Keywords: *Congress, Congressional authority, Constitution*

Justice Stephen Field
Ex parte Garland,
71 U.S. 333, 381 (1866)
It is not within the constitutional power of Congress thus to inflict punishment beyond the reach of executive clemency.

Keywords: *Congressional authority, Executive clemency, Oaths, Pardons, Punishment*

Justice Noah Swayne
Smythe v. Fiske,
90 U.S. 374, 380 (1874)
A thing may be within the letter of a statute and not within its meaning, and within its meaning though not within its letter. The intention of the lawmaker is the law.

Keywords: *Legislative intent, Statutory interpretation*

Chief Justice Morrison Waite
Munn v. Illinois,
94 U.S. 113, 134 (1876)
For protection against abuses by legislatures the people must resort to the polls, not to the courts.

Keywords: *Courts, Legislative abuse, Legislatures, People, Political recourse, Polls*

Chief Justice Morrison Waite
Reynolds v. United States,
98 U.S. 145, 164 (1878)
Congress was deprived of all legislative power over mere opinion, but was left free to reach actions which were in violation of social duties or subversive of good order.

Keywords: *Congress, Legislative power, Opinion, Public order, Social duties, Subversive*

Justice Joseph Bradley
Civil Rights Cases,
109 U.S. 3, 11 (1883)
To adopt appropriate legislation for correcting the effects of such prohibited State laws and State acts, and thus to render them effactually null, void, and innocuous. This is the legislative power conferred upon Congress [by the Fourteenth Amendment], and this is the whole of it. It does not invest Congress with power to legislate upon subjects which are within the domain of State legislation; but to provide modes of relief against State legislation, or State action, of the kind referred to. It does not authorize Congress to create a code of municipal law for the regulation of private rights; but to provide modes of redress against the operation of State laws, and the action of State officers executive or judicial, when these are subversive of the fundamental rights specified in the amendment.

Keywords: *Congress, Congressional*

power, *Federalism, Fourteenth Amendment, Fundamental rights, Legislative authority, Legislative power, Legislature, Municipal law, State legislation, States, Private rights, Public officials, Redress*

Justice Stephen Field, dissenting
Powell v. Pennsylvania,
127 U.S. 678, 696 (1888)
If the courts could not in such cases examine into the real character of the act, but must accept the declaration of the legislature as conclusive, the most valued rights of the citizen would be subject to the arbitrary control of a temporary majority of such bodies, instead of being protected by the guarantees of the Constitution.
Keywords: *Arbitrary control, Citizens' rights, Constitutional guarantees, Courts, Democracy, Legislative intent, Legislature, Majority*

Justice David Brewer
United States v. Ballin,
144 U.S. 1, 7 (1892)
The two houses of congress are legislative bodies representing larger constituencies. Power is not vested in any one individual, but in the aggregate of the members who compose the body, and its action is not the action of any separate member or number of members, but the action of the body as a whole.
Keywords: *Bicameral, Congress, Constituency, Legislative power*

Justice John Marshall Harlan
Hennington v. Georgia,
163 U.S. 299, 304 (1896)
The whole theory of our government, federal and state, is hostile to the idea

that questions of Legislative authority may depend . . . upon opinions of judges as to the wisdom or want of wisdom in the enactment of laws under powers clearly conferred upon the legislature.
Keywords: *Constitutional theory, Federalism, Judges, Judicial authority, Legislative authority, Political theory, Separation of powers, Wisdom*

Justice Oliver Wendell Holmes, dissenting
Hammer v. Dagenhart,
247 U.S. 251, 277 (1918)
It would not be argued today that the power to regulate does not include the power to prohibit. Regulation means the prohibition of something, and when interstate commerce is the matter to be regulated I cannot doubt that the regulation may prohibit any part of such commerce that Congress sees fit to forbid.
Keywords: *Congress, Interstate commerce, Legislative authority, Legislative power, Police power, Regulations*

Justice Willis Van Devanter
McGrain v. Daugherty,
273 U.S. 135, 175 (1927)
A legislative body cannot legislate wisely or effectively in the absence of information respecting the conditions which the legislation is intended to affect or change; and where the legislative body does not itself possess the requisite information—which not infrequently is true—recourse must be had to others who do possess it.
Keywords: *Legislative authority, Legislative body, Legislative information, Legislative process*

Justice Oliver Wendell Holmes, dissenting
Panhandle Oil Co. v. Mississippi ex rel Knox,
277 U.S. 218, 223 (1928)
The power to tax is not the power to destroy while this Court sits.
Keywords: *Power, Regulation, Taxation*

Justice Pierce Butler
Champlin Refining Co. v. Corporation Commission,
286 U.S. 210, 234 (1932)
The unconstitutionality of a part of an act does not necessarily defeat or affect the validity of its remaining provisions. Unless it is evident that the Legislature would not have enacted those provisions which are within its power, independently of that which is not, the invalid part may be dropped if what is left is fully operative as a law.
Keywords: *Congressional intent, Constitutionality, Judicial review, Legislation, Severability*

Chief Justice Charles Evans Hughes
Panama Refining Co. v. Ryan,
293 U.S. 388, 421 (1935)
Undoubtedly legislation must often be adapted to complex conditions involving a host of details with which the national legislature cannot deal directly. The constitution has never been regarded as denying to the Congress the necessary resources of flexibility and practicality, which will enable it to perform its function in laying down policies and establishing standards, while leaving to selected instrumentalities the making of subordinate rules within prescribed limits and the determina-

tion of facts to which the policy as declared by the legislature is to apply. Without capacity to give authorizations of that sort we should have the anomaly of a legislative power which in many circumstances calling for its exertion would be but a futility.
Keywords: *Complex conditions, Congressional authority, Delegation, Instrumentalities, Legislation, Legislative power, Public policies, Standards, Subordinate rules*

Chief Justice Charles Evans Hughes
Townsend v. Yeomans,
301 U.S. 441, 451 (1937)
. . . the Legislature, acting within its sphere, is presumed to know the needs of the people. . . . Whether or not special inquiries should be made is a matter for the legislative discretion.
Keywords: *Legislative authority, Legislative discretion, Legislature, People*

Justice Harlan Fiske Stone
United States v. Carolene Products Co.,
304 U.S. 144, 152 (1938)
Even in the absence of such aids, the existence of facts supporting the legislative judgment is to be presumed, for regulatory legislation affecting ordinary commercial transactions is not to be pronounced unconstitutional unless in the light of the facts made known or generally assumed it is of such a character as to preclude the assumption that it rests upon some rational basis within the knowledge and experience of the legislators.
Keywords: *Commercial transactions, Judicial review, Legislative experience, Legislative intent, Legislative*

judgment, Legislative knowledge, Rational basis, Regulation, Regulatory legislation

Justice Harlan Fiske Stone
Apex Hosiery Co. v. Leader,
310 U.S. 469, 488–489 (1940)
Failure of Congress to alter the act after it had been judicially construed, and the enactment by Congress of legislation which implicitly recognizes the judicial construction as effective, is persuasive of legislative recognition that the judicial construction is the correct one. This is the more so where, as here, the application of the statute . . . has brought forth sharply conflicting views both on the court and in Congress, and where after the matter has been fully brought to the attention of the public and the Congress, the latter has not seen fit to change the statute.
Keywords: *Congress, Constitutional conflict, Judicial construction, Judicial review, Separation of powers, Statute, Statutory intent, Statutory interpretation*

Justice Felix Frankfurter
Federal Trade Commission v. Bunte Brothers Inc.,
312 U.S. 349, 353 (1941)
Translation of an implication drawn from the special aspects of one statute to a totally different statute is treacherous business.
Keywords: *Statutory interpretation*

Justice Harlan Fiske Stone, dissenting
Hines v. Davidowitz,
312 U.S. 52, 75 (1941)
At a time when the exercise of the federal power is being rapidly expanded through congressional action, it is difficult to overstate the importance of safeguarding against such diminution of state power by vague inferences as to what Congress might have intended if it had considered the matter or by reference to our own conceptions of a policy which Congress has not expressed and which is not plainly to be inferred from the legislation which it has enacted.
Keywords: *Congress, Congressional action, Congressional intent, Federalism, Federal power, Legislation, Public policy, State power*

Justice Harlan Fiske Stone
Opp Cotton Mills, Inc. v. Administrator of Wage and Hour Division,
312 U.S. 126, 145 (1941)
While fact finding may be and often is a step in the legislative process, the constitution does not require that Congress should find for itself every fact upon which it bases legislation. . . . In an increasingly complex society Congress obviously could not perform its functions if it were obliged to find all the facts subsidiary to the basic conclusions which support the defined legislative policy. . . . The constitution, viewed as a continuously operative charter of government, is not to be interpreted as demanding the impossible or the impracticable. The essentials of the legislative function are the determination of the legislative policy and its formulation as a rule of conduct. Those essentials are preserved when congress specifies the basic conclusions of fact upon ascertainment of which, from relevant data by a designated administrative agency, it ordains

that its statutory command is to be effective.

Keywords: *Administrative agency, Complex society, Congress, Congressional authority, Constitution, Fact finding, Government information charter, Legislative function, Legislative policy, Legislative process, Statutory command, Statutory intent*

Justice Felix Frankfurter, dissenting
United States v. Monia,
317 U.S. 424, 432 (1943)
A statute, like other living organisms, derives significance and sustenance from its environment, from which it cannot be severed without being mutilated.

Keywords: *Statute, Statutory significance*

Justice Felix Frankfurter, concurring
Martin v. Struthers,
319 U.S. 141, 153–154 (1943)
. . . it is not our business to require legislatures to extend the area of prohibition or regulation beyond the demands of revealed abuses. And the greatest leeway must be given to the legislative judgment of what those demands are. The right to legislate implies the right to classify.

Keywords: *Legislative authority, Legislative intent, Legislative judgment, Regulations, Separation of powers, Statutory interpretation*

Justice Felix Frankfurter
Goesaert v. Cleary,
335 U.S. 464, 466 (1948)
The Constitution does not require legislatures to reflect sociological insight, or shifting social standards, any more than

it requires them to keep abreast of the latest scientific standards.

Keywords: *Legislative authority, Legislative intent, Legislative process, Science, Social standards, Sociology*

Justice Robert Jackson, concurring
United States v. Spelar,
338 U.S. 217, 225 (1949)
While congressional incoherence of thought or of speech is not unconstitutional and Congress can use a contrariety of terms to describe the same thing, we should pay Congress the respect of not assuming lightly that it indulges in inconsistencies of speech which make the English language almost meaningless. There is some reason to think the inconsistency lies in the Court's rendering of the statutes rather than in the way Congress has written them.

Keywords: *Congressional intent, Legal definitions, Judicial review, Legislative authority, Statutes, Statutory construction*

Justice Felix Frankfurter, concurring
American Communications Association v. Douds,
339 U.S. 382, 419 (1950)
Legislation, in order to effectuate its purposes, may deal with radiations beyond the immediate incidence of a mischief.

Keywords: *Legislation, Legislative intent*

Justice Felix Frankfurter
Tenney v. Brandhove,
341 U.S. 367, 377 (1951)
The claim of an unworthy purpose does not destroy the [Speech and Debate]

privilege. Legislators are immune from deterrents to the uninhibited discharge of their legislative duty, not for their private indulgence but for the public good. One must not expect uncommon courage even in legislators.

Keywords: *Congressional authority, Legislative courage, Legislative duties, Legislative immunity, Legislators, Representatives, Speech and Debate Clause*

Justice Felix Frankfurter
Tenney v. Brandhove,
341 U.S. 367, 378 (1951)
In times of political passion, dishonest or vindictive motives are readily attributed to legislative conduct and as readily believed.

Keywords: *Legislative authority, Legislative conduct, Legislative confidence, Legislative legitimacy, Politics, Public opinion*

Justice Robert Jackson
Morissete v. United States,
342 U. S. 246, 263 (1952)
. . . where Congress borrows terms of art in which are accumulated the legal tradition and meaning of centuries of practice, it presumably knows and adopts the cluster of ideas that were attached to each borrowed word in the body of learning from which it was taken and the meaning its use will convey to the judicial mind unless otherwise instructed.

Keywords: *Congress, Ideas, Judicial mind, Learning, Legal tradition, Words*

Justice Felix Frankfurter
Bell v. United States,
349 U.S. 81, 83–84 (1955)
When Congress has the will it has no difficulty in expressing it—when it has the will, that is, of defining what it desires to make the unit of prosecution and, more particularly, to make each stick in a faggot a single criminal unit. When Congress leaves to the judiciary the task of imputing to Congress an undeclared will, the ambiguity should be resolved in favor of lenity. And this not out of any sentimental consideration, or for want of sympathy with the purpose of Congress in proscribing evil or anti-social conduct. It may fairly be said to be a presupposition of our law to resolve doubts in the enforcement of a penal code against the imposition of a harsher punishment. This in no wise implies that language used in criminal statutes should not be read with the saving grace of common sense with which other enactments, not cast in technical language, are to be read. Nor does it assume that offenders against the law carefully read the penal code before they embark on crime. It merely means that if congress does not fix the punishment for a federal offense clearly and without ambiguity, doubt will be resolved against turning a single transaction into multiple offenses, when we have no more to go on than the present case furnishes.

Keywords: *Antisocial conduct, Congress, Congressional expression, Congressional intent, Congressional will,*

Constitutional ambiguity, Criminal law, Delegation, Enforcement, Federal offense, Judiciary, Penal code, Prosecution, Punishment, Statutory language

Chief Justice Earl Warren
Watkins v. United States,
354 U.S. 178, 187–188 (1957)
It is unquestionably the duty of all citizens to cooperate with Congress in its efforts to obtain the facts needed for intelligent legislative action. It is their unremitting obligation to respond to subpoenas, to respect the dignity of the Congress and its committees and to testify fully with respect to matters within the province of proper investigation. This, of course, assumes that the constitutional rights of witnesses will be respected by the Congress as they are in a court of justice. The Bill of Rights is applicable to investigations as to all forms of governmental action.
Keywords*: Bill of Rights, Citizenship, Congressional committees, Congressional dignity, Constitutional rights, Court of justice, Duty, Governmental action, Legislative investigations, Legislative process, Subpoenas, Testify, Witnesses*

Justice John Marshall Harlan
United States v. Price,
361 U.S. 304, 313 (1960)
. . . the views of a subsequent congress form a hazardous basis for inferring the intent of an earlier one.

Keywords: *Congressional intent*

Chief Justice Earl Warren
United States v. O'Brien,
391 U.S. 367, 384 (1968)
Inquiries into Congressional motives or purposes are a hazardous matter. When the issue is simply the interpretation of legislation, the Court will look to statements by legislators for guidance as to the purpose of the legislature, because the benefit to sound decision-making in this circumstance is thought sufficient to risk the possibility of misreading Congress' purpose. It is entirely a different matter when we are asked to void a statute that is, under well-settled criteria, constitutional on its face, on the basis of what fewer than a handful of Congressmen said about it. What motivates one legislator to make a speech about a statute is not necessarily what motivates scores of others to enact it, and the stakes are sufficiently high for us to eschew guesswork. We decline to void essentially on the ground that it is unwise legislation which Congress had the undoubted power to enact and which could be reenacted in its exact form if the same or another legislator made a wiser speech about it.
Keywords: *Congressional decision-making, Congressional intent, Congressional motives, Congressional record, Judicial authority, Judicial review, Legislative history, Legislation, Legislators, Members of Congress, Statute*

Justice Byron White, dissenting
United States v. Brewster,
408 U.S. 501, 563 (1972)
The Speech or Debate Clause is an allocation of power. It authorizes Congress to call offending members to account in their appropriate Houses. A statute that represents an abdication of that power is in my view impermissible. I return to the beginning. The Speech or Debate Clause does not immunize corrupt Congressmen. It reserves the power to discipline in the Houses of Congress. I would insist that those Houses develop their own institutions and procedures for dealing with those in their midst who would prostitute the legislative process.
Keywords: *Congressional power, Constitutional authority, Delegation, Judicial authority, Legislative process, Legislative self-management, Members of Congress, Representatives, Speech and Debate Clause, Statutory intent*

Justice Byron White
Gravel v. United States,
408 U.S. 606, 616–617 (1972)
. . . it is literally impossible, in view of the complexities of the modern legislative process, with Congress almost constantly in session and matters of legislative concern constantly proliferating, for Members of Congress to perform their legislative tasks without the help of aides and assistants; the day-to-day work of such aides is so critical to the Members' performance that they must be treated as the latter's alter egos; and if they are not so recognized, the central role of the Speech or Debate Clause—to prevent in-

timidation of legislators by the Executive and accountability before a possibly hostile judiciary—will inevitably be diminished and frustrated. . . .
Keywords: *Congressional process, Executive branch, Judicial review, Legislative process, Legislative tasks, Legislators, Members of Congress, Separation of powers, Speech and Debate Clause*

Justice William Brennan, dissenting
Gravel v. United States,
408 U.S. 606, 652 (1972)
I agree with the Court that not every task performed by a legislator is privileged; intervention before Executive departments is one that is not. But the informing function carries a far more persuasive claim to the protections of the [Speech or Debate] Clause. It has been recognized by this Court as something generally done by Congressmen, the Congress itself has established special concessions designed to lower the cost of such communication, and, most important, the function furthers several well-recognized goals of representative government. To say in the face of these facts that the informing function is not privileged merely because it is not necessary to the internal deliberations of Congress is to give the Speech or Debate Clause an artificial and narrow reading unsupported by reason. . . .
Keywords: *Congress, Congressional communication, Executive department, Legislative privilege, Legislative process, Legislative tasks, Legislators, Member of Congress, Political philosophy, Representative govern-*

ment, Separation of powers, Speech and Debate Clause

Justice John Paul Stevens, concurring
Washington v. Davis,
426 U.S. 229, 253 (1976)
A law conscripting clerics should not be invalidated because an atheist voted for it.
Keywords: *Atheist, Judicial review, Law, Legislative history, Legislative record, Legislator, Religion*

Justice William Brennan, dissenting
National League of Cities v. Usery,
426 U.S. 833, 880 (1976)
We are left then with a catastrophic judicial body blow at Congress' power under the Commerce Clause. Even if Congress may nevertheless accomplish its objectives . . . there is an ominous portent of disruption of our constitutional structure implicit in today's mischievous decision. I dissent.
Keywords: *Commerce Clause, Congress, Congressional authority, Congressional intent, Congressional objectives, Congressional power, Constitutional authority, Judicial authority, Judicial review, Separation of powers*

Justice Potter Stewart
New Jersey v. Portash,
440 U.S. 450, 459 (1979)
Testimony given in response to a grant of legislative immunity is the essence of coerced testimony. In such cases there is no question whether physical or psychological pressures overrode the defendant's will; the witness is told to talk or face the government's coercive sanctions, notably, a conviction for contempt.
Keywords: *Contempt, Defendant, Legislative immunity, Legislative process, Sanctions, Testimony, Witness*

Justice Potter Stewart
Transamerica Mortgage Advisors, Inc. v. Lewis,
444 U.S. 11, 20 (1979)
Even settled rules of statutory construction could yield, of course, to persuasive evidence of a contrary legislative intent.
Keywords: *Judicial review, Legislative intent, Statutory construction*

Justice William Rehnquist, dissenting
Harrison v. PPG Industries Inc.,
446 U.S. 578, 595 (1980)
The effort to determine Congressional intent here might better be entrusted to a detective than to a judge.
Keywords: *Congressional intent, Judicial review, Judges*

Justice Lewis Powell, concurring
Fullilove v. Klutznick,
448 U.S. 448, 502–503 (1980)
Congress is not an adjudicatory body called upon to resolve specific disputes between competing adversaries. Its constitutional role is to be representative rather than impartial, to make policy rather than to apply settled principles of law. . . . Congress is not expected to act as though it were duty bound to find facts and make conclusion of law. The creation of national rules for the governance of our society simply does not entail the same concept of recordmaking

that is appropriate to a judicial or administrative proceeding. Congress has no responsibility to confine its vision to the facts and evidence adduced by particular parties. Instead, its special attribute as a Legislative body lies in its broader mission to investigate and consider all facts and opinions that may be relevant to the resolution of an issue. One appropriate source is the information and expertise that Congress acquires in the consideration and enactment of earlier legislation. After Congress has legislated repeatedly in an area of national concern, its members gain experience that may reduce the need for fresh hearings or prolonged debate when Congress again considers action in that area.

Keywords: *Adjudicatory body, Administrative proceeding, Congress, Debate, Information, Legislative process, Legislature, Public policy, Recordmaking, Separation of powers*

Justice Byron White, dissenting
Northern Pipeline Construction Co. v. Marathon Pipe Line Co.,
458 U.S. 50, 118–119 (1982)
The real question is not whether Congress was justified in establishing a specialized bankruptcy court, but rather whether it was justified in failing to create a specialized, Art. III bankruptcy court. My own view is that the very fact of extreme specialization may be enough, and certainly has been enough in the past, to justify the creation of a legislative court. Congress may legitimately consider the effect on the federal judiciary of the addition of several hundred specialized judges: We are, on the whole,

a body of generalists. The addition of several hundred specialists may substantially change, whether for good or bad, the character of the federal bench. Moreover, Congress may have desired to maintain some flexibility in its possible future responses to the general problem of bankruptcy. There is no question that the existence of several hundred bankruptcy judges with life tenure would have severely limited Congress' future options. Furthermore, the number of bankruptcies may fluctuate, producing a substantially reduced need for bankruptcy judges. Congress may have thought that, in that event, a bankruptcy specialist should not as a general matter serve as a judge in the countless nonspecialized cases that come before the federal district courts. It would then face the prospect of large numbers of idle federal judges. Finally, Congress may have believed that the change from bankruptcy referees to Art. I judges was far less dramatic, and so less disruptive of the existing bankruptcy and constitutional court systems, than would be a change to Art. III judges.

Keywords: *Article I judges, Article III courts, Bankruptcy, Bankruptcy courts, Congress, Judges, Legislative intent*

Justice Byron White, dissenting
Immigration and Naturalization Service v. Chadha,
462 U.S. 919, 967–968 (1983)
The prominence of the legislative veto mechanism in our contemporary political system and its importance to Congress can hardly be overstated. It has

become a central means by which Congress secures the accountability of executive and independent agencies. Without the legislative veto, Congress is faced with a Hobson's choice: either to refrain from delegating the necessary authority, leaving itself with a hopeless task of writing laws with the requisite specificity to cover the endless special circumstances across the entire policy landscape, or in the alternative, to abdicate its lawmaking function to the executive branch and independent agencies. To choose the former leaves major national problems unresolved; to opt for the latter risks unaccountable policymaking by those not elected to fill that role. Accordingly, over the past five decades, the legislative veto has been placed in nearly 200 statutes. The device is known in every field of governmental concern: reorganization, budgets, foreign affairs, war powers, and regulation of trade, safety, energy, the environment and the economy.

Keywords: *Administrative agencies, Independent agencies, Legislative process, Legislative veto, Legislature, Public policy, Separation of powers*

Justice Sandra Day O'Connor, dissenting
South Dakota v. Dole,
483 U.S. 203, 215 (1987)

When Congress appropriates money to build a highway, it is entitled to insist that the highway be a safe one. But it is not entitled to insist as a condition of the use of highway funds that the State impose or change regulations in other areas of the State's social and economic life because of an attenuated or tangential relationship to highway use or safety. Indeed, if the rule were otherwise, the Congress could effectively regulate almost any area of a State's social, political, or economic life on the theory that use of the interstate transportation system is somehow enhanced. If, for example, the United States were to condition highway moneys upon moving the state capital, I suppose it might argue that interstate transportation is facilitated by locating local governments in places easily accessible to interstate highways—or, conversely, that highways might become overburdened if they had to carry traffic to and from the state capital. In my mind, such a relationship is hardly more attenuated than the one which the Court finds supports [for the National Minimum Drinking Age Amendment].

Keywords: *Appropriations, Ends/ means, Federalism, Public financing, Public policy, Regulations, States' rights*

Justice Byron White, dissenting
Barnes v. Glen Theatre, Inc.,
501 U.S. 560, 590–591 (1991)

Legislators do not just randomly select certain conduct for proscription; they have reasons for doing so, and those reasons illuminate the purpose of the law that is passed. Indeed, a law may have multiple purposes. The purpose of forbidding people to appear nude in parks, beaches, hot dog stands, and like public places is to protect others from offense. But that could not possibly be the purpose of preventing nude dancing in theaters and barrooms, since the viewers are exclusively consenting adults who pay money to see these dances. The purpose of the proscription in these contexts is to protect the viewers from what the State believes is the harmful message that nude dancing communicates.

Keywords: *Adults, Conduct, Dance, First Amendment, Legislators, Legislative intent, Legislative purpose, Nudity, Police power*

Justice Antonin Scalia
College Savings Bank v. Florida Prepaid Postsecondary Education Expense Board,
527 U.S. ___, ___ (1999)
Legislative flexibility on the part of Congress will be the touchstone of federalism when the capacity to support combustion becomes the acid test of a fire extinguisher.

Congressional flexibility is desirable, of course—but only within the bounds of federal power established by the Constitution. Beyond those bounds (the theory of our Constitution goes), it is a menace.

Keywords: *Congress, Constitutional theory, Federalism, Federal power, Legislative flexibility*

Justice Sandra Day O'Connor, concurring
Chicago v. Morales,
527 U.S. ___, ___ (1999)
This Court has never held that the intent of the drafters determines whether a law is vague.

Keywords: *Judicial review, Legislative drafters, Statutory intent, Statutory interpretation*

2. The Enforcers

Article II of the Constitution outlines the powers of the executive branch. Chapter 2 likewise focuses on the presidency along with its inherent strengths and weaknesses. Read in conjunction with chapter 12, the researcher will get a more complete picture of how this branch works.

Justice Joseph Story
Martin v. Mott,
25 U.S. 19, 33 (1827)
Every public officer is presumed to act in obedience to his duty, until the contrary is shown; and, a fortiori, this presumption ought to be favorably applied to the chief magistrate of the Union.
Keywords: *Officer, Chief magistrate*

Justice Smith Thompson
Kendall v. United States ex rel Stokes,
37 U.S. 524, 610 (1838)
There are certain political duties imposed upon many officers in the executive department, the discharge of which is under the direction of the President. But it would be an alarming doctrine, that congress cannot impose upon any executive officer any duty they may think proper, which is not repugnant to any rights secured and protected by the constitution; and in such cases, the duty and responsibility grow out of and are subject to the control of the law, and not to the direction of the President. And this is emphatically the case, where the duty enjoined is of a mere ministerial character.
Keywords: *Congress, Executive department, Political duties, President, Public officials*

Chief Justice William Howard Taft
Myers v. United States,
272 U.S. 52, 134 (1926)
[The President] must place in each member of his official family, and his chief executive subordinates, implicit faith. The moment that he loses confidence in the intelligence, ability, judgment or loyalty of any one of them, he must have the power to remove him without delay. To require him to file charges and submit them to the consideration of the Senate might make impossible that unity and co-ordination in executive administration essential to effective action.
Keywords: *Character, Chief executive, Executive branch administration, Executive branch officials, Removal, Senate*

Justice George Sutherland
United States v. Belmont,
301 U.S. 324, 330 (1937)
That the negotiations, acceptance of the assignment and agreements and understandings in respect thereof were within the competence of the President may not be doubted. Governmental power over internal affairs is distributed between the national government and the several states. Governmental power over exter-

nal affairs is not distributed, but is vested exclusively in the national government. And in respect of what was done here, the Executive had authority to speak as the sole organ of that government.

Keywords: *External affairs, Foreign affairs, Governmental power, Internal affairs, National government, President, Presidential authority, Presidential competence, States*

Justice Robert Jackson
Wickard v. Filburn,
317 U.S. 111, 118 (1942)
To hold that a speech by a cabinet officer, which failed to meet judicial ideals of clarity, precision, and exhaustiveness, may defeat a policy embodied in an act of Congress, would invest communication between administrators and the people with perils heretofore unsuspected.

Keywords: *Administrators, Cabinet officer, Congressional intent, Executive branch, Judicial limitations*

Justice Frank Murphy, dissenting
Endicott Johnson Corp. v. Perkins,
317 U.S. 501, 510 (1943)
Because of the varied and important responsibilities of a quasi-judicial nature that have been entrusted to administrative agencies in the regulation of our political and economic life, their activities should not be subjected to unwarranted and ill-advised intrusions by the judicial branch of the government. Yet, if they are freed of all restraint upon inquisitorial activities and are allowed uncontrolled discretion in the exercise of the sovereign power of government to in-

vade private affairs through the use of the subpoena, to the extent required or sought in situations like the one before us and other inquiries of much broader scope, under the direction of well-meaning but over-zealous officials they may at times become instruments of intolerable oppression and injustice.

Keywords: *Administrative agencies, Judiciary, Oppression, Quasi-judicial, Sovereignty, Subpoena*

Justice Potter Stewart, concurring
New York Times Co. v. United States,
403 U.S. 713, 728–730 (1971)
If the Constitution gives the Executive a large degree of unshared power in the conduct of foreign affairs and the maintenance of our national defense, then under the Constitution the Executive must have the largely unshared duty to determine and preserve the degree of internal security necessary to exercise that power successfully. It is an awesome responsibility, requiring judgment and wisdom of a high order. I should suppose that moral, political, and practical considerations would dictate that a very first principle of that wisdom would be an insistence upon avoiding secrecy for its own sake. For when everything is classified, then nothing is classified, and the system becomes one to be disregarded by the cynical or the careless, and to be manipulated by those intent on self-protection or self-promotion. I should suppose, in short, that the hallmark of a truly effective internal security system would be the maximum possible disclosure, recognizing that secrecy can best be preserved only when credibility is truly

maintained. But be that as it may, it is clear to me that it is the constitutional duty of the Executive—as a matter of sovereign prerogative and not as a matter of law as the courts know law—through the promulgation and enforcement of executive regulations, to protect the confidentiality necessary to carry out its responsibilities in the fields of international relations and national defense.

Keywords: *Confidentiality, Executive branch, Foreign affairs, Internal security, International relations, National defense, Political responsibility, Secrecy, Sovereignty, Wisdom*

Chief Justice Warren Burger
United States v. Nixon,
418 U.S. 683, 706 (1974)
Absent a claim of need to protect military, diplomatic, or sensitive national security secrets, we find it difficult to accept the argument that even the very important interest in confidentiality of Presidential communications is significantly diminished by production of such material for *in camera* inspection with all the protection that a district court will be obliged to provide.

Keywords: *Diplomatic, Military, National security, Presidential communications*

Justice William Brennan
Nixon v. Administrator of General Services,
433 U.S. 425, 459 (1977)
The overwhelming bulk of the 42 million pages of documents and the 880 tape recordings pertain, not to appellant's private communications, but to the official conduct of his Presidency. Most of the 42 million pages were prepared and seen by others and were widely circulated within the government. Appellant concedes that he saw no more than 200,000 items, and we do not understand him to suggest that his privacy claim extends to items he never saw.

Keywords: *Executive privilege, Presidency, Presidential archives, Privacy, Private communications*

Justice John Paul Stevens, concurring
Nixon v. Administrator of General Services,
433 U.S. 425, 486 (1977)
Appellant resigned his office under unique circumstances and accepted a pardon for any offenses committed while in office. By so doing, he placed himself in a different class from all other Presidents. Even though unmentioned, it would be unrealistic to assume that historic facts of this consequence did not affect the legislative decision.

Keywords: *History, Legislative intent, Pardon, Presidency, Presidential resignation*

Chief Justice Warren Burger, dissenting
Nixon v. Administrator of General Services,
433 U.S. 425, 520 (1977)
The consequences of this development on what a President expresses to others in writing and orally are incalculable; perhaps even more crucial is the inhibiting impact on those to whom the President turns for information and for counsel, whether they are officials in the government, business or labor leaders, or for-

eign diplomats and statesmen. I have little doubt that Title I—and the Court's opinion—will be the subject of careful scrutiny and analysis in the foreign offices of other countries whose representatives speak to a President on matters they prefer not to put in writing, but which may be memorialized by a President or an aide. Similarly, Title I may well be a "ghost" at future White House conferences, with conferees choosing their words more cautiously because of the enlarged prospect of compelled disclosure to others.

Keywords: *Counsel, Diplomacy, Executive privilege, Foreign affairs, Information, Presidential aides, Presidential communications, Privacy, Secrecy, Security*

Justice William Rehnquist, dissenting
Nixon v. Administrator of General Services,
433 U.S. 425, 545 (1977)

. . . today's decision countenances the power of any future Congress to seize the official papers of an outgoing President as he leaves the inaugural stand. In so doing, it poses a real threat to the ability of future Presidents to receive candid advice and to give candid instructions. This result, so at odds with our previous case law on the separation of powers, will daily stand as a veritable sword of Damocles over every succeeding President and his advisers.

Keywords: *Case law, Congressional power, Presidency, Presidential advisors, Presidential communications, Separation of powers*

Justice Lewis Powell
Nixon v. Fitzgerald,
457 U.S. 731, 757 (1982)

A rule of absolute immunity for the President will not leave the Nation without sufficient protection against misconduct on the part of the chief executive. There remains the constitutional remedy of impeachment. In addition, there are formal and informal checks on Presidential action that do not apply with equal force to other executive officials. The President is subjected to constant scrutiny by the press. Vigilant oversight by Congress also may serve to deter Presidential abuses of office, as well as to make credible the threat of impeachment. Other incentives to avoid misconduct may include a desire to earn re-election, the need to maintain prestige as an element of Presidential influence, and a President's traditional concern for his historical stature.

Keywords: *Abuse of office, Congressional oversight, Election, Executive officials, Immunity, Impeachment, President, Presidential misconduct, Press*

Chief Justice Warren Burger, dissenting
Harlow v. Fitzgerald,
457 U.S. 800, 827–828 (1982)

We—judges collectively—have held that the common law provides us with absolute immunity for ourselves with respect to judicial acts, however erroneous or ill-advised. Are the lowest ranking of 27,000 or more judges, thousands of prosecutors, and thousands of congressional aides—an aggregate of not less than 75,000 in all—entitled to greater protection than two senior aides of a President?

Keywords: *Common law, Immunity, Judges, Presidential aides*

Justice Antonin Scalia, dissenting
Morrison v. Olson,
487 U.S. 654, 709 (1988)
It is not for us to determine, and we have presumed to determine, how much of the purely executive powers of government must be within the full control of the President. The Constitution prescribes that they all are.

Keywords: *Congressional authority, Executive power, Presidential authority*

3. The Least Dangerous Branch

The quite concise Article III of the Constitution outlines the judicial power. In Chapter 3 significant space is devoted to shedding light on how the judges of the Supreme Court should and do decide cases.

Justice James Iredell, seriatim
Ware v. Hylton,
3 U.S. 199, 256–257 (1796)
In delivering my opinion on this important case, I feel myself deeply affected by the awful situation in which I stand. The uncommon magnitude of the subject, its novelty, the high expectation it has excited, and the consequences with which a decision may be attended, have all impressed me with their fullest force. I have trembled left by an ill informed or precipitate opinion of mine, either the honour, the interest, or the safety of the United States should suffer or be endangered on the one hand, or the just rights and proper security of any individual on the other. In endeavouring to form the opinion I shall now deliver, I am sure the great object of my heart has been to discover the true principles upon which a decision ought to be given, unbiassed by any other consideration than the most sacred regard to justice.
Keywords: *Judicial authority, Judicial opinions, Justice, Political system, Principles*

Chief Justice John Marshall
Marbury v. Madison,
5 U.S. 137, 177 (1803)
It is emphatically the province and duty of the judicial department to say what the law is. Those who apply the rule to particular cases, must of necessity expound and interpret that rule. If two laws conflict with each other, the courts must decide on the operation of each.
Keywords: *Judicial authority, Judicial duty, Judicial review*

Chief Justice John Marshall
Trustees of Dartmouth College v. Woodward,
17 U.S. 518, 644 (1819)
. . . although a particular and a rare case may not, in itself, be of sufficient magnitude to induce a rule, yet it must be governed by the rule, when established, unless some plain and strong reason for excluding it can be given. It is not enough to say, that this particular case was not in the mind of the convention, when the article was framed, nor of the American people, when it was adopted. It is necessary to go further, and to say that, had this particular case been suggested, the language would have been so varied, as to exclude it, or it would have been made a special exception.
Keywords: *Framers, Language, Legislative intent, Rules*

Justice Joseph Story, dissenting
Houston v. Moore,
18 U.S. 1, 48 (1820)
Sitting here, we are not at liberty to add one jot of power to the national government beyond what the people have granted by the constitution; and, on the other hand, we are bound to support that constitution as it stands, and to give a fair and rational scope to all the powers which it clearly contains.
Keywords: *Constitution, Judicial power, Liberty, National government*

Chief Justice John Marshall
United States v. Wiltberger,
18 U.S. 76, 105 (1820)
Probability is not a guide which a court, in construing a penal statute, can safely take.
Keywords: *Judicial role, Penal code, Statutory interpretation*

Chief Justice John Marshall
Cohens v. Virginia,
19 U.S. 264, 404 (1821)
The judiciary cannot, as the legislature may, avoid a measure because it approaches the confines of the constitution. We cannot pass it by because it is doubtful. With whatever doubts, with whatever difficulties, a case may be attended, we must decide it, if it be brought before us. We have no more right to decline the exercise of jurisdiction which is given, than to usurp that which is not given. The one or the other would be treason to the constitution.
Keywords: *Constitutional confines, Judicial authority, Jurisdiction, Legislative authority*

Justice Bushrod Washington, dissenting
Ogden v. Saunders,
25 U.S. 213, 267–268 (1827)
That the derangement of the words, and even sentences of a law, may sometimes be tolerated, in order to arrive at the apparent meaning of the legislature, to be gathered from other parts, or from the entire scope of the law, I shall not deny.
Keywords: *Legislative intent, Statutory construction, Statutory interpretation*

Justice Henry Baldwin, concurring
Cherokee Nation v. Georgia,
30 U.S. 1, 41 (1831)
Where its terms are plain, I should, as a dissenting judge, deem it judicial sacrilege to put my hands on any of its provisions, and arrange or construe them according to any fancied use, object, purpose, or motive, which, by an ingenious train of reasoning, I might bring my mind to believe was the reason for its adoption by the sovereign power, from whose hands it comes to me as the rule and guide to my faith, my reason, and judicial oath. In taking out, putting in, or varying the plain meaning of a word or expression, to meet the results of my poor judgment, as to the meaning and intention of the great charter, which alone imparts to me my power to act as a judge of its supreme injunctions, I should feel myself acting upon it by judicial amendments, and not as one of its executors. I will not add unto these things; I will not take away from the words of this book of prophecy; I will not impair the force or obligation

of its enactments, plain and unqualified in its terms, by resorting to the authority of names; the decisions of foreign courts; or a reference to books or writers. The plain ordinances are a safe guide to my judgment. When they admit of doubt, I will connect the words with the practice, usages, and settled principles of this government, as administered by its fathers before the adoption of the constitution: and refer to the received opinion and fixed understanding of the high parties who adopted it; the usage and practice of the new government acting under its authority; and the solemn decisions of this court, acting under its high powers and responsibility: nothing fearing that in so doing, I can discover some sound and safe maxims of American policy and jurisprudence, which will always afford me light enough to decide on the constitutional powers of the federal and state governments, and all tribunals acting under their authority.

Keywords: *Constitutional power, Courts, Federalism, Judgment, Judicial oath, Judicial role, Language, Maxims, Principles, Reasoning, Sovereignty*

Justice Henry Baldwin
Groves v. Slaughter,
40 U.S. 449, 517 (1841)
... wherever slavery exists, by the laws of a state, slaves are property in every constitutional sense, and for every purpose, whether as subjects of taxation, as the basis of representation, as articles of commerce, or fugitives from service. To consider them as persons merely, and not property, is, in my settled opinion, the first step towards state of things to be avoided only by a firm adherence to the fundamental principles of the state and federal governments, in relation to this species of property. If the first step taken be a mistaken one, the successive ones will be fatal to the whole system. I have taken my stand on the only position which, in my judgment, is impregnable; and feel confident in its strength, however it may be assailed in public opinion, here or elsewhere.

Keywords: *Constitution, Persons, Principles, Property, Public opinion, Slavery, States*

Chief Justice Roger Taney
Aldridge v. Williams,
44 U.S. 9 (1845)
In expounding this law, the judgment of the court cannot, in any degree, be influenced by the construction placed upon it by individual members of Congress in the debate which took place on its passage, nor by the motives or reasons assigned by them for supporting or opposing amendments that were offered. The law as it passed is the will of the majority of both houses, and the only mode in which that will is spoken is in the act itself; and we must gather their intention from the language there used, comparing it, when any ambiguity exists, with the laws upon the same subject, and looking, if necessary, to the public history of the times in which it was passed.

Keywords: *Courts, Congressional intent, History, Judicial process, Language, Law*

Justice Levi Woodbury, dissenting
Luther v. Borden,
48 U.S. 1, 52–53 (1849)
. . . if the people, in the distribution of powers under the constitution, should ever think of making judges supreme arbiters in political controversies, when not selected by nor, frequently, amenable to them, nor at liberty to follow such various considerations in their judgments as belong to mere political questions, they will dethrone themselves and lose one of their own invaluable birthrights; building up in this way—slowly, but surely—a new sovereign power in the republic, in most respects irresponsible and unchangeable for life, and one more dangerous, in theory at least, than the worst elective oligarchy in the worst of times.
Keywords: *Judges, Judicial review, Liberty, Political controversies, Oligarchy, Power, Republic, Sovereignty*

Chief Justice Roger Taney
Dred Scott v. Sandford,
60 U.S. 393, 426 (1857)
No one, we presume, supposes that any change in public opinion or feeling, in relation to this unfortunate race, in the civilized nations of Europe or in this country, should induce the court to give to the words of the Constitution a more liberal construction in their favor than they were intended to bear when the instrument was framed and adopted. Such an argument would be altogether inadmissible in any tribunal called on to interpret it. If any of its provisions are deemed unjust, there is a mode prescribed in the instrument itself by which

it may be amended, but while it remains unaltered, it must be construed now as it was understood at the time of its adoption.
Keywords: *Constitutional interpretation, Court, Liberal construction, Original intent, Public opinion, Public sentiment, Race*

Justice Peter Daniel, concurring
Dred Scott v. Sandford,
60 U.S. 393, 475 (1856)
Now, the following are truths which a knowledge of the history of the world, and particularly of that of our own country, compels us to know—that the African negro race never have been acknowledged as belonging to the family of nations; that as amongst them there never has been known or recognised by the inhabitants of other countries anything partaking of the character of nationality, or civil or political polity; that this race has been by all the nations of Europe regarded as subjects of capture or purchase; as subjects of commerce or traffic; and that the introduction of that race into every section of this country was not as members of civil or political society, but as slaves, as property in the strictest sense of the term.
Keywords: *Civil society, History, Political society, Property, Race, Slavery, Truth*

Chief Justice Salmon Chase
License Tax Cases,
72 U.S. 462, 469 (1866)
This court can know nothing of public policy except from the Constitution and

the laws, and the course of administration and decision. It has no legislative powers. It cannot amend or modify any legislative acts. It cannot examine questions as expedient or inexpedient, as politic or impolitic. Considerations of that sort must, in general, be addressed to the legislature. Questions of policy determined there are concluded here.

Keywords: *Constitutional authority, Public policy, Judicial administration, Judicial powers, Judicial review, Legislative authority, Legislative powers, Legislative responsibilities, Separation of powers*

Chief Justice Salmon Chase
Ex parte McCardle,
74 U.S. 506, 514 (1868)

Without jurisdiction the court cannot proceed at all in any cause. Jurisdiction is power to declare the law, and when it ceases to exist, the only function remaining to the court is that of announcing the fact and dismissing the cause.

Keywords: *Judicial authority, Judicial review, Jurisdiction*

Chief Justice Salmon Chase
Veazie Bank v. Fenno,
75 U.S. 533, 548 (1869)

The judicial cannot prescribe to the legislative department of the government limitations upon the exercise of its acknowledged power.

Keywords: *Governmental limitations, Judicial authority, Judicial power, Legislative power*

Justice William Strong
Blyew v. United States,
80 U.S. 581, 593 (1871)

We cannot be expected to be ignorant of the condition of things which existed when the statute was enacted, or of the evils which it was intended to remedy.

Keywords: *Congressional intent, Judicial process, Judicial review, Legislative history, Statutory construction, Statutory interpretation, Statutory remedies*

Justice Nathan Clifford, dissenting
Loan Association v. Topeka,
87 U.S. 655, 669 (1874)

Courts cannot nullify an act of the State legislature on the vague ground that they think it opposed to a general latent spirit supposed to pervade or underlie the constitution, where neither the terms nor the implications of the instrument disclose any such restriction. Such a power is denied to the courts, because to concede it would be to make the courts sovereign over both the constitution and the people, and convert the government into a judicial despotism.

Keywords: *Constitutional limitations, Judicial authority, Judicial despotism, Judicial review, Legislatures, Separation of powers, States*

Justice William Strong
Washington Market Co. v. Hoffman,
101 U.S. 112 (1879)

We are not at liberty to construe any statute so as to deny effect to any part of its language. It is a cardinal rule of statutory construction that significance and effect shall, if possible, be accorded to every word.

Keywords: *Judicial review, Liberty, Statutory construction, Statutory interpretation, Statutory language*

Justice John Marshall Harlan
Mugler v. Kansas,
123 U.S. 623, 661 (1887)

The courts are not bound by mere forms,

nor are they to be misled by mere pretences. They are at liberty—indeed, are under a solemn duty—to look at the substance of things, whenever they enter upon the inquiry whether the legislature has transcended the limits of its authority. If, therefore, a statute purporting to have been enacted to protect the public health, the public morals, or the public safety, has no real or substantial relation to those objects, or is a palpable invasion of rights secured by the fundamental law, it is the duty of the courts to so adjudge, and thereby given effect to the Constitution.

Keywords: *Judicial authority, Judicial duty, Judicial process, Judicial review, Legislative authority, Legislative intent, Statutory overreaching*

Justice Samuel Miller
Cunningham v. Neagle,
135 U.S. 1, 59 (1890)

It would be a great reproach to the system of government of the United States, declared to be within its sphere sovereign and supreme, if there is to be found within the domain of its powers no means of protecting the judges, in the conscientious and faithful discharge of their duties, from the malice and hatred of those upon whom their judgments may operate unfavorably.

Keywords: *Judges, Judicial power, Judicial protection, Public opinion, Sovereignty*

Justice Stephen Field, dissenting
Baltimore & Ohio Railroad Co. v. Baugh,
149 U.S. 368, 401 (1893)

I am aware that what has been termed the general law of the country—which is often little less than what the judge advancing the doctrine thinks at the time should be the general law on a particular subject—has been often advanced in judicial opinions of this court to control a conflicting law of a state. I admit that learned judges have fallen into the habit of repeating this doctrine as a convenient mode of brushing aside the law of a state in conflict with their views. And I confess that, moved and governed by the authority of the great names of those judges, I have, myself, in many instances, unhesitatingly and confidently, but I think now erroneously, repeated the same doctrine. But, notwithstanding the great names which may be cited in favor of the doctrine, and notwithstanding the frequency with which the doctrine has been reiterated, there stands, as a perpetual protest against its repetition, the Constitution of the United States, which recognizes and preserves the autonomy and independence of the states—independence in their legislative and independence in their judicial departments. Supervision over either the legislative or the judicial action of the states is in no case permissible except as to matters by the constitution specifically authorized or delegated to the United States. Any interference with either, except as thus permitted, is an invasion of the authority of the state and, to that extent, a denial of its independence.

Keywords: *Doctrine, Federalism, General law, Independence, Judges, Judicial authority, Judicial review, Jurisprudence, State autonomy*

Justice Oliver Wendell Holmes, dissenting
Northern Securities Company v. United States,
193 U.S. 197, 364–365 (1904)

Great cases like hard cases make bad law.

For great cases are called great not by reason of their real importance in shaping the law of the future, but because of some accident of immediate, overwhelming interest which appeals to the feelings and distorts the judgment. These immediate interests exercise a kind of hydraulic pressure which makes what previously was clear seem doubtful, and before which even well-settled principles of law will bend.

Keywords: *Cases, Judicial judgments, Legal principles*

Justice Oliver Wendell Holmes, dissenting
Lochner v. New York,
198 U.S. 45, 75 (1905)
This case is decided upon an economic theory which a large part of the country does not entertain. If it were a question whether I agreed with that theory, I should desire to study it further and long before making up my mind. But I do not conceive that to be my duty, because I strongly believe that my agreement or disagreement has nothing to do with the right of a majority to embody their opinions in law. It is settled by various decisions of this court that state constitutions and state laws may regulate life in many ways which we as legislators might think as injudicious, or if you like as tyrannical, as this, and which, equally with this, interfere with the liberty to contract.

Keywords: *Contract, Economic theory, Judicial role, Liberty, Opinions, States*

Justice Oliver Wendell Holmes, dissenting
Lochner v. New York,
198 U.S. 45, 76 (1905)
General propositions do not decide concrete cases.

Keywords: *Cases, Theories*

Justice William Moody
Twining v. New Jersey,
211 U.S. 78, 106–107 (1908)
Under the guise of interpreting the constitution we must take care that we do not import into the discussion our own personal views of what would be wise, just and fitting rules of government to be adopted by a free people and confound them with constitutional limitations.

Keywords: *Constitutional interpretation, Constitutional limitations, Free people, Judicial authority, Judicial power, Judicial review, Personal views*

Justice John Marshall Harlan
Monongahela Bridge Co. v. United States,
216 U.S. 177, 195 (1910)
. . . the Courts have rarely, if ever, felt themselves so restrained by technical rules, that they could not find some remedy, consistent with the law, for acts, whether done by government or by individual persons, that violated natural justice or were hostile to the fundamental principles devised for the protection of the essential rights of property.

Keywords: *Fundamental principles, Judicial authority, Judicial review, Natural justice, Property, Technical rules*

Justice Joseph Lamar
Gompers v. Bucks Stove & Range Co.,
221 U.S. 418, 450 (1911)
If a party can make himself a judge of the validity of orders which have been issued,

and by his own act of disobedience set them aside, then are the courts impotent, and what the constitution now fittingly calls the "judicial power of the United States" would be a mere mockery.

Keywords: *Constitutional authority, Judicial authority, Judicial overreaching, Judicial power*

Justice Oliver Wendell Holmes
United States v. Jin Fuey Moy,
241 U.S. 394, 401 (1916)

A statute must be construed, if fairly possible, so as to avoid not only the conclusion that it is unconstitutional, but also grave doubts upon that score.

Keywords: *Constitutionality, Statutory interpretation*

Justice Oliver Wendell Holmes, dissenting
Southern Pacific v. Jensen,
244 U.S. 205, 221 (1917)

. . . judges do and must legislate, but they can do so only interstitially. They are confined from molar to molecular motions.

Keywords: *Judges, Judicial authority, Judicial legislation, Judicial power*

Justice Oliver Wendell Holmes
New York Trust Co. v. Eisner,
256 U.S. 345, 349 (1921)

. . . a page of history is worth a volume of logic.

Keywords: *History, Judicial role, Logic*

Justice Oliver Wendell Holmes
Diaz v. Gonzalez,
261 U.S. 102, 105–106 (1923)

This Court has stated many times the deference due to the understanding of the local courts upon matters of purely local concern. . . . This is especially true in dealing with the decisions of a Court inheriting and brought up in a different system from that which prevails here. When we contemplate such a system from the outside it seems like a wall of stone, every part even with all the others, except so far as our own local education may lead us to see subordinations to which we are accustomed. But to one brought up within it, varying emphasis, tacit assumptions, unwritten practices, a thousand influences gained only from life, may give to the different parts wholly new values that logic and grammar never could have gotten from the books.

Keywords: *Comparative legal systems, Customs, Localities, Traditions*

Chief Justice William Howard Taft
Layne & Bowler Corp. v. Western Well Works, Inc.,
261 U.S. 387, 393 (1923)

If it be suggested that as much effort and time as we have given to the consideration of the alleged conflict would have enabled us to dispose of the case before us on the merits, the answer is that it is very important that we be consistent in not granting the writ of certiorari except in cases involving principles the settlement of which is of importance to the public as distinguished from that of the parties, and in cases where there is a real and embarrassing conflict of opinion and authority between the circuit courts of appeal.

Keywords: *Certiorari, Controversy, Judicial opinions, Judiciary, Merits, Parties, Principles, Public interest*

Justice Oliver Wendell Holmes
Irwin v. Gavit,
268 U.S. 161, 168 (1925)
Neither are we troubled by the question where to draw the line. That is the question in pretty much everything worth arguing in the law. Day and night, youth and age are only types.
Keywords: *Judicial competence, Judicial process, Legal process*

Justice Oliver Wendell Holmes
Bain Peanut Co. of Texas v. Pinson,
282 U.S. 499, 501 (1931)
The interpretation of constitutional principles must not be too literal. We must remember that the machinery of government would not work if it were not allowed a little play in its joints.
Keywords: *Constitutional interpretation, Constitutional principles, Government*

Justice Louis Brandeis
Burnet v. Coronado Oil & Gas Co.,
285 U.S. 393, 407–408 (1932)
Stare decisis is usually the wise policy, because in most matters it is more important that the applicable rule of law be settled than that it be settled right. . . . This is commonly true even where the error is a matter of serious concern, providing correction can be had by legislation. But in cases involving the Federal Constitution, where correction through legislative action is practically impossible, this Court has often overruled its earlier decisions. The Court bows to the lessons of experience and the force of better reasoning, recognizes that the process of trial and error, so fruitful in the physical sciences, is

appropriate also in the judicial function.
Keywords: *Constitutional questions, Experience, History, Judicial function, Legislation, Rule of law, Stare decisis*

Justice George Sutherland
Helvering v. Stockholms Enskilda Bank,
293 U.S. 84, 92 (1934)
This may be in the nature of a legal fiction; but legal fictions have an appropriate place in the administration of the law when they are required by the demands of convenience and justice.
Keywords: *Administration of law, Justice, Legal fiction*

Justice Owen Roberts
United States v. Butler,
297 U.S. 1, 62–63 (1936)
When an act of Congress is appropriately challenged in the courts as not conforming to the constitutional mandate, the judicial branch of the Government has only one duty—to lay the article of the Constitution which is invoked beside the statute which is challenged and to decide whether the latter squares with the former. All the court does, or can do, is to announce its considered judgment upon the question. The only power it has, if such it may be called, is the power of judgment. This court neither approves nor condemns any legislative policy. Its delicate and difficult office is to ascertain and declare whether the legislation is in accordance with, or in contravention of, the provisions of the Constitution; and having done that, its duty ends.
Keywords: *Congress, Constitutionality, Judicial review, Judiciary, Legislative policy, Statutes*

Justice Harlan Fiske Stone, dissenting
United States v. Butler,
297 U.S. 1, 78–79 (1936)
The power of courts to declare a statute unconstitutional is subject to two guiding principles of decision which ought never to be absent from judicial consciousness. One is that courts are concerned only with the power to enact statutes, not with their wisdom. The other is that while unconstitutional exercise of power by the executive and legislative branches of the government is subject to judicial restraint, the only check upon our own exercise of power is our own sense of self-restraint. For the removal of unwise laws from the statute books appeal lies not to the courts but to the ballot and to the processes of democratic government.
Keywords: *Checks and balances, Constitutionality, Democratic system, Electoral process, Judicial consciousness, Judicial power, Judicial review, Separation of powers, Statutes, Unwise laws*

Justice Louis Brandeis
Ashwander v. Tennessee Valley Authority,
297 U.S. 288, 347 (1936)
The Court will not pass on a constitutional question, although properly presented by the record, if there is also present some other ground on which the case may be disposed of. This rule has found some varied application. Thus, if a case can be decided on either of two grounds, one involving a constitutional question, the other a question of statutory construction or general law, the Court will decide on the latter.

Keywords: *Constitutionality, General law, Judicial review, Judiciary, Statutory construction*

Chief Justice Charles Evans Hughes
Morgan v. United States,
298 U.S. 468, 481 (1936)
The one who decides must hear.
Keywords: *Fairness, Judging, Judicial process*

Justice George Sutherland, dissenting
West Coast Hotel Co. v. Parrish,
300 U.S. 379, 402 (1937)
Self-restraint belongs in the domain of will and not of judgment, the check upon the judge is that imposed of his oath of office, by the Constitution, and by his own conscience and informed convictions.
Keywords*: Conscience, Constitution, Convictions, Judge, Judgment, Oath, Self-restraint*

Chief Justice Charles Evans Hughes
National Labor Relations Board v. Jones & Laughlin Steel Corporation,
301 U.S. 1, 30 (1937)
The cardinal principle of statutory construction is to save and not to destroy. We have repeatedly held that as between two possible interpretations of a statute, by one of which it would be unconstitutional and the other valid, our plain duty is to adopt that which will save the act. Even to avoid a serious doubt the rule is the same.
Keywords: *Constitutionality, Judicial review, Plain duty, Principles, Statutory construction, Statutory interpretation*

**Justice Harlan Fiske Stone,
dissenting in part**
Wright v. United States,
302 U.S. 583, 607 (1938)
The court has hitherto consistently held
that a literal reading of a provision of the
constitution which defeats a purpose
evident when the instrument is read as a
whole, is not to be favored.
Keywords: *Constitutional interpretation, Judicial process*

Justice Hugo Black, concurring
Coleman v. Miller,
307 U.S. 433, 459 (1939)
Congress, possessing exclusive power
over the amending process, cannot be
bound by and is under no duty to accept
the pronouncements upon that exclusive
power by this court or by the Kansas
courts. Neither State nor Federal courts
can review that power. Therefore, any
judicial expression amounting to more
than mere acknowledgment of exclusive
Congressional power over the political
process of amendment is a mere admonition to the Congress in the nature of
an advisory opinion, given wholly without constitutional authority.
Keywords: *Advisory opinions,
Amending process, Congress, Constitutional authority, Judicial power,
Political process*

Justice Felix Frankfurter, concurring
Coleman v. Miller,
307 U.S. 433, 462 (1939)
It is not our function, and it is beyond our
power, to write legal essays or to give legal opinions, however solemnly requested
and however great the national emergency.

Keywords: *Advisory opinions, Judicial authority, Judicial function, Legal essays, Legal opinions, National
emergency*

Chief Justice Charles Evans Hughes
United States v. Borden Company,
308 U.S. 188, 198 (1939)
It is a cardinal principle of construction
that repeals by implication are not favored. When there are two acts upon the
same subject, the rule is to give effect to
both if possible.
Keywords: *Statutory authority,
Statutory construction, Statutory interpretation*

Chief Justice Charles Evans Hughes
*Chicot County Drainage District v. Baxter
State Bank,*
308 U.S. 371, 374 (1940)
The courts below have proceeded on the
theory that the Act of Congress, having
been found to be unconstitutional, was
not a law; that it was inoperative, conferring no rights and imposing no duties. It
is quite clear, however, that such broad
statements as to the effect of a determination of unconstitutionality must be taken
with qualifications. The actual existence
of a statute, prior to such a determination,
is an operative fact and may have consequences which cannot justly be ignored.
The past cannot always be erased by a
new judicial declaration. The effect of the
subsequent ruling as to invalidity may
have to be considered in various aspects,—with respect to particular relations, individual and corporate, and particular conduct, private and official.
Keywords: *Congressional acts, Con-*

stitutionality, Judicial authority, Judicial declarations, Judicial review, Statutory interpretation

Justice Felix Frankfurter
Helvering v. Hallock,
309 U.S. 106, 119 (1940)
It would require very persuasive circumstances enveloping congressional silence to debar this Court from reexamining its own doctrines.
Keywords: *Congressional intent, Congressional silence, Doctrines, Judicial doctrines, Judicial process*

Justice Felix Frankfurter
Federal Communications Commission v. Pottsville Broadcasting Co.,
309 U.S. 134, 146 (1940)
. . . courts are not charged with general guardianship against all potential mischief in the complicated tasks of government.
Keywords*: Governmental function, Governmental mischief, Judicial authority, Judicial function, Judicial oversight*

Justice Hugo Black
Bridges v. California,
314 U.S. 252, 270–271 (1942)
The assumption that respect for the judiciary can be won by shielding judges from published criticism wrongly appraises the character of American public opinion. For it is a prized American privilege to speak one's mind, although not always with perfect good taste, on all public institutions. And an enforced silence, however limited, solely in the name of preserving the dignity of the bench, would probably engender resentment, suspicion, and contempt much more than it would enhance respect.
Keywords: *Free speech, Judges, Judicial criticism, Judicial independence, Judiciary, Public opinion*

Justice Hugo Black
United States v. Bethlehem Steel Corporation,
315 U.S. 289, 308–309 (1942)
. . . indignation based on the notions of morality of this or any other court cannot be judicially transmuted into a principle of law of greater force than the expressed will of Congress.
Keywords*: Congressional will, Judicial function, Legal principles, Morality*

Justice Felix Frankfurter, dissenting
Pearce v. Commissioner of Internal Revenue,
315 U.S. 543, 558 (1942)
In law as in life lines have to be drawn. But the fact that a line has to be drawn somewhere does not justify its being drawn anywhere. The line must follow some direction of policy, whether rooted in logic or experience. Lines should not be drawn simply for the sake of drawing lines.
Keywords*: Judicial formulas, Judicial restraint, Legal limitations*

Justice Stanley Reed
Jones v. Opelika,
316 U.S. 584, 593–594 (1942)
Courts, no more than Constitutions, can intrude into the consciences of men or compel them to believe contrary to their faith or think contrary to their convictions. . . .

Keywords: Conscience, Constitutional limitations, Faith, Judicial authority, Religion, Thought

Justice Robert Jackson, dissenting
Williams v. North Carolina,
317 U.S. 287, 324 (1942)
. . . I had supposed that our judicial responsibility is for the regularity of the law, not for the regularity of pedigrees.
Keywords: Legal consistency, Judicial authority, Judicial legitimacy, Judicial process, Judicial responsibility, Marriage

Justice Felix Frankfurter, dissenting
West Virginia Board of Education v. Barnette,
319 U.S. 624, 646–647 (1943)
One who belongs to the most vilified and persecuted minority in history is not likely to be insensible to the freedoms guaranteed by our Constitution. Were my purely personal attitude relevant, I should wholeheartedly associate myself with the general libertarian views in the Court's opinion, representing as they do the thought and action of a lifetime. But as judges we are neither Jew nor Gentile, neither Catholic nor agnostic. . . .
Keywords: Constitutional freedoms, History, Judicial authority, Judicial legitimacy, Libertarian views, Persecuted minorities, Religion

Justice Owen Roberts, dissenting
Smith v. Allwright,
321 U.S. 649, 669 (1944)
The reason for my concern is that the in-

stant decision, overruling that announced about nine years ago, tends to bring adjudications of this tribunal into the same class as a restricted railroad ticket, good for this day and train only. I have no assurance, in view of current decisions, that the opinion announced today may not shortly be repudiated and overruled by justices who deem they have new light on the subject.
Keywords: Judicial authority, Judicial function, Legal precedents, Stare decisis

Justice Frank Murphy
Commissioner of Internal Revenue v. Scottish American Investment Co.,
323 U.S. 119, 124 (1944)
The judicial eye must not in the first instance rove about searching for evidence to support other conflicting inferences and conclusions which the judges or the litigants may consider more reasonable or desirable. It must be cast directly and primarily upon the evidence in support of those made by the tax court.
Keywords: Judicial decision making, Judicial process

Justice Owen Roberts, concurring
Precision Instrument Manufacturing Co. v. Automotive Maintenance Machinery Co.,
324 U.S. 806, 820 (1945)
The case ought not to have been taken by this Court. It involves merely the application of acknowledged principles of law to the facts disclosed by the record. Decision here settles nothing save the merits or demerits of the conduct of the respective parties. In my

view it is not the function of this court to weigh the facts for the third time in order to choose between litigants, where appraisal of the conduct of each must affect the result.

Keywords: *Appellate process, Conduct, Judicial function, Legal principles*

Chief Justice Harlan Fiske Stone
Federation of Labor v. McAdory,
325 U.S. 450, 470 (1945)
Most courts conceive it to be their duty to construe a statute, whenever reasonably possible, so that it may be constitutional rather than unconstitutional.

Keywords: *Constitutionality, Court practice, Judicial function, Statutory interpretation*

Justice Felix Frankfurter
New York v. United States,
326 U.S. 572, 583 (1946)
The process of Constitutional adjudication does not thrive on conjuring up horrible possibilities that never happen in the real world and devising doctrines sufficiently comprehensive in detail to cover the remotest contingency.

Keywords: *Adjudication, Legal doctrines, Slippery slope*

Justice Wiley Rutledge, dissenting
United States v. United Mine Workers of America,
330 U.S. 258, 363 (1947)
At times in our system the way in which courts perform their function becomes as important as what they do in the result. In some respects matters of procedure constitute the very essence of ordered liberty under the constitution.

Keywords: *Constitutional expecta-tions, Judicial function, Judicial process, Liberty, Procedure*

Justice Robert Jackson
Gulf Oil Corp. v. Gilbert,
330 U.S. 501, 508–509 (1947)
Administrative difficulties follow for courts when litigation is piled up in congested centers instead of being handled at its origin. Jury duty is a burden that ought not to be imposed upon the people of a community which has no relation to the litigation. In cases which touch the affairs of many persons, there is reason for holding the trial in their view and reach rather than in remote parts of the country where they can learn of it by report only. There is a local interest in having localized controversies decided at home. There is an appropriateness, too, in having the trial of a diversity case in a forum that is at home with the state law that must govern the case, rather than having a court in some other forum untangle problems in conflict of laws, and in law foreign to itself.

Keywords: *Caseload, Community interests, Forum, Judicial administration, Jury duty, Litigation, Local interests, State law*

Justice Hugo Black, dissenting
Francis v. Southern Pacific Co.,
333 U.S. 445, 453 (1948)
. . . if judges make rules of law, it would seem that they should keep their minds open in order to exercise a continuing and helpful supervision over the manner in which their laws serve the public. Experience might prove that a rule created by judges should never have

been created at all, or that their rule, though originally sound, had become wholly unsuited to new physical and social conditions developed by a dynamic society. A revaluation of social and economic interests affected by the old rule might reveal the unwisdom of its expansion or imperatively require its revision or abandonment.

Keywords: *Experience, Judges, Judicial activism, Judicial authority, Judicial legitimacy, Judicial restraint, Legal rules, Societal interests*

Justice Felix Frankfurter, concurring
American Federation of Labor v. American Sash & Door Co.,
335 U.S. 538, 555–556 (1949)
The Court is not saved from being oligarchic because it professes to act in the service of humane ends. As history amply proves, the judiciary is prone to misconceive the public good by confounding private notions with constitutional requirements, and such misconceptions are not subject to legitimate displacement by the will of the people except at too slow a pace. Judges appointed for life whose decisions run counter to prevailing opinion cannot be voted out of office and supplanted by men of views more consonant with it. They are even farther removed from democratic pressures by the fact that their deliberations are in secret and remain beyond disclosure either by periodic reports or by such a modern device for securing responsibility to the electorate as the "press conference." But a democracy need not rely on the courts to save it from its own unwisdom. If it is alert—and without alertness by the people there can be no enduring democracy—unwise or unfair legislation can readily be removed from the statute books. It is by such vigilance over its representatives that democracy proves itself.

Keywords: *Constitutional requirements, Democracy, History, Judges, Judicial function, Judicial independence, Judicial process, Legislation, Lifetime tenure, Oligarchy, Political process, Public interest, Statutes, Wisdom*

Justice Hugo Black, dissenting
H.P. Hood & Sons v. DuMond,
336 U.S. 525, 558 (1949)
It requires more than invocation of the spectre of "Balkanization" and eulogy of the Constitution's framers to prove that there is a gnat's heel difference in the burdens imposed on commerce by the two laws.

Keywords: *Commerce, Commerce clause, Framers, Judicial process, Judicial review*

Justice Felix Frankfurter
Maryland v. Baltimore Radio Show,
338 U.S. 912, 918 (1950)
A case may raise an important question but the record may be cloudy. It may be desirable to have different aspects of an issue further illumined by the lower courts. Wise adjudication has its own time for ripening.

Keywords: *Adjudication, Case record, Judicial process, Remand, Ripeness*

Justice Felix Frankfurter, dissenting
United States v. Rabinowitz,
339 U.S. 56, 69 (1950)
It is true . . . of journeys in the law that the place you reach depends on the direction you are taking. And so, where

one comes out on a case depends on where one goes in.

Keywords: Judicial decision making, Judicial outcomes, Judicial process

Justice Robert Jackson, concurring
McGrath v. Kristensen,
340 U.S. 162, 178 (1950)

Perhaps Dr. Johnson really went to the heart of the matter when he explained a blunder in his dictionary—"ignorance, sir, ignorance." But an escape less self-deprecating was taken by Lord Westbury, who, it is said, rebuffed a barrister's reliance upon an earlier opinion of his lordship: "I can only say that I am amazed that a man of my intelligence should have been guilty of giving such an opinion." If there are other ways of gracefully and good-naturedly surrendering former views to a better considered position, I invoke them all.

Keywords: Humility, Judicial errors

Justice Felix Frankfurter, concurring
Dennis v. United States,
341 U.S. 494, 525 (1951)

History teaches that the independence of the judiciary is jeopardized when courts become embroiled in the passions of the day and assume primary responsibility in choosing between competing political, economic and social pressures.

Keywords: History, Judicial independence, Judicial responsibilities, Political pressures, Societal concerns

Justice Robert Jackson
Sacher v. United States,
343 U.S. 1, 12 (1952)

That contempt power over counsel, summary or otherwise, is capable of abuse is certain. Men who make their way to the bench sometimes exhibit vanity, irascibility, narrowness, arrogance, and other weaknesses to which human flesh is heir. Most judges, however, recognize and respect courageous, forthright lawyerly conduct. They rarely mistake overzeal or heated words of a man fired with a desire to win, for the contemptuous conduct which defies rulings and deserves punishment. They recognize that our profession necessarily is a contentious one and they respect the lawyer who makes a strenuous effort for his client.

Keywords: Contempt, Counsel, Judges, Judicial abuse, Punishment, Zealous lawyers

Justice Felix Frankfurter, dissenting
Sacher v. United States,
343 U.S. 1, 37–38 (1952)

Criminal justice is concerned with the pathology of the body politic. In administering the criminal law, judges wield the most awesome surgical instruments of society. A criminal trial, it has been well said, should have the atmosphere of the operating room. The presiding judge determines the atmosphere. He is not an umpire who enforces the rules of a game, or merely a moderator between contestants. If he is adequate to his functions, the moral authority which he radiates will impose the indispensable standards of dignity and austerity upon all those who participate in a criminal trial.

Keywords: Criminal justice, Criminal trial, Dignity, Judges, Judicial authority, Judicial function

Justice Robert Jackson
Orloff v. Willoughby,
345 U.S. 83, 93–94 (1953)
. . . judges are not given the task of running the Army. The responsibility for setting up channels through which such grievances can be considered and fairly settled rests upon the Congress and upon the President of the United States and his subordinates. The military constitutes a specialized community governed by a separate discipline from that of the civilian. Orderly government requires that the judiciary be as scrupulous not to interfere with legitimate Army matters as the Army must be scrupulous not to intervene in judicial matters.
Keywords: *Civilian, Commander in chief, Congressional authority, Judicial authority, Military*

Justice Robert Jackson, concurring
United States v. Public Utilities Commission of California,
345 U.S. 295, 319 (1953)
I should concur in this result if the Court could reach it by analysis of the statute instead of by psychoanalysis of Congress. When we decide from legislative history, including statements of witnesses at hearings, what Congress probably had in mind, we must put ourselves in the place of a majority of Congressmen and act according to the impression we think this history should have made on them. Never having been a Congressman, I am handicapped in that weird endeavor. That process seems to me not interpretation of a statute but creation of a statute.
Keywords: *Congressional intent, Judicial legislating, Judicial psychoana-lyzing, Legislative history, Legislative record, Statutory analysis, Statutory interpretation, Witnesses*

Justice Felix Frankfurter, concurring
Terry v. Adams,
345 U.S. 461, 472 (1953)
Whenever the law draws a line between permissive and forbidden conduct cases are bound to arise which are not obviously on one side or the other. These dubious situations disclose the limited utility of the figure of speech, a "line," in the law. Drawing a "line" is necessarily exercising a judgment, however confined the conscientious judgment may be within the bounds of constitutional and statutory provisions, the course of decisions, and the presuppositions of the judicial process. If "line" is in the main a fruitful tool for dividing the sheep from the goats, it must not be forgotten that since the "line" is figurative the place of this or that case in relation to it cannot be ascertained externally but is a matter of the mind.
Keywords: *Conduct, Constitutional authority, Judicial process, Judicial restraint, Judicial test, Statutory purpose*

Chief Justice Earl Warren
Brown v. Board of Education,
349 U.S. 294, 301 (1955)
. . . with all deliberate speed. . . .
Keywords: *Due process, Judicial formula, Judicial remedy*

Justice Felix Frankfurter, dissenting
Trop v. Dulles,
356 U.S. 86, 120 (1958)
It is not easy to stand aloof and allow

want of wisdom to prevail, to disregard one's own strongly held view of what is wise in the conduct of affairs. But it is not the business of this Court to pronounce policy. It must observe a fastidious regard for limitations on its own power, and this precludes the Court's giving effect to its own notions of what is wise or politic. That self-restraint is of the essence in the observance of the judicial oath, for the Constitution has not authorized the judges to sit in judgment on the wisdom of what Congress and the Executive Branch do.

Keywords: *Constitutional authority, Judicial authority, Judicial function, Judicial oath, Judicial power, Judicial review, Judicial self-restraint, Wisdom*

Justice John Marshall Harlan, dissenting
Michalic v. Cleveland Tankers, Inc.,
364 U.S. 325, 332–333 (1960)
At the opening of a term which finds the court's docket crowded with more important and difficult litigation than in many years, it is not without irony that we should be witnessing among the first matters to be heard a routine negligence . . . case involving only issues of facts. I continue to believe that such cases, distressing and important as they are for unsuccessful plaintiffs, do not belong in this Court.

Keywords: *Caseload, Criticism, Judicial function, Litigation*

Justice Felix Frankfurter, dissenting
Monroe v. Pape,
365 U.S. 167, 241 (1961)
[Judicial s]elf-limitation is not a matter of technical nicety, nor judicial timidity. It reflects the recognition that to no small degree the effectiveness of the legal order depends upon the infrequency with which it solves its problems by resorting to determinations of ultimate power. Especially is this true where the circumstances under which those ultimate determinations must be made are not conducive to the most mature deliberation and decision.

Keywords: *Judicial function, Judicial power, Judicial self-restraint, Legal system, Rule of law*

Justice William Douglas, dissenting
Glidden Co. v. Zdanok,
370 U.S. 530, 598–599 (1962)
Judges of the Article III courts work by standards and procedures which are either specified in the Bill of Rights or supplied by well-known historic precedents. Article III courts are law courts, equity courts, and admiralty courts—all specifically named in Article III. They sit to determine "cases" or "controversies." But Article I courts have no such restrictions. They need not be confined to "cases" or "controversies" but can dispense legislative largesse. Their decisions may affect vital interests; yet like legislative bodies, zoning commissions, and other administrative bodies they need not observe the same standards of due process required in trials of Article III "cases" or "controversies."

Keywords: *Article I courts, Article III judges, Bill of Rights, Cases and controversies, Due process, History, Judicial power, Legislative power, Precedents, Quasi-judicial, Quasi-legislative*

Justice Tom Clark, dissenting
Douglas v. California,
372 U.S. 353, 359 (1963)
With this new fetish for indigency the Court piles an intolerable burden on the State's judicial machinery. Indeed, if the Court is correct it may be that we should first clean up our own house. We have afforded indigent litigants much less protection than has California. Last Term we received over 1,200 in forma pauperis applications in none of which had we appointed attorneys or required a record. Some were appeals of right. Still we denied the petitions or dismissed the appeals on the moving paper alone. At the same time we had hundreds of paid cases in which we permitted petitions or appeals to be filed with not only records but briefs by counsel, after which they were disposed of in due course.
Keywords: *Appellate process, Caseload, Indigency, In forma pauperis, Judicial function*

Justice John Marshall Harlan, dissenting
Wesberry v. Sanders,
376 U.S. 1, 48 (1964)
Today's decision has portents for our society and the Court itself which should be recognized. This is not a case in which the Court vindicates the kind of individual rights that are assured by the Due Process Clause of the Fourteenth Amendment, whose "vague contours" of course leave much room for constitutional developments necessitated by changing conditions in a dynamic society. Nor is this a case in which an emergent set of facts requires the Court to frame new principles to protect recognized constitutional rights. The claim for judicial relief in this case strikes at one of the fundamental doctrines of our system of government, the separation of powers. In upholding that claim, the Court attempts to effect reforms in a field which the Constitution, as plainly as can be, has committed exclusively to the political process. . . . This Court, no less than all other branches of the Government, is bound by the Constitution. The Constitution does not confer on the Court blanket authority to step into every situation where the political branch may be thought to have fallen short. The stability of this institution ultimately depends not only upon its being alert to keep the other branches of government within constitutional bounds but equally upon recognition of the limitations on the Court's own functions in the constitutional system. . . . What is done today saps the political process. The promise of judicial intervention in matters of this sort cannot but encourage popular inertia in efforts for political reform through the political process, with the inevitable result that the process is itself weakened. By yielding to the demand for a judicial remedy in this instance, the Court in my view does a disservice both to itself and to the broader values of our system of government.
Keywords: *Constitutional development, Constitutional interpretation, Constitutional limitations, Constitutional principles, Constitutional rights, Due process, Fourteenth Amendment, Individual rights, Judicial authority, Judicial intervention, Judicial relief, Judicial remedy, Political process, Political reform, Separation of powers*

Justice Potter Stewart, concurring
Jacobellis v. Ohio,
378 U.S. 184, 197 (1964)
I shall not today attempt further to define the kinds of material I understand
to be embraced within that shorthand
description; and perhaps I could never
succeed in intelligibly doing so. But I
know it when I see it, and the motion
picture involved in this case is not that.
Keywords: *Legal guidelines, Motion
pictures, Pornography*

Justice William Douglas, concurring
Memoirs v. Massachusetts,
383 U.S. 413, 427–428 (1966)
Every time an obscenity case is to be argued here, my office is flooded with letters and postal cards urging me to protect the community or the Nation by
striking down the publication. The messages are often identical even down to
commas and semicolons. The inference
is irresistible that they were all copied
from a school or church blackboard. Doz-
ens of postal cards often are mailed from
the same precinct. The drives are inces-
sant and the pressures are great. Happily
we do not bow to them. I mention them
only to emphasize the lack of popular
understanding of our constitutional system. Publications and utterances were
made immune from majoritarian control
by the First Amendment, applicable to
the States by reason of the Fourteenth.
No exceptions were made, not even for
obscenity.
Keywords: *First Amendment, Fourteenth Amendment, Free press, Free
speech, Judicial criticism, Majority
rule, Obscenity, Public opinion, States*

Justice John Marshall Harlan, dissenting
Flast v. Cohen,
392 U.S. 83, 132 (1968)
I appreciate that this Court does not ordinarily await the mandate of other
branches of the Government, but it seems
to me that the extraordinary character of
public actions, and of the mischievous,
if not dangerous, consequences they involve for the proper functioning of our
constitutional system, and in particular
of the federal courts, makes such judicial forbearance the part of wisdom.
Keywords: *Constitutional system, Federal courts, Judicial forbearance, Judicial wisdom, Separation of powers*

Justice Hugo Black, concurring
Epperson v. Arkansas,
393 U.S. 97, 114 (1968)
However wise this Court may be or may
become hereafter, it is doubtful that, sitting in Washington, it can successfully
supervise and censor the curriculum of
every public school in every hamlet and
city in the United States. I doubt that our
wisdom is so nearly infallible.
Keywords: *Curriculum, Education,
Judicial power, Judicial wisdom, Public schools*

Justice John Marshall Harlan, dissenting
Shapiro v. Thompson,
394 U.S. 618, 677 (1969)
Today's decision, it seems to me, reflects
to an unusual degree the current notion
that this Court possesses a peculiar wisdom all its own whose capacity to lead
this Nation out of its present troubles is
contained only by the limits of judicial
ingenuity in contriving new constitu-

tional principles to meet each problem as it arises. For anyone who, like myself, believes that it is an essential function of this Court to maintain the constitutional divisions between state and federal authority and among the three branches of the Federal Government, today's decision is a step in the wrong direction. This resurgence of the expansive view of "equal protection" carries the seeds of more judicial interference with the state and federal legislative process, much more than does the judicial application of "due process" according to traditional concepts, about which some members of this Court have expressed fears as to its potentialities for setting us up as judges "at large."

Keywords: *Due process, Equal protection, Federalism, Judicial interference, Judiciary, Legislative process, Separation of powers*

Chief Justice Earl Warren
Powell v. McCormack,
395 U.S. 486, 549 (1969)
Our system of government requires that federal courts on occasion interpret the Constitution in a manner at variance with the construction given the document by another branch. The alleged conflict that such an adjudication may cause cannot justify the courts' avoiding their constitutional responsibility.

Keywords: *Constitutional interpretation, Judicial function, Judicial review, Separation of powers*

Justice Thurgood Marshall
Grayned v. Rockford,
408 U.S. 104, 110 (1972)
Condemned to the use of words, we can never expect mathematical certainty from our language.

Keywords: *Language, Words*

Justice William Brennan, dissenting
United States v. Brewster,
408 U.S. 501, 550 (1972)
Our duty is to Nation and Constitution, not Congress.

Keywords: *Congress, Constitutional authority, Judicial legitimacy, Judicial responsibilities*

Justice Lewis Powell
United States v. United States District Court,
407 U.S. 297, 320 (1972)
We cannot accept the Government's argument that internal security matters are too subtle and complex for judicial evaluation. Courts regularly deal with the most difficult issues of our society. There is no reason to believe that federal judges will be insensitive to or uncomprehending of the issues involved in domestic security cases. Certainly courts can recognize that domestic security surveillance involves different considerations from the surveillance of "ordinary crime." If the threat is too subtle or complex for our senior law enforcement officers to convey its significance to a court, one may question whether there is probable cause for surveillance.

Keywords: *Crime, Domestic security, Federal judges, Internal security, Judicial evaluation, Law enforcement, Probable cause, Societal issues, Surveillance*

Justice Harry Blackmun
Roe v. Wade,
410 U.S. 113, 125 (1973)
. . . when, as here, pregnancy is a significant fact in the litigation, the normal 266-

day human gestation period is so short that the pregnancy will come to term before the usual appellate process is complete. If that termination makes a case moot, pregnancy litigation seldom will survive much beyond the trial stage, and appellate review will be effectively denied. Our laws should not be that rigid.... Pregnancy provides a classic justification for a conclusion of non-mootness.

Keywords: Abortion, Appellate process, Appellate review, Human gestation, Legal flexibility, Litigation, Moot issue, Pregnancy, Principle

Chief Justice Warren Burger
Gilligan v. Morgan,
413 U.S. 1, 10–11 (1973)
It would be difficult to think of a clearer example of the type of governmental action that was intended by the Constitution to be left to the political branches directly responsible—as the Judicial Branch is not—to the electoral process. Moreover, it is difficult to conceive of an area of governmental activity in which the courts have less competence. The complex, subtle, and professional decisions as to the composition, training, equipping, and control of a military force are essentially professional military judgments, subject always to civilian control of the Legislative and Executive Branches. The ultimate responsibility for these decisions is appropriately vested in branches of the government which are periodically subject to electoral accountability. It is this power of oversight and control of military force by elected representatives and officials which underlies our entire constitutional system. ...

Keywords: Civilian, Constitutional

authority, Electoral accountability, Judicial authority, Judicial competence, Military, Oversight, Political branches, Representative democracy

Justice Potter Stewart, dissenting
Pittsburgh Press Co. v. Pittsburgh Commission on Human Relations,
413 U.S. 376, 402 (1973)
So long as Members of this Court view the First Amendment as no more than a set of "values" to be balanced against other "values," that Amendment will remain in grave jeopardy.

Keywords: Constitutional balancing, Constitutional interpretation, Constitutional rights, First Amendment, Values

Justice William Brennan, dissenting
DeFunis v. Odegaard,
416 U.S. 312, 350 (1974)
Although the Court should, of course, avoid unnecessary decisions of constitutional questions, we should not transform principles of avoidance of constitutional decisions into devices for sidestepping resolution of difficult cases.

Keywords: Constitutional adjudication, Constitutional questions, Judicial process, Judicial responsibilities, Principles

Justice William Rehnquist
Ross v. Moffitt,
417 U.S. 600, 617 (1974)
The suggestion that a State is responsible for providing counsel to one petitioning this Court simply because it initiated the prosecution which led to the judgment sought to be reviewed is unsupported by either reason or authority.

Keywords: Appellate review, Consti-

tutional authority, Counsel, Prosecution, States

Chief Justice Warren Burger
United States v. Richardson,
418 U.S. 166, 179–180 (1974)
As our society has become more complex, our numbers more vast, our lives more varied and our resources more strained, citizens increasingly request the intervention of the courts on a greater variety of issues than at any period of our national development. The acceptance of new categories of judicially cognizable injury has not eliminated the basic principle that to invoke judicial power the claimant must have a "personal stake in the outcome". . . or a "particular concrete injury" . . . "that he has sustained . . . a direct injury" . . . in short, something more than "generalized grievances."
Keywords: *Grievances, Injury, Judicial function, Judicial power, Justice, Principles, Public expectations, Resources, Society*

Justice William Douglas, dissenting
Warth v. Seldin,
422 U.S. 490, 519 (1975)
The mounting caseload of federal courts is well known. But cases such as this one reflect festering sores in our society; and the American dream teaches that if one reaches high enough and persists there is a forum where justice is dispensed. I would lower the technical barriers and let the courts serve that ancient need.
Keywords: *History, Judicial caseload, Judicial forum, Judicial function, Justice, Rule of law, Societal problems*

Justice Harry Blackmun, dissenting
Beal v. Doe,
432 U.S. 438, 463 (1977)
There is another world "out there," the existence of which the Court, I suspect, either chooses to ignore or fears to recognize. And so the cancer of poverty will continue to grow. This is a sad day for those who regard the Constitution as a force that would serve justice to all even-handedly and, in so doing, would better the lot of the poorest among us.
Keywords: *Criticism, Equal protection, Judiciary, Justice, Opinion, Poverty*

Justice William Brennan
Nixon v. Administrator of General Services,
433 U.S. 425, 484 (1977)
. . . this Court is not free to invalidate Acts of Congress based upon inferences that we may be asked to draw from our personalized reading of the contemporary scene or recent history.
Keywords: *Congressional intent, History, Judicial authority, Judicial legitimacy, Judicial restraint, Judicial review, Legislation, Statutory interpretation*

Justice William Rehnquist, dissenting
Orr v. Orr,
440 U.S. 268, 300 (1979)
Much as "Caesar had his Brutus; Charles the First his Cromwell," Congress and the States have this Court to ensure that their legislative Acts do not run afoul of the limitations imposed by the United States Constitution. But this Court has neither a Brutus nor a Cromwell to impose a similar discipline on it. While our "right of expounding the Constitution"

is confined to "cases of a Judiciary Nature," we are empowered to determine for ourselves when the requirements of Art. III are satisfied.

Keywords: *Article III, Cases, Checks and balances, Congress, Judicial activism, Judicial authority, Judicial restraint, Judicial review, Legislation, States*

Justice William Rehnquist
Bell v. Wolfish,
441 U.S. 520, 563 (1979)

There was a time not too long ago when the federal judiciary took a completely "hands-off" approach to the problem of prison administration. In recent years, however, these courts largely have discarded this "hands-off" attitude and have waded into this complex arena. The deplorable conditions and Draconian restrictions of some of our Nation's prisons are too well known to require recounting here, and the federal courts rightly have condemned these sordid aspects of our prison systems. But many of these same courts have, in the name of the Constitution, become increasingly enmeshed in the minutiae of prison operations. Judges, after all, are human. They, no less than others in our society, have a natural tendency to believe that their individual solutions to often intractable problems are better and more workable than those of the persons who are actually charged with and trained in the running of the particular institution under examination. But under the Constitution, the first question to be answered is not whose plan is best, but in what branch of the Government is lodged the authority to initially devise the plan. This does not mean that constitutional rights are not to be scrupulously observed. It does mean, however, that the inquiry of federal courts into prison management must be limited to the issue of whether a particular system violates any prohibition of the Constitution or, in the case of a federal prison, a statute. The wide range of "judgment calls" that meet constitutional and statutory requirements are confided to officials outside of the Judicial Branch of Government.

Keywords: *Constitutional rights, Judging, Judicial authority, Judicial limitations, Judicial process, Judiciary, Prison administration, Statutory requirements*

Justice John Paul Stevens
Chapman v. Houston Welfare Rights Org.,
441 U.S. 600, 608 (1979)

As in all cases of statutory construction, our task is to interpret the words of these statutes in light of the purposes Congress sought to serve.

Keywords: *Congressional intent, Judicial interpretation, Statutory construction*

Justice Thurgood Marshall, dissenting
Personnel Administrator of Massachusetts v. Feeney,
442 U.S. 256, 282 (1979)

Absent an omniscience not commonly attributed to the judiciary, it will often be impossible to ascertain the sole or even dominant purpose of a given statute.

Keywords: *Judicial authority, Judicial insight, Judicial wisdom, Statutory interpretation, Statutory intent*

Justice Lewis Powell, dissenting
Columbus Board of Education v. Penick,
443 U.S. 449, 487–488 (1979)
The time has come for a thoughtful re-examination of the proper limits of the role of courts in confronting the intractable problems of public education in our complex society. Proved discrimination by state or local authorities should never be tolerated, and it is a first responsibility of the judiciary to put an end to it where it has been proved. But many courts have continued also to impose wide-ranging decrees, and to retain on-going supervision over school systems. Local and state legislative and administrative authorities have been supplanted or relegated to initiative-stifling roles as minions of the courts. Indeed, there is reason to believe that some legislative bodies have welcomed judicial activism with respect to a subject so inherently difficult and so politically sensitive that the prospect of others confronting it seems inviting. Federal courts no longer should encourage this deference by the appropriate authorities—no matter how willing they may be to defer. Courts are the branch least competent to provide long-range solutions acceptable to the public and most conducive to achieving both diversity in the classroom and quality education.
Keywords: Courts, Education, Judicial activism, Judicial remedies, Legislatures, Politics, Society

Justice Harry Blackmun, dissenting
Harris v. McRae,
448 U.S. 297, 348–349 (1980)
There is "condescension" in the Court's holding that "she may go elsewhere for her abortion"; this is "disingenuous and alarming"; the Government "punitively impresses upon a needy minority its own concepts of the socially desirable, the publicly acceptable, and the morally sound"; the "financial argument, of course, is specious"; there truly is "another world 'out there,' the existence of which the Court, I suspect, either chooses to ignore or fears to recognize"; the "cancer of poverty will continue to grow"; and "the lot of the poorest among us," once again, and still, is not to be bettered.
Keywords: Abortion, Criticism, Indigence, Minority, Moral, Opinion, Poverty

Justice William Rehnquist, dissenting
Richmond Newspapers, Inc. v. Virginia,
448 U.S. 555, 604 (1980)
In the Gilbert and Sullivan operetta "Iolanthe," the Lord Chancellor recites: "The Law is the true embodiment of everything that's excellent, It has no kind of fault or flaw, And I, my Lords, embody the Law." It is difficult not to derive more than a little of this flavor from the various opinions supporting the judgment in this case.
Keywords: Criticism, Judicial opinions, Opera, Personality

Justice William Rehnquist, dissenting
Richmond Newspapers, Inc. v. Virginia,
448 U.S. 555, 605–606 (1980)
The proper administration of justice in any nation is bound to be a matter of the highest concern to all thinking citizens. But to gradually rein in, as this Court has done over the past generation, all of the

ultimate decisionmaking power over how justice shall be administered, not merely in the federal system but in each of the 50 States, is a task that no Court consisting of nine persons, however gifted, is equal to. Nor is it desirable that such authority be exercised by such a tiny numerical fragment of the 220 million people who compose the population of this country.
Keywords: *Citizens, Judicial authority, Judicial legitimacy, Judicial limitations, Judicial power, Judicial restraint, Justice*

Justice William Rehnquist
Valley Forge Christian College v. Americans United,
454 U.S. 464, 473 (1982)
Were the federal courts merely publicly funded forums for the ventilation of public grievances or the refinement of jurisprudential understandings, the concept of "standing" would be quite unnecessary. But the "cases and controversies" language of Art. III forecloses the conversion of courts of the United States into judicial versions of college debating forums.
Keywords: *Article III, Cases and controversies, Grievances, Judicial function, Jurisprudence, Public institution, Standing*

Chief Justice Warren Burger
Plyler v. Doe,
457 U.S. 202, 242 (1982)
. . . the Constitution does not constitute us as "Platonic Guardians" nor does it vest in this Court the authority to strike down laws because they do not meet our standards of desirable social policy, "wisdom," or "common sense."

Keywords: *Judicial activism, Judicial authority, Judicial review, Judicial restraint, Policy, Wisdom*

Justice Byron White, dissenting
Northern Pipeline Construction Co. v. Marathon Pipe Line Co.,
458 U.S. 50, 116–117 (1982)
. . . no one seriously argues that the Bankruptcy Act of 1978 represents an attempt by the political branches of government to aggrandize themselves at the expense of the third branch or an attempt to undermine the authority of constitutional courts in general. Indeed, the congressional perception of a lack of judicial interest in bankruptcy matters was one of the factors that led to the establishment of the bankruptcy courts: Congress feared that this lack of interest would lead to a failure by federal district courts to deal with bankruptcy matters in an expeditious manner. Bankruptcy matters are, for the most part, private adjudications of little political significance. Although some bankruptcies may indeed present politically controversial circumstances or issues, Congress has far more direct ways to involve itself in such matters than through some sort of subtle, or not so subtle, influence on bankruptcy judges.
Keywords: *Adjudications, Article III courts, Bankruptcy courts, Congress, Congressional intent, Judges, Judicial authority*

Justice Sandra Day O'Connor, dissenting
Akron v. Akron Center for Reproductive Health, Inc.,
462 U.S. 416, 453–454 (1983)
The trimester or "three-stage" approach

adopted by the Court in *Roe*, and, in a modified form, employed by the Court to analyze the regulations in these cases, cannot be supported as a legitimate or useful framework for accommodating the woman's right and the State's interests. The decision of the Court today graphically illustrates why the trimester approach is a completely unworkable method of accommodating the conflicting personal rights and compelling state interests that are involved in the abortion context.
Keywords*: Abortion, Personal rights, Precedent, State interests*

Justice William Brennan, dissenting
Marsh v. Chambers,
463 U.S. 783, 795–796 (1983)

. . . disagreement with the Court requires that I confront the fact that some 20 years ago, in a concurring opinion in one of the cases striking down official prayer and ceremonial Bible reading in the public schools, I came very close to endorsing essentially the result reached by the Court today. Nevertheless, after much reflection, I have come to the conclusion that I was wrong then and that the Court is wrong today.
Keywords*: Bible reading, Judicial corrections, Opinions, Prayer, Public schools, Religion*

Justice Sandra Day O'Connor, concurring
Brockett v. Spokane Arcades, Inc.,
472 U.S. 491, 510 (1985)

Speculation by a federal court about the meaning of a state statute in the absence of prior state court adjudication is particularly gratuitous when, as is the case here, the state courts stand willing to address questions of state law on certification from a federal court.
Keywords*: Adjudication, Federal courts, State courts, State statutes*

Justice Byron White, dissenting
Thornburgh v. American College of Obstetricians & Gynecologists,
476 U.S. 747, 786–787 (1986)

The rule of *stare decisis* is essential if case-by-case judicial decisionmaking is to be reconciled with the principle of the rule of law, for when governing legal standards are open to revision in every case, deciding cases becomes a mere exercise of judicial will, with arbitrary and unpredictable results. But *stare decisis* is not the only constraint upon judicial decisionmaking. Cases—like this one—that involve our assumed power to set aside on grounds of unconstitutionality a state or federal statute representing the democratically expressed will of the people call other considerations into play. Because the Constitution itself is ordained and established by the people of the United States, constitutional adjudication by this Court does not, in theory at any rate, frustrate the authority of the people to govern themselves through institutions of their own devising and in accordance with principles of their own choosing. But decisions that find in the Constitution principles or values that cannot fairly be read into that document usurp the people's authority, for such decisions represent choices that the people have never made and that they cannot disavow through corrective legislation. For this reason, it is essential that this Court maintain the power to restore authority to its proper possessors by correcting constitutional decisions that, on reconsideration, are found to be mistaken.

Keywords: *Constitutional adjudication, Constitutional principles, Constitutionality, Judicial authority, Judicial legitimacy, Judicial process, Judicial review, Judicial will, Legislation, Rule of law, Self-government, Stare decisis*

Justice Byron White, dissenting
Thornburgh v. American College of Obstetricians & Gynecologists,
476 U.S. 747, 813–814 (1986)
The decision today appears symptomatic of the Court's own insecurity over its handiwork in *Roe v. Wade* and the cases following that decision. Aware that in *Roe* it essentially created something out of nothing and that there are many in this country who hold that decision to be basically illegitimate, the Court responds defensively. Perceiving, in a statute implementing the State's legitimate policy of preferring childbirth to abortion, a threat to or criticism of the decision in *Roe v. Wade*, the majority indiscriminately strikes down statutory provisions that in no way contravene the right recognized in *Roe*. I do not share the warped point of view of the majority, nor can I follow the tortuous path the majority treads in proceeding to strike down the statute before us.

Keywords: *Abortion, Childbirth, Criticism, Judicial authority, Judicial legitimacy, Judicial review, Judicial will, Legislative intent, Roe, Statutory interpretation*

Justice Byron White
Bowers v. Hardwick,
478 U.S. 186, 194–195 (1986)
Nor are we inclined to take a more expansive view of our authority to discover new fundamental rights imbedded in the Due Process Clause. The Court is most vulnerable and comes nearest to illegitimacy when it deals with judge-made constitutional law having little or no cognizable roles in the language or design of the Constitution. . . . There should be therefore great resistance to expanding the substantive reach of those Clauses, particularly if it requires redefining the category of rights deemed to be fundamental. Otherwise the Judiciary necessarily takes to itself further authority to govern the country without express constitutional authority.

Keywords: *Constitutional authority, Due Process Clause, Judicial authority, Judge-made law*

Justice Thurgood Marshall, dissenting
United States v. Salerno,
481 U.S. 739, 767 (1987)
Throughout the world today there are men, women, and children interned indefinitely, awaiting trials which may never come or which may be a mockery of the word, because their governments believe them to be "dangerous." Our Constitution, whose construction began two centuries ago, can shelter us forever from the evils of such unchecked power. Over 200 years it has slowly, through our efforts, grown more durable, more expansive, and more just. But it cannot protect

us if we lack the courage, and the self-restraint, to protect ourselves. Today a majority of the Court applies itself to an ominous exercise in demolition. Theirs is truly a decision which will go forth without authority, and come back without respect.

Keywords: *Bail, Courage, Dangerous citizens, Judicial authority, Judicial legitimacy, Trial, Unchecked power*

Justice Lewis Powell, concurring
Rankin v. McPherson,
483 U.S. 378, 392 (1987)
It is not easy to understand how this case has assumed constitutional dimensions and reached the Supreme Court of the United States. The fact that the case is here, however, illustrates the uniqueness of our Constitution and our system of judicial review: courts at all levels are available and receptive to claims of injustice, large and small, by any and every citizen of this country.

Keywords: *Constitutional adjudication, Judicial review, Justice, Legal recourse*

Justice William Brennan, dissenting
Michael H. v. Gerald D.,
491 U.S. 110, 157 (1989)
The atmosphere surrounding today's decision is one of make-believe. Beginning with the suggestion that the situation confronting us here does not repeat itself every day in every corner of the country, moving on to the claim that it is tradition alone that supplies the details of the liberty that the Constitution protects, and passing finally to the notion that the Court always has recognized a cramped vision of "the family," today's decision lets stand California's pro-nouncement that Michael—whom blood tests show to a 98 percent probability to be Victoria's father—is not Victoria's father. When and if the Court awakes to reality, it will find a world very different from the one it expects.

Keywords: *Family, Judicial legitimacy, Liberty, Tradition*

Justice Byron White
Missouri v. Jenkins,
495 U.S. 33, 51 (1990)
. . . the imposition of a tax increase by a federal court was an extraordinary event. In assuming for itself the fundamental and delicate power of taxation the District Court not only intruded on local authority but circumvented it altogether. Before taking such a drastic step the District Court was obliged to assure itself that no permissible alternative would have accomplished the required task.

Keywords: *Federalism, Judicial authority, Judicial legitimacy, Judicial remedies, Local authority, Separation of powers, Taxation*

Justice Anthony Kennedy, concurring
Missouri v. Jenkins,
495 U.S. 33, 75 (1990)
If, however, judicial discretion is to provide the sole limit on judicial remedies, that discretion must counsel restraint. Ill-considered entry into the volatile field of taxation is a step that may place at risk the legitimacy that justifies judicial independence.

Keywords: *Judicial authority, Judicial discretion, Judicial independence, Judicial legitimacy, Judicial remedies, Taxation*

Justice Anthony Kennedy, concurring
Missouri v. Jenkins,
495 U.S. 33, 81 (1990)
This case is a stark illustration of the ever-present question whether ends justify means. Few ends are more important than enforcing the guarantee of equal educational opportunity for our Nation's children. But rules of taxation that override state political structures not themselves subject to any constitutional infirmity raise serious questions of federal authority, questions compounded by the odd posture of a case in which the Court assumes the validity of a novel conception of desegregation remedies we never before have approved. The historical record of voluntary compliance with the decree of *Brown v. Board of Education* is not a proud chapter in our constitutional history, and the judges of the District Courts and Courts of Appeals have been courageous and skillful in implementing its mandate. But courage and skill must be exercised with due regard for the proper and historic role of the courts.
Keywords: *Children, Constitutional democracy, Desegregation, Education, Ends/means, Equal opportunity, Judicial authority, Judicial discretion, Judicial history, Judicial legitimacy, Judicial remedies, States' rights, Taxation*

Justice Harry Blackmun, dissenting
Lucas v. South Carolina Coastal Council,
505 U.S. 1003, 1036 (1992)
Today the Court launches a missile to kill a mouse.
Keywords: *Frustration, Opinion*

Justice Harry Blackmun, dissenting
Lucas v. South Carolina Coastal Council,
505 U.S. 1003, 1060 (1992)
. . . I find no clear and accepted "historical compact" or "understanding of our citizens" justifying the Court's new takings doctrine. Instead, the Court seems to treat history as a grab bag of principles, to be adopted where they support the Court's theory and ignored where they do not. If the Court decided that the early common law provides the background principles for interpreting the Takings Clause, then regulation, as opposed to physical confiscation, would not be compensable. If the Court decided that the law of a later period provides the background principles, then regulation might be compensable, but the Court would have to confront the fact that legislatures regularly determined which uses were prohibited, independent of the common law, and independent of whether the uses were lawful when the owner purchased. What makes the Court's analysis unworkable is its attempt to package the law of two incompatible eras and peddle it as historical fact.
Keywords: *Common law, Confiscation, History, Legislatures, Principles, Property, Regulation, Taking doctrine*

Justice Sandra Day O'Connor, dissenting
Vernonia School District 47J v. Acton,
515 U.S. 646, 686 (1995)
It cannot be too often stated that the greatest threats to our constitutional freedoms come in times of crisis. But we must also stay mindful that not all government responses to such times are hysterical overreactions; some crises are quite real, and when they are, they serve

precisely as the compelling state interest that we have said may justify a measured intrusion on constitutional rights. The only way for judges to mediate these conflicting impulses is to do what they should do anyway: stay close to the record in each case that appears before them, and make their judgments based on that alone.

Keywords: *Constitutional freedoms, Constitutional threats, Crisis, Governmental process, Judicial process, State interest*

Justice Antonin Scalia, dissenting
Regions Hospital v. Shalala,
522 U.S. 448, 468–469 (1998)
Most judicial constructions of statutes solve textual problems; today's construction creates textual problems, in order to solve a practical one. The problem to which the Secretary's implausible reading of the statute is the solution is simply this: Though the Secretary had plenty of time to correct any erroneous determinations before the three-year revision window closed, she (or more precisely her predecessor) neglected to do so. We obligingly pull her chestnuts from the fire by accepting a reading of the statute that is implausible.

Keywords: *Executive branch, Judicial construction, Statutes, Statutory interpretation, Textual problems*

Justice Antonin Scalia, dissenting
Clinton v. City of New York,
524 U.S. 417, 469 (1998)
The title of the Line Item Veto Act, which was perhaps designed to simplify for public comprehension, or perhaps merely to comply with the terms of a campaign pledge, has succeeded in faking out the Supreme Court.

Keywords: *Campaign pledge, Electoral process, Legislative intent, Line item veto, Public comprehension, Public opinion*

Justice Antonin Scalia, concurring
Department of Commerce v. United States House of Representatives,
525 U.S. ___, ___ (1999)
. . . Justice Stevens' interpretation creates a statute in which Congress swallows a camel and strains out a gnat.

Keywords: *Congress, Opinion, Statutory interpretation*

Justice Anthony Kennedy, dissenting
Davis v. Monroe County Board of Education,
526 U.S. ___, ___ (1999)
Perhaps the most grave, and surely the most lasting, disservice of today's decision is that it ensures the Court's own disregard for the federal balance soon will be imparted to our youngest citizens. The Court clears the way for the federal government to claim center stage in America's classrooms. Today's decision mandates to teachers instructing and supervising their students the dubious assistance of federal court plaintiffs and their lawyers and makes the federal courts the final arbiters of school policy and of almost every disagreement between students. Enforcement of the federal right recognized by the majority means that federal influence will permeate everything from curriculum decisions to day-to-day classroom logistics and interactions. After today,

Johnny will find that the routine problems of adolescence are to be resolved by invoking a federal right to demand assignment to a desk two rows away.

Keywords: *Adolescence, Classroom, Dispute resolution, Federal balance, Federal courts, Federal rights, School policy, Students, Teachers*

Justice John Paul Stevens, dissenting
Sutton v. United Air Lines, Inc.,
527 U.S. ___, ___(1999)
The vision of appellate judges is sometimes subconsciously obscured by a concern that their decision will legalize issues best left to the private sphere or will magnify the work of an already-overburdened judiciary. Although these concerns may help to explain the Court's decision to chart its own course—rather than to follow the one that has been well marked by Congress, by the overwhelming consensus of circuit judges, and by the Executive officials charged with the responsibility of administering the ADA—they surely do not justify the Court's crabbed vision of the territory covered by this important statute.

Keywords: *ADA, Administrative law, Appellate judges, Congressional intent, Judicial intent, Overburdened judiciary*

4. The Sacred Parchment

Chapter 4 is about the words and phrases, the spirit and intention of the federal Constitution. As Chief Justice John Marshall reminds us, it is the Constitution we are expounding. Here we find clues as to how the limited self-government has survived more than two hundred years.

Justice James Iredell
Calder v. Bull,
3 U.S. 386, 399 (1798)
If any act of Congress, or of the Legislature of a state, violates . . . constitutional provisions, it is unquestionably void; though, I admit, that as the authority to declare it void is of a delicate and awful nature, the Court will never resort to that authority, but in a clear and urgent case. If, on the other hand, the Legislature of the Union, or the legislature of any member of the union, shall pass a law, within the general scope of their constitutional power, the Court cannot pronounce it to be void, merely because it is, in their judgment, contrary to the principles of natural justice. The ideas of natural justice are regulated by no fixed standard: the ablest and the purest men have differed upon this subject; and all that the Court could properly say, in such an event, would be, that the Legislature (possessed of an equal right of opinion) had passed an act which, in the opinion of the judges, was inconsistent with the abstract principles of natural justice.

Keywords: Constitutionality, Judges, Judicial authority, Judicial power, Judicial review, Legislation, Natural justice, State legislature

Chief Justice John Marshall
Marbury v. Madison,
5 U.S. 137, 176 (1803)
That the people have an original right to establish, for their future government, such principles as, in their operation, shall most conduce to their own happiness, is the basis, on which the whole American fabric has been erected.
Keywords: Democracy, Happiness, People, Principles

Chief Justice John Marshall
Bank of United States v. Deveaux,
9 U.S. 61, 87 (1809)
A constitution, from its nature, deals in generals, not in detail. Its framers cannot perceive minute distinctions which arise in the progress of the nation, and therefore confine it to the establishment of broad and general principles.
Keywords: Constitutional intent, Constitutional theory, Framers, Principles, Progress

Justice Joseph Story
Terrett v. Taylor,
13 U.S. 43, 50 (1815)
The dissolution of the regal government no more destroyed the right to possess or enjoy this property than it did the right

of any other corporation or individual to his or its own property. The dissolution of the form of government did not involve in it a dissolution of civil rights, or an abolition of the common law under which the inheritances of every man in the state were held. The state itself succeeded only to the rights of the crown; and, we may add, with many a flower of prerogative struck from its hands. It has been asserted as a principle of the common law that the division of an empire creates no forfeiture of previously vested rights of property.

Keywords: *Civil rights, Common law, Dissolving government, Monarchy, Principles, Property, States*

Justice Joseph Story
Martin v. Hunter's Lessee,
14 U.S. 304, 344 (1816)
The courts of the United States can, without question, revise the proceedings of the executive and legislative authorities of the states, and if they are found to be contrary to the constitution, may declare them to be of no legal validity. Surely the exercise of the same right over judicial tribunals is not a higher or more dangerous act of sovereign power.

Keywords: *Checks and balances, Judicial authority, Judicial review, Judiciary, Sovereignty*

Chief Justice John Marshall
Sturges v. Crowninshield,
17 U.S. 122, 202–203 (1819)
. . . although the spirit of an instrument, especially of a constitution, is to be respected not less than its letter, yet the spirit is to be collected chiefly from its words. It would be dangerous in the extreme, to infer from extrinsic circumstances, that a case for which the words of an instrument expressly provide, shall be exempted from its operation. Where words conflict with each other, where the different clauses of an instrument bear upon each other, and would be inconsistent, unless the natural and common import of words be varied, construction becomes necessary, and a departure from the obvious meaning of words, is justifiable. But if, in any case, the plain meaning of a provision, not contradicted by any other provision in the same instrument, is to be disregarded, because we believe the framers of that instrument could not intend what they say, it must be one in which the absurdity and injustice of applying the provision to the case, would be so monstrous, that all mankind would, without hesitation, unite in rejecting the application.

Keywords: *Constitution, Constitutional conflict, Constitutional interpretation, Letter, Plain meaning, Spirit, Words*

Chief Justice John Marshall
Cohens v. Virginia,
19 U.S. 264, 387–388 (1821)
. . . a constitution is framed for ages to come, and is designed to approach immortality as nearly as human institutions can approach it. Its course cannot always be tranquil. It is exposed to storms and tempests, and its framers must be unwise statesmen indeed, if they have not provided it, as far as its nature will permit, with the means of self-preservation from the perils it may be destined to en-

counter. No government ought to be so defective in its organization, as not to contain within itself the means of securing the execution of its own laws against other dangers than those which occur every day. Courts of justice are the means most usually employed; and it is reasonable to expect that a government should repose on its own Courts, rather than others.

Keywords: *Constitution, Constitutional self-preservation, Courts of justice, Framers, Future, Governmental organization, Human institutions, Judiciary*

Chief Justice John Marshall
Cohens v. Virginia,
19 U.S. 264, 416 (1821)

Dismissing the unpleasant suggestion, that any motives which may not be fairly avowed, or which ought not to exist, can ever influence a State or its Courts, the necessity of uniformity, as well as correctness in expounding the constitution and laws of the United States, would itself suggest the propriety of vesting in some single tribunal the power of deciding, in the last resort, all cases in which they are involved.

Keywords: *Constitutional interpretation, Constitutional uniformity, Judicial review, States*

Chief Justice John Marshall
Gibbons v. Ogden,
22 U.S. 1, 188 (1824)

What do gentlemen mean, by a strict construction? If they contend only against that enlarged construction, which would extend words beyond their natural and obvious import, we might question the application of the term, but should not controvert the principle. If they contend for that narrow construction which, in support of some theory not to be found in the constitution, would deny to the government those powers which the words of the grant, as usually understood, import, and which are consistent with the general views and objects of the instrument; for that narrow construction, which would cripple the government, and render it unequal to the object for which it is declared to be instituted, and to which the powers given, as fairly understood, render it competent; then we cannot perceive the propriety of this strict construction, nor adopt it as the rule by which the constitution is to be expounded.

Keywords: *Constitutional interpretation, Governmental powers, Principle, Strict construction*

Chief Justice John Marshall
Gibbons v. Ogden,
22 U.S. 1, 222 (1824)

Powerful and ingenious minds, taking, as postulates, that the powers expressly granted to the government of the Union, are to be contracted by construction, into the narrowest possible compass, and that the original powers of the States are retained, if any possible construction will retain them, may, by a course of well digested, but refined and metaphysical reasoning, founded on these premises, explain away the constitution of our country, and leave it, a magnificent structure, indeed, to look at, but totally unfit for use. They may so entangle and perplex the understanding, as to obscure principles, which were before thought quite plain, and induce doubts where, if the mind were to pursue its own course, none would be perceived. In such a case, it is peculiarly necessary to recur to safe and fundamental principles to sustain those principles, and when sustained, to make them the tests of the arguments to be examined.

Keywords: *Constitutional construction, Constitutional interpretation, Constitutional powers, Framers, Principles, State powers*

Chief Justice Marshall, concurring
Ogden v. Saunders,
25 U.S. 213, 355 (1827)

In framing an instrument, which was intended to be perpetual, the presumption is strong, that every important principle introduced into it is intended to be perpetual also; that a principle expressed in terms to operate in all future time, is intended so to operate.

Keywords: *Constitution, Constitutional construction, Constitutional value, Framers, Future, Perpetual, Principle*

Chief Justice John Marshall
Brown v. Maryland,
25 U.S. 419, 437 (1827)

In performing the delicate and important duty of constructing clauses in the constitution of our country, which involve conflicting powers of the government of the Union, and of the respective states, it is proper to take a view of the literal meaning of the words to be expounded, of their connection with other words, and of the general objects to be accomplished by the prohibitory clause, or by the grant of power.

Keywords: *Constitution, Constitutional conflict, Constitutional construction, Constitutional language, Federalism, Framers, Separation of powers*

Justice Philip Barbour
Mayor, Aldermen and Commonality of New York v. Miln,
36 U.S. 102, 137 (1837)

All experience shows, that the same measures, or measures scarcely distinguishable from each other, may flow from distinct powers; but this does not prove that the powers are identical. Although the means used in their execution may sometimes approach each other, so nearly as to be confounded, there are other situations in which they are sufficiently distinct to establish their individuality.

Keywords: *Experience, Intent, Powers*

Justice Henry Baldwin, concurring
Briscoe v. Bank of Kentucky,
36 U.S. 257, 268 (1837)

The framers of the constitution did not speak in terms known only in local history, laws or usages, nor infuse into the instrument local definitions, the expressions of historians, or the phraseology peculiar to the habits, institutions or legislation of the several states. Speaking in language intended to be "uniform throughout the United States," the terms used were such as had been long defined, well understood in policy, legislation and jurisprudence, and capable of being referred to some authoritative standard meaning; otherwise, the constitution would be open to such a construction of its terms as might be found in any history of a colony, a state, or their laws, however contradictory the mass might be in the aggregate.

Keywords: *Constitution, Constitutional conflict, Definitions, Framers, History, Jurisprudence, Language, Legislation, Locality, Policy, Uniformity*

Chief Justice Roger Taney
Holmes v. Jennison,
39 U.S. 540, 570–571 (1840)
In expounding the constitution of the United States, every word must have its due force, and appropriate meaning; for it is evident from the whole instrument, that no word was unnecessarily used, or needlessly added. The many discussions which have taken place upon the construction of the constitution, have proved the correctness of this proposition; and shown the high talent, the caution, and the foresight of the illustrious men who framed it. Every word appears to have been weighed with the utmost deliberation, and its force and effect to have been fully understood.

Keywords: *Constitutional construction, Constitutional interpretation, Constitutional language, Framers*

Chief Justice Roger Taney
Dred Scott v. Sandford,
60 U.S. 393, 439 (1856)
The Constitution has always been remarkable for the felicity of its arrangement of different subjects, and the perspicuity and appropriateness of the language it uses.

Keywords: *Constitutional construction, Constitutional language*

Chief Justice Roger Taney
Dred Scott v. Sandford,
60 U.S. 393, 405 (1857)
. . . we must not confound the rights of citizenship which a state may confer within its own limits, and the rights of citizenship as a member of the Union. It does not by any means follow, because he has all the rights and privileges of a citizen of a State, that he must be a citizen of the United States. He may have all the rights and privileges of a citizen of a State, and yet not be entitled to the rights and privileges of a citizen in any other State.

Keywords: *Citizenship, Rights and privileges, States, Union*

Justice Benjamin Curtis, dissenting
Dred Scott v. Sandford,
60 U.S. 393, 620–621 (1856)
To engraft on any instrument a substantive exception not found in it, must be admitted to be a matter attended with great difficulty. And the difficulty increases with the importance of the instrument, and the magnitude and complexity of the interests involved in its construction. To allow this to be done with the Constitution, upon reasons purely political, renders its judicial interpretation impossible—because judicial tribunals, as such, cannot decide upon political considerations. Political reasons have not the requisite certainty to afford rules of juridical interpretation. They are different in different men. They are different in the same

men at different times. And when a strict interpretation of the Constitution, according to the fixed rules which govern the interpretation of laws, is abandoned, and the theoretical opinions of individuals are allowed to control its meaning, we have no longer a Constitution; we are under the government of individual men, who for the time being have power to declare what the Constitution is, according to their own views of what it ought to mean. When such a method of interpretation of the Constitution obtains, in place of a republican Government, with limited and defined powers, we have a Government which is merely an exponent of the will of Congress; or what, in my opinion, would not be preferable, an exponent of the individual political opinions of the members of this court.

Keywords: *Congressional will, Constitution, Constitutional interpretation, Judges, Judicial interpretation, Political, Republic, Strict interpretation*

Justice David Davis
Ex parte Milligan,
71 U.S. 2, 120–121 (1866)
The Constitution of the United States is a law for rulers and people, equally in war and in peace, and covers with the shield of its protection all classes of men, at all times and under all circumstances. No doctrine, involving more pernicious consequences, was ever invented by the wit of man than that any of its provisions can be suspended during any of the great exigencies of government. Such a doctrine leads directly to anarchy or despotism, but the theory of necessity on which it is based is false; for the government, within the Constitution, has all the powers granted to it which are necessary to preserve its existence. . . .

Keywords: *Anarchy, Constitution, Despotism, Exigencies, Uniformity*

Justice Nathan Clifford, dissenting
Legal Tender Cases,
79 U.S. 457, 579 (1870)
Delegated power ought never to be enlarged beyond the fair scope of its terms, and that rule is emphatically applicable in the construction of the Constitution. Restrictions may at times be inconvenient, or even embarrassing, but the power to remove the difficulty by amendment is vested in the people, and if they do not exercise it the presumption is that the inconvenience is a less evil than the mischief to be apprehended if the restriction should be removed and the power extended, or that the existing inconvenience is the least of the two evils; and it should never be forgotten that the government ordained and established by the Constitution is a government "of limited and enumerated powers," and that to depart from the true import and meaning of those powers is to establish a new Constitution or to do for the people what they have not chosen to do for themselves, and to usurp the functions of a legislator and desert those of an expounder of the law.

Keywords: *Constitutional construction, Constitutional restrictions, Delegated powers, Limited government, Self-government*

Justice Stephen Field, dissenting
Legal Tender Cases,
79 U.S. 457, 655–656 (1870)
I am aware of the rule that the opinions and intentions of individual members of the Convention, as expressed in its debates and proceedings, are not to control the construction of the plain language of the Constitution or narrow down the powers which that instrument confers. Members, it is said, who did not participate in the debate may have entertained different views from those expressed. The several State conventions to which the Constitution was submitted may have differed widely from each other and from its framers in their interpretation of its clauses. We all know that opposite opinions on many points were expressed in the conventions, and conflicting reasons were urged both for the adoption and the rejection of that instrument.
Keywords: *Constitutional construction, Constitutional debate, Constitutional interpretation, Constitutional powers, Framers, State constitutional conventions*

Justice Stephen Field, dissenting
Legal Tender Cases,
79 U.S. 457, 680–681 (1870)
I do not yield to any one in honoring and reverencing the noble and patriotic men who were in the councils of the nation during the terrible struggle with the rebellion. To them belong the greatest of all glories in our history,—that of having saved the Union, and that of having emancipated a race. For these results they will be remembered and honored so long

as the English language is spoken or read among men. But I do not admit that a blind approval of every measure which they may have thought essential to put down the rebellion is any evidence of loyalty to the country. The only loyalty which I can admit consists in obedience to the Constitution and laws made in pursuance of it. It is only by obedience that affection and reverence can be shown to a superior having a right to command. So thought our great Master when he said to his disciples: "If ye love me, keep my commandments."
Keywords: *Civil War, Constitutional obedience, History, Judicial responsibilities, Loyalty, Patriotism, Race, Rebellion*

Justice Joseph Bradley
Ex parte Siebold,
100 U.S. 371, 393 (1879)
We may mystify any thing. But if we take a plain view of the words of the Constitution, and give to them a fair and obvious interpretation, we cannot fail in most cases of coming to a clear understanding of its meaning. We shall not have far to seek. We shall find it on the surface, and not in the profound depths of speculation.
Keywords: *Constitution, Constitutional interpretation, Constitutional language, Constitutional speculation, Plain meaning*

Justice Joseph Bradley
Boyd v. United States,
116 U.S. 616, 635 (1886)
It may be that it is the obnoxious thing in its mildest and least repulsive form;

but illegitimate and unconstitutional practices get their first footing in that way, namely, by silent approaches and slight deviations from legal modes of procedures.

Keywords: *Constitutional deviations, Legal procedures, Unconstitutionality*

Justice Stephen Field
Norton v. Shelby County,
118 U.S. 425, 442 (1886)
An unconstitutional act is not law; it confers no rights; it imposes no duties; it affords no protection; it creates no office; it is as inoperative as though it had never been passed.

Keywords: *Constitutionality, Unconstitutional laws*

Justice David Brewer, dissenting
Fong Yue Ting v. United States,
149 U.S. 698, 737–738 (1893)
It is said that the power here asserted is inherent in sovereignty. This doctrine of powers inherent in sovereignty is one both indefinite and dangerous. Where are the limits to such powers to be found, and by whom are they to be pronounced? Is it within legislative capacity to declare the limits? If so, then the mere assertion of an inherent power creates it, and despotism exists. May the courts establish the boundaries? Whence do they obtain the authority for this? Shall they look to the practices of other nations to ascertain the limits? The governments of other nations have elastic powers—ours is fixed and bounded by a written constitution. The expulsion of a race may be within the inherent powers of a despotism. His-

tory, before the adoption of this constitution, was not destitute of examples of the exercise of such a power; and its framers were familiar with history, and wisely, as it seems to me, they gave to this government no general power to banish. Banishment may be resorted to as punishment for crime; but among the powers reserved to the people and not delegated to the government is that of determining whether whole classes in our midst shall, for no crime but that of their race and birthplace, be driven from our territory.

Keywords: *Banishment, Constitution, Crime, Delegation, Despotism, Framers, Judicial authority, Legislative authority, Powers, Punishment, Race, Sovereignty*

Justice Horace Gray, dissenting
Sparf v. United States,
156 U.S. 51, 169 (1895)
. . . all questions of constitutional construction are largely a historical question.

Keywords: *Constitutional construction, Constitutional interpretation, Constitutional questions, History*

Justice David Brewer
In re Debs,
158 U.S. 564, 591 (1895)
Constitutional provisions do not change, but their operation extends to new matters, as the modes of business and the habits of life of the people vary with each succeeding generation.

Keywords: *Constitutional change, Constitutional evolution, Constitutional interpretation, Generations, Habits*

Justice John Marshall Harlan, dissenting
Plessy v. Ferguson,
163 U.S. 537, 559 (1896)
In view of the Constitution, in the eyes of the law, there is in this country no superior, dominant, ruling class of citizens. There is no caste here. Our constitution is colorblind, and neither knows nor tolerates classes among citizens.
Keywords: *Caste, Citizenship, Class division, Constitution, Discrimination, Equality, Race*

Justice John Harlan Marshall, dissenting
Hawaii v. Mankichi,
190 U.S. 197, 241 (1903)
. . . it has been announced by some statesmen that the Constitution should be interpreted to mean not what its words naturally, or usually, or even plainly, import, but what the apparent necessities of the hour, or the apparent majority of the people, at a particular time, demand at the hands of the judiciary. I cannot assent to any such view of the Constitution.
Keywords: *Constitutional interpretation, Exigencies, Judicial legitimacy, Plain meaning*

Justice Oliver Wendell Holmes, dissenting
Hyde v. United States,
225 U.S. 347, 391 (1912)
It is one of the misfortunes of the law that ideas become encysted in phrases and thereafter for a long time cease to provoke further analysis.
Keywords: *History, Law, Phrases*

Justice Oliver Wendell Holmes
Gompers v. United States,
233 U.S. 604, 610 (1914)
. . . the provisions of the constitution are not mathematical formulas having their essence in their form; they are organic living institutions transplanted from English soil. Their significance is vital not formal; it is to be gathered not simply by taking the words and a dictionary, but by considering their origin and the line of their growth.
Keywords: *Constitution, Constitutional provisions, Language, Organic institutions*

Justice Oliver Wendell Holmes
Missouri v. Holland,
252 U.S. 416, 433 (1920)
. . . when we are dealing with words that also are a constituent act, like the Constitution of the United States, we must realize that they have called into life a being the development of which could not have been foreseen completely by the most gifted of its begetters. It was enough for them to realize or to hope that they had created an organism; it has taken a century and has cost their successors much sweat and blood to prove that they created a nation. The case before us must be considered in the light of our whole experience and not merely in that of what was said a hundred years ago.
Keywords: *Constitution, Experiences, History, Language, Nationbuilding, Organism, Words*

Justice Oliver Wendell Holmes, dissenting
Adkins v. Children's Hospital,
261 U.S. 525, 570 (1923)
The criterion of constitutionality is not whether we believe the law to be for the public good.

Keywords: *Constitutionality, Public good, Statutory intent*

Justice Louis Brandeis, dissenting
Myers v. United States,
272 U.S. 52, 293 (1926)
The doctrine of the separation of powers was adopted by the convention of 1787, not to promote efficiency but to preclude the exercise of arbitrary power. The purpose was, not to avoid friction, but, by means of the inevitable friction incident to the distribution of the governmental powers among three departments, to save the people from autocracy.
Keywords: *Arbitrary power, Autocracy, Checks and balances, Governmental powers, Separation of powers*

Justice Oliver Wendell Holmes
Westfall v. United States,
274 U.S. 256, 259 (1927)
. . . when it is necessary in order to prevent an evil to make the law embrace more than the precise thing to be prevented it may do so.
Keywords: *Constitutional permission, Ends/means, Legislative intent, Statutory interpretation*

Justice Benjamin Cardozo
Snyder v. Massachusetts,
291 U.S. 97, 114 (1934)
A fertile source of perversion in constitutional theory is the tyranny of labels.
Keywords: *Classification, Constitutional theory, Tyranny*

Justice Benjamin Cardozo
Carter v. Carter Coal Co.,
298 U.S. 238, 327 (1936)
A great principle of constitutional law is not susceptible of comprehensive statement in an adjective.
Keywords: *Constitutional interpretation, Constitutional law, Language, Principles*

Justice George Sutherland
United States v. Curtiss-Wright Export Corporation,
299 U.S. 304, 327–328 (1936)
A legislative practice such as we have here, evidenced not only by occasional instances, but marked by the movement of a steady stream for a century and a half of time, goes a long way in the direction of proving the presence of unassailable ground for the constitutionality of the practice, to be found in the origin and history of the power involved, or in its nature, or in both combined.
Keywords: *Constitutionality, History, Legislative power, Legislative practice*

Chief Justice Charles Evans Hughes
Anniston Mfg. Co. v. Davis,
301 U.S. 337, 353 (1937)
Constitutional questions are not to be decided hypothetically.
Keywords: *Constitutional adjudication, Constitutional questions*

Justice Stanley Reed
James Stewart & Co. v. Sadrakula,
309 U.S. 94, 99 (1940)
The Constitution does not command that every vestige of the laws of the former sovereignty must vanish. On the contrary its language has long been interpreted so as to permit the continuance until abrogated of those rules existing at the time of the surrender of sovereignty which govern the rights of the occupants of the territory transferred.

Keywords: Constitution, Constitutional language, History, Sovereignty, Territory

Justice Harlan Fiske Stone
United States v. Darby,
312 U.S. 100, 124 (1941)
From the beginning and for many years the [Tenth] Amendment has been construed as not depriving the national government of authority to resort to all means for the exercise of a granted power which are appropriate and plainly adapted to the permitted end.
Keywords: Ends/means, Federal authority, National government, Tenth Amendment

Justice William Douglas, dissenting
Federal Trade Commission v. Bunte Brothers Inc.,
312 U.S. 349, 359 (1941)
Mere non-use does not subtract from power which has been granted.
Keywords: Power, Reserved power

Justice William Douglas
Olsen v. Nebraska,
313 U.S. 236, 246 (1941)
We are not concerned with the wisdom, need, or appropriateness of the legislation. There is no necessity for the state to demonstrate before us that evil persists despite the competition which attends the bargaining in this field. In final analysis, the only constitutional prohibitions or restraints which respondents have suggested for the invalidation of this legislation are those notions of public policy embedded in earlier decisions of this Court but which, as Mr. Justice Holmes long admonished, should not be read into the Constitution.
Keywords: Constitutional restrictions, Judicial review, Legislative intent, Legislative wisdom, States' rights

Justice Harlan Fiske Stone
United States v. Classic,
313 U.S. 299, 316 (1941)
. . . in determining whether a provision of the constitution applies to a new subject matter, it is of little significance that it is one with which the framers were not familiar. For in setting up an enduring framework of government they undertook to carry out for the indefinite future and in all the vicissitudes of the changing affairs of men, those fundamental purposes which the instrument itself discloses. Hence we read its words, not as we read legislative codes which are subject to continuous revision with the changing course of events, but as the revelation of the great purposes which were intended to be achieved by the constitution as a continuing instrument of government.
Keywords: Constitutional adjudication, Constitutional intent, Constitutional interpretation, Constitutional provisions, Framers, Language, Legislation

Justice Felix Frankfurter, dissenting
Bridges v. California,
314 U.S. 252, 283–284 (1942)
The Constitution was not conceived as a doctrinaire document, nor was the Bill of Rights intended as a collection of popular slogans. We are dealing with instruments of government.

Keywords: *Bill of Rights, Constitution, Government instruments, Slogans*

Justice Felix Frankfurter
Scripps-Howard Radio v. Federal Communications Commission,
316 U.S. 4, 15 (1942)
Courts and administrative agencies are not to be regarded as competitors in the task of safeguarding the public interest.
Keywords: *Administrative law, Judicial review, Public interest, Separation of powers*

Justice Felix Frankfurter, dissenting
West Virginia State Board of Education v. Barnette,
319 U.S. 624, 670 (1943)
Our constant preoccupation with the constitutionality of legislation rather than its wisdom tends to the preoccupation of the American mind with a false value. The tendency of focusing attention on constitutionality is to make constitutionality synonymous with wisdom, to regard law as all right if it is constitutional.
Keywords: *Constitutionality, Judicial review, Legislative wisdom*

Justice Wiley Rutledge, concurring
Screws v. United States,
325 U.S. 91, 133–134 (1945)
To the Constitution state officials and the states themselves owe first obligation. The federal power lacks no strength to reach their malfeasance in office when it infringes constitutional rights. If that is a great power, it is one generated by the Constitution and the Amendments, to which the states have assented and their officials owe prime allegiance.

Keywords: *Constitutional history, Constitutional rights, Federalism, Malfeasance, States' rights*

Chief Justice Harlan Fiske Stone
Federation of Labor v. McAdory,
325 U.S. 450, 462 (1945)
A law which is constitutional as applied in one manner may, it is true, violate the constitution when applied in another.
Keywords: *Constitutionality, Constitutional law, Judicial review*

Justice Felix Frankfurter
Colegrove v. Green,
328 U.S. 549, 556 (1946)
The remedy for unfairness in districting is to secure state legislatures that will apportion properly, or to invoke the ample powers of Congress. The Constitution has many commands that are not enforceable by courts because they clearly fall outside the conditions and purposes that circumscribe judicial action.
Keywords: *Congressional power, Districting, Judicial authority, Judicial legitimacy, Judicial remedies, State legislatures*

Justice Wiley Rutledge
United States v. Standard Oil Co.,
332 U.S. 301, 313 (1947)
We would not deny the government's basic premise of the law's capacity for growth, or that it must include the creative work of judges. Soon all law would become antiquated strait jacket and then dead letter, if that power were lacking. And the judicial hand would stiffen in mortmain if it had no part in the work of creation. But in the federal scheme our

part in that work, and the part of the other federal courts, outside the constitutional area is more modest than that of state courts, particularly in the freedom to create new common law liabilities. . . .

Keywords: *Common law, Constitutional growth, Federalism, Judges, Judicial authority, State courts*

Justice Felix Frankfurter, concurring
Kovacs v. Cooper,
336 U.S. 77, 90–91 (1949)

A footnote hardly seems to be an appropriate way of announcing a new constitutional doctrine, and the Carolene footnote did not purport to announce any new doctrine; incidentally, it did not have the concurrence of a majority of the Court.

Keywords: *Constitutional doctrine, Judicial footnote, Judicial opinions, Precedent*

Justice Robert Jackson, concurring
Youngstown Sheet & Tube Company v. Sawyer,
343 U.S. 579, 635 (1952)

The actual art of governing under our Constitution does not and cannot conform to judicial definitions of the power of any of its branches based on isolated clauses or even single Articles torn from context. While the Constitution diffuses power the better to secure liberty, it also contemplates that practice will integrate the dispersed powers into a workable government. It enjoins upon its branches separateness but interdependence, autonomy but reciprocity. Presidential powers are not fixed but fluctuate, depending upon their disjunction or conjunction with those of Congress.

Keywords: *Congressional power, Constitutional power, Delegation, Governing, Presidential power, Separation of powers*

Chief Justice Earl Warren
Brown v. Board of Education,
349 U.S. 294, 300 (1955)

. . . it should go without saying that the vitality of these constitutional principles cannot be allowed to yield simply because of disagreement with them.

Keywords: *Constitutional debate, Constitutional principles*

Justice Felix Frankfurter
Ullman v. United States,
350 U.S. 422, 428 (1956)

Nothing new can be put into the Constitution except through the amendatory process. Nothing old can be taken out without the same process.

Keywords: *Amending process, Constitutional change*

Justice Felix Frankfurter
Ullman v. United States,
350 U.S. 422, 428 (1956)

As no constitutional guarantee enjoys preference, so none should suffer subordination or deletion.

Keywords: *Constitutional guarantees, Constitutional interpretation*

Justice Tom Clark
Mapp v. Ohio,
367 U.S. 643, 657 (1961)

There is no war between the Constitution and common sense.

Keywords: *Common sense, Constitution, Constitutional conflict*

Justice Tom Clark
Mapp v. Ohio,
367 U.S. 643, 659 (1961)
Nothing can destroy a government more quickly than its failure to observe its own laws, or worse, its disregard of the character of its own existence.
Keywords: *Governmental authority, Governmental legitimacy, Rule of law*

Justice William Brennan
Baker v. Carr,
369 U.S. 186, 210–211 (1962)
The nonjusticiability of a political question is primarily a function of the separation of powers. Much confusion results from the capacity of the "political question" label to obscure the need for case-by-case inquiry. Deciding whether a matter has in any measure been committed by the Constitution to another branch of government, or whether the action of that branch exceeds whatever authority has been committed, is itself a delicate exercise in constitutional interpretation, and is a responsibility of this Court as ultimate interpreter of the Constitution.
Keywords: *Constitutionality adjudication, Constitutional interpretation, Judicial review, Nonjusticiability, Political questions, Separation of powers*

Justice Felix Frankfurter, dissenting
Baker v. Carr,
369 U.S. 186, 270 (1962)
. . . there is not under our Constitution a judicial remedy for every political mischief, for every undesirable exercise of legislative power. The Framers carefully and with deliberate forethought refused so to enthrone the judiciary.

Keywords: *Constitution, Framers, Judicial authority, Judicial legitimacy, Judicial remedies, Legislative power, Political abuse*

Justice Hugo Black
Wesberry v. Sanders,
376 U.S. 1, 18 (1964)
While it may not be possible to draw congressional districts with mathematical precision, that is no excuse for ignoring our Constitution's plain objective of making equal representation for equal numbers of people the fundamental goal for the House of Representatives. That is the high standard of justice and common sense which the Founders set for us.
Keywords: *Apportionment, Common sense, Congressional districts, Equal representation, Founders, House of Representatives, Justice*

Justice John Marshall Harlan, dissenting
Wesberry v. Sanders,
376 U.S. 1, 30 (1964)
There is dubious propriety in turning to the "historical context" of constitutional provisions which speak so consistently and plainly. But, as one might expect when the Constitution itself is free from ambiguity, the surrounding history makes what is already clear even clearer.
Keywords: *Constitutional interpretation, Constitutional provisions, Historical context*

Justice Hugo Black, concurring in part, dissenting in part
South Carolina v. Katzenbach,
383 U.S. 301, 360–361 (1966)
I see no reason to read into the Constitution meanings it did not have when it

was adopted and which have not been put into it since. The proceedings of the original Constitutional convention show beyond all doubt that the power to veto or negative state laws was denied Congress. On several occasions proposals were submitted to the convention to grant this power to Congress. These proposals were debated extensively and on every occasion when submitted for vote they were overwhelmingly rejected. The refusal to give Congress this extraordinary power to veto state laws was based on the belief that if such power resided in Congress the States would be helpless to function as effective governments. Since that time neither the Fifteenth Amendment nor any other Amendment to the Constitution has given the slightest indication of a purpose to grant Congress the power to veto state laws either by itself or its agents. Nor does any provision in the Constitution endow the federal courts with power to participate with state legislative bodies in determining what state policies shall be enacted into law. The judicial power to invalidate a law in a case or controversy after the law has become effective is a long way from the power to prevent a State from passing a law. I cannot agree with the Court that Congress—denied a power in itself to veto a state law—can delegate this same power to the Attorney General or the District Court for the District of Columbia. For the effect on the States is the same in both cases—they cannot pass their laws without sending their agents to the City of Washington to plead to federal officials for their advance approval. **Keywords:** *Congressional authority, Constitution, Constitutional conven-tion, Delegation, Federalism, Fifteenth Amendment, Framers, Judicial re-view, Legislative veto, State laws, State legislatures*

Justice Hugo Black, dissenting
Turner v. United States,
396 U.S. 398, 426 (1970)
The Framers of our Constitution and Bill of Rights were too wise, too pragmatic, and too familiar with tyranny to attempt to safeguard personal liberty with broad, flexible words and phrases like "fair trial," "fundamental decency," and "reasonable-ness." Such stretchy, rubberlike terms would have left judges constitutionally free to try people charged with crime under will-o'-the-wisp standards improvised by different judges for different defendants. Neither the Due Process Clause nor any other constitutional language vests any judge with such power. Our Constitution was not written in the sands to be washed away by each wave of new judges blown in by each successive political wind that brings new political administrations into temporary power. Rather, our Constitution was fashioned to perpetuate liberty and justice by marking clear, explicit, and lasting constitutional boundaries for trials. **Keywords:** *Bill of Rights, Constitu-tion, Constitutional boundaries, Con-stitutional language, Crime, Due process, Framers, Judicial limitations, Judicial process, Justice, Liberty, Tyranny*

Chief Justice Warren Burger
Williams v. Illinois,
399 U.S. 235, 239 (1970)
While neither the antiquity of a prac-tice nor the fact of steadfast legislative

and judicial adherence to it through the centuries insulates it from constitutional attack. . . .

Keywords: *Constitutional adjudication, History, Judicial adherence, Legislative adherence, Precedent, Tradition*

Justice Byron White, concurring and dissenting
Coolidge v. New Hampshire,
403 U.S. 443, 520–521 (1971)

It may be that constitutional law cannot be fully coherent and that constitutional principles ought not always be spun out to their logical limits, but this does not mean that we should cease to strive for clarity and consistency of analysis. Here the Court has a ready opportunity, one way or another, to bring clarity and certainty to a body of law that lower courts and law enforcement officials often find confusing. Instead, without apparent reason, it only increases their confusion by clinging to distinctions that are both unexplained and inexplicable.

Keywords: *Constitutional interpretation, Constitutional law, Constitutional principles, Judicial legitimacy, Judicial responsibility*

Justice Lewis Powell, concurring
United States v. Richardson,
418 U.S. 166, 188 (1974)

I . . . believe that repeated and essentially head-on confrontations between the life-tenured branch and the representative branches of government will not, in the long run, be beneficial to either. The public confidence essential to the former and the vitality critical to the latter may well erode if we do not exercise self-restraint

in the utilization of our power to negative the actions of the other branches. We should be ever mindful of the contradictions that would arise if a democracy were to permit at large oversight of the elected branches of government by a nonrepresentative, and in large measure insulated, judicial branch.

Keywords: *Checks and balances, Democracy, Judicial authority, Judicial legitimacy, Judicial restraint, Public confidence, Representative branches, Separation of powers*

Justice William Douglas, dissenting
United States v. Richardson,
418 U.S. 166, 200 (1974)

From the history of [Art. I § 9, cl. 7] it is apparent that the Framers inserted it in the Constitution to give the public knowledge of the way public funds are expended. No one has a greater "personal stake" in policing this protective measure than a taxpayer. Indeed, if a taxpayer may not raise the question, who may do so?

Keywords: *Article I, Constitution, Framers, Public funds, Taxpayers*

Justice William Douglas, dissenting
Schlesinger v. Reservists Committee to Stop the War,
418 U.S. 208, 232–233 (1974)

We tend to overlook the basic political and legal reality that the people, not the bureaucracy, are the sovereign. Our Federal government was created for the security and happiness of the people. Executives, lawmakers, and members of the Judiciary are inferior in the sense that they are in office only to carry out and execute the constitutional regime.

Keywords: *Constitutional authority, Executive limitations, Federal government, Happiness, Judicial limitations, Legal reality, Legislative limitations, Political reality, Self-government, Security, Sovereignty*

Justice William Douglas, dissenting
Schlesinger v. Reservists Committee to Stop the War,
418 U.S. 208, 234 (1974)
The interest of citizens in guarantees written in the Constitution seems obvious. Who other than citizens has a better right to have the Incompatibility clause enforced? It is their interests that the Incompatibility clause was designed to protect. The Executive branch under our regime is not a fiefdom or principality competing with the Legislative as another center of power. It operates within a constitutional framework, and it is that constitutional framework that these citizens want to keep intact. That is, in my view, their rightful concern.
Keywords: *Citizens, Constitutional authority, Constitutional guarantees, Executive branch, Incompatibility Clause, Legislative branch*

Justice Byron White, concurring in part, dissenting in part
Buckley v. Valeo,
424 U.S. 1, 280–281 (1976)
There is no doubt that the development of the administrative agency in response to modern legislative and administrative need has placed severe strain on the separation-of-powers principle in its pristine formulation. Any notion that the Constitution bans any admixture of powers that might be deemed legislative, executive, and judicial has had to give way. The independent agency has survived attacks from various directions: that it exercises invalidly delegated legislative power; that it invalidly exercises judicial power; and that its functions are so executive in nature that its members must be subject to Presidential control. Until now, however, it has not been insisted that the commands of the Appointments Clause must also yield to permit congressional appointments of members of a major agency. With the Court, I am not convinced that we should create a broad exception to the requirements of that Clause that all officers of the United States be appointed in accordance with its terms.
Keywords: *Administrative agencies, Appointments, Delegation, Judicial power, Separation of powers*

Justice John Paul Stevens
Mathews v. Diaz,
426 U.S. 67, 81 (1976)
Any rule of constitutional law that would inhibit the flexibility of the political branches of government to respond to changing world conditions should be adopted only with the greatest caution.
Keywords: *Constitutional evolution, Constitutional rules, Political branches, Separation of powers*

Justice John Paul Stevens
Bishop v. Woods,
426 U.S. 341, 349–350 (1976)
We must accept the harsh fact that numerous individual mistakes are inevitable in the day-to-day administration of

our affairs. The United States Constitution cannot feasibly be construed to require federal judicial review for every such error.

Keywords: *Constitution, Governmental operations, Judicial remedies, Judicial review*

Chief Justice Warren Burger, dissenting
Nixon v. Administrator of General Services,
433 U.S. 425, 513 (1977)
If separation-of-powers principles can be so easily evaded, then the constitutional separation is a sham.

Keywords: *Constitutional legitimacy, Constitutional principles, Separation of powers*

Justice Thurgood Marshall, concurring
Pruneyard Shopping Center v. Robins,
447 U.S. 74, 93 (1980)
The constitutional terms "life, liberty, and property" do not derive their meaning solely from the provisions of positive law. They have a normative dimension as well, establishing a sphere of private autonomy which government is bound to respect.

Keywords: *Autonomy, Liberty, Life, Positive law, Privacy, Property*

Justice William Rehnquist, dissenting
Wallace v. Jaffree,
472 U.S. 38, 112 (1985)
If a constitutional theory has no basis in the history of the amendment it seeks to interpret, is difficult to apply and yields unprincipled results, I see little use in it.

Keywords: *Constitutional history, Constitutional interpretation, Constitutional principles, Constitutional theory*

Justice William Rehnquist
Daniels v. Williams,
474 U.S. 327, 332 (1986)
Our Constitution deals with the large concerns of the governors and the governed, but it does not purport to supplant traditional tort law in laying down rules of conduct to regulate liability for injuries that attend living together in society.

Keywords: *Conduct, Constitution, Tort law, Liability, Social community*

Justice Byron White, dissenting
Thornburgh v. American College of Obstetricians & Gynecologists,
476 U.S. 747, 789 (1986)
As its prior cases clearly show . . . this Court does not subscribe to the simplistic view that constitutional interpretation can possibly be limited to the "plain meaning" of the Constitution's text or to the subjective intention of the Framers. The Constitution is not a deed setting forth the precise metes and bounds of its subject matter; rather, it is a document announcing fundamental principles in value-laden terms that leave ample scope for the exercise of normative judgment by those charged with interpreting and applying it.

Keywords: *Constitutional interpretation, Framers, Original intent, Plain meaning, Principles, Strict construction, Values*

Justice Harry Blackmun, concurring and dissenting
Webster v. Reproductive Health Services, Inc.,
492 U.S. 490, 558 (1989)
To overturn a constitutional decision is a rare and grave undertaking. To overturn

a constitutional decision that secured a fundamental personal liberty to millions of persons would be unprecedented in our 200 years of constitutional history.

Keywords: *History, Liberty, Precedence, Stare decisis*

Justice Antonin Scalia, dissenting
Riverside v. McLaughlin,
500 U.S. 44, 59–60 (1991)
The story is told of the elderly judge who, looking back over a long career, observes with satisfaction that "when I was young, I probably let stand some convictions that should have been overturned, and when I was old I probably set aside some that should have stood; so overall, justice was done." I sometimes think that is an appropriate analog to this Court's constitutional jurisprudence, which alternately creates rights that the Constitution does not contain and denies rights that it does.

Keywords: *Constitutional jurisprudence, Judicial legitimacy, Rights*

Justice Sandra Day O'Connor
New York v. United States,
505 U.S. 144, 187 (1992)
Some truths are so basic that, like the air around us, they are easily overlooked. Much of the Constitution is concerned with setting forth the form of our government, and the courts have traditionally invalidated measures deviating from that form. The result may appear "formalistic" in a given case to partisans of the measure at issue, because such measures are typically the product of the era's perceived necessity. But the Constitution protects us from our own best intentions: it divides power among sovereigns and among branches of government precisely so that we may resist the temptation to concentrate power in one location as an expedient solution to the crisis of the day.

Keywords: *Checks and balances, Constitutional authority, Constitutional restraints, Judicial review, Separation of powers, Sovereignty*

Justice Sandra Day O'Connor
Planned Parenthood of Southeastern Pennsylvania v. Casey,
505 U.S. 833, 901 (1992)
Our Constitution is a covenant running from the first generation of Americans to us and then to future generations. It is a coherent succession.

Keywords: *Constitutional value, Future generations*

Justice Anthony Kennedy, concurring
U.S. Term Limits, Inc. v. Thornton,
514 U.S. 779, 838–839 (1995)
Federalism was our Nation's own discovery. The Framers split the atom of sovereignty. It was the genius of their idea that our citizens would have two political capacities, one state and one federal, each protected from incursion by the other. The resulting Constitution created a legal system unprecedented in form and design, establishing two orders of government, each with its own direct relationship, its own privity, its own set of mutual rights and obligations to the people who sustain it and are governed by it. It is appropriate to recall these origins, which instruct us as to the nature

of the two different governments created and confirmed by the Constitution.

Keywords: *Federalism, Framers, Legal system, National government, Sovereignty, States*

Justice Clarence Thomas, dissenting
U.S. Term Limits, Inc. v. Thornton,
514 U.S. 779, 846 (1995)
Our system of government rests on one overriding principle: All power stems from the consent of the people. To phrase the principle in this way, however, is to be imprecise about something important to the notion of "reserved" powers. The ultimate source of the Constitution's authority is the consent of the people of each individual State, not the consent of the undifferentiated people of the Nation as a whole.

Keywords: *Constitutional authority, People, Principle, Reserved power, States*

Justice Clarence Thomas, concurring
McIntyre v. Ohio Elections Commission,
514 U.S. 334, 360 (1995)
. . . the simple fact that the Framers engaged in certain conduct does not necessarily prove that they forbade its prohibition by the government.

Keywords: *Conduct, Constitutional intent, Constitutional limitations, Framers, History, Prohibited conduct*

Justice Clarence Thomas, concurring
Bennis v. Michigan,
516 U.S. 442, 454 (1996)
. . . the Federal Constitution does not prohibit everything that is intensely undesirable.

Keywords: *Constitutional limitations, Constitutional prohibitions*

Justice Anthony Kennedy, concurring
Clinton v. City of New York,
524 U.S. 417, 450 (1998)
Liberty is always at stake when one or more of the branches seek to transgress the separation of powers.

Keywords: *Liberty, Separation of powers*

Justice Anthony Kennedy
Alden v. Maine,
527 U.S. ___, ___ (1999)
In apparent attempt to disparage a conclusion with which it disagrees, the dissent attributes our reasoning to natural law. We seek to discover, however, only what the Framers and those who ratified the Constitution sought to accomplish when they created a federal system. We appeal to no higher authority than the Charter which they wrote and adopted. Theirs was the unique insight that freedom is enhanced by the creation of two governments, not one. We need not attach a label to our dissenting colleagues' insistence that the constitutional structure adopted by the founders must yield to the politics of the moment. Although the Constitution begins with the principle that sovereignty rests with the people, it does not follow that the National Government becomes the ultimate, preferred mechanism for expressing the people's will. The States exist as a refutation of that concept. In choosing to ordain and establish the Constitution, the people insisted upon a federal structure for the very pur-

pose of rejecting the idea that the will of the people in all instances is expressed by the central power, the one most remote from their control. The Framers of the Constitution did not share our dissenting colleagues' belief that the Congress may circumvent the federal design by regulating the States directly when it pleases to do so, including by a proxy in which individual citizens are authorized to levy upon the state treasuries absent the States' consent to jurisdiction.

Keywords: *Congress, Congressional power, Federalism, Framers, Freedom, National government, Natural law, Sovereignty, States*

Justice David Souter, dissenting
Alden v. Maine,
527 U.S. ___, ___ (1999)

It would be hard to imagine anything more inimical to the republican conception, which rests on the understanding of its citizens precisely that the government is not above them, but of them, its actions being governed by law just like their own. Whatever justification there may be for an American government's immunity from private suit, it is not dignity.

Keywords: *Citizens, Governmental immunity, Private suit, Republican government, Rule of law*

5. Expectations and Deliverance

This chapter explores the historical and political role of the United States. Here you will discern the nature of a constitutional republic and how it has evolved to meet the expectations of its diverse citizenry.

Chief Justice John Marshall
McCulloch v. Maryland,
17 U.S. 316, 431 (1819)
That the power to tax involves the power to destroy; that the power to destroy may defeat and render useless the power to create; that there is a plain repugnance, in conferring on one government a power to control the constitutional measures of another, which other, with respect to those very measures, is declared to be supreme over that which exerts the control, are propositions not to be denied.
Keywords: *Governmental power, Taxation*

Chief Justice John Marshall
Loughborough v. Blake,
18 U.S. 317, 324 (1820)
The difference between requiring a continent, with an immense population, to submit to be taxed by a government having no common interest with it, separated from it by a vast ocean, restrained by no principle of apportionment, and associated with it by no common feelings; and permitting the representatives of the American people, under the restrictions of our constitution, to tax a part of the society, which is either in a state of infancy advancing to manhood, looking forward to complete equality so soon as that state of manhood shall be attained, as is the case with the territories; or which has voluntarily relinquished the right of representation, and has adopted the whole body of Congress for its legitimate government, as is the case with the district, is too obvious not to present itself to the minds of all.
Keywords: *Apportionment, Congress, Constitutional restrictions, Representatives, Taxation, Territories*

Justice William Johnson
Anderson v. Dunn,
19 U.S. 204, 226 (1821)
No one is so visionary as to dispute the assertion, that the sole end and aim of all our institutions is the safety and happiness of the citizen. But the relation between the action and the end, is not always so direct and palpable as to strike the eye of every observer. The science of government is the most abstruse of all sciences; if, indeed, that can be called a science which has but few fixed principles, and practically consists in little more than the exercise of a sound discretion, applied to the exigencies of the state as they arise. It is the science of experiment.
Keywords: *Democratic experimentation, Ends/means, Government, Happiness, Principles, Safety*

Justice William Johnson
Anderson v. Dunn,
19 U.S. 204, 232 (1821)
The most absolute tyranny could not subsist where men could not be trusted with power because they might abuse it, much less a government which has no other basis than the sound morals, moderation, and good sense of those who compose it. Unreasonable jealousies not only blight the pleasures, but dissolve the very texture of society.
Keywords: *Morals, Power, Society, Tyranny*

Chief Justice John Marshall, concurring
Ogden v. Saunders,
25 U.S. 213, 345 (1827)
Superior strength may give the power, but cannot give the right.
Keyword: *Power*

Chief Justice John Marshall
Barron v. City of Baltimore,
32 U.S. 243, 247 (1833)
The constitution was ordained and established by the people of the United States for themselves, for their own government, and not for the government of the individual states. Each state established a constitution for itself, and, in that constitution, provided such limitations and restrictions on the powers of its particular government as its judgment dictated.
Keywords: *Constitution, Self-government, State constitutions, States*

Justice John McLean, dissenting
Dred Scott v. Sandford,
60 U.S. 393, 545 (1856)
It is refreshing to turn to the early inci-

dents of our history, and learn wisdom from the acts of the great men who have gone to their account.
Keywords: *History, Leaders, Wisdom*

Justice Benjamin Curtis, dissenting
Dred Scott v. Sandford,
60 U.S. 393, 576 (1856)
That Constitution was ordained and established by the people of the United States, through the action, in each State, or those persons who were qualified by its laws to act thereon, in behalf of themselves and all other citizens of that State. In some of the States . . . colored persons were among those qualified by law to act on this subject. These colored persons were not only included in the body of "the people of the United States," by whom the Constitution was ordained and established, but in at least five of the States they had the power to act, and doubtless did act, by their suffrages, upon the question of its adoption. It would be strange, if we were to find in that instrument anything which deprived of their citizenship any part of the people of the United States who were among those by whom it was established.
Keywords: *Citizenship, Constitution, Race, Representatives, Self-government, States, Suffrage*

Chief Justice Roger Taney
Ableman v. Booth,
62 U.S. 506, 525 (1858)
Now, it certainly can be no humiliation to the citizen of a republic to yield a ready obedience to the laws as administered by the constituted authorities. On the con-

trary, it is among his first and highest duties as a citizen, because free government cannot exist without it. Nor can it be inconsistent with the dignity of a sovereign State to observe faithfully, and in the spirit of sincerity and truth, the compact into which it voluntarily entered when it became a State of this Union. On the contrary, the highest honor of sovereignty is untarnished faith. And certainly no faith could be more deliberately and solemnly pledged than that which every State has plighted to the other States to support the Constitution as it is, in all its provisions, until they shall be altered in the manner which the Constitution itself prescribes.

Keywords: *Citizen, Compact, Constitutional support, Free government, Governmental confidence, Laws, Obedience, Republic, Sovereignty, States*

Justice John Campbell
Rector, Church Wardens, and Vestrymen v. Philadelphia,
65 U.S. 300, 302 (1860)
All laws, all political institutions, are dispositions for the future, and their professed object is to afford a steady and permanent security to the interests of society.

Keywords: *Laws, Political institutions, Security, Society*

Justice David Davis
Ex parte Milligan,
71 U.S. 2, 125 (1866)
Wicked men, ambitious of power, with hatred of liberty and contempt of law, may fill the place once occupied by Washington and Lincoln; and if this right is conceded, and the calamities of war again befall us, the dangers to human liberty are frightful to contemplate.

Keywords: *Ambition, Contempt, Leadership, Liberty, Lincoln (Abraham), Power, War, Washington (George)*

Justice William Strong
Legal Tender Cases,
79 U.S. 457, 530 (1870)
Men have bought and sold, borrowed and lent, and assumed every variety of obligations contemplating that payment might be made with such notes. Indeed, legal tender treasury notes have become the universal measure of values. If now, by our decision, it be established that these debts and obligations can be discharged only by gold coin; if, contrary to the expectation of all parties to these contracts, legal tender notes are rendered unavailable, the government has become an instrument of the grossest injustice; all debtors are loaded with an obligation it was never contemplated they should assume; a large percentage is added to every debt, and such must become the demand for gold to satisfy contracts, that ruinous sacrifices, general distress, and bankruptcy may be expected.

Keywords: *Bankruptcy, Contracts, Custom, Debt, Debtors, Economy, Gold, Injustice, Legal tender, Treasury notes, Value*

Justice Joseph Bradley, concurring
Legal Tender Cases,
79 U.S. 457, 563 (1870)
It is absolutely essential to independent national existence that government should have a firm hold on the two great sovereign instrumentalities of the sword

and the purse, and the right to wield them without restriction on occasions of national peril. In certain emergencies government must have at its command, not only the personal services—the bodies and lives—of its citizens, but the lesser, though not less essential, power of absolute control over the resources of the country. Its armies must be filled, and its navies manned, by the citizens in person. Its material of war, its munitions, equipment, and commissary stores must come from the industry of the country. This can only be stimulated into activity by a proper financial system, especially as regards the currency.

Keywords: Citizens, Currency, Economy, Emergency power, Financial system, Military, National government, Purse, Sovereignty, Sword, War

Chief Justice Salmon Chase, dissenting
Legal Tender Cases,
79 U.S. 457, 579 (1870)
. . . many are persuaded by their representations that the forced circulation is not only a necessity but a benefit. But the apparent benefit is a delusion and the necessity imaginary. In their legitimate use, the notes are hurt not helped by being made a legal tender. The legal tender quality is only valuable for the purposes of dishonesty. Every honest purpose is answered as well and better without it.

Keywords: Economy, Legal tender, Treasury notes

Justice Stephen Field, dissenting
Legal Tender Cases,
79 U.S. 457, 652–653 (1870)
The statesmen who framed the Consti-

tution understood this principle as well as it is understood in our day. They had seen in the experience of the Revolutionary period the demoralizing tendency, the cruel injustice, and the intolerable oppression of a paper currency not convertible on demand into money, and forced into circulation by legal tender provisions and penal enactments. When they therefore were constructing a government for a country, which they could not fail to see was destined to be a mighty empire, and have commercial relations with all nations, a government which they believed was to endure for ages, they determined to recognize in the fundamental law as the standard of value, that which ever has been and always must be recognized by the world as the true standard, and thus facilitate commerce, protect industry, establish justice, and prevent the possibility of a recurrence of the evils which they had experienced and the perpetration of the injustice which they had witnessed.

Keywords: Commerce, Currency, Framers, Fundamental law, Justice, Legal tender, Principles, Value

Justice Joseph Bradley, dissenting
In re Slaughter-House Cases,
83 U.S. 36, 112–113 (1872)
The States have not now, if they ever had, any power to restrict their citizenship to any classes or persons. A citizen of the United States has a perfect constitutional right to go to and reside in any State he chooses, and to claim citizenship therein, and an equality of rights with every other citizen; and the whole power of the nation is pledged to sustain him in that

right. He is not bound to cringe to any superior, or to pray for any act of grace, as a means of enjoying all the rights and privileges enjoyed by other citizens. And when the spirit of lawlessness, mob violence, and sectional hate can be so completely repressed as to give full practical effect to this right, we shall be a happier nation, and a more prosperous one than we now are.

Keywords: *Citizenship, Constitutional rights, Equality, Lawlessness, Privileges, States*

Justice Noah Swayne, dissenting
In re Slaughter-House Cases,
83 U.S. 36, 128 (1872)
The prejudices and apprehension as to the central government which prevailed when the Constitution was adopted were dispelled by the light of experience. The public mind became satisfied that there was less danger of tyranny in the head than of anarchy and tyranny in the members.

Keywords: *Constitution, Experience, Federal government, Tyranny, States*

Justice Samuel Miller
Citizens' Savings & Loan Association v. Topeka,
87 U.S. 655, 663 (1874)
The theory of our governments . . . is opposed to the deposit of unlimited power anywhere. The executive, the legislative, and the judicial branches of these governments are all of limited and defined powers.

Keywords: *Defined power, Executive branch, Governmental theory, Judicial power, Legislative power, Limited power*

Justice Samuel Miller
Citizens' Savings & Loan Association v. Topeka,
87 U.S. 655, 663 (1874)
The power to tax is . . . the strongest, the most pervading of all the powers of government, reaching directly or indirectly to all classes of the people.

Keywords: *Governmental power, Taxation*

Chief Justice Morrison Waite
Minor v. Happersett,
88 U.S. 162, 175 (1874)
Nothing is more evident than that the greater must include the less.

Keywords: *Inclusivity, Philosophy*

Justice John Marshall Harlan, dissenting
Civil Rights Cases,
109 U.S. 3, 59 (1883)
. . . government has nothing to do with social, as distinguished from technically legal, rights of individuals. No government ever has brought, or ever can bring, its people into social intercourse against their wishes. Whether one person will permit or maintain social relations with another is a matter with which government has no concern. I agree that if one citizen chooses not to hold social intercourse with another, he is not and cannot be made amenable to the law for his conduct in that regard; for no legal right of a citizen is violated by the refusal of others to maintain merely social relations with him, even upon grounds of race.

Keywords: *Citizens, Conduct, Governmental limitations, Race, Social relations, Social rights*

Justice Samuel Miller
Ku Klux Cases,
110 U.S. 651, 657–658 (1884)
That a government whose essential character is republican, whose executive head and legislative body are both elective, whose numerous and powerful branch of the legislature is elected by the people directly, has no power by appropriate laws to secure this election from the influence of violence, of corruption, and of fraud, is a proposition so startling as to arrest attention and demand the gravest consideration. If this government is anything more than a mere aggregation of delegated agents of other states and governments, each of which is superior to the general government, it must have the power to protect the elections on which its existence depends, from violence and corruption. If it has not this power, it is left helpless before the two great natural and historical enemies of all republics, open violence and insidious corruption.
Keywords: *Corruption, Delegation, Electoral process, Federalism, Representative democracy, Republican government, States, Violence*

Justice Stanley Matthews
Yick Wo v. Hopkins,
118 U.S. 356, 369–370 (1886)
When we consider the nature and the theory of our institutions of government, the principles upon which they are supposed to rest, and review the history of their development, we are constrained to conclude that they do not mean to leave room for the play and action of purely personal and arbitrary power. Sovereignty itself is, of course, not subject to law, for it is the author and source of law; but in our system, while sovereign powers are delegated to the agencies of government, sovereignty itself remains with the people, by whom and for whom all government exists and acts. And the law is the definition and limitation of power. It is, indeed, quite true, that there must always be lodged somewhere, and in some person or body, the authority of final decision; and in many cases of mere administration the responsibility is purely political, no appeal lying except to the ultimate tribunal of the public judgment, exercised either in the pressure of opinion or by means of suffrage.
Keywords: *Delegation, Governmental institutions, Governmental theory, History, Political, Power, Principles, Public opinion, Self-government, Sovereignty, Suffrage*

Justice Joseph Bradley
Mormon Church v. United States,
136 U.S. 1, 49 (1890)
The organization of a community for the spread and practice of polygamy is, in a measure, a return to barbarism. It is contrary to the spirit of Christianity and of the civilization which Christianity has produced in the western world.
Keywords: *Barbarism, Christianity, Community, Domestic relations, Family, Marriage, Polygamy, Western world*

Justice John Marshall Harlan, dissenting
United States v. E.C. Knight Co.,
156 U.S. 1, 33 (1895)
The jurisdiction of the general govern-

ment extends over every foot of territory within the United States.
Keywords: *Constitutional authority, Jurisdiction, National government, Scope of power, Territory*

Justice Rufus Peckham
Lochner v. New York,
198 U.S. 45, 64 (1905)
It is impossible for us to shut our eyes to the fact that many of the laws of this character, while passed under what is claimed to be the police power for the purpose of protecting the public health or welfare, are, in reality, passed from other motives. We are justified in saying so when, from the character of the law and the subject upon which it legislates, it is apparent that the public health or welfare bears but the most remote relation to the law.
Keywords: *Congressional intent, Police power, Public health, Public welfare, Statutes, Statutory interpretation*

Justice Oliver Wendell Holmes, dissenting
Lochner v. New York,
198 U.S. 45, 76 (1905)
Every opinion tends to become a law.
Keywords: *Jurisprudence, Opinions, Philosophy*

Justice Oliver Wendell Holmes
Rock Island, A. & L.R. Co. v. United States,
254 U.S. 141, 143 (1920)
Men must turn square corners when they deal with the government.
Keywords: *Governmental intrusion, Governmental process*

Chief Justice William Howard Taft
Bailey v. Drexel Furniture Co.,
259 U.S. 20, 38 (1922)
The difference between a tax and a penalty is sometimes difficult to define, and yet the consequences of the distinction in the required method of their collection often are important. Where the sovereign enacting the law has power to impose both tax and penalty the difference between revenue production and mere regulation may be immaterial, but not so when one sovereign can impose a tax only, and the power of regulation rests in another. Taxes are occasionally imposed in the discretion of the legislature on proper subjects with the primary motive of obtaining revenue from them and with the incidental motive of discouraging them by making their continuance onerous. They do not lose their character as taxes because of the incidental motive. But there comes a time in the extension of the penalizing features of the so-called tax when it loses its character as such and becomes a mere penalty with the characteristics of regulation and punishment.
Keywords: *Congressional intent, Legislative discretion, Penalties, Punishment, Regulation, Revenue, Sovereignty, Taxation*

Justice George Sutherland
Massachusetts v. Mellon,
262 U.S. 447, 487 (1923)
The administration of any statute, likely to produce additional taxation to be imposed upon a vast number of taxpayers, the extent of whose several liability is indefinite and constantly changing, is

essentially a matter of public and not of individual concern. If one taxpayer may champion and litigate such a cause, then every other taxpayer may do the same, not only in respect of the statute here under review but also in respect of every other appropriation act and statute whose administration requires the outlay of public money, and whose validity may be questioned.

Keywords: *Public concern, Public finance, Statutory implementation, Taxation, Taxpayers*

Justice Louis Brandeis
Quaker City Cab Co. v. Pennsylvania,
277 U.S. 389, 410 (1928)
. . . there are still intelligent, informed, just-minded and civilized persons who believe that the rapidly growing aggregation of capital through corporations constitutes an insidious menace to the liberty of the citizen; that it tends to increase the subjection of labor to capital; that, because of the guidance and control necessarily exercised by great corporations upon those engaged in business, individual initiative is being impaired and creative power will be lessened; that the absorption of capital by corporations, and their perpetual life, may bring evils similar to those which attended mortmain. . . .

Keywords: *Capital, Citizens, Corporations, Labor, Liberty*

Justice Louis Brandeis, dissenting
Olmstead v. United States,
277 U.S. 438, 485 (1928)
Decency, security, and liberty alike demand that government officials shall be subjected to the same rules of conduct that are commands to the citizen. In a government of laws, existence of the government will be imperiled if it fails to observe the law scrupulously. Our government is the potent, the omnipresent teacher. For good or for ill, it teaches the whole people by its example. Crime is contagious. If the government becomes a lawbreaker, it breeds contempt for law; it invites every man to become a law unto himself; it invites anarchy.

Keywords: *Anarchy, Citizens, Contempt of law, Government officials, Governmental authority, Governmental confidence, Governmental lawlessness, Governmental legitimacy, Liberty, Rule of law, Security*

Chief Justice Charles Evans Hughes
Home Building & Loan Association v. Blaisdell,
290 U.S. 398, 425 (1934)
Emergency does not create power. Emergency does not increase granted power or remove or diminish the restrictions imposed upon power granted or reserved.

Keywords: *Constitutional authority, Constitutional question, Emergency powers, Reserved powers*

Justice Benjamin Cardozo
Baldwin v. G.A.F. Seelig, Inc.,
294 U.S. 511, 523 (1935)
Economic welfare is always related to health, for there can be no health if men are starving. Let such an exception be admitted, and all that a state will have to do in times of stress and strain is to say that its farmers and merchants and

workmen must be protected against competition from without, lest they go upon the poor relief lists or perish altogether. To give entrance to that excuse would be to invite a speedy end of our national solidarity. The Constitution was framed under the dominion of a political philosophy less parochial in range. It was framed upon the theory that the peoples of the several states must sink or swim together, and that in the long run prosperity and salvation are in union and not division.

Keywords: Competition, Constitution, Economic welfare, Health, National solidarity, Political philosophy, Prosperity, States, Unity

Justice Benjamin Cardozo
Chas. C. Steward Machine Co. v. Davis,
301 U.S. 548, 589–590 (1937)
Every rebate from a tax when conditioned upon conduct is in some measure a temptation. But to hold that motive or temptation is equivalent to coercion is to plunge the law in endless difficulties.

Keywords: Coercion, Conduct, Governmental authority, Rebate, Tax

Justice Benjamin Cardozo
Helvering v. Davis and Steward Machine Co.,
301 U.S. 619, 641 (1937)
Needs that were narrow or parochial a century ago may be interwoven in our day with the well-being of the Nation. What is critical or urgent changes with the times.

Keywords: Change, History, National well-being

Justice Harlan Fiske Stone
Helvering v. Gerhardt,
304 U.S. 405, 416 (1938)
. . . any allowance of a tax immunity for the protection of state sovereignty is at the expense of the sovereign power of the nation to tax. Enlargement of the one involves diminution of the other. When enlargement proceeds beyond the necessity of protecting the state, the burden of the immunity is thrown upon the national government with benefit only to a privileged class of taxpayers.

Keywords: National government, Privileged class, Tax, Tax immunity, State sovereignty

Justice Harlan Fiske Stone
Helvering v. Gerhardt,
304 U.S. 405, 419 (1938)
In a period marked by a constant expansion of government activities and the steady multiplication of the complexities of taxing systems, it is perhaps too much to expect that the judicial pronouncements marking the boundaries of state immunity should present a completely logical pattern.

Keywords: Government activities, Government expansion, Judicial processes, State immunity, Taxation

Justice Hugo Black, concurring
Helvering v. Gerhardt,
304 U.S. 405, 427 (1938)
There is not, and there cannot be, any unchanging line of demarcation between essential and nonessential governmental functions. Many governmental functions of today have at some time in the past been nongovernmental. The

genius of our government provides that, within the sphere of constitutional action, the people—acting not through the courts but through their elected legislative representatives—have the power to determine as conditions demand, what services and functions the public welfare requires.

Keywords: *Constitutional actions, Governmental functions, Legislative branch, Public welfare*

Justice Hugo Black
Smith v. Texas,
311 U.S. 128, 130 (1940)

It is part of the established tradition in the use of juries as instruments of public justice that the jury be a body truly representative of the community. For racial discrimination to result in the exclusion from jury service of otherwise qualified groups not only violates our constitution and the laws enacted under it but is at war with our basic concepts of a democratic society and a representative government.

Keywords: *Community, Democracy, Discrimination, Jury, Public justice, Race, Representative government*

Justice Owen Roberts
United States v. Cooper Corporation,
312 U.S. 600, 604 (1941)

The United States is a juristic person in the sense that it has capacity to sue upon contracts made with it or in vindication of its property rights.

Keywords: *Capacity, Contracts, Juristic person, Property rights, United States*

Justice Owen Roberts, concurring
Ex parte Mitsuye Endo,
323 U.S. 283, 309 (1944)

I think it inadmissible to suggest that some inferior public servant exceeded the authority granted by executive order in this case. Such a basis of decision will render easy the evasion of law and the violation of constitutional rights, for when conduct is called in question the obvious response will be that, however much the superior executive officials knew, understood, and approved the conduct of their subordinates, those subordinates in fact lacked a definite mandate so to act. It is to hide one's head in the sand to assert that the detention of relator resulted from an excess of authority by subordinate officials.

Keywords: *Conduct, Constitutional rights, Executive branch, Executive order, Public official, Subordinate official*

Chief Justice Harlan Fiske Stone
Hooven & Allison Co. v. Evatt,
324 U.S. 652, 671–672 (1945)

The term "United States" may be used in any one of several senses. It may be merely the name of a sovereign occupying the position analogous to that of other sovereigns in the family of nations. It may designate the territory over which the sovereignty of the United States extends, or it may be the collective name of the states which are united by and under the Constitution.

Keywords: *Constitutional organization, Nation-states, Sovereign, States, Territory, United States*

Justice Frank Murphy, dissenting
Screws v. United States,
325 U.S. 91, 160 (1945)
Evil men are rarely given power; they take it over from better men to whom it had been entrusted.
Keywords: *Evil, Philosophy, Power, Trust*

Chief Justice Harlan Fiske Stone
Bigelow v. RKO Radio Pictures,
327 U.S. 251, 265 (1946)
The most elementary conceptions of justice and public policy require that the wrongdoer shall bear the risk of the uncertainty which his own wrong has created.
Keywords: *Justice, Public policy, Wrongdoer*

Justice William Douglas
United States v. Columbia Steel Corp.,
334 U.S. 495, 536 (1948)
Industrial power should be decentralized. It should be scattered into many hands so that the fortune of the people will not be dependent on the whim or caprice, the political prejudice, the emotional stability of a few self-appointed men. The fact that they are not vicious men, but respectable and social-minded is irrelevant. That is the philosophy and command of the Sherman Act. It was founded on a theory of hostility to the concentration in private hands of power so great that only a government of the people should have it.
Keywords: *Decentralized power, Industrial power, Philosophy, Political prejudice, Power*

Justice Robert Jackson
H.P. Hood & Sons v. DuMond,
336 U.S. 525, 534–535 (1949)
The Commerce Clause is one of the most prolific sources of national power and an equally prolific source of conflict with legislation of the state. While the Constitution vests in Congress the power to regulate commerce among the states, it does not say what the states may or may not do in the absence of congressional action, nor how to draw the line between what is and what is not commerce among the states. Perhaps even more than by interpretation of its written word, this Court has advanced the solidarity and prosperity of this Nation by the meaning it has given to these great silences of the Constitution.
Keywords: *Commerce Clause, Congress, Congressional action, Constitutional silence, Legislation, National power, State power*

Justice Robert Jackson
H.P. Hood & Sons v. DuMond,
336 U.S. 525, 539 (1949)
Our system, fostered by the Commerce clause, is that every farmer and every craftsman shall be encouraged to produce by the certainty that he will have free access to every market in the Nation, that no home embargoes will withhold his export, and no foreign state will by customs duties or regulations exclude them. Likewise, every consumer may look to the free competition from every producing area in the Nation to protect him from exploitation by any. Such was the vision of the Founders; such has been

the doctrine of this Court which has given it reality.

Keywords: *Commerce Clause, Consumer, Customs, Duties, Economic system, Embargoes, Founders, Free access, Free competition, Markets, Regulations*

Justice William Douglas
Day-Brite Lighting, Inc. v. Missouri,
342 U.S. 421, 423 (1952)
Our recent decisions make plain that we do not sit as a super-legislature to weigh the wisdom of legislation nor to decide whether the policy which it expresses offends the public welfare. The legislative power has limits. . . . But the state legislatures have constitutional authority to experiment with new techniques; they are entitled to their own standard of the public welfare; they may within extremely broad limits control practices in the business-labor field, so long as specific constitutional prohibitions are not violated and so long as conflicts with valid and controlling federal laws are avoided.

Keywords: *Constitutional authority, Constitutional prohibitions, Controlling law, Judicial authority, Judicial legislating, Judicial power, Judicial restraint, Legislative power, Public welfare, State legislatures, Super legislature*

Justice Sherman Minton
Adler v. Board of Education,
342 U.S. 485, 493 (1952)
A teacher works in a sensitive area in a schoolroom. There he shapes the attitude of young minds towards the society in which they live. In this, the state has a

vital concern. It must preserve the integrity of the schools. That the school authorities have the right and the duty to screen the officials, teachers, and employees as to their fitness to maintain the integrity of the schools as a part of ordered society, cannot be doubted. One's associates, past and present, as well as one's conduct, may properly be considered in determining fitness and loyalty. From time immemorial, one's reputation has been determined in part by the company he keeps. In the employment of officials and teachers of the school system, the state may very properly inquire into the company they keep, and we know of no rule, constitutional or otherwise, that prevents the state, when determining the fitness and loyalty of such persons, from considering the organizations and persons with whom they associate.

Keywords: *Acquaintances, Employees, Employment, Integrity, Loyalty, Reputation, School, Society, States, Teacher*

Justice William Douglas, dissenting
Adler v. Board of Education,
342 U.S. 485, 510 (1952)
What happens under this law is typical of what happens in a police state. Teachers are under constant surveillance; their pasts are combed for signs of disloyalty; their utterances are watched for clues to dangerous thoughts. A pall is cast over the classrooms. There can be no real academic freedom in that environment. Where suspicion fills the air and holds scholars in line for fear of their jobs, there can be no exercise of the free intellect. Supineness and dogmatism take the

place of inquiry. A "party line"—as dangerous as the "party line" of the communists—lays hold. It is the "party line" of the orthodox view, of the conventional thought, of the accepted approach. A problem can no longer be pursued with impunity to its edges. Fear stalks the classroom. The teacher is no longer a stimulant to adventurous thinking; she becomes instead a pipe line for safe and sound information. A deadening dogma takes the place of free inquiry. Instruction tends to become sterile; pursuit of knowledge is discouraged; discussion often leaves off where it should begin.

Keywords: *Classrooms, Conventional thought, Dogmatism, Education, Knowledge, Loyalty, Police state, Surveillance, Teachers, Thoughts*

Justice Hugo Black, dissenting
Rutkin v. United States,
343 U.S. 130, 141 (1952)
It seems illusory to believe, as the majority apparently does, that the burden on honest American taxpayers will be lightened by a governmental policy of pursuing extortioners in futile efforts to collect income taxes. I venture the guess that this one trial has cost United States taxpayers more money than the government will collect in taxes from extortioners in the next twenty-five years.

Keywords: *Extortion, Income tax, Public policy, Taxpayers*

Justice Robert Jackson, dissenting
Ray v. Blair,
343 U.S. 214, 234 (1952)
The demise of the whole electoral system would not impress me as a disaster. At its best it is a mystifying and distorting factor in presidential elections which may resolve a popular defeat into an electoral victory. At its worst it is open to local corruption and manipulation, once so flagrant as to threaten the stability of the country. To abolish it and substitute direct election of the president, so that every vote wherever cast would have equal weight in calculating the result, would seem to me a gain for simplicity and integrity of our governmental processes.

Keywords: *Constitutional stability, Corruption, Electoral system, Governmental process, Political stability, Presidential elections*

Justice Robert Jackson, concurring
United States v. Kahriger,
345 U.S. 22, 36 (1953)
The United States has a system of taxation by confession. That a people so numerous, scattered and individualistic annually assesses itself with a tax liability, often in highly burdensome amounts, is a reassuring sign of the stability and vitality of our system of self-government. It will be a sad day for the revenues if the good will of the people toward the their taxing system is frittered away in efforts to accomplish by taxation moral reforms that cannot be accomplished by direct legislation.

Keywords: *Governmental stability, Public policy, Public revenue, Self-government, Taxation, Tax compliance, Tax liability*

Chief Justice Earl Warren
United States v. Harriss,
347 U.S. 612, 625 (1954)
Present-day legislative complexities are

such that individual members of Congress cannot be expected to explore the myriad pressures to which they are regularly subjected. Yet full realization of the American ideal of government by elected representatives depends to no small extent on their ability to properly evaluate such pressures. Otherwise the voice of the people may all too easily be drowned out by the voice of special interest groups seeking favored treatment while masquerading as proponents of the public weal.

Keywords: *Congress, Governmental complexity, Interest groups, Legislative process, Legislative representatives, Lobbying, Political pressure*

Justice Felix Frankfurter, dissenting
Baker v. Carr,
369 U.S. 186, 269–270 (1962)
This is not only an euphoric hope. It implies a sorry confession of judicial impotence in place of a frank acknowledgment that there is not under the Constitution a judicial remedy for every political mischief, for every undesirable exercise of legislative power. The Framers carefully and with deliberate forethought refused so to enthrone the judiciary. In this situation, as in others of like nature, appeal for relief does not belong here. Appeal must be to an informed, civically militant electorate. In a democratic society like ours, relief must come through an aroused popular conscience that sears the conscience of the people's representatives.

Keywords: *Electoral process, Framers, Judicial authority, Judicial legitimacy, Judicial remedies, Legislative*

power, Political mischief, Public opinion, Self-government

Justice William Douglas
Gray v. Sanders,
372 U.S. 368, 381 (1963)
The conception of political equality from the Declaration of Independence, to Lincoln's Gettysburg Address, to the Fifteenth, Seventeenth, and Nineteenth Amendments can mean only one thing—one person, one vote.

Keywords: *Declaration of Independence, Electoral process, Equality, Fifteenth Amendment, Gettysburg Address, Lincoln (Abraham), Nineteenth Amendment, Political equality, Seventeenth Amendment, Voting*

Justice William Douglas, dissenting
Wright v. Rockefeller,
376 U.S. 52, 66 (1964)
Racial electoral registers, like religious ones, have no place in a society that honors the Lincoln tradition—"of the people, by the people, for the people." Here the individual is important, not his race, his creed, or his color. The principle of equality is at war with the notion that District A must be represented by a negro, as it is with the notion that District B must be represented by a caucasian, District C by a Jew, District D by a Catholic, and so on.

Keywords: *Creed, Electoral process, Equality, Lincoln (Abraham), Race, Religion*

Justice Potter Stewart, dissenting
In re Gault,
387 U.S. 1, 79 (1967)
In the last 70 years many dedicated men

and women have devoted their professional lives to the enlightened task of bringing us out of the dark world of Charles Dickens in meeting our responsibilities to the child in our society. The result has been the creation in this century of a system of juvenile and family courts in each of the 50 states. There can be no denying that in many areas the performance of these agencies has fallen disappointingly short of the hopes and dreams of the courageous pioneers who first conceived them. For a variety of reasons, the reality has sometimes not even approached the ideal, and much remains to be accomplished in the administration of public juvenile and family agencies—in personnel, in planning, in financing, perhaps in the formulation of wholly new approaches.

Keywords: Agencies, Children, Dickens (Charles), Family courts, Juvenile courts, Juvenile justice, Legal reform, Social reform, States

Justice Hugo Black
Williams v. Rhodes,
393 U.S. 23, 32 (1968)
There is . . . no reason why two parties should retain a permanent monopoly on the right to have people vote for or against them. Competition in ideas and governmental policies is at the core of our electoral process and of the First Amendment freedoms. New parties struggling for their place must have the time and opportunity to organize in order to meet reasonable requirements for ballot position, just as the old parties have had in the past.

Keywords: Ballot position, Electoral

process, First Amendment, Political parties, Voting

Justice Abe Fortas, concurring
Kirkpatrick v. Preisler,
394 U.S. 526, 538 (1969)
Arithmetically, it is possible to achieve division of a State into districts of precisely equal size, as measured by the decennial census or any other population base. To carry out this theoretical possibility, however, a legislature might have to ignore the boundaries of common sense, running the congressional district line down the middle of the corridor of an apartment house or even dividing the residents of a single-family house between two districts. The majority opinion does not suggest so extreme a practical application of its teaching, and I mention it only because the example may dramatize the fallacy of inflexible insistence upon mathematical exactness, with no tolerance for reality.

Keywords: Census, Congressional districts, Judicial formulas, Legislature, States

Justice William Douglas
Boykin v. Alabama,
395 U.S. 238, 242–243 (1969)
Ignorance, incomprehension, coercion, terror, inducements, subtle or blatant threats might be a perfect cover-up of unconstitutionality.

Keywords: Coercion, Constitutionality, Inducements, Terror, Threats

Justice Hugo Black, dissenting
In re Winship,
397 U.S. 358, 385 (1970)
. . . the States, to the extent they are not

restrained by the provisions in [the Constitution], were to be left free to govern themselves in accordance with their own views of fairness and decency. Any legislature presumably passes a law because it thinks the end result will help more than hinder and will thus further the liberty of the society as a whole. The people, through their elected representatives, may of course be wrong in making those determinations, but the right of self-government that our Constitution preserves is just as important as any of the specific individual freedoms preserved in the Bill of Rights. The liberty of government by the people in my opinion, should never be denied by this Court except when the decision of the people as stated in laws passed by their chosen representatives, conflicts with the express or necessarily implied commands of our Constitution.

Keywords: *Bill of Rights, Express powers, Fairness, Federalism, Freedoms, Implied powers, Judicial authority, Legislative process, Legislatures, Liberty, Representatives, Self-government, Society, States*

Chief Justice Warren Burger
Gordon v. Lance,
403 U.S. 1, 6 (1971)
Certainly any departure from strict majority rule gives disproportionate power to the minority. But there is nothing in the language of the Constitution, our history, or our cases that requires that a majority always prevail on every issue. The Federal Constitution itself provides that a simple majority vote is insufficient on some issues.

Keywords: *Case law, Constitutional language, Electoral process, Judicial history, Majority power, Minority power, Voting*

Justice William Douglas, concurring
New York Times Co. v. United States,
403 U.S. 713, 724 (1971)
Secrecy in government is fundamentally anti-democratic, perpetuating bureaucratic errors. Open debate and discussion of public issues are vital to our national health.

Keywords: *Bureaucracy, Debate, Democracy, Openness, Public issues, Secrecy*

Justice Byron White
Stanley v. Illinois,
405 U.S. 645, 656 (1972)
. . . one might fairly say of the Bill of Rights in general, and the Due Process Clause in particular, that they were designed to protect the fragile values of a vulnerable citizenry from the overbearing concern for efficiency and efficacy that may characterize praiseworthy government officials no less, and perhaps more, than mediocre ones.

Keywords: *Bill of Rights, Citizenry, Constitutional safeguards, Due process, Governmental officials, Values*

Justice William Brennan, dissenting
Gravel v. United States,
408 U.S. 606, 651–652 (1972)
Though I fully share these and related views on the educational values served by the informing function, there is yet another, and perhaps more fundamental, interest at stake. It requires no citation of authority to state that public con-

cern over current issues—the war, race relations, governmental invasions of privacy—has transformed itself in recent years into what many believe is a crisis of confidence, in our system of government and its capacity to meet the needs and reflect the wants of the American people. Communication between Congress and the electorate tends to alleviate that doubt by exposing and clarifying the workings of the political system, the policies underlying new laws and the role of the Executive in their administration. To the extent that the informing function succeeds in fostering public faith in the responsiveness of Government, it is not only an "ordinary" task of the legislator but one that is essential to the continued vitality of our democratic institutions.

Keywords: *Communication, Congress, Democratic institutions, Electorate, Governmental confidence, Information, Legislators, Policies, Political system, Social issues*

Per Curiam
O'Brien v. Brown,
409 U.S. 1, 4 (1972)
No case is cited to us in which any federal court has undertaken to interject itself into the deliberative process of a national political convention. . . .

Keywords: *Case law, Electoral process, Federal courts, Political conventions*

Justice Lewis Powell
San Antonio Independent School District v. Rodriguez,
411 U.S. 1, 54 (1973)
. . . if local taxation for local expenditure is an unconstitutional method of providing for education, then it may be an equally impermissible means of providing other necessary services customarily financed largely from local property taxes, including local police and fire protection, public health and hospitals, and public utility facilities of various kinds. We perceive no justification for such a severe denigration of local property taxation and control. . . .

Keywords: *Taxation, Public finance, Governmental services, Property tax*

Justice Byron White, concurring
Smith v. Goguen,
415 U.S. 566, 586–587 (1974)
There is no doubt in my mind that it is well within the powers of Congress to adopt and prescribe a national flag and to protect the integrity of that flag. Congress may provide for the general welfare, control interstate commerce, provide for the common defense, and exercise any powers necessary and proper for those ends. These powers, and the inherent attributes of sovereignty as well, surely encompass the designation and protection of a flag. It would be foolishness to suggest that the men who wrote the Constitution thought they were violating it when they specified a flag for the new Nation, just as they had for the Union under the Articles of Confederation. It is a fact of history that flags have been associated with nations and with government at all levels, as well as with tribes and families. It is also a historical fact that flags, including ours, have played an important and useful role in human affairs. One need not explain

fully a phenomenon to recognize its existence and in this case to concede that the flag is an important symbol of nationhood and unity, created by the Nation and endowed with certain attributes. Conceived in this light, I have no doubt about the validity of laws designating and describing the flag and regulating its use, display, and disposition. The United States has created its own flag, as it may. The flag is a national property, and the Nation may regulate those who would make, imitate, sell, possess, or use it. I would not question those statutes which proscribe mutilation, defacement, or burning of the flag or which otherwise protect its physical integrity, without regard to whether such conduct might provoke violence. Neither would I find it beyond congressional power, or that of state legislatures, to forbid attaching to or putting on the flag any words, symbols, or advertisements. All of these objects, whatever their nature, are foreign to the flag, change its physical character, and interfere with its design and function. There would seem to be little question about the power of Congress to forbid the mutilation of the Lincoln Memorial or to prevent overlaying it with words or other objects. The flag is itself a monument, subject to similar protection.

Keywords: *Articles of Confederation, Congressional authority, Congressional power, Constitutional history, Desecration, Ends/means, Flag, Framers, General welfare, Human affairs, Interstate commerce, Monuments, National property, Necessary and proper, Sovereignty, State legislatures, Symbolism*

Justice William Rehnquist, dissenting
Smith v. Goguen,
415 U.S. 566, 602–603 (1974)
The significance of the flag, and the deep emotional feelings it arouses in a large part of our citizenry, cannot be fully expressed in the two dimensions of a lawyer's brief or of a judicial opinion. But if the Government may create private proprietary interests in written work and in musical and theatrical performances by virtue of copyright laws, I see no reason why it may not, for all of the reasons mentioned, create a similar governmental interest in the flag by prohibiting even those who have purchased the physical object from impairing its physical integrity. For what they have purchased is not merely cloth dyed red, white, and blue, but also the one visible manifestation of two hundred years of nationhood—a history compiled by generations of our forebears and contributed to by streams of immigrants from the four corners of the globe, which has traveled a course since the time of this country's origin that could not have been "foreseen . . . by the most gifted of its begeters." The permissible scope of government regulation of this unique physical object cannot be adequately dealt with in terms of the law of private property or by a highly abstract, scholastic interpretation of the First Amendment. Massachusetts has not prohibited Goguen from wearing a sign sewn to the seat of his pants expressing in words his low opinion of the flag, of the country, or anything else. It has prohibited him from wearing there a particular symbol of extraordinary significance and content, for which significance and

content Goguen is in no wise responsible. The flag of the United States is not just another "thing," and it is not just another "idea"; it is not primarily an idea at all.
Keywords: *Citizenry, Copyright, Desecration, Expression, First Amendment, Flag, Free speech, History, Governmental regulations, Nationhood, Political criticism, Private interests, Property, Symbolism*

Justice Byron White
American Party of Texas v. White,
415 U.S. 767, 794 (1974)
. . . we cannot agree that the State, simply because it defrays the expenses of party primary elections, must also finance the efforts of every nascent political group seeking to organize itself and unsuccessfully attempting to win a place on the general election ballot.
Keywords: *Electoral process, Party primaries, Political parties, Public financing, States*

Per Curiam
Buckley v. Valeo,
424 U.S. 1, 21 (1976)
A contribution serves as a general expression of support for the candidate and his views, but does not communicate the underlying basis for the support. The quantity of communication by the contributor does not increase perceptibly with the size of his contribution, since the expression rests solely on the undifferentiated, symbolic act of contributing. At most, the size of the contribution provides a very rough index of the intensity of the contributor's support for the candidate. A limitation on the amount of money a person may give to a candidate or campaign organization thus involves little direct restraint on his political communication, for it permits the symbolic expression of support evidenced by a contribution but does not in any way infringe the contributor's freedom to discuss candidates and issues. While contributions may result in political expression if spent by a candidate or an association to present views to the voters, the transformation of contributions into political debate involves speech by someone other than the contributor.
Keywords: *Associations, Campaign contributions, Candidates, Electoral process, Free expression, Free speech, Political communication, Political debate, Political participation, Political support, Political symbolism, Voters*

Justice William Rehnquist, concurring in part, dissenting in part
Buckley v. Valeo,
424 U.S. 1, 293–294 (1976)
. . . Congress. . . . has enshrined the Republican and Democratic Parties in a permanently preferred position, and has established requirements for funding minor-party and independent candidates to which the two major parties are not subject. Congress would undoubtedly be justified in treating the Presidential candidates of the two major parties differently from minor-party or independent Presidential candidates, in view of the long demonstrated public support of the former. But because of the First Amendment overtones of the appellants' Fifth Amendment equal protection claim, something more than a merely

rational basis for the difference in treatment must be shown, as the Court apparently recognizes. I find it impossible to subscribe to the Court's reasoning that because no third party has posed a credible threat to the two major parties in Presidential elections since 1860, Congress may by law attempt to assure that this pattern will endure forever.

Keywords: *Campaign financing, Candidates, Electoral process, Equal protection, Fifth Amendment, First Amendment, Judicial credibility, Minor political parties, Political parties, Presidential politics*

Justice Thurgood Marshall
Illinois Elections Board v. Socialist Workers Party,
440 U.S. 173, 185–186 (1979)
The States' interest in screening out frivolous candidates must be considered in light of the significant role that third parties have played in the political development of the Nation. . . . an election campaign is a means of disseminating ideas as well as attaining political office. [Overbroad] restrictions on ballot access jeopardize this form of political expression.

Keywords: *Ballots, Campaign, Candidates, Electoral process, First Amendment, Political communication, Political expression, Political ideas, Political parties, States*

Justice Lewis Powell
Ambach v. Norwick,
441 U.S. 68, 76 (1979)
The importance of public schools in the preparation of individuals for participation as citizens, and in the preservation of the values on which our society

rests, long has been recognized by our decisions. . . .

Keywords: *Citizens, Democracy, Education, Judicial history, Public schools, Society, Teachers, Values*

Justice Lewis Powell
Ambach v. Norwick,
441 U.S. 68, 79 (1979)
Through both the presentation of course materials and the example he sets, a teacher has an opportunity to influence the attitudes of students toward government, the political process, and a citizen's social responsibilities. This influence is crucial to the continued good health of a democracy.

Keywords: *Citizens, Curriculum, Democracy, Education, Governmental awareness, Political attitudes, Political process, Public schools, Society, Teachers, Values, Virtues*

Justice Lewis Powell
Ambach v. Norwick,
441 U.S. 68, 80 (1979)
. . . a State properly may regard all teachers as having an obligation to promote civic virtues and understanding in their classes, regardless of the subject taught.

Keywords: *Citizens, Civics, Education, Governmental awareness, Public schools, Society, States, Teachers, Values, Virtues*

Justice Lewis Powell, dissenting
Rome v. United States,
446 U.S. 156, 206 (1980)
If there were reason to believe that today's decision would protect the voting rights of minorities in any way, perhaps this case could be viewed as one

where the Court's ends justify dubious analytical means. But the District Court found, and no one denies, that for at least 17 years there has been no voting discrimination by the city of Rome. Despite this record, the Court today continues federal rule over the most local decisions made by this small city in Georgia. Such an outcome must vitiate the incentive for any local government in a State covered by the Act to meet diligently the Act's requirements. Neither the Framers of the Fifteenth Amendment nor the Congress that enacted the Voting Rights Act could have intended that result.

Keywords: *Discrimination, Electoral process, Federalism, Fifteenth Amendment, Framers, Judicial authority, Judicial legitimacy, Minorities, Voting rights*

Justice William Rehnquist, dissenting
Rome v. United States,
446 U.S. 156, 219 (1980)

The Constitution imposes no obligation on local governments to erect institutional safeguards to ensure the election of a black candidate. Nor do I believe that Congress can do so, absent a finding that this obligation would be necessary to remedy constitutional violations on the part of the local government.

Keywords: *Constitutional restraints, Discrimination, Electoral process, Federalism, Local government, Minority representation*

Justice John Paul Stevens, concurring
Mobile v. Bolden,
446 U.S. 55, 92 (1980)

. . . a political decision that is supported by valid and articulable justifications cannot be invalid simply because some participants in the decisionmaking process were motivated by a purpose to disadvantage a minority group.

Keywords: *Discrimination, Legislative intent, Political decision, Minority group, Public policy*

Justice Thurgood Marshall, dissenting
Mobile v. Bolden,
446 U.S. 55, 134–135 (1980)

. . . it is beyond dispute that a standard based solely upon the motives of official decisionmakers creates significant problems of proof for plaintiffs and forces the inquiring court to undertake an unguided, tortuous look into the minds of officials in the hope of guessing why certain policies were adopted and others rejected. . . . An approach based on motivation creates the risk that officials will be able to adopt policies that are the products of discriminatory intent so long as they sufficiently mask their motives through the use of subtlety and illusion.

Keywords: *Discrimination, Legislative intent, Public officials, Public policy*

Chief Justice Warren Burger, dissenting
Schad v. Mount Ephraim,
452 U.S. 61, 87 (1981)

Citizens should be free to choose to shape their community so that it embodies their conception of the "decent life." This will sometimes mean deciding that certain forms of activity—factories, gas stations, sports stadia, bookstores, and surely live nude shows—will not be allowed. That a community is willing to tolerate such a commercial use as a convenience store, a gas station, a pharmacy, or a delicatessen does not compel it also to tolerate every other "commercial use," including pornography peddlers and live nude shows.

Keywords: *Citizens, Commerciality, Communities, Decency, Nudity, Pornography*

Justice William Rehnquist
Santosky v. Kramer,
455 U.S. 745, 770 (1982)

I believe that few of us would care to live in a society where every aspect of life was regulated by a single source of law, whether that source be this Court or some other organ of our complex body politic. But today's decision certainly moves us in that direction. By parsing the New York scheme and holding one narrow provision unconstitutional, the majority invites further federal-court intrusion into every facet of state family law. If ever there were an area in which federal courts should heed the admonition of Justice Holmes that "a page of history is worth a volume of logic," it is in the area of domestic relations. This area has been left to the States from time immemorial, and not without good reason.

Keywords: *Body politic, Domestic relations, Experience, Family law, Federalism, History, Holmes (Oliver Wendell), Judicial authority, Judicial legitimacy, Judicial review, Logic, Society, States, Totalitarian*

Chief Justice Warren Burger
Plyler v. Doe,
457 U.S. 202, 243 (1982)

The Court's holding today manifests the justly criticized judicial tendency to attempt speedy and wholesale formulation of "remedies" for the failures—or simply the laggard pace—of the political processes of our system of government.

Keywords: *Democracy, Judicial Activism, Judicial authority, Judicial legitimacy, Judicial remedies, Political process, Separation of powers*

Justice Byron White, dissenting
Nixon v. Fitzgerald,
457 U.S. 731, 797 (1982)

The remedies in which the Court finds comfort were never designed to afford relief for individual harms. Rather, they were designed as political safety-valves. Politics and history, however, are not the domain of the courts; the courts exist to assure each individual that he, as an individual, has enforceable rights that he may pursue to achieve a peaceful redress of his legitimate grievances.

Keywords: *Grievances, History, Judicial authority, Judicial legitimacy, Judicial remedies, Politics, Rights*

Justice Harry Blackmun
Thornburgh v. American College of Obstetricians & Gynecologists,
476 U.S. 747, 771–772 (1986)

Constitutional rights do not always have easily ascertainable boundaries, and controversy over the meaning of our Nation's most majestic guarantees frequently has been turbulent. As judges, however, we are sworn to uphold the law even when its content gives rise to bitter dispute. We recognized at the very beginning of our opinion in *Roe* that abortion raises moral and spiritual questions over which honorable persons can disagree sincerely and profoundly. But those disagreements did not then and do not now relieve us of our duty to apply the Constitution faithfully.

Keywords: *Abortion, Constitutional rights, Freedom, Judicial authority, Liberties, Morality, Spiritualism*

Justice Antonin Scalia, dissenting
Edwards v. Aguillard,
482 U.S. 578, 636–637 (1987)

. . . while it is possible to discern the objective "purpose" of a statute (i. e., the public good at which its provisions appear to be directed), or even the formal motivation for a statute where that is explicitly set forth (as it was, to no avail, here), discerning the subjective motivation of those enacting the statute is, to be honest, almost always an impossible task. The number of possible motivations, to begin with, is not binary, or indeed even finite. In the present case, for example, a particular legislator need not have voted for the Act either because he wanted to foster religion or because he wanted to improve education. He may have thought the bill would provide jobs for his district, or may have wanted to make amends with a faction of his party he had alienated on another vote, or he may have been a close friend of the bill's sponsor, or he may have been repaying a favor he owed the majority leader, or he may have hoped the Governor would appreciate his vote and make a fundraising appearance for him, or he may have been pressured to vote for a bill he disliked by a wealthy contributor or by a flood of constituent mail, or he may have been seeking favorable publicity, or he may have been reluctant to hurt the feelings of a loyal staff member who worked on the bill, or he may have been settling an old score with a legislator who opposed the bill, or he may have been mad at his wife who opposed the bill, or he may have been intoxicated and utterly unmotivated when the vote was called, or he may have accidentally voted "yes" instead of "no," or, of course, he may have had (and very likely did have) a combination of some of the above and many other motivations. To look for the sole purpose of even a single legislator is probably to look for something that does not exist.

Keywords: *Legislation, Legislators, Political process, Public good, Statutory intent, Statutory interpretation*

Justice Antonin Scalia, dissenting
Morrison v. Olson,
487 U.S. 654, 713–714 (1988)

Besides weakening the Presidency by reducing the zeal of his staff, it must also be obvious that the institution of the independent counsel enfeebles him more directly in his constant confrontation with Congress, by eroding his public support. Nothing is so politically effective as the ability to charge that one's opponent and his associates are not merely wrongheaded, naïve, ineffective, but, in all probability "crooks." And nothing so effectively gives an appearance of validity to such charges as a Justice Department investigation and, even better, prosecution. The present statute provides ample means for that sort of attack, assuring that massive and lengthy investigations will occur, not merely when the Justice Department in the application of its usual standards believes they are called for, but whenever it cannot be said that there are "no reasonable grounds to believe" they are called for. The statute's highly visible procedures assure, moreover, that unlike most investigations these will be widely known and prominently displayed. Thus, in the 10 years since the institution of the independent counsel was established by law, there have been nine highly publicized investigations, a source of constant political damage to two administrations.

Keywords: *Congress, Independent counsel, Investigations, Oversight, Presidency, Presidential aides, Separation of powers*

Justice William Brennan, dissenting
DeShaney v. Winnebago County Department of Social Services,
489 U.S. 189, 212 (1989)

. . . inaction can be every bit as abusive of power as action, that oppression can result when a State undertakes a vital duty and then ignores it.

Keywords: *Abuse of power, Due process, Duty, Government services, Oppression, Social services, State*

Justice Antonin Scalia, dissenting
Treasury Employees v. Von Raab,
489 U.S. 656, 686–687 (1989)

I do not believe for a minute that the driving force behind these drug-testing rules was any of the feeble justifications put forward by counsel here and accepted by the Court. . . . What better way to show that the Government is serious about its "war on drugs" than to subject its employees on the front line of that war to this invasion of their privacy and affront to their dignity? To be sure, there is only a slight chance that it will prevent some serious public harm resulting from Service employee drug use, but it will show to the world that the [Customs] Service is "clean," and—most important of all—will demonstrate the determination of the Government to eliminate this scourge of our society! I think it obvious that this justification is unacceptable; that the impairment of individual liberties cannot be the means of making a point; that symbolism, even symbolism for so worthy a cause as the abolition of unlawful drugs, cannot validate an otherwise unreasonable search.

Keywords: *Drug testing, Drug use, Liberties, Politics, Public employees, Public relations, Search, Symbolism, War on drugs*

Justice John Paul Stevens, dissenting
Texas v. Johnson,
491 U.S. 397, 439 (1989)

The ideas of liberty and equality have been an irresistible force in motivating leaders like Patrick Henry, Susan B. Anthony, and Abraham Lincoln, schoolteachers like Nathan Hale and Booker T. Washington, the Philippine Scouts who fought at Bataan, and the soldiers who scaled the bluff at Omaha Beach. If those ideas are worth fighting for—and our history demonstrates that they are—it cannot be true that the flag that uniquely symbolizes their power is not itself worthy of protection from unnecessary desecration.

Keywords: *American flag, Desecration, Equality, Heroes, History, Leaders, Liberty, Symbolism*

Justice William Brennan, dissenting
Michigan Department of State Police v. Sitz,
496 U.S. 444, 459 (1990)
. . . consensus that a particular law enforcement technique serves a laudable purpose has never been the touchstone of constitutional analysis.
Keywords: *Constitutional analysis, Constitutional legitimacy, Law enforcement, Police, Political consensus, Public relations*

Justice Antonin Scalia, concurring
Cruzan v. Director, Missouri Department of Health,
497 U.S. 261, 293 (1990)
. . . I would have preferred that we announce, clearly and promptly, that the federal courts have no business in this field; that American law has always accorded the State the power to prevent, by force if necessary, suicide—including suicide by refusing to take appropriate measures necessary to preserve one's life; that the point at which life becomes "worthless," and the point at which the means necessary to preserve it become "extraordinary" or "inappropriate," are neither set forth in the Constitution nor known to the nine Justices of this Court any better than they are known to nine people picked at random from the Kansas City telephone directory; and hence, that even when it is demonstrated by clear and convincing evidence that a patient no longer wishes certain measures to be taken to preserve her life, it is up to the citizens of Missouri to decide, through their elected representatives, whether that wish will be honored. It is quite impossible (because the Constitution says nothing about the matter) that those citizens will decide upon a line less lawful than the one we would choose; and it is unlikely (because we know no more about "life-and-death" than they do) that they will decide upon a line less reasonable.
Keywords: *Federal courts, Federalism, Judicial authority, Judicial legitimacy, Life, Representative democracy, Right to die, States, Suicide*

Justice Anthony Kennedy, concurring
United States v. Lopez,
514 U.S. 549, 581 (1995)
While it is doubtful that any State, or indeed any reasonable person, would argue that it is wise policy to allow students to carry guns on school premises, considerable disagreement exists about how best to accomplish that goal.
Keywords: *Education, Ends/Means, Firearms, Public policy, Reasonable persons, Schools, States, Wisdom*

Justice Sandra Day O'Connor, concurring
Washington v. Glucksberg,
117 S. Ct. 2302, 2303 (1997)
There is no reason to think the democratic process will not strike the proper balance between the interests of terminally ill, mentally competent individuals who would seek to end their suffering and the State's interests in protecting those who might seek to end life mistakenly or under pressure.
Keywords: *Death, Democratic process, Health, Mentally competent, Police power, Right to die, State interests, Terminally ill*

Justice Antonin Scalia, concurring
National Endowment for the Arts
v. Finley,
524 U.S. 569, 598 (1998)
It is the very business of government to favor and disfavor points of view on (in modern times, at least) innumerable subjects which is the main reason we have decided to elect those who run the government, rather than save money by making their posts hereditary.
Keywords: *Political process, Representative government*

Justice Antonin Scalia, dissenting
Chicago v. Morales,
527 U.S. ___, ___ (1999)
. . . in our democratic system, how much harmless conduct to proscribe is not a judgment to be made by the courts. So long as constitutionally guaranteed rights are not affected, and so long as the proscription has a rational basis, all sorts of perfectly harmless activity by millions of perfectly innocent people can be forbidden—riding a motorcycle without a safety helmet, for example, starting a campfire in a national forest, or selling a safe and effective drug not yet approved by the FDA. All of these acts are entirely innocent and harmless in themselves, but because of the risk of harm that they entail, the freedom to engage in them has been abridged. The citizens of Chicago have decided that depriving themselves of the freedom to "hang out" with a gang member is necessary to eliminate pervasive gang crime and intimidation—and that the elimination of the one is worth the deprivation of the other. This Court has no business second-guessing either the degree of necessity or the fairness of the trade.
Keywords: *Citizens, Conduct, Constitutional rights, Democratic system, Freedom, Gang members, Judicial authority, Judicial judgment, Rational basis, Risk of harm*

6. The Good of the Fifty

Chapter 6 explores the unique nature of federalism as it relates directly to states' rights. You will find excerpts about the demise and rebirth of the Tenth Amendment. The subject matter, perhaps more than any other, sheds considerable light into the philosophical leanings of individual justices.

Justice Samuel Chase
Calder v. Bull,
3 U.S. 386, 387–388 (1798)
I cannot subscribe to the omnipotence of a state Legislature, or that it is absolute and without control; although its authority should not be expressly restrained by the constitution, or fundamental law of the state. . . . There are certain vital principles in our free Republican governments, which will determine and overrule an apparent and flagrant abuse of legislative power; as to authorize manifest injustice by positive law; or to take away that security for personal liberty, or private property, for the protection whereof the government was established. An ACT of the Legislature (for I cannot call it a law) contrary to the great first principles of the social compact, cannot be considered a rightful exercise of legislative authority. . . . The genius, the nature, and the spirit, of our state governments, amount to a prohibition of such acts of legislation; and the general principles of law and reason forbid them.
Keywords: *Compact, Constitutional authority, Federalism, Legislative abuse, Legislative authority, Liberties, Positive law, Principles, Property, Republican government, State legislatures*

Chief Justice John Marshall
McCulloch v. Maryland,
17 U.S. 316, 429–430 (1819)
If we measure the power of taxation residing in a state, by the extent of sovereignty which the people of a single state possess, and can confer on its government, we have an intelligible standard, applicable to every case to which the power may be applied. We have a principle which leaves the power of taxing the people and property of a state unimpaired; which leaves to a state the command of all its resources, and which places beyond its reach, all those powers which are conferred by the people of the United States on the government of the union, and all those means which are given for the purpose of carrying those powers into execution. We have a principle which is safe for the states, and safe for the union. We are relieved, as we ought to be, from clashing sovereignty; from interfering powers; from a repugnancy between a right in one government to pull down what there is an acknowledged right in another to build up; from the incompatibility of a right in one government to destroy what there is a right in another to preserve. We are not

driven to the perplexing inquiry, so unfit for the judicial department, what degree of taxation is the legitimate use, and what degree may amount to the abuse of the power.

Keywords: *Abuse of power, Federalism, Principles, Resources, Self-government, Sovereignty, States, Taxation*

Chief Justice Roger Taney
Dred Scott v. Sandford,
60 U.S. 393, 416 (1856)
The legislation of the States therefore shows, in a manner not to be mistaken, the inferior and subject condition of that race at the time the Constitution was adopted, and long afterwards, throughout the thirteen States by which that instrument was framed; and it is hardly consistent with the respect due to these States, to suppose that they regarded at that time, as fellow-citizens and members of the sovereignty, a class of beings whom they had thus stigmatized; whom, as we are bound, out of respect to the State sovereignties, to assume they had deemed it just and necessary thus to stigmatize, and upon whom they had impressed such deep and enduring marks of inferiority and degradation; or, that when they met in convention to form the Constitution, they looked upon them as a portion of their constituents, or designed to include them in the provisions so carefully inserted for the security and protection of the liberties and rights of their citizens. It cannot be supposed that they intended to secure to them rights, and privileges, and rank, in the new political body throughout the Union, which

every one of them denied within the limits of its own dominion.

Keywords: *Citizens, Constitutional history, Discrimination, Liberties, Privileges, Race, Rights, Sovereignty, State legislatures*

Justice Benjamin Curtis, dissenting
Dred Scott v. Sandford,
60 U.S. 393, 585 (1856)
It may be further objected, that if free colored persons may be citizens of the United States, it depends only on the will of a master whether he will emancipate his slave, and thereby make him a citizen. Not so. The master is subject to the will of the State. Whether he shall be allowed to emancipate his slave at all; if so, on what conditions; and what is to be the political status of the freed man, depend, not on the will of the master, but on the will of the State, upon which the political status of all its native-born inhabitants depends.

Keywords: *Citizens, Emancipation, Masters, Political status, Race, Slavery, State authority*

Chief Justice Salmon Chase
Texas v. White,
74 U.S. 700, 725–726 (1868)
The Constitution, in all its provisions, looks to an indestructible Union, composed of indestructible States. When, therefore, Texas became one of the United States, she entered into an indissoluble relation. All the obligations of perpetual union, and all the guaranties of republican government in the Union, attached at once to the State. The act which consummated her admission into

the Union was something more than a compact; it was the incorporation of a new member into the political body. And it was final. The union between Texas and the other States was as complete, as perpetual, and as indissoluble as the union between the original States. There was no place for reconsideration, or revocation, except through revolution, or through consent of the States.

Keywords: *Admission, Perpetual union, Political body, Revolution, Statehood, United States*

Justice Ward Hunt
United States v. Baltimore & Ohio Railroad Co.,
84 U.S. 322, 327 (1872)

The right of the States to administer their own affairs through their legislative, executive, and judicial departments, in their own manner through their own agencies, is conceded by the uniform decisions of this court and by the practice of the Federal government from its organization. This carries with it an exemption of those agencies and instruments, from the taxing power of the Federal government. If they may be taxed lightly, they may be taxed heavily; if justly, oppressively. Their operation may be impeded and may be destroyed, if any interference is permitted.

Keywords: *Federal government, Federalism, Judicial history, States, States' rights, Taxation*

Justice Stephen Field, dissenting
Ex parte Virginia,
100 U.S. 339, 368 (1879)

In the consideration of questions growing out of these amendments much confusion has arisen from a failure to distinguish between the civil and the political rights of citizens. Civil rights are absolute and personal. Political rights, on the other hand, are conditioned and dependent upon the discretion of the elective or appointing power, whether that be the people acting through the ballot, or one of the departments of their government. The civil rights of the individual are never to be withheld, and may be always judicially enforced. The political rights which he may enjoy, such as holding office and discharging a public trust, are qualified because their possession depends on his fitness, to be adjudged by those whom society has clothed with the elective authority.

Keywords: *Appointive power, Ballots, Civil rights, Elective authority, Elective power, Electoral process, Judicial authority, Political rights*

Justice Stephen Field, dissenting
Ex parte Clarke,
100 U.S. 399, 410 (1879)

It is true that Congress may authorize a particular State officer to perform a particular duty; but if he declines to do so, it does not follow that he may be coerced or punished for his refusal.

Keywords: *Congressional authority, Congressional orders, Federalism, Punishment, State officers*

Justice Henry Brown
Holden v. Hardy,
169 U.S. 366, 387 (1898)

. . . while the cardinal principles of justice are immutable, the methods by which justice is administered are subject to constant fluctuation, and that the constitution of the United States, which is necessarily and to a large extent inflexible, and exceedingly difficult of amendment, should not be so construed as to deprive the states of the power to so amend their laws as to make them conform to the wishes of the citizens, as they may deem best for the public welfare, without bringing them into conflict with the supreme law of the land.

Keywords: *Administration of justice, Amending process, Constitutional authority, Justice, Principles, Public expectations, Public welfare, States, Supreme law*

Justice Horace Lurton
Coyle v. Smith,
221 U.S. 559, 573 (1911)
. . . when a new State is admitted into the Union, it is so admitted with all of the powers of sovereignty and jurisdiction which pertain to the original States, and . . . such powers may not be constitutionally diminished, impaired or shorn away by any conditions, compacts or stipulations embraced in the act under which the new state came into the Union, which would not be valid and effectual if the subject of congressional legislation after admission.

Keywords: *Admission, Compacts, Congressional authority, Constitutional authority, Sovereignty, Statehood, State power, States*

Justice George Sutherland
Frost & Frost Trucking Co. v. Railroad Commission,
271 U.S. 583, 593–594 (1926)
It would be a palpable incongruity to strike down an act of state legislation which, by words of express divestment, seeks to strip the citizen of rights guaranteed by the federal Constitution, but to uphold an act by which the same result is accomplished under the guise of a surrender of a right in exchange for a valuable privilege which the state threatens otherwise to withhold. It is not necessary to challenge the proposition that, as a general rule, the state, having power to deny a privilege altogether, may grant it upon such conditions as it sees fit to impose. But the power of the state in that respect is not unlimited; and one of the limitations is that it may not impose conditions which require the relinquishment of constitutional rights. If the state may compel the surrender of one constitutional right as a condition of its favor, it may, in like manner, compel a surrender of all. It is inconceivable that guaranties embedded in the Constitution of the United States may thus be manipulated out of existence.

Keywords: *Citizens, Constitutional guarantees, Constitutional rights, Constitutionality, Judicial review, Privileges, State legislation, State powers*

Justice Oliver Wendell Holmes, dissenting
Tyson & Brothers–United Theatre Ticket Offices v. Banton,
273 U.S. 418, 446 (1927)
. . . [a] state Legislature can do whatever it sees fit to do unless it is restrained by some express prohibition in the Constitution of the United States or of the State, and that Courts should be careful not to extend such prohibitions beyond their obvious meaning by reading into them

conceptions of public policy that the particular Court may happen to entertain.
Keywords: *Constitutional restraints, Judicial limitations, Public policy, State legislature*

Justice Louis Brandeis, dissenting
New State Ice Co. v. Liebmann,
285 U.S. 262, 311 (1932)
To stay experimentation in things social and economic is a grave responsibility. Denial of the right to experiment may be fraught with serious consequences to the nation. It is one of the happy incidents of the federal system that a single courageous state may, if its citizens choose, serve as a laboratory; and try novel social and economic experiments without risk to the rest of the country.
Keywords: *Experimentation, Laboratories of democracy, Novel ideas, Political process, Public policy, States*

Justice Owen Roberts
Nebbia v. New York,
291 U.S. 502, 537 (1934)
So far as the requirement of due process is concerned, and in the absence of other constitutional restriction, a state is free to adopt whatever economic policy may reasonably be deemed to promote public welfare, and to enforce that policy by legislation adapted to its purpose. The courts are without authority either to declare such policy, or, when it is declared by the legislative arm, to override it.
Keywords: *Constitutional restrictions, Due process, Economic policies, Judicial authority, Judicial legitimacy, Judicial restraint, Legislative process, Public welfare, States*

Justice Benjamin Cardozo, concurring
A.L.A. Schechter Poultry Corp. v. United States,
295 U.S. 495, 554 (1935)
Activities local in their immediacy do not become interstate and national because of distant repercussions. What is near and what is distant may at times be uncertain. . . . There is no penumbra of uncertainty obscuring judgment here. To find immediacy or directness here is to find it almost everywhere. If centripetal forces are to be isolated to the exclusion of the forces that oppose and counteract them, there will be an end to our federal system.
Keywords: *Centripetal forces, Federal system, Interstate activities, Local activities, Penumbra of uncertainty*

Justice William Douglas, dissenting
New York v. United States,
326 U.S. 572, 594 (1946)
The notion that the sovereign position of the States must find its protection in the will of a transient majority of Congress is foreign to and a negation of our constitutional system. There will often be vital regional interests represented by no majority in Congress. The Constitution was designed to keep the balance between the States and the nation outside the field of legislative controversy.
Keywords: *Congressional powers, Constitutional balances, Majority power, Representation, Sovereignty, States*

Justice Felix Frankfurter, concurring
Louisiana ex rel Francis v. Resweber,
329 U.S. 459, 471 (1947)
. . . this Court must abstain from interference with State action no matter how

strong one's personal feeling of revulsion against a State's insistence on its pound of flesh.

Keywords: *Judicial authority, Judicial restraint, State policies, States, Wisdom*

Justice John Marshall Harlan
Baker v. Carr,
369 U.S. 186, 332 (1962)
I can find nothing in the Equal Protection Clause or elsewhere in the Federal Constitution which expressly or impliedly supports the view that state legislatures must be so structured as to reflect with approximate equality the voice of every voter. Not only is that proposition refuted by history . . . but it strikes deep into the heart of our federal system.

Keywords: *Constitutional restraint, Electoral process, Equal Protection Clause, Express powers, Federal system, History, Implied powers, State legislatures, Voting*

Justice John Marshall Harlan
Baker v. Carr,
369 U.S. 186, 334 (1962)
. . . there is nothing in the Federal Constitution to prevent a State, acting not irrationally, from choosing any electoral legislative structure it thinks best suited to the interests, temper, and custom of its people.

Keywords: *Citizens, Constitutional restraint, Custom, Electoral process, Federal system, Legislative structure, State legislatures*

Justice John Marshall Harlan
Reynolds v. Sims,
377 U.S. 533, 603 (1964)
Can it be seriously contended that the legislatures of the States, almost two-thirds of those concerned, would have ratified an amendment which might render their own State constitutions unconstitutional?

Keywords: *Amendment process, Federalism, State constitutions, State legislatures, States*

Justice Potter Stewart, concurring
Ginsberg v. New York,
390 U.S. 629, 649–650 (1968)
I think a State may permissibly determine that, at least in some precisely delineated areas, a child—like someone in a captive audience—is not possessed of that full capacity for individual choice which is the presumption of First Amendment guarantees. It is only upon such a premise, I would suppose, that a State may deprive children of other rights—the right to marry, for example, or the right to vote—deprivations that would be constitutionally intolerable for adults.

Keywords: *Adults, Capacity, Children, Choice, Constitutional rights, First Amendment, Marriage, States, Voting*

Justice Abe Fortas
Epperson v. Arkansas,
393 U.S. 97, 104 (1968)
Judicial interposition in the operation of the public school system of the Nation raises problems requiring care and restraint. Our courts, however, have not failed to apply the First Amendment's mandate in our educational system where essential to safeguard the fundamental values of freedom of speech and inquiry and of belief. By and large, pub-

lic education in our Nation is committed to the control of state and local authorities. Courts do not and cannot intervene in the resolution of conflicts which arise in the daily operation of school systems and which do not directly and sharply implicate basic constitutional values.

Keywords: Beliefs, Constitutional values, Education, First Amendment, Free speech, Judicial authority, Judicial remedies, Judicial restraint, Schools

Justice Potter Stewart, concurring
Epperson v. Arkansas,
393 U.S. 97, 116 (1968)
It is one thing for a State to determine that "the subject of higher mathematics, or astronomy, or biology" shall or shall not be included in its public school curriculum. It is quite another thing for a State to make it a criminal offense for a public school teacher so much as to mention the very existence of an entire system of respected human thought. That kind of criminal law, I think, would clearly impinge upon the guarantees of free communication contained in the First Amendment, and made applicable to the States by the Fourteenth.

Keywords: Criminal offense, Curriculum, First Amendment, Fourteenth Amendment, Free speech, Schools, States, Teachers, Thoughts

Justice Potter Stewart
Dandridge v. Williams,
397 U.S. 471, 487 (1970)
We do not decide today that the Maryland regulation is wise, that it best fulfills the relevant social and economic objectives that Maryland might ideally espouse, or that a more just and humane system could not be devised. Conflicting claims of morality and intelligence are raised by opponents and proponents of almost every measure, certainly including the one before us. But the intractable economic, social, and even philosophical problems presented by public welfare assistance programs are not the business of this Court. The Constitution may impose certain procedural safeguards upon systems of welfare administration. But the Constitution does not empower this Court to second-guess state officials charged with the difficult responsibility of allocating limited public welfare funds among the myriad of potential recipients.

Keywords: Constitutional limitations, Constitutional safeguards, Economic objectives, Judicial authority, Morality, Procedure, Public funding, Public policy, Public welfare, Social objectives, State regulation, Welfare administration

Justice William Rehnquist
Sosna v. Iowa,
419 U.S. 393, 407 (1975)
A State such as Iowa may quite reasonably decide that it does not wish to become a divorce mill for unhappy spouses who have lived there as short a time as appellant had when she commenced her action in the state court after having long resided elsewhere.

Keywords: Divorce, Domestic relations, Domicile, Family law, Marriage, Spousal relations, States

Justice William Rehnquist
National League of Cities v. Usery,
426 U.S. 833, 845 (1976)
It is one thing to recognize the authority of Congress to enact laws regulating in-

dividual businesses necessarily subject to the dual sovereignty of the government of the Nation and of the State in which they reside. It is quite another to uphold a similar exercise of congressional authority not directed to private citizens, but to the States as States. We have repeatedly recognized that there attributes of sovereignty attaching to every state government which may not be impaired by Congress, not because Congress may lack an affirmative grant of legislative authority to reach the matter, but because the Constitution prohibits it from exercising the authority in that manner.

Keywords: *Business, Citizens, Congressional authority, Congressional limitations, Constitutional authority, Regulations, Sovereignty, States, Statutory legitimacy*

Justice William Rehnquist, dissenting
In re Primus,
436 U.S. 412, 445–446 (1978)

I cannot share the Court's confidence that the danger of such consequences is minimized simply because a lawyer proceeds from political conviction rather than for pecuniary gain. A State may reasonably fear that a lawyer's desire to resolve "substantial civil liberties questions" may occasionally take precedence over his duty to advance the interests of his client. It is even more reasonable to fear that a lawyer in such circumstances will be inclined to pursue both culpable and blameless defendants to the last ditch in order to achieve his ideological goals. Although individual litigants, including the ACLU, may be free to use the courts for such purposes, South Carolina is likewise free to restrict the activities of the members of its Bar who attempt to persuade them to do so.

Keywords: *ACLU, Civil liberties, Ideology, Judicial legitimacy, Lawyers, Litigants, Political beliefs, Regulations, States*

Justice Sandra Day O'Connor, concurring in part, dissenting in part
Federal Energy Regulatory Commission v. Mississippi,
456 U.S. 742, 776 (1982)

State legislative and administrative bodies are not field offices of the national bureaucracy. Nor are they think tanks to which Congress may assign problems for extended study. Instead, each State is sovereign within its own domain, governing its citizens and providing for their general welfare. While the Constitution and federal statutes define the boundaries of that domain, they do not harness state power for national purposes.

Keywords: *Congress, Constitution, General welfare, National government, Sovereignty, State government, State powers*

Justice Sandra Day O'Connor, dissenting
Akron v. Akron Center for Reproductive Health, Inc.,
462 U.S. 416, 460–461 (1983)

The state interest in potential human life is likewise extant throughout pregnancy. In *Roe,* the Court held that although the State had an important and legitimate interest in protecting potential life, that interest could not become compelling until the point at which the fetus was viable. The difficulty with this analysis is clear: potential life is no less potential in the first weeks of pregnancy than it is at viability or afterward. At any stage in pregnancy, there is the potential for human life.

Keywords: *Fetus, Human life, Judicial analysis, Judicial legitimacy, Potential life, Pregnancy, Roe, State interest*

Justice Lewis Powell, dissenting
Garcia v. San Antonio Metropolitan Transit Authority,
469 U.S. 528, 566–567 (1985)
. . . political success is not relevant to the question whether the political processes are the proper means of enforcing constitutional limitations. The fact that Congress generally does not transgress constitutional limits on its power to reach state activities does not make judicial review any less necessary to rectify the cases in which it does do so. The States' role in our system of government is a matter of constitutional law, not of legislative grace.

Keywords: *Congress, Constitutional law, Constitutional limitations, Government, Judicial process, Judicial review, Political process, Political success, States*

Justice Sandra Day O'Connor, dissenting
Garcia v. San Antonio Metropolitan Transit Authority,
469 U.S. 528, 580 (1985)
The Court today surveys the battle scene of federalism and sounds a retreat. Like JUSTICE POWELL, I would prefer to hold the field and, at the very least, render a little aid to the wounded.

Keywords: *Federalism, Judicial process*

Chief Justice Warren Burger, dissenting
Thornburgh v. American College of Obstetricians & Gynecologists,
476 U.S. 747, 783 (1986)
Yet today the Court astonishingly goes so far as to say that the State may not even require that a woman contemplating an abortion be provided with accurate medical information concerning the risks inherent in the medical procedure which she is about to undergo and the availability of state-funded alternatives if she elects not to run those risks. Can anyone doubt that the State could impose a similar requirement with respect to other medical procedures? Can anyone doubt that doctors routinely give similar information concerning risks in countless procedures having far less impact on life and health, both physical and emotional than an abortion, and risk a malpractice lawsuit if they fail to do so?

Keywords: *Abortion, Doctors, Malpractice, Medical alternatives, Medical procedure, Patients, Public financing, States*

Justice John Paul Stevens, dissenting
Cruzan v. Director, Missouri Department of Health,
497 U.S. 261, 356–357 (1990)
However commendable may be the State's interest in human life, it cannot pursue that interest by appropriating Nancy Cruzan's life as a symbol for its own purposes. Lives do not exist in abstraction from persons, and to pretend otherwise is not to honor but to desecrate

the State's responsibility for protecting life. A State that seeks to demonstrate its commitment to life may do so by aiding those who are actively struggling for life and health. In this endeavor, unfortunately, no State can lack for opportunities: there can be no need to make an example of tragic cases like that of Nancy Cruzan.

Keywords: *Human life, State interests, Symbolism*

Justice Anthony Kennedy
Federal Trade Commission v. Ticor Title Insurance Co.,
504 U.S. 621, 636 (1992)
States must accept political responsibility for actions they intend to undertake. It is quite a different matter, however, for federal law to compel a result that the States do not intend, but for which they are held to account. Federalism serves to assign political responsibility, not to obscure it. Neither federalism nor political responsibility is well served by a rule that essential national policies are displaced by state regulations intended to achieve more limited ends.

Keywords: *Ends/means, Federalism, Federal law, Political responsibility, Regulations, States*

Justice Sandra Day O'Connor
New York v. United States,
505 U.S. 144, 188 (1992)
States are not mere political subdivisions of the United States. State governments are neither regional offices nor administrative agencies of the Federal government. The positions occupied by state officials appear nowhere on the Federal Government's most detailed organizational chart. The Constitution instead "leaves to the several States a residuary and inviolable sovereignty," [The Federalist No. 39] reserved explicitly to the States by the Tenth Amendment. . . . Whatever the outer limits of that sovereignty may be, one thing is clear: the Federal Government may not compel the States to enact or administer a federal regulatory program. . . . The Constitution enables the Federal Government to preempt state regulation contrary to federal interests, and it permits the Federal Government to hold out incentives to the States as a means of encouraging them to adopt suggested regulatory schemes.

Keywords: *Constitutional authority, Federalism, National government, Political subdivisions, Regulations, Sovereignty, States, Tenth Amendment*

Justice Antonin Scalia, dissenting
United States v. Virginia,
518 U.S. 515, 566–567 (1996)
Much of the Court's opinion is devoted to deprecating the closed-mindedness of our forebears with regard to women's education, and even with regard to the treatment of women in areas that have nothing to do with education. Closed-minded they were—as every age is, including our own, with regard to matters it cannot guess, because it simply does not consider them debatable. The virtue of a democratic system with a First Amendment is that it readily enables the people, over time, to be persuaded that what they took for granted is not so, and to change their laws accordingly. That

system is destroyed if the smug assurances of each age are removed from the democratic process and written into the Constitution. So to counterbalance the Court's criticism of our ancestors, let me say a word in their praise: they left us free to change. The same cannot be said of this most illiberal Court, which has embarked on a course of inscribing one after another of the current preferences of the society (and in some cases only the counter-majoritarian preferences of the society's law-trained elite) into our Basic Law. Today it enshrines the notion that no substantial educational value is to be served by an all-men's military academy—so that the decision by the people of Virginia to maintain such an institution denies equal protection to women who cannot attend that institution but can attend others. Since it is entirely clear that the Constitution of the United States—the old one—takes no sides in this educational debate, I dissent.

Keywords: *Counter-majoritarianism, Education, Equal protection, First Amendment, Gender, Higher education, History, Judicial criticism, Political process, Social preferences, Women*

Chief Justice William Rehnquist, dissenting
Chandler v. Miller,
520 U.S. 305, 328 (1997)
Nothing in the Fourth Amendment or in any other part of the Constitution prevents a State from enacting a statute whose principal vice is that it may seem misguided or even silly to the members of this Court.

Keywords: *Fourth Amendment, Judicial review, States' rights, Statutory limitations*

Justice John Paul Stevens, concurring
Washington v. Glucksberg,
117 S. Ct. 2302, 2305 (1997)
History and tradition provide ample support for refusing to recognize an open ended constitutional right to commit suicide. Much more than the State's paternalistic interest in protecting the individual from the irrevocable consequences of an ill advised decision motivated by temporary concerns is at stake. There is truth in John Donne's observation that "No man is an island." The State has an interest in preserving and fostering the benefits that every human being may provide to the community—a community that thrives on the exchange of ideas, expressions of affection, shared memories and humorous incidents as well as on the material contributions that its members create and support. The value to others of a person's life is far too precious to allow the individual to claim a constitutional entitlement to complete autonomy in making a decision to end that life.

Keywords: *Community, Constitutional entitlement, Constitutional rights, Health, History, Life, Personal autonomy, Right to die, State interests, Suicide, Tradition*

Justice Ruth Bader Ginsburg
Arizonans for Official English v. Arizona,
520 U.S. 43, 79 (1997)
Warnings against premature adjudication of constitutional questions bear heightened attention when a federal

court is asked to invalidate a State's law, for the federal tribunal risks friction generating error when it endeavors to construe a novel state act not yet reviewed by the State's highest court.

Keywords: *Adjudication, Constitutional questions, Federal courts, State courts, State laws*

Justice John Paul Stevens
Saenz v. Roe,
526 U.S. ___, ___ (1999)
. . . States . . . do not have any right to select their citizens.

Keywords: *Citizens, States*

Justice Anthony Kennedy
Alden v. Maine,
527 U.S. ___, ___ (1999)
Private suits against nonconsenting States—especially suits for money damages—may threaten the financial integrity of the States. It is indisputable that, at the time of the founding, many of the States could have been forced into insolvency but for their immunity from private suits for money damages. Even today, an unlimited congressional power to authorize suits in state court to levy upon the treasuries of the States for compensatory damages, attorney's fees, and even punitive damages could create staggering burdens, giving Congress a power and a leverage over the States that is not

contemplated by our constitutional design. The potential national power would pose a severe and notorious danger to the States and their resources.

Keywords: *Compensatory damages, Congressional power, Constitutional design, Financial integrity, Monetary damages, National power, Private suits, States*

Justice David Souter, dissenting
Alden v. Maine,
527 U.S. ___, ___ (1999)
The resemblance of today's state sovereign immunity to the *Lochner* era's industrial due process is striking. The Court began this century by imputing immutable constitutional status to a conception of economic self-reliance that was never true to industrial life and grew insistently fictional with the years, and the Court has chosen to close the century by conferring like status on a conception of state sovereign immunity that is true neither to history nor to the structure of the Constitution. I expect the Court's late essay into immunity doctrine will prove the equal of its earlier experiment in laissez-faire, the one being as unrealistic as the other, as indefensible, and probably as fleeting.

Keywords: *Constitutional status, Economic self-reliance, Immunity, Laissez-faire, Lochner, Sovereignty, States*

7. Due Process and Equal Protection

The Fourteenth Amendment is the focus of this chapter; in particular the political use and constitutional controversies of the Due Process and Equal Rights doctrines.

Justice Benjamin Curtis
Den ex dem Murray v. Hoboken Land & Improvement Co.,
59 U.S. 272, 276–277 (1856)
The constitution contains no description of those processes which it was intended to allow or forbid. It does not even declare what principles are to be applied to ascertain whether it be due process. It is manifest that it was not left to the legislative power to enact any process which might be devised. The article is a restraint on the legislative as well as on the executive and judicial powers of the government, and cannot be so construed as to leave congress free to make any process "due process of law," by its mere will. To what principles, then, are we to resort to ascertain whether this process, enacted by congress, is due process? To this the answer must be twofold. We must examine the constitution itself, to see whether this process be in conflict with any of its provisions. If not found to be so, we must look to those settled usages and modes of proceeding existing in the common and statute law of England, before the emigration of our ancestors, and which are shown not to have been unsuited to their civil and political condition by having been acted on by them after the settlement of this country.
Keywords: *Congress, Constitutional processes, Constitutional restraint, Due process, History, Judicial proceedings, Legal history*

Justice Stanley Matthews
Hurtado v. California,
110 U.S. 516, 537 (1884)
. . . any legal proceeding enforced by public authority, whether sanctioned by age and custom, or newly devised in the discretion of the legislative power in furtherance of the general public good, which regards and preserves principles of liberty and justice, must be held to be due process of law.
Keywords: *Due process, Justice, Legal proceedings, Legislative power, Liberty, Public authority, Public good*

Justice Henry Brown
Plessy v. Ferguson,
163 U.S. 537, 551–552 (1896)
The argument . . . assumes that social prejudices may be overcome by legislation, and that equal rights cannot be secured to the negro except by an enforced commingling of the two races. We cannot accept this proposition. If the two races are to meet upon terms of social

equality, it must be the result of natural affinities, a mutual appreciation of each other's merits, and a voluntary consent of individuals. . . . Legislation is powerless to eradicate racial instincts or to abolish distinctions based upon physical differences, and the attempt to do so can only result in accentuating the difficulties of the present situation. If the civil and political rights of both races be equal one cannot be inferior to the other civilly or politically. If one race be inferior to the other socially, the constitution of the United States cannot put them upon the same plane.

Keywords: *Civil rights, Equal rights, Legislation, Prejudice, Political rights, Racial equality, Racial instincts, Social equality*

Justice John Marshall Harlan, dissenting
Plessy v. Ferguson,
163 U.S. 537, 559 (1896)
. . . in view of the Constitution, in the eyes of the law, there is in this country no superior, dominant, ruling class of citizens. There is no caste there. Our Constitution is color-blind, and neither knows nor tolerates classes among citizens.

Keywords: *Caste, Citizens, Equality, Race, Color-blind constitution*

Justice Oliver Wendell Holmes, dissenting
Lochner v. New York,
198 U.S. 45, 75 (1905)
The 14th Amendment does not enact Mr. Herbert Spencer's Social Statistics.

Keywords: *Due process, Fourteenth Amendment, Sociology, Spencer (Herbert)*

Justice David Brewer
Muller v. Oregon,
208 U.S. 412, 421 (1908)
That woman's physical structure and the performance of maternal functions place her at a disadvantage in the struggle for subsistence is obvious. This is especially true when the burdens of motherhood are upon her. Even when they are not, by abundant testimony of the medical fraternity continuance for a long time on her feet at work, repeating this from day to day, tends to injurious effects upon the body, and, as healthy mothers are essential to vigorous offspring, the physical well-being of woman becomes an object of public interest and care in order to preserve the strength and vigor of the race. . . . Still again, history discloses the fact that woman has always been dependent upon man.

Keywords: *Gender equality, Motherhood, Science*

Justice Mahlon Pitney
Coopage v. Kansas,
236 U.S. 1, 14 (1915)
Included in the right of personal liberty and the right of private property . . . is the right to make contracts for the acquisition of property. . . . An interference with this liberty so serious as that now under consideration, and so disturbing of equality of right, must be deemed to be arbitrary, unless it be supportable as a reasonable exercise of the police power of the state.

Keywords: *Contracts, Equality, Liberty, Police power, Property rights, State*

Justice William Day
Buchanan v. Warley,
245 U.S. 60, 81–81 (1917)
It is urged that this proposed segregation will promote the public peace by preventing race conflicts. Desirable as this is, and important as is the preservation of the public peace, this aim cannot be accomplished by laws or ordinances which deny rights created or protected by the federal Constitution. It is said that such acquisitions by colored persons depreciate property owned in the neighborhood by white persons. But property may be acquired by undesirable white neighbors or put to disagreeable though lawful uses with like results.
Keywords: *Civil rights, Colored persons, Laws, Legislative intent, Neighborhoods, Ordinances, Property rights, Segregation, Tranquility, White persons*

Justice Oliver Wendell Holmes
Jackman v. Rosenbaum Co.,
260 U.S. 22, 31 (1922)
The Fourteenth Amendment, itself a historical product, did not destroy history for the States and substitute mechanical compartments of law all exactly alike. If a thing has been practiced for two hundred years by common consent, it will need a strong case for the Fourteenth Amendment to affect it. . . .
Keywords: *Fourteenth Amendment, History, Precedent, States, Tradition*

Chief Justice Charles Evans Hughes
Missouri ex rel Gaines v. Canada,
305 U.S. 337, 349–350 (1938)
The basic consideration is not as to what sort of opportunities, other States provide, or whether they are as good as those in Missouri, but as to what opportunities Missouri itself furnishes to white students and denies to negroes solely upon the ground of color. The admissibility of laws separating the races in the enjoyment of privileges afforded by the State rests wholly upon the equality of the privileges which the laws give to the separated groups within the State. The question here is not of a duty of the State to supply legal training, or of the quality of the training which it does supply, but of its duty when it provides such training to furnish it to the residents of the State upon the basis of an equality of right. By the operation of the laws of Missouri a privilege has been created for white law students which is denied to negroes by reason of their race. The white resident is afforded legal education within the State; the negro resident having the same qualifications is refused it there and must go outside the State to obtain it. That is a denial of the equality of legal right to the enjoyment of the privilege which the State has set up, and the provision for the payment of tuition fees in another State does not remove the discrimination.
Keywords: *Discrimination, Equal rights, Law students, Legal education, Privileges, Race, States*

Justice Robert Jackson
United States v. Willow River Power Co.,
324 U.S. 499, 502 (1945)
. . . not all economic interests are "property rights"; only those economic advan-

tages are "rights" which have the law back of them, and only when they are so recognized may courts compel others to forbear from interfering with them or to compensate for their invasion.

Keywords: *Compensation, Economic interest, Property rights*

Justice Wiley Rutledge, dissenting
United States v. United Mine Workers of America,
330 U.S. 258, 374 (1947)
One who does not know until the end of litigation what his procedural rights in trial are, or may have been, has no such rights.

Keywords: *Litigation, Procedural rights*

Justice Robert Jackson, concurring
Railway Express Agency, Inc. v. New York,
336 U.S. 106, 112–113 (1949)
. . . there is no more effective practical guaranty against arbitrary and unreasonable government than to require that the principles of law which officials would impose upon a majority must be imposed generally. Conversely, nothing opens the door to arbitrary action so effectively as to allow those officials to pick and choose only a few to whom they will apply legislation and thus to escape the political retribution that might be visited upon them if larger numbers were affected.

Keywords: *Arbitrary action, Majority, Political accountability, Principles, Public officials*

Justice Felix Frankfurter, dissenting
Irvine v. California,
347 U.S. 128, 147 (1954)
Since due process is not a mechanical

yardstick, it does not afford mechanical answers. In applying the Due Process Clause judicial judgment is involved in an empiric process in the sense that results are not predetermined or mechanically ascertainable. But that is a very different thing from conceiving the results as ad hoc decisions in the opprobrious sense of ad hoc. Empiricism implies judgment upon variant situations by the wisdom of experience. Ad hocness in adjudication means treating a particular case by itself and not in relation to the meaning of a course of decisions and the guides they serve for the future. There is all the difference in the world between disposing of a case as though it were a discrete instance and recognizing it as part of the process of judgment, taking its place in relation to what went before and further cutting a channel for what is to come.

Keywords: *Due process, Empiricism, Experience, Judicial judgment, Wisdom*

Chief Justice Earl Warren
Hernandez v. Texas,
347 U.S. 475, 482 (1954)
Circumstances or chance may well dictate that no persons in a certain class will serve on a particular jury or during some particular period. But it taxes our credulity to say that mere chance resulted in there being no members of this class among the over six thousand jurors called in the past 25 years. The result bespeaks discrimination, whether or not it was a conscious decision on the part of any individual jury commissioner.

Keywords: *Discrimination, Jury duty*

Justice William Douglas
Williamson v. Lee Optical of Oklahoma, Inc.,
348 U.S. 483, 488 (1955)
The day is gone when this court uses the Due Process Clause of the Fourteenth Amendment to strike down state laws, regulatory of business and industrial conditions, because they may be unwise, improvident, or out of harmony with a particular school of thought.
Keywords: *Due process, Fourteenth Amendment, Judicial review, Philosophy, Regulation, State laws, Work environment*

Chief Justice Earl Warren
McGowan v. Maryland,
366 U.S. 420, 425–426 (1961)
Although no precise formula has been developed, the Court has held that the Fourteenth Amendment permits the States a wide scope of discretion in enacting laws which affect some groups of citizens differently than others. The constitutional safeguard is offended only if the classification rests on grounds wholly irrelevant to the achievement of the State's objective. State legislatures are presumed to have acted within their constitutional power despite the fact that, in practice, their laws result in some inequality. A statutory discrimination will not be set aside if any state of facts reasonably may be conceived to justify it.
Keywords: *Classifications, Constitutional power, Constitutional safeguards, Federalism, Fourteenth Amendment, Judicial formulas, Legislative intent, State objectives, States, Statutory discrimination*

Justice John Marshall Harlan, dissenting
Poe v. Ullman,
366 U.S. 497, 542–543 (1961)
Due process has not been reduced to any formula; its content cannot be determined by reference to any code. The best that can be said is that through the course of this Court's decisions it has represented the balance which our Nation, built upon postulates of respect for the liberty of the individual, has struck between that liberty and the demands of organized society. If the supplying of content to this Constitutional concept has of necessity been a rational process, it certainly has not been one where judges have felt free to roam where unguided speculation might take them. The balance of which I speak is the balance struck by this country, having regard to what history teaches are the traditions from which it developed as well as the traditions from which it broke. That tradition is a living thing. A decision of this Court which radically departs from it could not long survive, while a decision which guilds on what has survived is likely to be sound. No formula could serve as a substitute, in this area, for judgment and restraint.

It is this outlook which has led the Court continually to perceive distinctions in the imperative character of Constitutional provisions, since that character must be discerned from a particular provision's larger context. and inasmuch as this context is one not of words, but of history and purposes, the full scope of the liberty guaranteed by the Due Process Clause cannot be found in or limited by the precise terms of the specific guarantees elsewhere provided in the Constitution. This "liberty" is not a series of isolated points pricked out in terms of the taking of property; the freedom of speech, press, and religion; the right to keep and bear arms, the freedom from unreasonable searches and seizures; and so on. It is a rational continuum which, broadly speaking, includes a freedom from all substantial arbitrary impositions and purposeless restraints . . . and which also recognizes, what a reasonable and sensitive judgment must, that certain interests require particularly careful scrutiny of the state needs asserted to justify their abridgment.

Keywords: *Arbitrary impositions, Due process, Freedom, History, Judicial authority, Judicial formula, Judicial interpretation, Judicial legitimacy, Judicial restraint, Liberty, Rational process, Societal needs*

Justice John Marshall Harlan, dissenting
Douglas v. California,
372 U.S. 353, 362 (1963)
Laws such as these do not deny equal protection to the less fortunate for one essential reason: the Equal Protection Clause does not impose on the States "an affirmative duty to lift the handicaps flowing from differences in economic circumstances." To so construe it would be to read into the Constitution a philosophy of leveling that would be foreign to many of our basic concepts of the proper relations between government and society. The State may have a moral obligation to eliminate the evils of poverty, but it is not required by the Equal Protection

Clause to give to some whatever others can afford.

Keywords: *Constitutional philosophy, Economic conditions, Equal protection, Governmental philosophy, Moral obligation, Poverty, States*

Justice Potter Stewart, concurring
McLaughlin v. Florida,
379 U.S. 184, 198 (1964)
. . . I cannot conceive of a valid legislative purpose under our Constitution for a state law which makes the color of a person's skin the test of whether his conduct is a criminal offense. . . . There might be limited room under the Equal Protection Clause for a civil law requiring the keeping of racially segregated public records for statistical or other valid purposes. . . . But we deal here with a criminal law which imposes criminal punishment. And I think it is simply not possible for a state law to be valid under our Constitution which makes the criminality of an act depend upon the race of the actor. Discrimination of that kind is invidious per se.

Keywords: *Civil law, Conduct, Criminality, Discrimination, Equal protection, Invidious discrimination, Legislative purpose, Punishment, Race, Segregation, State law*

Justice William Douglas
Harper v. Virginia Board of Elections,
383 U.S. 663, 668 (1966)
Wealth, like race, creed, or color, is not germane to one's ability to participate intelligently in the electoral process.

Keywords: *Color, Creed, Electoral*

process, Race, Voter qualifications, Wealth

Justice Hugo Black, concurring
Duncan v. Louisiana,
391 U.S. 145, 168 (1968)
Due process, according to my Brother Harlan, is to be a phrase with no permanent meaning, but one which is found to shift from time to time in accordance with judges' predilections and understanding of what is best for the country. . . . It is impossible for me to believe that such unconfined power is given to judges in our Constitution that is a written one in order to limit governmental power.
Keywords: *Due process, Governmental power, Judicial authority, Judicial predilection, Judicial wisdom, Philosophy*

Justice John Marshall Harlan, dissenting
Duncan v. Louisiana,
391 U.S. 145, 177–178 (1968)
Due process was not restricted to rules fixed in the past. . . . Nor did it impose nationwide uniformity in details. . . .
Keywords: *Due process, Rules, Uniformity*

Justice Potter Stewart
Jones v. Alfred H. Mayer Company,
392 U.S. 409, 441–443 (1968)
Just as the Black Codes, enacted after the Civil War to restrict the free exercise of those rights, were substitutes for the slave system, so the exclusion of Negroes from white communities became a substitute for the Black Codes. And when racial discrimination herds men into ghettos and makes their ability to buy property turn on the color of their

skin, then it too is a relic of slavery.
Keywords: *Black codes, Property rights, Racial discrimination, Slavery*

Justice Byron White
Hunter v. Erickson,
393 U.S. 385, 391 (1969)
The majority needs no protection against discrimination. . . .
Keywords: *Discrimination, Majority*

Justice John Marshall Harlan
Benton v. Maryland,
395 U.S. 784, 808 (1969)
Today *Palko* becomes another casualty in the so far unchecked march toward "incorporating" much, if not all, of the Federal Bill of Rights into the Due Process Clause.
Keywords: *Bill of Rights, Due process, Incorporation, Judicial authority*

Justice William Brennan, dissenting
Evans v. Abney,
396 U.S. 435, 453 (1970)
I have no doubt that a public park may constitutionally be closed down because it is too expensive to run or has become superfluous, or for some other reason, strong or weak, or for no reason at all. But under the Equal Protection Clause a State may not close down a public facility solely to avoid its duty to desegregate that facility.
Keywords: *Desegregation, Discrimination, Equal protection, Public finance, Public parks, States*

Chief Justice Warren Burger
Swann v. Charlotte-Mecklenburg Board of Education,
402 U.S. 1, 24 (1971)
The constitutional command to desegre-

gate schools does not mean that every school in every community must always reflect the racial composition of the school system as a whole.

Keywords: *Community, Constitutional command, Desegregation, Education, Judicial remedies, Racial composition, Schools*

Chief Justice Warren Burger
Swann v. Charlotte-Mecklenburg Board of Education,
402 U.S. 1, 25 (1971)
. . . the use made of mathematical ratios was no more than a starting point in the process of shaping a remedy, rather than an inflexible requirement.

Keywords: *Judicial formulas, Judicial remedies*

Chief Justice Warren Burger
Swann v. Charlotte-Mecklenburg Board of Education,
402 U.S. 1, 28 (1971)
Absent a constitutional violation there would be no basis for judicially ordering assignment of students on a racial basis. All things being equal, with no history of discrimination, it might well be desirable to assign pupils to schools nearest their homes. But all things are not equal in a system that has been deliberately constructed and maintained to enforce racial segregation. The remedy for such segregation, may be administratively awkward, inconvenient, and even bizarre in some situations and may impose burdens on some; but all awkwardness and inconvenience cannot be avoided in the interim period when remedial adjustments are being made to

eliminate the dual school systems. No fixed or even substantially fixed guidelines can be established as to how far a court can go, but it must be recognized that there are limits. The objective is to dismantle the dual school system.

Keywords: *Constitutional violation, Desegregation, Discrimination, Education, History, Judicial order, Judicial remedies, Racial composition, Racial segregation, Schools*

Justice Lewis Powell
San Antonio Independent School District v. Rodriguez,
411 U.S. 1, 41 (1973)
No scheme of taxation, whether the tax is imposed on property, income, or purchases of goods and services, has yet been devised which is free of all discriminatory impact. In such a complex arena in which no perfect alternatives exist, the Court does well not to impose too rigorous a standard of scouting lest all local fiscal schemes become subjects of criticism under the Equal Protection Clause.

Keywords: *Discrimination, Education, Equal protection, Judicial standards, Public financing, Taxation*

Justice Lewis Powell, concurring in part, dissenting in part
Keyes v. School District No. 1,
413 U.S. 189, 227–228 (1973)
Public schools are creatures of the State, and whether the segregation is state-created or state-assisted or merely state-perpetuated should be irrelevant to constitutional principle. The school board exercises pervasive and continuing responsibility over the long-range planning as

well as the daily operations of the public school system. It sets policies on attendance zones, faculty employment and assignments, school construction, closings and consolidations, and myriad other matters. School board decisions obviously are not the sole cause of segregated school conditions. But if, after such detailed and complete public supervision, substantial school segregation still persists, the presumption is strong that the school board, by its acts or omissions, is in some part responsible. Where state action and supervision are so pervasive and where, after years of such action, segregated schools continue to exist within the district to a substantial degree, this Court is justified in finding a prima facie case of a constitutional violation. The burden then must fall on the school board to demonstrate it is operating an "integrated school system."

Keywords: *Constitutionality, Constitutional principle, Constitutional violation, Discrimination, Education, Integration, Public schools, School boards, Segregation, States*

Justice William Rehnquist, dissenting
Sugarman v. Dougall,
413 U.S. 634, 657 (1973)
Our society, consisting of over 200 million individuals of multitudinous origins, customs, tongues, beliefs, and cultures, is, to say the least, diverse. It would hardly take extraordinary ingenuity for a lawyer to find "insular and discrete" minorities at every turn in the road. Yet, unless the Court can precisely define and constitutionally justify both the terms and analysis it uses, these decisions to-

day stand for the proposition that the Court can choose a "minority" it "feels" deserves "solicitude" and thereafter prohibit the States from classifying that "minority" differently from the "majority." I cannot find, and the Court does not cite, any constitutional authority for such a "ward of the Court" approach to equal protection.

Keywords: *Constitutional authority, Culture, Diversity, Equal protection, Judicial authority, Majority rights, Minority rights*

Justice Thurgood Marshall, dissenting
Milliken v. Bradley,
418 U.S. 717, 814–815 (1974)
... public opposition, no matter how strident, cannot be permitted to divert this Court from the enforcement of the constitutional principles at issue in this case. Today's holding, I fear, is more a reflection of a perceived public mood that we have gone far enough in enforcing the Constitution's guarantee of equal justice than it is the product of neutral principles of law. In the short run, it may seem to be the easier course to allow our great metropolitan areas to be divided up each into two cities—one white, the other black—but it is a course, I predict, our people will ultimately regret.

Keywords: *Equal protection, Neutral principles, Public opinion, Race, Segregation*

Justice John Paul Stevens, dissenting
Meachum v. Fano,
427 U.S. 215, 230 (1976)
But neither the Bill of Rights nor the laws of sovereign States create the liberty

which the Due Process Clause protects. The relevant constitutional provisions are limitations on the power of the sovereign to infringe on the liberty of the citizen. The relevant state laws either create property rights, or they curtail the freedom of the citizen who must live in an ordered society. Of course, law is essential to the exercise and enjoyment of individual liberty in a complex society. But it is not the source of liberty, and surely not the exclusive source. . . . I had thought it self-evident that all men were endowed by their Creator with liberty as one of the cardinal unalienable rights. It is that basic freedom which the Due Process Clause protects, rather than the particular rights or privileges conferred by specific laws or regulations.

Keywords: *Bill of Rights, Constitutional provisions, Due Process Clause, Freedom, Liberty, Ordered society, Privileges, Property rights, State laws, State sovereignty, Unalienable rights*

Justice William Brennan
Craig v. Boren,
429 U.S. 190, 204 (1976)
It is unrealistic to expect either members of the judiciary or state officials to be well versed in the rigors of experimental or statistical technique. But this merely illustrates that proving broad sociological propositions by statistics is a dubious business, and one that inevitably is in tension with the normative philosophy that underlies the Equal Protection Clause.

Keywords: *Equal protection, Experimental technique, Judiciary, Philoso-phy, Public officials, Sociology, Statistical technique*

Justice Byron White, dissenting
Ingraham v. Wright,
430 U.S. 651, 696–697 (1977)
The majority's conclusion that a damages remedy for excessive corporal punishment affords adequate process rests on the novel theory that the State may punish an individual without giving him any opportunity to present his side of the story, as long as he can later recover damages from a state official if he is innocent. The logic of this theory would permit a State that punished speeding with a one-day jail sentence to make a driver serve his sentence first without a trial and then sue to recover damages for wrongful imprisonment. Similarly, the State could finally take away a prisoner's good-time credits for alleged disciplinary infractions and require him to bring a damages suit after he was eventually released. There is no authority for this theory, nor does the majority purport to find any, in the procedural due process decisions of this Court.

Keywords: *Corporal Punishment, Damages, Judicial authority, Judicial legitimacy, Judicial logic, Procedural due process, State officials, States*

Justice William Rehnquist, dissenting
Trimble v. Gordon,
430 U.S. 762, 779 (1977)
. . . we are constantly subjected to the human temptation that any law containing a number of imperfections denies equal protection simply because those

who drafted it could have made it a fairer or better law.

Keywords: *Equal protection, Fairness, Legislative value, Temptation*

Justice Byron White, dissenting
Moore v. East Cleveland,
431 U.S. 494, 544 (1977)
That the Court has ample precedent for the creation of new constitutional rights should not lead it to repeat the process at will. The Judiciary, including this Court, is the most vulnerable and comes nearest to illegitimacy when it deals with judge-made constitutional law having little or no cognizable roots in the language or even the design of the Constitution. Realizing that the present construction of the Due Process Clause represents a major judicial gloss on its terms, as well as on the anticipation of the Framers, and that much of the underpinning for the broad, substantive application of the Clause disappeared in the conflict between the Executive and the Judiciary in the 1930s and 1940s, the Court should be extremely reluctant to breathe still further substantive content into the Due Process Clause so as to strike down legislation adopted by a State or city to promote its welfare. Whenever the Judiciary does so, it unavoidably pre-empts for itself another part of the governance of the country without express constitutional authority.

Keywords: *Constitutional authority, Constitutional language, Constitutional rights, Due Process Clause, Framers, Judicial legitimacy, Judiciary, Precedent, Judicial review, Substantive due process, Welfare*

Justice Harry Blackmun
Baldwin v. Montana Fish & Game Commission,
436 U.S. 371, 388 (1978)
Whatever rights or activities may be "fundamental" under the Privilege and Immunities Clause, we are not persuaded, and hold, that elk hunting by nonresidents in Montana is not one of them.

Keywords: *Fundamental rights, Hunting, Privilege and immunities*

Justice Harry Blackmun, concurring
University of California Regents v. Bakke,
438 U.S. 265, 407 (1978)
In order to get beyond racism, we must first take account of race. There is no other way. And in order to treat some persons equally, we must treat them differently.

Keywords: *Equality, Race, Racism*

Justice Thurgood Marshall, dissenting
Bell v. Wolfish,
441 U.S. 520, 567 (1979)
By its terms, the Due Process Clause focuses on the nature of deprivations, not on the persons inflicting them.

Keywords: *Deprivations, Due process, Liberty*

Justice Potter Stewart
Personnel Administrator of Massachusetts v. Feeney,
442 U.S. 256, 277 (1979)
Invidious discrimination does not become less so because the discrimination is of a lesser magnitude. Discriminatory intent is simply not amenable to calibration.

Keywords: *Discrimination, Discriminatory intent*

Chief Justice Warren Burger
Parham v. J.R.,
442 U.S. 584, 608 (1979)
What process is constitutionally due cannot be divorced from the nature of the ultimate decision that is being made.
Keywords*: Due process*

Justice William Brennan, dissenting
Parham v. J.R.,
442 U.S. 584, 638–639 (1979)
Children incarcerated in public mental institutions are constitutionally entitled to a fair opportunity to contest the legitimacy of their confinement. They are entitled to some champion who can speak on their behalf and who stands ready to oppose a wrongful commitment. Georgia should not be permitted to deny that opportunity and that champion simply because the children's parents or guardians wish them to be confined without a hearing. The risk of erroneous commitment is simply too great unless there is some form of adversary review. And fairness demands that children abandoned by their supposed protectors to the rigors of institutional confinement be given the help of some separate voice.
Keywords*: Children, Confinement, Due process, Fairness, Guardians, Hearing, Mental institutions, Parens patriae, Parents*

Justice Lewis Powell, dissenting
Columbus Board of Education v. Penick,
443 U.S. 449, 489 (1979)
After all, and in spite of what many view as excessive government regulation, we are a free society—perhaps the most free of any in the world. Our people instinc-

tively resent coercion, and perhaps most of all when it affects their children and the opportunities that only education affords them. It is now reasonably clear that the goal of diversity that we call integration, if it is to be lasting and conducive to quality education, must have the support of parents who so frequently have the option to choose where their children will attend school. Courts, of course, should confront discrimination wherever it is found to exist. But they should recognize limitations on judicial action inherent in our system and also the limits of effective judicial power. The primary and continuing responsibility for public education, including the bringing about and maintaining of desired diversity, must be left with school officials and public authorities.
Keywords*: Children, Coercion, Discrimination, Diversity, Education, Equal protection, Free society, Integration, Judicial action, Judicial power, Parents, Public authorities, Regulation, School, School officials*

Justice Potter Stewart, plurality
Mobile v. Bolden,
446 U.S. 55, 74 (1980)
. . . past discrimination cannot, in the manner of original sin, condemn governmental action that is not itself unlawful.
Keywords*: Discrimination, Governmental action, Historical discrimination*

Justice Thurgood Marshall, dissenting
Mobile v. Bolden,
446 U.S. 55, 139 (1980)
Like outright racial hostility, selective racial indifference reflects a belief that the

concerns of the minority are not worthy of the same degree of attention paid to problems perceived by whites.

Keywords: Discrimination, Minority interests, Racial hostility, Racial indifference

Justice Potter Stewart, dissenting
Fullilove v. Klutznick,
448 U.S. 448, 522–523 (1980)

"Our constitution is color-blind . . ." *Plessy v. Fergusson* (Harlan, J., dissenting). His colleagues disagreed with him, and held that a statute that required the separation of people on the basis of their race was constitutionally valid because it was a "reasonable" exercise of legislative power and had been "enacted in good faith for the promotion [of] the public good." Today, the Court upholds a statute that accords a preference to citizens who are "Negroes, Spanish-speaking, Orientals, Indians, Eskimos, and Aleuts," for much the same reasons. I think today's decision is wrong for the same reason that *Plessy v. Ferguson* was wrong.

Keywords: Color-blind constitution, Judicial review, Legislative good faith, Legislative power, Preferences, Race, Statutory intent

Justice William Rehnquist
Michael M. v. Superior Court,
450 U.S. 464, 473 (1981)

Because virtually all of the significant harmful and inescapably identifiable consequences of teenage pregnancy fall on the young female, a legislature acts well within its authority when it elects to punish only the participant who, by nature, suffers few of the consequences of his conduct. It is hardly unreasonable for a legislature acting to protect minor females to exclude them from punishment. Moreover, the risk of pregnancy itself constitutes a substantial deterrence to young females. No similar natural sanctions deter males. A criminal sanction imposed solely on males thus serves to roughly "equalize" the deterrents on the sexes.

Keywords: Conduct, Deterrence, Equal protection, Gender rights, Legislative intent, Men, Punishment, Teenage pregnancy, Young women

Justice William Brennan, dissenting
Michael M. v. Superior Court,
450 U.S. 464, 494–496 (1981)

Until very recently, no California court or commentator had suggested that the purpose of California's statutory rape law was to protect young women from the risk of pregnancy. Indeed, the historical development of [the statute] demonstrates that the law was initially enacted on the premise that young women, in contrast to young men, were to be deemed legally incapable of consenting to an act of sexual intercourse. Because their chastity was considered particularly precious, those young women were felt to be uniquely in need of the State's protection. In contrast, young men were assumed to be capable of making such decisions for themselves; the law therefore did not offer them any special protection.

Keywords: Chastity, Equal protection, Pregnancy, Sexual intercourse, State protection, Statutory history, Statutory rape, Young men, Young women

Justice Lewis Powell, dissenting
Mississippi University for Women v. Hogan,
458 U.S. 718, 735 (1982)
The Court's opinion bows deeply to conformity. Left without honor—indeed, held unconstitutional—is an element of diversity that has characterized much of American education and enriched much of American life. The Court in effect holds today that no State now may provide even a single institution of higher learning open only to women students.
Keywords: Conformity, Constitutionality, Diversity, Education, Gender equality, Higher education, States

Justice Lewis Powell, dissenting
Mississippi University for Women v. Hogan,
458 U.S. 718, 741–742 (1982)
By applying heightened equal protection analysis to this case, the Court frustrates the liberating spirit of the Equal protection Clause. It prohibits the States from providing women with an opportunity to choose the type of university they prefer. And yet it is these women whom the Court regards as the victims of an illegal, stereotyped perception of the role of women in our society. The Court reasons this way in a case in which no woman has complained, and the only complainant is a man who advances no claims on behalf of anyone else. His claim, it should be recalled, is not that he is being denied a substantive educational opportunity, or even the right to attend an all-male or a coeducational college. It is only that the colleges open to him are located at inconvenient distances.
Keywords: College, Education, Equal protection, Gender equality, Societal issues, States

Chief Justice Warren Burger
Palmore v. Sidoti,
466 U.S. 429, 433 (1984)
Private biases may be outside the reach of the law, but the law cannot, directly or indirectly, give them effect.
Keywords: Biases, Discrimination, Liberty, Prejudice, Reach of law

Justice Sandra Day O'Connor, concurring in part, dissenting in part
Ford v. Wainwright,
477 U.S. 399, 429 (1986)
. . . I consider it self-evident that once society has validly convicted an individual of a crime and therefore established its right to punish, the demands of due process are reduced accordingly.
Keywords: Criminal conviction, Due process, Punishment, Societal rights

Justice Byron White
Bowers v. Hardwick,
478 U.S. 186, 196 (1986)
The law, however, is constantly based on notions of morality, and if all laws representing essentially moral choices are to be invalidated under the Due Process Clause, the courts will be very busy indeed.
Keywords: Due process, Moral choices, Morality

Justice Antonin Scalia, concurring
Richmond v. J. A. Croson, Co.,
488 U.S. 469, 528 (1989)
Racial preferences appear to "even the score" (in some small degree) only if one embraces the proposition that our society is appropriately viewed as divided into races, making it right that an injustice rendered in the past to a black man

should be compensated for by discriminating against a white. Nothing is worth that embrace.

Keywords: *Discrimination, Injustice, Race, Racial preferences*

Justice Antonin Scalia, concurring
Cruzan v. Director, Missouri Department of Health,
497 U.S. 261, 300–301 (1990)
What I have said above is not meant to suggest that I would think it desirable, if we were sure that Nancy Cruzan wanted to die, to keep her alive by the means at issue here. I assert only that the Constitution has nothing to say about the subject. To raise up a constitutional right here, we would have to create out of nothing (for it exists neither in text nor tradition) some constitutional principle whereby, although the State may insist that an individual come in out of the cold and eat food, it may not insist that he take medicine; and although it may pump his stomach empty of poison he has ingested, it may not fill his stomach with food he has failed to ingest. Are there, then, no reasonable and humane limits that ought not to be exceeded in requiring an individual to preserve his own life? There obviously are, but they are not set forth in the Due Process Clause. What assures us that those limits will not be exceeded is the same constitutional guarantee that is the source of most of our protection—what protects us, for example, from being assessed a tax of 100% of our income above the subsistence level, from being forbidden to drive cars, or from being required to send our children to school for 10 hours a day, none

of which horribles is categorically prohibited by the Constitution. Our salvation is the Equal Protection Clause, which requires the democratic majority to accept for themselves and their loved ones what they impose on you and me. This Court need not, and has no authority to, inject itself into every field of human activity where irrationality and oppression may theoretically occur, and if it tries to do so, it will destroy itself.

Keywords: *Constitutional guarantee, Constitutional principle, Constitutional rights, Constitutional silence, Democratic majority, Due process, Equal protection, Humanity, Judicial authority, Judicial legitimacy, Right to die, Science, State*

Chief Justice William Rehnquist
Rust v. Sullivan,
500 U.S. 173, 194 (1991)
To hold that the Government unconstitutionally discriminates on the basis of viewpoint when it chooses to fund a program dedicated to advance certain permissible goals because the program, in advancing those goals, necessarily discourages alternate goals would render numerous government programs constitutionally suspect. When Congress established a National Endowment for Democracy to encourage other countries to adopt democratic principles, it was not constitutionally required to fund a program to encourage competing lines of political philosophy such as Communism and Fascism. Petitioners' assertions ultimately boil down to the position that, if the government chooses to subsidize one protected right, it must subsidize analogous

counterpart rights. But the Court has soundly rejected that proposition.

Keywords: *Constitutionality, Democratic principles, Policy goals, Political philosophy, Public financing, Public policy, Protected rights, Subsidies, Viewpoints*

Justice Antonin Scalia, concurring in part, dissenting in part
United States v. Fordice,
505 U.S. 717, 758 (1992)

It is my view that the requirement of compelled integration . . . does not apply to higher education.

Keywords: *Colleges, Desegregation, Discrimination, Education, Higher education, Integration, Judicial remedies*

Justice Antonin Scalia, dissenting
Romer v. Evans,
517 U.S. 620, 639 (1996)

The central thesis of the Court's reasoning is that any group is denied equal protection when, to obtain advantage (or, presumably, to avoid disadvantage), it must have recourse to a more general and hence more difficult level of political decisionmaking than others. The world has never heard of such a principle, which is why the Court's opinion is so long on emotive utterance and so short on relevant legal citation. And it seems to me most unlikely that any multilevel democracy can function under such a principle. For whenever a disadvantage is imposed, or conferral of a benefit is prohibited, at one of the higher levels of democratic decisionmaking (i.e., by the state legislature rather than local government, or by the people at large in the state constitution rather than the legislature), the affected group has (under this theory) been denied equal protection.

Keywords: *Benefits, Democracy, Equal protection, Federalism, Judicial decision making, Political decision making, State legislatures*

Justice Antonin Scalia, dissenting
Chicago v. Morales,
527 U.S.___, ___ (1999)

Of course every activity, even scratching one's head, can be called a "constitutional right" if one means by that term nothing more than the fact that the activity is covered (as all are) by the Equal Protection Clause, so that those who engage in it cannot be singled out without "rational basis." But using the term in that sense utterly impoverishes our constitutional discourse. We would then need a new term for those activities—such as political speech or religious worship—that cannot be forbidden even with rational basis.

Keywords: *Constitutional discourse, Constitutional rights, Equal Protection Clause, Political speech, Rational basis, Religious worship*

8. Opinions, Dissents, and Recorders

Although the First Amendment protection of speech, assembly, and press are fairly specific this has been one of the more politically controversial areas of the Supreme Court. Like the next chapter, these topics are particularly interesting as evidence of personal conflict between idealism and reality struggle to dominate the Court.

Justice Mahlon Pitney
*International News Service
v. Associated Press,*
248 U.S. 215, 234 (1918)
It is not to be supposed that the framers of the Constitution, when they empowered Congress "to promote the progress of science and useful arts, by securing for limited times to authors and inventors the exclusive right to their respective writings and discoveries". . . , intended to confer upon one who might happen to be the first to report a historic event the exclusive right for any period to spread the knowledge of it.
Keywords: *Congressional powers, Copyright, First Amendment, Framers, Historical events, News, Press, Reporting*

Justice Oliver Wendell Holmes
Schenck v. United States,
249 U.S. 47, 52 (1919)
We admit that in many places and in ordinary times the defendants in saying all that was said in the circular would have been within their constitutional rights. But the character of every act depends upon the circumstances in which it is done. . . . The most stringent protection of free speech would not protect a man in falsely shouting fire in a theatre and causing a panic. . . . The question in every case is whether the words used are used in such circumstances and are of such a nature as to create a clear and present danger that they will bring about the substantive evils that Congress has a right to prevent. It is a question of proximity and degree.
Keywords: *Clear and present danger, Congressional limitations, Constitutional rights, False speech, Free speech, Incitement, Lies, Police powers, Proximity, Untruths*

Justice Oliver Wendell Holmes, dissenting
Abrams v. United States,
250 U.S. 616, 628 (1919)
It is only the present danger of immediate evil or an intent to bring about that warrants Congress in setting a limit to the expression of opinion where private rights are not concerned. Congress certainly cannot forbid all effort to change the mind of the country. Now nobody can suppose that the surreptitious publishing of a silly leaflet by an unknown man, without more, would present any

immediate danger that its opinion would hinder the success of the government arms or have any appreciable tendency to do so.

Keywords: *Congressional limitations, Expression of opinion, First Amendment, Freedom of expression, Free speech, Incitement, Press, Private rights, Publishing*

Justice Oliver Wendell Holmes, dissenting
Abrams v. United States,
250 U.S. 616, 630 (1919)
Persecution for the expression of opinions seems to me perfectly logical. If you have doubt of your premises or your power and want a certain result with all your heart you naturally express your wishes in law and sweep away all opposition. But when men have realized that time has upset many fighting faiths, they may come to believe even more than they believe the very foundations of their own conduct that the ultimate good desired is better reached by free trade in ideas— that the best test of truth is the power of the thought to get itself accepted in the competition of the market, and that truth is the only ground upon which their wishes safely can be carried out. That at any rate is the theory of our Constitution.

Keywords: *Constitutional theory, Expression of opinion, Faith, First Amendment, Free speech, Ideas, Market competition, Opinions*

Justice Oliver Wendell Holmes, dissenting
Gitlow v. New York,
268 U.S. 652, 673 (1925)
If in the long run the beliefs expressed in a proletarian dictatorship are destined to be accepted by the dominant forces of the community, the only meaning of free speech is that they should be given their chance and have their way.

Keywords: *Beliefs, Dictatorship, Free speech*

Justice Louis Brandeis
Whitney v. California,
274 U.S. 357, 375–376 (1927)
Those who won our independence believed that the final end of the State was to make men free to develop their faculties; and that in its government the deliberative forces should prevail over the arbitrary. They valued liberty both as an end and as a means. They believed liberty to be the secret of happiness and courage to be the secret of liberty. They believed that freedom to think as you will and to speak as you think are means indispensable to the discovery and spread of political truth; that without free speech and assembly discussion would be futile; that with them, discussion affords ordinarily adequate protection against the dissemination of noxious doctrine; that the greatest menace to freedom is an inert people; that public discussion is a political duty; and that this should be a fundamental principle of the American government. But they knew that order cannot be secured merely through fear of punishment for its infraction; that fear breeds repression; that repression breeds hate; that hate menaces stable government; that the path of safety lies in the opportunity to discuss freely supposed grievances and proposed remedies; and that the fitting remedy for evil counsels is good ones. Believing in the power of reason as applied through public discussion,

they eschewed silence coerced by law—the argument of force in its worst form. Recognizing the occasional tyrannies of governing majorities, they amended the Constitution so that free speech and assembly should be guaranteed.

Keywords: *Deliberative process, Fear, Founders, Free assembly, Freedom, Free speech, Governmental processes, Grievances, Hate, Liberty, Majorities, Political duty, Political truths, Public discussion, Repression, Tyrannies*

Justice Louis Brandeis
Whitney v. California,
274 U.S. 357, 377 (1927)

To courageous, self-reliant men, with confidence in the power of free and fearless reasoning applied through the processes of popular government, no danger flowing from speech can be deemed clear and present, unless the incidence of the evil apprehended is so imminent that it may befall before there is opportunity for full discussion. If there be time to expose through discussion the falsehood and fallacies, to avert the evil by the processes of education, the remedy to be applied is more speech, not enforced silence.

Keywords: *Clear and present, Democracy, Falsehoods, Free speech, Governmental process, Imminent danger, Popular government*

Chief Justice Charles Evans Hughes
Near v. Minnesota ex rel Olson,
283 U.S. 697, 721 (1931)

The recognition of authority to impose previous restraint upon publication in order to protect the community against the circulation of charges of misconduct, and especially of official misconduct, necessarily would carry with it the admission of the authority of the censor against which the constitutional barrier was erected. The preliminary freedom, by virtue of the very reason for its existence, does not depend, as this Court has said, on proof of truth.

Keywords: *Censorship, Constitutional limitations, Free press, Prior restraint*

Chief Justice Charles Evans Hughes
DeJonge v. Oregon,
299 U.S. 353, 365 (1937)

The greater the importance of safeguarding the community from incitements to the overthrow of our institutions by force and violence, the more imperative is the need to preserve inviolate the constitutional rights of free speech, free press and free assembly in order to maintain the opportunity for free political discussion, to the end that government may be responsive to the will of the people and that changes, if desired, may be obtained by peaceful means. Therein lies the security of the Republic, the very foundation of constitutional government.

Keywords: *Constitutional government, Democracy, Free assembly, Free press, Free speech, Incitement, Police power, Political discussion, Republic, Will of the people*

Justice Owen Roberts
Schneider v. New Jersey,
308 U.S. 147, 151 (1939)

In every case . . . where legislative abridgment of [First Amendment] rights is asserted, the courts should be astute to examine the effect of the challenged legislation. Mere legislative preferences or beliefs respecting matters of public convenience may well support regulation directed at other personal activities, but be insufficient to justify such as diminishes the exercise of rights so vital to the maintenance of democratic institutions. And so, as cases arise, the delicate and difficult task falls upon the courts to weigh the circumstances and to appraise the substantiality of the reasons advanced in support of the regulation of the free enjoyment of the rights.

Keywords: *Democratic institutions, First Amendment, Judicial review, Legislative preferences, Personal activities, Public convenience, Regulation, Rights*

Justice Owen Roberts
Schneider v. New Jersey,
308 U.S. 147, 162 (1939)
We are of opinion that the purpose to keep the streets clean is insufficient to justify an ordinance which prohibits a person rightfully on a public street from handing literature to one willing to receive it. Any burden imposed upon the city authorities in cleaning and caring for the streets as an indirect consequence of such distribution results from the constitutional protection of the freedom of speech and press. This constitutional protection does not deprive a city of all power to prevent street littering. There are obvious methods of preventing littering. Amongst these is the punishment of those who actually throw papers on the street.

Keywords: *Constitutional limitations, Constitutional protections, Free press, Free speech, Littering, Ordinance, Police power*

Justice Felix Frankfurter
Milk Wagon Drivers Union of Chicago v. Meadowmoor Co.,
312 U.S. 287, 293 (1941)
It must never be forgotten . . . that the Bill of Rights was the child of the enlightenment. Back of the guarantee of free speech lay faith in the power of an appeal to reason by all the peaceful means for gaining access to the mind. It was in order to avert force and explosions due to restrictions upon rational modes of communication that the guarantee of free speech was given a generous scope. But utterance in a context of violence can lose its significance as an appeal to reason and become part of an instrument of force. Such utterance was not meant to be sheltered by the constitution.

Keywords: *Bill of Rights, Communication, Free speech, History, Reason, Utterance, Violence*

Justice Stanley Reed, dissenting
Milk Wagon Drivers Union of Chicago v. Meadowmoor Co.,
312 U.S. 287, 320 (1941)
Free speech may be absolutely prohibited only under the most pressing national emergencies. Those emergencies must be of the kind that justify the suspension of the writ of *habeas corpus* or the suppression of the right of trial by jury.

Keywords: *Free speech, Habeas corpus, National emergencies, Right to jury*

Justice Hugo Black
Bridges v. California,
314 U.S. 252, 268 (1942)
It must be recognized that public interest is much more likely to be kindled by a controversial event of the day than by a generalization, however penetrating, of the historian or scientist.
Keywords: *Current affairs, Public interest*

Justice Frank Murphy, dissenting
Jones v. Opelika,
316 U.S. 584, 620 (1942)
If the guaranties of freedom of speech and freedom of the press are to be preserved, municipalities should not be free to raise general revenue by taxes on the circulation of information and opinion in non commercial causes; other sources can be found, the taxation of which will not choke off ideas.
Keywords: *Commercial, Free press, Free speech, Municipalities, Revenue, Taxation*

Justice Robert Jackson
West Virginia State Board of Education v. Barnette,
319 U.S. 624, 642 (1943)
If there is any fixed star in our constitutional constellation, it is that no official, high or petty, can prescribe what shall be orthodox in politics, nationalism, religion, or other matters of opinion or force citizens to confess by word or act their faith therein.
Keywords: *First Amendment, Free press, Free religion, Free speech, Governmental limitations*

Justice Frank Murphy, concurring
Baumgartner v. United States,
322 U.S. 665, 679 (1944)
American citizenship is not a right granted on a condition subsequent that the naturalized citizen refrain in the future from uttering any remark or adopting an attitude favorable to his original homeland or those there in power, no matter how distasteful such conduct may be to most of us. He is not required to imprison himself in an intellectual or spiritual strait-jacket; nor is he obliged to retain a static mental attitude. Moreover, he does not lose the precious right of citizenship because he subsequently dares to criticize his adopted government in vituperative or defamatory terms.
Keywords: *Citizenship, Conduct, Free speech, Immigration, Naturalization*

Justice Wiley Rutledge, concurring
Pennekamp v. Florida,
328 U.S. 331, 370 (1946)
One can have no respect for a newspaper which is careless with facts and with insinuations founded in its carelessness.
Keywords: *Facts, Free press, Journalism, Newspapers, Reporting*

Justice William Douglas
Craig v. Harney,
331 U.S. 367, 374 (1947)
A trial is a public event. What transpires in the court room is public property. If a transcript of the court proceedings had been published, we suppose none would claim that the judge could punish the publisher for contempt. And we can see no difference though the conduct of the

attorneys, of the jury, or even of the judge himself, may have reflected on the court. Those who see and hear what transpired can report it with impunity. There is no special perquisite of the judiciary which enables it, as distinguished from other institutions of democratic government, to suppress, edit, or censor events which transpire in proceedings before it.

Keywords: *Censorship, Courtroom, Court proceedings, Criminal trial, Judge, Jury, Transcript, Public trial, Publisher*

Justice Stanley Reed
Winters v. New York,
333 U.S. 507, 510 (1948)
The line between the informing and the entertaining is too elusive for the protection of that basic right. Everyone is familiar with instances of propaganda through fiction. What is one man's amusement, teaches another's doctrine. Though we can see nothing of any possible value to society in these magazines, they are as much entitled to the protection of free speech as the best of literature.

Keywords: *Entertainment, Free speech, Informing the public, Propaganda*

Justice Felix Frankfurter, dissenting
Saia v. New York,
334 U.S. 558, 563 (1948)
The native power of human speech can interfere little with the self protection of those who do not wish to listen. They may easily move beyond earshot, just as those who do not choose to read need not have their attention bludgeoned by undesired reading matter. And so utterances by speech or pen can neither be forbidden nor licensed, save in the familiar classes of exceptional situations. But modern devices for amplifying the range and volume of the voice, or its recording, afford easy, too easy, opportunities for aural aggression. If uncontrolled, the result is intrusion into cherished privacy. The refreshment of mere silence, or meditation, or quiet conversation, may be disturbed or precluded by noise beyond one's personal control.

Keywords: *Aural aggression, Privacy, Silence, Speech, Technology, Utterances*

Justice Felix Frankfurter, dissenting
Saia v. New York,
334 U.S. 558, 565 (1948)
The men whose labors brought forth the Constitution of the United States had the street outside Independence Hall covered with earth so that their deliberations might not be disturbed by passing traffic. Our democracy presupposes the deliberative process as a condition of thought and of responsible choice by the electorate. To the Founding Fathers it would hardly seem a proof of progress in the development of our democracy that the blare of sound trucks must be treated as a necessary medium in the deliberative process.

Keywords: *Deliberative process, Democracy, Framers, Speech*

Justice Stanley Reed
Kovacs v. Cooper,
336 U.S. 77, 88–89 (1949)
The preferred position of freedom of

speech in a society that cherishes liberty for all does not require legislators to be insensible to claims by citizens to comfort and convenience. That more people may be more easily and cheaply reached by sound trucks is not enough to call forth constitutional protection for what those charged with public welfare reasonably think is a nuisance when easy means of publicity are open. . . . There is no restriction upon the communication of ideas or discussion of issues by the human voice, by newspapers, by pamphlets, by dodgers. We think that the need for reasonable protection in the homes or business houses from distracting noises of vehicles equipped with such sound amplifying devices justifies the ordinance.

Keywords: Amplifiers, Communication, Constitutional protections, Free speech, Ideas, Nuisance, Publicity, Public welfare

Justice William Douglas
Terminiello v. Chicago,
337 U.S. 1, 4 (1949)
. . . a function of free speech under our system of government is to invite dispute. It may indeed best serve its high purpose when it induces a condition of unrest, creates dissatisfaction with conditions as they are, or even stirs people to anger. Speech is often provocative and challenging. It may strike at prejudices and preconceptions and have profound unsettling effects as it presses for acceptance of an idea. That is why freedom of speech, though not absolute . . . is nevertheless protected against censorship or punishment, unless shown likely to produce a clear and present danger of a serious substantive evil that rises far above public inconvenience, annoyance, or unrest.

Keywords: Censorship, Clear and present danger, Disputes, Free speech, Ideas, Incitement

Justice William Douglas, dissenting
Beauharnais v. Illinois,
343 U.S. 250, 286–287 (1952)
Emotions sway speakers and audiences alike. Intemperate speech is a distinctive characteristic of man. Hotheads blow off and release destructive energy in the process. They shout and rave, exaggerating weaknesses, magnifying error, viewing with alarm. So it has been from the beginning; and so it will be throughout time.

Keywords: Audience, Emotions, History, Speakers, Speech

Justice John Marshall Harlan
Konigsberg v. State Bar of California,
366 U.S. 36, 49 (1961)
. . . we reject the view that freedom of speech and association as protected by the First and Fourteenth Amendments are "absolutes," not only in the undoubted sense that where the constitutional protection exists it must prevail, but also in the sense that the scope of that protection must be gathered solely from a literal reading of the First Amendment.

Keywords: Absolute rights, Constitutional interpretation, Constitutional protections, First Amendment, Fourteenth Amendment, Free association, Free speech

Justice William Brennan
New York Times Co. v. Sullivan,
376 U.S. 254, 279 (1964)
A rule compelling the critic of official conduct to guarantee the truth of all his factual assertions—and to do so on pain of libel judgments virtually unlimited in amount—leads to a comparable "self-censorship." Allowance of the defense of truth, with the burden of proving it on the defendant, does not mean that only false speech will be deterred. Under such a rule, would-be critics of official conduct may be deterred from voicing their criticism, even though it is believed to be true and even though it is in fact true, because of doubt whether it can be proved in court or fear of the expense of having to do so. The rule dampens the vigor and limits the variety of public debate. It is inconsistent with the First Amendment.
Keywords: *Censorship, Critics, Factual assertions, False speech, First Amendment, Official conduct, Speech, Truth*

Justice William Brennan
Garrison v. Louisiana,
379 U.S. 64, 73 (1964)
Debate on public issues will not be uninhibited if the speaker must run the risk that it will be proved in court that he spoke out of hatred; even if he did speak out of hatred, utterances honestly believed contribute to the free interchange of ideas and the ascertainment of truth.
Keywords: *Debate, Free speech, Ideas, Litigation, Public issues, Speaker, Truth, Utterances*

Chief Justice Earl Warren
Zemel v. Rusk,
381 U.S. 1, 16 (1965)
. . . the prohibition of unauthorized entry into the White House diminishes the citizen's opportunities to gather information he might find relevant to his opinion of the way the country is being run, but that does not make entry into the White House a First Amendment right. The right to speak and publish does not carry with it the unrestrained right to gather information.
Keywords: *First Amendment limitations, Information gathering, Right to speak*

Chief Justice Earl Warren, concurring
Estes v. Texas,
381 U.S. 532, 571 (1965)
The televising of trials would cause the public to equate the trial process with the forms of entertainment regularly seen on television and with the commercial objectives of the television industry.
Keywords: *Criminal justice, Television, Trials*

Chief Justice Earl Warren, concurring
Estes v. Texas,
381 U.S. 532, 574 (1965)
Broadcasting in the courtroom would give the television industry an awesome power to condition the public mind either for or against an accused. By showing only those parts of its films or tapes which depict the defendant or his witnesses in an awkward or unattractive position, television directors could give the community, state or country a false and unfavorable impression of the man on trial. Moreover, if the case should end in a mistrial, the showing of selected

portions of the trial, or even of the whole trial, would make it almost impossible to select an impartial jury for a second trial.

Keywords: *Broadcasting, Courtroom, Criminal justice, Defendant, Jury, Television, Witnesses*

Chief Justice Earl Warren, concurring
Estes v. Texas,
381 U.S. 532, 585–586 (1965)

. . . television is one of the great inventions of all time and can perform a large and useful role in society. But the television camera, like other technological innovations, is not entitled to pervade the lives of everyone in disregard of constitutionally protected rights. The television industry, like other institutions, has a proper area of activities and limitations beyond which it cannot go with its cameras. That area does not extend into an American courtroom. On entering that hallowed sanctuary, where the lives, liberty and property of people are in jeopardy, television representatives have only the rights of the general public, namely, to be present, to observe the proceedings, and thereafter, if they choose, to report them.

Keywords: *Constitutional rights, Courtroom, Liberty, Technology, Television*

Justice William Douglas, concurring
Memoirs v. Massachusetts,
383 U.S. 413, 432 (1966)

As I read the First Amendment, judges cannot gear the literary diet of an entire nation to whatever tepid stuff is incapable of triggering the most demented mind. The First Amendment demands more than a horrible example or two of the perpetrator of a crime of sexual violence, in whose pocket is found a pornographic book, before it allows the Nation to be saddled with a regime of censorship.

Keywords: *Censorship, Crime, First Amendment, Judges, Pornography, Sexual violence*

Justice Tom Clark
Sheppard v. Maxwell,
384 U.S. 333, 350 (1966)

A responsible press has always been regarded as the handmaiden of effective judicial administration, especially in the criminal field. Its function in this regard is documented by an impressive record of service over several centuries. The press does not simply publish information about trials but guards against the miscarriage of justice by subjecting the police, prosecutors, and judicial processes to extensive public scrutiny and criticism.

Keywords: *Criminal justice, Judicial administration, Judicial process, Miscarriage of justice, Police, Press, Prosecutors, Trials*

Justice Tom Clark
Sheppard v. Maxwell,
384 U.S. 333, 362–363 (1966)

Due process requires that the accused receive a trial by an impartial jury free from outside influences. Given the pervasiveness of modern communications and the difficulty of effacing prejudicial publicity from the minds of the jurors, the trial courts must take strong measures to ensure that the balance is never weighed against the accused. And appellate tribunals have the duty to make an independent evaluation of the circumstances. Of course, there is nothing that proscribes the press from reporting events that transpire in the courtroom. But where there is a reasonable likelihood that prejudicial news prior to trial will prevent a fair trial, the judge should continue the case until the threat abates, or transfer it to another county not so permeated with publicity. . . . If publicity during the proceedings threatens the fairness of the trial, a new trial should be ordered. But we must remember that reversals are but palliatives; the cure lies in those remedial measures that will prevent the prejudice at its inception. The courts must take such steps by rule and regulation that will protect their processes from prejudicial outside interferences. Neither prosecutors, counsel for defense, the accused, witnesses, court staff nor enforcement officers coming under the jurisdiction of the court should be permitted to frustrate its function. Collaboration between counsel and the press as to information affecting the fairness of a criminal trial is not only subject to regulation, but is highly censurable and worthy of disciplinary measures.

Keywords: *Accused, Appellate tribunals, Court staff, Criminal trial, Defense counsel, Due process, Fair and impartial jury, Judicial remedies, Jurors, Law enforcement officers, Press, Prosecutors, Trial courts, Witnesses*

Justice William Douglas, dissenting
Adderley v. Florida,
385 U.S. 39, 56 (1966)

. . . by allowing these orderly and civilized protests against injustice to be suppressed, we only increase the forces of frustration which the conditions of second-class citizenship are generating amongst us.

Keywords: *First Amendment, Free assembly, Free speech, Injustice, Protests, Second-class citizenship*

Justice Abe Fortas
Tinker v. Des Moines Independent School District,
393 U.S. 503, 511 (1969)

In our system, state-operated schools may not be enclaves of totalitarianism. School officials do not possess absolute authority over their students. Students in school as well as out of school are "persons" under our Constitution. They are possessed of fundamental rights which the State must respect, just as they themselves must respect their obligations to the State. In our system, students may not be regarded as closed-circuit recipients of only that which the State chooses to communicate. They may not be confined to the expression of those sentiments that are officially approved. In the absence of a specific showing of constitutionally valid reasons to regulate their speech, students are entitled to freedom of expression of their views.

Keywords: *Education, First Amendment, Free expression, Free speech, Fundamental rights, School officials, States, Students, Totalitarianism*

Justice Abe Fortas
Tinker v. Des Moines Independent School District,
393 U.S. 503, 513 (1969)
Freedom of expression would not truly exist if the right could be exercised only in an area that a benevolent government has provided as a safe haven for crackpots.
Keywords: *First Amendment, Free expression, Government regulations*

Justice Thurgood Marshall
Stanley v. Georgia,
394 U.S. 557, 565 (1969)
If the First Amendment means anything, it means that a State has no business telling a man, sitting alone in his own house, what books he may read or what films he may watch. Our whole constitutional heritage rebels at the thought of giving government the power to control men's minds.
Keywords: *Censorship, Film viewing, First Amendment, Heritage, Reading, States*

Per Curiam
Watts v. United States,
394 U.S. 705, 707 (1969)
The Nation undoubtedly has a valid, even an overwhelming, interest in protecting the safety of its Chief Executive and in allowing him to perform his duties without interference from threats of physical violence. Nevertheless, a statute such as this one, which makes criminal a form of pure speech, must be interpreted with the commands of the First Amendment clearly in mind. What is a threat must be distinguished from what is constitutionally protected speech.
Keywords: *Chief executive, Criminal speech, First Amendment, Safety, Speech, Statutory intent, Threats, Violence*

Per Curiam
Bradenburg v. Ohio,
395 U.S. 444, 447 (1969)
. . . later decisions have fashioned the principle that the constitutional guarantees of free speech and free press do not permit a State to forbid or proscribe advocacy of the use of force or of law violation except where such advocacy is directed to inciting or producing imminent lawless action and is likely to incite of produce such action.
Keywords: *Advocacy, Constitutional rights, Free speech, Imminent, Incitement*

Chief Justice Warren Burger
Rowan v. Post Office Department,
397 U.S. 728, 736 (1970)
In today's complex society we are inescapably captive audiences for many purposes, but a sufficient measure of individual autonomy must survive to permit every householder to exercise control over unwanted mail.
Keywords: *Autonomy, Household, Mail, Privacy, Society*

Chief Justice Warren Burger
Rowan v. Post Office Department,
397 U.S. 728, 736–737 (1970)
Weighing the highly important right to communicate against the very basic right

to be free from sights, sounds and tangible matter we do not want, it seems to us that a mailer's right to communicate must stop at the mailbox of an unreceptive addressee.
Keywords: *Basic rights, Communication, Mail, Privacy*

Chief Justice Warren Burger
Organization for a Better Austin v. Keefe,
402 U.S. 415, 419–420 (1971)
No prior decisions support the claim that the interest of an individual in being free from public criticism of his business practices in pamphlets or leaflets warrants use of the injunctive power of a court. Designating the conduct as an invasion of privacy is not sufficient to support an injunction against peaceful distribution of informational literature of the nature revealed by this record.
Keywords: *Business, Criticism, Distribution, Injunction, Leaflets, Literature, Pamphlets, Privacy*

Justice John Marshall Harlan
Cohen v. California,
403 U.S. 15, 24 (1971)
The constitutional right of free expression is powerful medicine in a society as diverse and populous as ours. It is designed and intended to remove governmental restraints from the arena of public discussion, putting the decision as to what views shall be voiced largely into the hands of each of us, in the hopes that use of such freedom will ultimately produce a more capable citizenry and more perfect polity and in the belief that no other approach would comport with the premise of individual dignity and choice upon which our political system rests.
Keywords: *Citizenry, Constitutional rights, Dignity, Free expression, Governmental restraints, Political system, Polity, Public discussion*

Justice John Marshall Harlan
Cohen v. California,
403 U.S. 15, 25 (1971)
For, while the particular four-letter word being litigated here is perhaps more distasteful than most others of its genre, it is nevertheless often true that one man's vulgarity is another's lyric. Indeed, we think it is largely because governmental officials cannot make principled distinctions in this area that the Constitution leaves matters of taste and style so largely to the individual.
Keywords: *Speech, Style, Swearing, Taste, Vulgarity*

Justice William Brennan
Rosenbloom v. Metromedia, Inc.,
403 U.S. 29, 43 (1971)
If a matter is a subject of public or general interest, it cannot suddenly become less so merely because a private individual is involved, or because in some sense the individual did not "voluntarily" choose to become involved. The public's primary interest is in the event; the public focus is on the conduct of the participant and the content, effect, and significance of the conduct, not the participant's prior anonymity or notoriety.
Keywords: *Anonymity, Notoriety, Private individual, Public interest*

Chief Justice Warren Burger, dissenting
New York Times Co. v. United States,
403 U.S. 713, 750 (1971)
It is not disputed that the Times has had unauthorized possession of the

documents for three to four months, during which it has had its expert analysts studying them, presumably digesting them and preparing the material for publication. During all of this time, the Times, presumably in its capacity as trustee of the public's "right to know," has held up publication for purposes it considered proper and thus public knowledge was delayed. No doubt this was for a good reason; the analysis of 7,000 pages of complex material drawn from a vastly greater volume of material would inevitably take time and the writing of good news stories takes time. But why should the United States Government, from whom this information was illegally acquired by someone, along with all the counsel, trial judges, and appellate judges be placed under needless pressure? After these months of deferral, the alleged "right to know" has somehow and suddenly become a right that must be vindicated instanter.

Keywords: *Free press, Judicial process, News, Newspapers, Publication, Right to know*

Justice Harry Blackmun, dissenting
New York Times Co. v. United States,
403 U.S. 713, 761 (1971)
The First Amendment, after all, is only one part of an entire Constitution. Article II of the great document vests in the Executive Branch primary power over the conduct of foreign affairs and places in that branch the responsibility for the Nation's safety. Each provision of the Constitution is important, and I cannot subscribe to a doctrine of unlimited absolutism for the First Amendment at the

cost of downgrading other provisions. First Amendment absolutism has never commanded a majority of this Court. What is needed here is a weighing, upon properly developed standards, of the broad right of the press to print and of the very narrow right of the Government to prevent. Such standards are not yet developed.

Keywords: *Constitution, Constitutional interpretation, Executive branch, First Amendment, Foreign affairs, Free press, National safety*

Justice Harry Blackmun, dissenting
New York Times Co. v. United States,
403 U.S. 713, 762 (1971)
I strongly urge, and sincerely hope, that these two newspapers will be fully aware of their ultimate responsibilities to the United States of America.

Keywords: *Free press, Newspapers, Responsible press*

Justice Byron White
Branzburg v. Hayes,
408 U.S. 665, 691 (1972)
It would be frivolous to assert—and no one does in these cases—that the First Amendment, in the interest of securing news or otherwise, confers a license on either the reporter or his news sources to violate valid criminal laws. Although stealing documents or private wiretapping could provide newsworthy information, neither reporter nor source is immune from conviction for such conduct, whatever the impact on the flow of news.

Keywords: *Criminal laws, Documents, First Amendment, News, Press, Reporter, Stealing, Wiretapping*

Chief Justice Warren Burger
Miller v. California,
413 U.S. 15, 32–33 (1973)
It is neither realistic nor constitutionally sound to read the First Amendment as requiring that the people of Maine or Mississippi accept depiction of conduct found tolerable in Las Vegas, or New York City. People in different States vary in their tastes and attitudes, and this diversity is not to be strangled by the absolutism of imposed uniformity.
Keywords: *Attitudes, Community standard, Conduct, Constitutional errors, Evidence, First Amendment, Jury, Obscenity, State, Tastes, Uniformity*

Chief Justice Warren Burger
Paris Adult Theatre I v. Slaton,
413 U.S. 49, 67 (1973)
Conduct or depictions of conduct that the state police power can prohibit on a public street do not become automatically protected by the Constitution merely because the conduct is moved to a bar or a "live" theatre stage, any more than a "live" performance of a man and woman locked in a sexual embrace at high noon in Times Square is protected by the Constitution because they simultaneously engage in a valid political dialogue.
Keywords: *Conduct, Police power, Political dialogue, Sexual embrace, State*

Justice William Douglas, dissenting
Pittsburgh Press Co. v. Pittsburgh Commission on Human Relations,
413 U.S. 376, 399 (1973)
. . . we have witnessed a growing tendency to cut down the literal require-ments of First Amendment freedoms so that those in power can squelch someone out of step. Historically, the miscreant has usually been an unpopular minority. Today it is a newspaper that does not bow to the spreading bureaucracy that promises to engulf us. It may be that we have become so stereotyped as to have earned that fate. But the First Amendment presupposes free-wheeling, independent people whose vagaries include ideas spread across the entire spectrum of thoughts and beliefs. I would let any expression in that broad spectrum flourish, unrestrained by Government, unless it was an integral part of action—the only point which in the Jeffersonian philosophy marks the permissible point of governmental intrusion.
Keywords: *Beliefs, First Amendment, Free press, Jeffersonian philosophy, Newspaper, Thoughts*

Justice Potter Stewart, dissenting
Pittsburgh Press Co. v. Pittsburgh Commission on Human Relations,
413 U.S. 376, 403 (1973)
The Court today holds that a government agency can force a newspaper publisher to print his classified advertising pages in a certain way in order to carry out governmental policy. After this decision, I see no reason why government cannot force a newspaper publisher to conform in the same way in order to achieve other goals thought socially desirable. And if government can dictate the layout of a newspaper's classified advertising pages today, what is there to prevent it from dictating the layout of the news pages tomorrow?
Keywords: *Advertising, Classifieds,*

First Amendment, Free press, News-paper, Publisher

Justice Byron White
Broadrick v. Oklahoma,
413 U.S. 601, 611–612 (1973)
It has long been recognized that the First Amendment needs breathing space and that statutes attempting to restrict or burden the exercise of First Amendment rights must be narrowly drawn and represent a considered legislative judgment that a particular mode of expression has to give way to other compelling needs of society.
Keywords: *Compelling needs, Expression, First Amendment, Legislative judgment*

Justice Byron White, concurring
Miami Herald Publishing Co. v. Tornillo,
418 U.S. 241, 259 (1974)
We have learned, and continue to learn, from what we view as the unhappy experiences of other nations where government has been allowed to meddle in the internal editorial affairs of newspapers. Regardless of how beneficent-sounding the purposes of controlling the press might be, we prefer "the power of reason as applied through public discussion" and remain intensely skeptical about those measures that would allow government to insinuate itself into the editorial rooms of this Nation's press.
Keywords: *First Amendment, Government, Newspapers, Press*

Justice Byron White, concurring
Miami Herald Publishing Co. v. Tornillo,
418 U.S. 241, 262–263 (1974)
One need not think less of the First Amendment to sustain reasonable methods for allowing the average citizen to redeem a falsely tarnished reputation. Nor does one have to doubt the genuine decency, integrity, and good sense of the vast majority of professional journalists to support the right of any individual to have his day in court when he has been falsely maligned in the public press. The press is the servant, not the master, of the citizenry, and its freedom does not carry with it an unrestricted hunting license to prey on the ordinary citizen.
Keywords: *Citizenry, First Amendment, Journalists, Press, Reputation*

Justice Harry Blackmun
Lehman v. Shaker Heights,
418 U.S. 298, 304 (1974)
Revenue earned from long-term commercial advertising could be jeopardized by a requirement that short-term candidacy or issue-oriented advertisements be displayed on car cards. Users would be subjected to the blare of political propaganda. There could be lurking doubts about favoritism, and sticky administrative problems might arise in parceling out limited space to eager politicians. In these circumstances, the managerial decision to limit car card space to innocuous and less controversial commercial and service oriented advertising does not rise to the dignity of a First Amendment violation. Were we to hold to the contrary, display cases in public hospitals, libraries, office buildings, military compounds, and other public facilities immediately would become Hyde Parks open to every would-be pamphleteer and politician. This the Constitution does not require.
Keywords: *Advertising, Candidacy,*

Favoritism, First Amendment, Pamphleteer, Political propaganda, Politicians, Public buildings

Justice Byron White
Cox Broadcasting Corp. v. Cohn,
420 U.S. 469, 491–492 (1975)
. . . in a society in which each individual has but limited time and resources with which to observe at first hand the operations of his government, he relies necessarily upon the press to bring to him in convenient form the facts of those operations. Great responsibility is accordingly placed upon the news media to report fully and accurately the proceedings of government, and official records and documents open to the public are the basic data of governmental operations. Without the information provided by the press most of us and many of our representatives would be unable to vote intelligently or to register opinions on the administration of government generally. With respect to judicial proceedings in particular, the function of the press serves to guarantee the fairness of trials and to bring to bear the beneficial effects of public scrutiny upon the administration of justice.
Keywords: *Government administration, Government operations, Government proceedings, News media, Oversight, Press, Society*

Justice Lewis Powell
Erznoznik v. Jacksonville,
422 U.S. 205, 213–214 (1975)
Clearly all nudity cannot be deemed obscene even as to minors. . . . Speech that is neither obscene as to youths nor subject to some other legitimate proscription can-

not be suppressed solely to protect the young from ideas or images that a legislative body thinks unsuitable for them.
Keywords: *Ideas, Minors, Nudity, Obscenity, Speech, Youths*

Per Curiam
Buckley v. Valeo,
424 U.S. 1, 19 (1976)
A restriction on the amount of money a person or group can spend on political communication during a campaign necessarily reduces the quantity of expression by restricting the number of issues discussed, the depth of their exploration, and the size of the audience reached. This is because virtually every means of communicating ideas in today's mass society requires the expenditure of money.
Keywords: *Audience, Campaign, Expenditures, Mass society, Money, Political communication*

Justice Potter Stewart, concurring
Virginia Pharmacy Board v. Virginia Consumer Council,
425 U.S. 748, 777–778 (1976)
In contrast to the press, which must often attempt to assemble the true facts from sketchy and sometimes conflicting sources under the pressure of publication deadlines, the commercial advertiser generally knows the product or service he seeks to sell and is in a position to verify the accuracy of his factual representations before he disseminates them. The advertiser's access to the truth about his product and its price substantially eliminates any danger that governmental regulation of false or misleading price or product advertising will chill accurate and nondescriptive commercial expres-

sion. There is, therefore, little need to sanction "some falsehood in order to protect speech that matters."

Keywords: *Advertising, Commercial expression, Press, Product, Publication, Service, Truth*

Justice Potter Stewart, dissenting
Young v. American Mini Theaters, Inc., 427 U.S. 50, 88 (1976)

Much speech that seems to be of little or no value will enter the marketplace of ideas, threatening the quality of our social discourse and, more generally, the serenity of our lives. But that is the price to be paid for constitutional freedom.

Keywords: *Constitutional protections, Freedoms, Ideas, Marketplace, Offensive speech, Social discourse*

Justice John Paul Stevens
Smith v. United States, 431 U.S. 291, 319–321 (1977)

I do not know whether the ugly pictures in this record have any beneficial value. The fact that there is a large demand for comparable materials indicates that they do provide amusement or information, or at least satisfy the curiosity of interested persons. Moreover, there are serious well-intentioned people who are persuaded that they serve a worthwhile purpose. Others believe they arouse passions that lead to the commission of crimes; if that be true, surely there is a mountain of material just within the protected zone that is equally capable of motivating comparable conduct. Moreover, the dire predictions about the baneful effects of these materials are disturbingly reminiscent of arguments formerly made about the availability of what are now valued as works of art. In the end, I believe we must rely on the capacity of the free marketplace of ideas to distinguish that which is useful or beautiful from that which is ugly or worthless.

Keywords: *Amusement, Art, Conduct, Criminality, Ideas, Marketplace, Passions*

Justice Lewis Powell, concurring
Federal Communications Commission v. Pacifica Foundation, 438 U.S. 726, 761 (1978)

I do not subscribe to the theory that the Justices of this Court are free generally to decide on the basis of its content which speech protected the First Amendment is most "valuable" and hence deserving of the most protection, and which is less "valuable" and hence deserving of less protection. In my view, the result in this case does not turn on whether Carlin's monologue, viewed as a whole, or the words that comprise it, have more or less "value" than a candidate's campaign speech. This is a judgment for each person to make, not one for the judges to impose upon him.

Keywords: *Campaign, Content, First Amendment, Judicial judgment, Speech, Value*

Justice William Brennan, dissenting
Federal Communications Commission v. Pacifica Foundation, 438 U.S. 726, 765–766 (1978)

Whatever the minimal discomfort suffered by a listener who inadvertently tunes into a program he finds offensive during the brief interval before he can simply extend his arm and switch stations of flick the "off" button, it is surely worth the candle to preserve the broadcaster's right to send, and the right of those interested to receive, a message entitled to full First Amendment protection.

Keywords: *Broadcaster, First Amendment, Listener, Offensive*

Justice Lewis Powell
Friedman v. Rogers,
440 U.S. 1, 12–13 (1979)
A trade name conveys no information about the price and nature of the services offered by an optometrist until it acquires meaning over a period of time by associations formed in the minds of the public between the name and some standard of price or quality. Because these ill-defined associations of trade names with price and quality information can be manipulated by the users of trade names, there is a significant possibility that trade names will be used to mislead the public.

Keywords: *Advertising, Commercial speech, Misleading, Trade name*

Justice William Brennan, dissenting
Brown v. Glines,
444 U.S. 348, 370–371 (1980)
. . . the Court has been deluded into unquestioning acceptance of the very flawed assumption that discipline and morale are enhanced by restricting peaceful communication of various viewpoints. Properly regulated as to time, place, and manner, petitioning provides a useful outlet for airing complaints and opinions that are held as strongly by citizens in uniform as by the rest of society. The forced absence of peaceful expression only creates the illusion of good order; underlying dissension remains to

flow into the more dangerous channels of incitement and disobedience. In that sense, military efficiency is only disserved when First Amendment rights are devalued.

Keywords: *Citizens, Discipline, Disobedience, Dissension, Expression, First Amendment, Military, Morale, Peaceful communication, Speech, Viewpoints*

Justice John Paul Stevens, concurring
Consolidated Edison Co. v. Public Service Commission,
447 U.S. 530, 544–545 (1980)
Any student of history who has been reprimanded for talking about the World Series during a class discussion of the First Amendment knows that it is incorrect to state that a "time, place, or manner restriction may not be based upon either the content or subject matter of speech."

Keywords: *First Amendment, Speech, Subject matter*

Chief Justice Warren Burger
Chandler v. Florida,
449 U.S. 560, 574–575 (1981)
An absolute constitutional ban on broadcast coverage of trials cannot be justified simply because there is a danger that, in some cases, prejudicial broadcast accounts of pretrial and trial events may impair the ability of jurors to decide the issue of guilt or innocence uninfluenced by extraneous matter. The risk of juror prejudice in some cases does not justify an absolute ban on news coverage of trials by the printed media; so also the risk of such prejudice does not warrant an

absolute constitutional ban on all broadcast coverage. A case attracts a high level of public attention because of its intrinsic interest to the public and the manner of reporting the event. The risk of juror prejudice is present in any publication of a trial, but the appropriate safeguard against such prejudice is the defendant's right to demonstrate that the media's coverage of his case—be it printed or broadcast—compromised the ability of the particular jury that heard the case to adjudicate fairly.

Keywords: *Broadcasting, Constitutional bans, Criminal justice, Defendant, Jurors, Media, News coverage, Pretrial publicity, Public attention, Trials*

Chief Justice Warren Burger, dissenting
Schad v. Mount Ephraim,
452 U.S. 61, 88 (1981)

To say that there is a First Amendment right to impose every form of expression on every community, including the kind of "expression" involved here, is sheer nonsense. To enshrine such a notion in the Constitution ignores fundamental values that the Constitution ought to protect. To invoke the First Amendment to protect the activity involved in this case trivializes and demeans that great Amendment.

Keywords: *Constitutional guarantees, Expression, First Amendment, Values*

Justice Byron White, concurring
Dun & Bradstreet, Inc. v. Greenmoss Builders,
472 U.S. 749, 767 (1985)

In a country like ours, where the people purport to be able to govern themselves through their elected representatives, adequate information about their government is of transcendent importance. That flow of intelligence deserves full First Amendment protection. Criticism and assessment of the performance of public officials and of government in general are not subject to penalties imposed by law. But these First Amendment values are not at all served by circulating false statements of fact about public officials. On the contrary, erroneous information frustrates these values. They are even more disserved when the statements falsely impugn the honesty of those men and women and hence lessen the confidence in government.

Keywords: *Criticism, False statements, First Amendment, Governmental confidence, Honesty, Political information, Representative government*

Justice William Brennan
Federal Election Commission v. Massachusetts Citizens for Life, Inc.,
479 U.S. 238, 264–265 (1986)

Our pursuit of other governmental ends, however, may tempt us to accept in small increments a loss that would be unthinkable if inflicted all at once. For this reason, we must be as vigilant against the modest diminution of speech as we are against its sweeping restriction. Where at all possible, government must curtail speech only to the degree necessary to meet the particular problem at hand, and must avoid infringing on speech that does not pose the danger that has prompted regulation.

Keywords: *First Amendment, Governmental ends, Regulation, Speech*

Chief Justice William Rehnquist
Hustler Magazine, Inc. v. Falwell,
485 U.S. 46, 55 (1988)

"Outrageousness" in the area of political and social discourse has an inherent subjectiveness about it which would allow a jury to impose liability on the basis of the jurors' tastes or views, or perhaps on the basis of their dislike of a particular expression. An "outrageousness" standard thus runs afoul of our long-standing refusal to allow damages to be awarded because the speech in question may have an adverse emotional impact on the audience.

Keywords: *Emotional impact, Expression, Jury, Political discourse, Social discourse, Speech*

Chief Justice William Rehnquist
Dallas v. Stanglin,
490 U.S. 19, 25 (1989)

It is possible to find some kernel of expression in almost every activity a person undertakes—for example, walking down the street or meeting one's friends at a shopping mall—but such a kernel is not sufficient to bring the activity within the protection of the First Amendment. We think the activity of these dance-hall patrons—coming together to engage in recreational dancing—is not protected by the First Amendment.

Keywords: *Dancing, Expression, First Amendment*

Justice Anthony Kennedy
Ward v. Rock Against Racism,
491 U.S. 781, 790 (1989)

Music is one of the oldest forms of human expression. From Plato's discourse in the Republic to the totalitarian state in our own times, rulers have known its capacity to appeal to the intellect and to the emotions, and have censored musical compositions to serve the needs of the state. The Constitution prohibits any like attempts in our own legal order. Music, as a form of expression and communication, is protected under the First Amendment.

Keywords: *Censorship, Constitutional limitations, Expression, First Amendment, Music*

Justice William Brennan, dissenting
Milkovich v. Lorain Journal Co.,
497 U.S. 1, 35 (1990)

Did NASA officials ignore sound warnings that the Challenger Space Shuttle would explode? Did Cuban-American leaders arrange for John Fitzgerald Kennedy's assassination? Was Kurt Waldheim a Nazi officer? Such questions are matters of public concern long before all the facts are unearthed, if they ever are. Conjecture is a means of fueling a national discourse on such questions and stimulating public pressure for answers from those who know more.

Keywords: *Conjecture, Free speech, National discourse, Public pressure*

Justice William Brennan, dissenting
Milkovich v. Lorain Journal Co.,
497 U.S. 1, 36 (1990)

Readers are as capable of independently evaluating the merits of such speculative conclusions as they are of evaluating the merits of pure opprobrium. Punishing such conjecture protects reputation only at the cost of expunging a genuinely useful mechanism for public debate.

Keywords: *First Amendment, Free press, Free speech, Public debate, Reputation, Thought*

Justice Anthony Kennedy
Masson v. New Yorker Magazine, Inc.,
501 U.S. 496, 514 (1991)
. . . writers and reporters, by necessity, alter what people say, at the very least to eliminate grammatical and syntactical infelicities. If every alteration constituted the falsity required to prove actual malice, the practice of journalism, which the First Amendment standard is designed to protect, would require a radical change, one inconsistent with our precedents and First Amendment principles.
Keywords: *Falsehoods, First Amendment, Grammatical errors, Journalism, Malice, Reporters, Writers*

Justice David Souter, concurring
Barnes v. Glen Theatre, Inc.,
501 U.S. 560, 581 (1991)
Although . . . performance dancing is inherently expressive, nudity per se is not. It is a condition, not an activity, and the voluntary assumption of that condition, without more, apparently expresses nothing beyond the view that the condition is somehow appropriate to the circumstances. But every voluntary act implies some such idea, and the implication is thus so common and minimal that calling all voluntary activity expressive would reduce the concept of expression to the point of the meaningless. A search for some expression beyond the minimal in the choice to go nude will often yield nothing: a person may choose nudity, for example, for maximum sun-

bathing. But when nudity is combined with expressive activity, its stimulative and attractive value certainly can enhance the force of expression, and a dancer's acts in going from clothed to nude, as in a strip-tease, are integrated into the dance and its expressive function.
Keywords: *Expression, Expressive activity, Nudity, Performance dancing*

Justice Anthony Kennedy, concurring
Simon & Schuster v. Crime Victims Board,
502 U.S. 105, 124 (1991)
Here, a law is directed to speech alone where the speech in question is not obscene, not defamatory, not words tantamount to an act otherwise criminal, not an impairment of some other constitutional right, not an incitement to lawless action, and not calculated or likely to bring about imminent harm the State has the substantive power to prevent. No further inquiry is necessary to reject the State's argument that the statute should be upheld.
Keywords: *Criminal, Defamatory, Imminent harm, Incitement, Obscene, Speech*

Justice John Paul Stevens, concurring
R.A.V. v. St. Paul,
505 U.S. 377, 422–423 (1992)
Our First Amendment decisions have created a rough hierarchy in the constitutional protection of speech. Core political speech occupies the highest, most protected position; commercial speech and nonobscene, sexually explicit speech are regarded as a sort of second-class expression; obscenity and fighting words receive the least protection of all. Assum-

ing that the Court is correct that this last class of speech is not wholly "unprotected," it certainly does not follow that fighting words and obscenity receive the same sort of protection afforded core political speech. Yet, in ruling that proscribable speech cannot be regulated based on subject matter, the Court does just that. Perversely, this gives fighting words greater protection than is afforded commercial speech. If Congress can prohibit false advertising directed at airline passengers without also prohibiting false advertising directed at bus passengers, and if a city can prohibit political advertisements in its buses, while allowing other advertisements, it is ironic to hold that a city cannot regulate fighting words based on "race, color, creed, religion or gender," while leaving unregulated fighting words based on "union membership ... or homosexuality." The Court today turns First Amendment law on its head: Communication that was once entirely unprotected (and that still can be wholly proscribed) is now entitled to greater protection than commercial speech—and possibly greater protection than core political speech.

Keywords: *Advertising, Commercial speech, False advertising, Fighting words, First Amendment, Nonobscene speech, Obscenity, Political advertising, Political speech, Proscribable speech, Sexually explicit speech*

Justice Antonin Scalia, dissenting
United States v. X-Citement Video, Inc.,
513 U.S. 64, 85 (1994)
The First Amendment will lose none of its value to a free society if those who

knowingly place themselves in the stream of pornographic commerce are obliged to make sure that they are not subsidizing child abuse.

Keywords: *Child abuse, Commerce, First Amendment, Police power, Pornography*

Justice John Paul Stevens
McIntyre v. Ohio Elections Commission,
514 U.S. 334, 357 (1995)
Under our Constitution, anonymous pamphleteering is not a pernicious, fraudulent practice, but an honorable tradition of advocacy and of dissent. Anonymity is a shield from the tyranny of the majority. It thus exemplifies the purpose behind the Bill of Rights, and of the First Amendment in particular: to protect unpopular individuals from retaliation—and their ideas from suppression—at the hand of an intolerant society. The right to remain anonymous may be abused when it shields fraudulent conduct. But political speech by its nature will sometimes have unpalatable consequences, and, in general, our society accords greater weight to the value of free speech than to the dangers of its misuse.

Keywords: *Advocacy, Anonymity, Bill of Rights, Dissent, First Amendment, Ideas, Intolerance, Majority, Pamphleteering, Political speech, Suppression, Tyranny*

Justice John Paul Stevens, concurring
Rubin v. Coors Brewing Co.,
514 U.S. 476, 497 (1995)
Any "interest" in restricting the flow of accurate information because of the per-

ceived danger of that knowledge is anathema to the First Amendment; more speech and a better-informed citizenry are among the central goals of the Free Speech Clause. Accordingly, the Constitution is most skeptical of supposed state interests that seek to keep people in the dark for what the government believes to be their own good.

Keywords: *Commercial speech, First Amendment, Free speech, Information, Police power*

Justice Anthony Kennedy, dissenting
Florida Bar v. Went For It, Inc.,
515 U.S., 618, 645 (1995)
Self-assurance has always been the hallmark of a censor.

Keywords: *Censorship, First Amendment*

9. In the Beginning

Although the First Amendment never explicitly uses the words "separation of church and state" this is the focus of this chapter. Diversity is the hallmark of the American experiment. Nowhere is this more evident than in religious freedoms and its inherent conflict with the status quo and majority philosophies.

Justice Samuel Miller
Watson v. Jones,
80 U.S. 679, 728 (1871)
The law knows no heresy, and is committed to the support of no dogma, the establishment of no sect.
Keywords: *Dogma, Establishment, Heresy, Sect*

Chief Justice Morrison Waite
Reynolds v. United States,
98 U.S. 145, 166 (1878)
Suppose one believed that human sacrifices were a necessary part of religious worship, would it be seriously contended that the civil government could not interfere to prevent a sacrifice? Or if a wife religiously believed it was her duty to burn herself upon the funeral pyre of a dead husband, would it be beyond the power of the civil government to prevent her carrying her belief into practice?
Keywords: *Civil government, Human sacrifice, Legislative power, Religion, Worship*

Chief Justice Morrison Waite
Reynolds v. United States,
98 U.S. 145, 167 (1878)
To permit [polygamy in the face of a bigamy law] would be to make the professed doctrines of religious beliefs superior to the law of the land, and in effect to permit every citizen to become a law unto himself. Government could exist only in name under such circumstances.
Keywords: *Bigamy, Citizen, Polygamy, Religious beliefs, Rule of law*

Justice Owen Roberts
Cantwell v. Connecticut,
310 U.S. 296, 303–304 (1940)
. . . the Amendment embraces two concepts—freedom to believe and freedom to act. The first is absolute, but in the nature of things, the second cannot be. . . . In every case the power to regulate must be so exercised as not, in attaining a permissible end, unduly to infringe the protected freedom.
Keywords: *Freedom, Free exercise, Regulations*

Justice Felix Frankfurter
Minersville School District v. Gobitis,
310 U.S. 586, 594–595 (1940)
The mere possession of religious convictions which contradict the relevant concerns of a political society does not relieve the citizen from the discharge of political responsibilities.
Keywords: *Citizens, Political respon-*

sibilities, Political society, Religious convictions

Justice Robert Jackson, concurring
Douglas v. Jeannette,
319 U.S. 157, 180–181 (1943)
Neither can I think it an essential part of freedom that religious differences be aired in language that is obscene, abusive, or inciting to retaliation. We have held that a Jehovah's Witness may not call a public officer a "god damned racketeer" and a "damned fascist," because that is to use "fighting words," and such are not privileged. How then can the Court today hold it a "high constitutional privilege" to go to homes, including those of devout Catholics on Palm Sunday morning, and thrust upon them literature calling their church a "whore" and their faith a "racket"? Nor am I convinced that we can have freedom of religion only by denying the American's deep-seated conviction that his home is a refuge from the pulling and hauling of the market place and the street. For a stranger to corner a man in his home, summon him to the door and put him in the position either of arguing his religion or of ordering one of unknown disposition to leave is a questionable use of religious freedom.
Keywords: *Fighting words, Freedom, Freedom of religion, Incitement, Jehovah's Witness, Obscene, Religious differences, Speech*

Justice Robert Jackson, concurring
Douglas v. Jeannette,
319 U.S. 157, 166 (1943)
Unless we are to reach judgments as did

Plato's men who were chained in a cave so that they saw nothing but shadows, we should consider the facts of the Douglas case at least as an hypothesis to test the validity of the conclusions in the other cases. This record shows us something of the strings as well as the marionettes. It reveals the problem of those in local authority when the right to proselyte comes in contact with what many people have an idea is their right to be let alone.
Keywords: *Privacy, Proselyte*

Justice Owen Roberts, dissenting
Follett v. McCormick,
321 U.S. 573, 581–583 (1944)
We cannot ignore what this decision involves. If the First Amendment grants immunity from taxation to the exercise of religion, it must equally grant a similar exemption to those who speak and to the press. It will not do to say that the Amendment, in the clause relating to religion, is couched in the imperative and, in the clause relating to freedom of speech and of press, is couched in the comparative. The amendment's prohibitions are equally sweeping. If exactions on the business or occupation of selling cannot be enforced against Jehovah's Witnesses they can no more be enforced against publishers or vendors of books, whether dealing with religion or other matters of information. The decision now rendered must mean that the guarantee of freedom of the press creates an immunity equal to that here upheld as to teaching or preaching religious doctrine. Thus the decision precludes nonoppressive, nondiscriminatory licensing or occupa-

tion taxes on publishers, and on news vendors as well, since, without the latter, the dissemination of views would be impossible. This court disavowed any such doctrine with respect to freedom of the press in *Grosjean v. American Press Co.* And it is unthinkable that those who publish and distribute for profit newspapers and periodicals should suggest that they are in a class apart, untouchable by taxation upon their enterprises for the support of the government which makes their activities possible . . . even in the field of religion alone, the implications of the present decision are startling. Multiple activities by which citizens earn their bread may, with equal propriety, be denominated an exercise of religion as may preaching or selling religious tracts. Certainly this Court cannot say that one activity is the exercise of religion and the other is not. The materials for judicial distinction do not exist. It would be difficult to deny the claims of those who devote their lives to the healing of the sick, to the nursing of the disabled, to the betterment of social and economic conditions, and to a myriad other worthy objects, that their respective callings, albeit they earn their living by pursuing them, are, for them, the exercise of religion. Such a belief, however earnestly and honestly held, does not entitle the believers to be free of contribution to the cost of government, which itself guarantees them the privilege of pursuing their callings without governmental prohibition or interference.

Keywords: *First Amendment, Governmental costs, Governmental prohibitions, Immunity, Jehovah's Witnesses, Newspapers, Periodicals, Preaching, Press, Publishers, Religion, Speech, Taxation, Teaching*

Justice William Douglas
United States v. Ballard,
322 U.S. 78, 86–87 (1944)

Men may believe what they cannot prove. They may not be put to the proof of their religious doctrines or beliefs. Religious experiences which are as real as life to some may be incomprehensible to others. Yet the fact that they may be beyond the ken of mortals does not mean that they can be made suspect before the law. Many take their gospel from the New Testament. But it would hardly be supposed that they could be tried before a jury charged with the duty of determining whether those teachings contained false representations. The miracles of the New Testament, the Divinity of Christ, life after death, the power of prayer are deep in the religious convictions of many. If one could be sent to jail because a jury in a hostile environment found those teachings false, little indeed would be left of religious freedom. The Fathers of the Constitution were not unaware of the varied and extreme views of religious sects, of the violence of disagreement among them, and of the lack of any one religious creed on which all men would agree. They fashioned a charter of government which envisaged the widest possible toleration of conflicting views. Man's relation to his God was made no concern of the state. He was granted the right to worship as he pleased and to answer to no man for the verity of his religious views.

Keywords: *Belief, Criminality, Divinity of Christ, Jury, Miracles, New Testament, Prayer, Religious convictions, Religious doctrines, Religious freedoms*

Justice Hugo Black, dissenting
In re Summers,
325 U.S. 561, 576 (1945)
It may be, as many people think, that Christ's gospel of love and submission is not suited to a world in which men still fight and kill one another. But I am not ready to say that a mere profession of belief in that gospel is a sufficient reason to keep otherwise well qualified men out of the legal profession, or to drive law-abiding lawyers of that belief out of the profession, which would be the next logical development.
Key Words: *Belief, First Amendment, Freedom of religion, Gospel, Legal practice, Profession, State regulations*

Justice Hugo Black
Everson v. Board of Education of Ewing TP,
330 U.S. 1, 18 (1947)
[The First] Amendment requires the state to be neutral in its relations with groups of religious believers and non-believers; it does not require the state to be their adversary. State power is no more to be used so as to handicap religions than it is to favor them.
Keywords: *First Amendment, Religion, Religious believers, Neutrality, States' rights*

Justice Robert Jackson, dissenting
Jordan v. De George,
341 U.S. 223, 241 (1951)
We should not forget that criminality is one thing—a matter of law—and that morality, ethics and religious teachings are another. Their relations have puzzled the best of men.
Keywords: Criminality, *Ethics, Morality, Religious teachings*

Justice William Douglas
Zorach v. Clauson,
343 U.S. 306, 312–313 (1952)
There cannot be the slightest doubt that the First Amendment reflects the philosophy that Church and State should be separated. . . . The First Amendment, however, does not say that in every and all respects there shall be a separation of Church and State. Rather, it studiously defines the manner, the specific ways, in which there shall be no concert or union or dependency one on the other. That is the common sense of the matter. Otherwise the state and religion would be aliens to each other—hostile, suspicious, and even unfriendly. Churches could not be required to pay even property taxes. Municipalities would not be permitted to render police or fire protection to religious groups. Policemen who helped parishioners into their places of worship would violate the Constitution. Prayers in our legislative halls; the appeals to the Almighty in the messages of the Chief Executive; the proclamations making Thanksgiving Day a holiday; "so help me God" in our courtroom oaths—these and all other references to the Almighty that run through our laws, our public rituals, our ceremonies would be flouting the First Amendment. A fastidious atheist or agnostic could even object to the supplication with which the Court opens each

session: "God save the United States and this Honorable Court."

Keywords: *Agnostic, Almighty, Atheist, Church, First Amendment, God, Legislative halls, Oaths, Prayer, Public rituals, Religion, Taxation*

Justice Robert Jackson, dissenting
Zorach v. Clauson,
343 U.S. 306, 324–325 (1952)

. . . I may challenge the Court's suggestion that opposition to this plan can only be antireligious, atheistic, or agnostic. My evangelistic brethren confuse an objection to compulsion with an objection to religion. It is possible to hold a faith with enough confidence to believe that what should be rendered to God does not need to be decided and collected by Caesar.

Keywords: *Agnostic, Antireligious, Atheistic, Caesar, Faith, God, Religion*

Chief Justice Earl Warren
Braunfeld v. Brown,
366 U.S. 599, 606–607 (1961)

Abhorrence of religious persecution and intolerance is a basic part of our heritage. But we are a cosmopolitan nation made up of people of almost every conceivable religious preference. These denominations number almost three hundred. Consequently, it cannot be expected, much less required, that legislators enact no law regulating conduct that may in some way result in an economic disadvantage to some religious sects and not to others because of the special practices of the various religions. We do not believe that such an effect is an absolute test for determining whether the legislation violates the freedom of religion protected by the First Amendment.

Keywords: *Conduct, Diversity, Economic disadvantage, First Amendment, Freedom of religion, Heritage, Intolerance, Legislation, Religion, Religious persecution*

Justice Hugo Black
Engel v. Vitale,
370 U.S. 421, 433–435 (1962)

It has been argued that to apply the Constitution in such a way as to prohibit state laws respecting an establishment of religious services in public schools is to indicate a hostility toward religion or toward prayer. Nothing, of course, could be more wrong. The history of man is inseparable from the history of religion. And perhaps it is not too much to say that since the beginning of that history many people have devoutly believed that "More things are wrought by prayer than this world dreams of." It was doubtless largely due to men who believed this that there grew up a sentiment that caused men to leave the cross-currents of officially established state religions and religious persecution in Europe and come to this country filled with the hope that they could find a place in which they could pray when they pleased to the God of their faith in the language they chose. And there were men of this same faith in the power of prayer who led the fight for adoption of our Constitution and also for our Bill of Rights with the very guarantees of religious freedom that forbid the sort of governmental activity which New York has attempted here. These men knew that the First Amendment, which tried to put an end to governmental control of religion and of prayer, was not written to destroy either. They knew rather that it was written to quiet well-justified fears which nearly all of them felt arising out of an awareness that governments of the past had shackled men's tongues to make them speak only the religious thoughts that government wanted them to speak and to pray only to the God that government wanted them to pray to. It is neither sacrilegious nor antireligious to say that each separate government in this country should stay out of the business of writing or sanctioning official prayers and leave that purely religious function to the people themselves and to those the people choose to look to for religious guidance.

Keywords: *Bill of Rights, Establishment Clause, First Amendment, God, Governmental activity, History, Hostility, Prayer, Public schools, Religion, Religious freedom, Sacrilegious*

Justice William Douglas, concurring
Engel v. Vitale,
370 U.S. 421, 441–442 (1962)

In New York the teacher who leads in prayer is on the public payroll; and the time she takes seems minuscule as compared with the salaries appropriated by state legislatures and Congress for chaplains to conduct prayers in the legislative halls. Only a bare fraction of the teacher's time is given to reciting [the] 22–word prayer, about the same amount of time that our Crier spends announcing the opening of our sessions and offering a prayer for this Court. Yet for me

the principle is the same, no matter how briefly the prayer is said, for in each of the instances given the person praying is a public official on the public payroll, performing a religious exercise in a governmental institution. It is said that the element of coercion is inherent in the giving of this prayer. If that is true here, it is also true of the prayer with which this Court is convened, and of those that open the Congress. Few adults, let alone children, would leave our courtroom or the Senate or the House while those prayers are being given. Every such audience is in a sense a "captive" audience.

Keywords: *Audience, Chaplains, Congress, Legislative halls, Prayer, Public school teacher, Religion*

Justice Potter Stewart, dissenting
Engel v. Vitale,
370 U.S. 421, 446–449 (1962)

At the opening of each day's Session of this Court we stand, while one of our officials invokes the protection of God. Since the days of John Marshall our Crier has said, "God save the United States and this Honorable Court." Both the Senate and the House of Representatives open their daily Sessions with prayer. Each of our Presidents, from George Washington to John F. Kennedy, has upon assuming his Office asked the protection and help of God.

The Court today says that the state and federal governments are without constitutional power to prescribe any particular form of words to be recited by any group of the American people on any subject touching religion. One of the stanzas of "The Star-Spangled Banner," made our National anthem by Act of Congress in 1931, contains these verses:

> "Blest with victory and peace, may the heav'n rescued land
>   Praise the Pow'r that hath made and preserved us a nation!
>   Then conquer we must, when our cause it is just, And this be our motto 'In God is our Trust.' "

In 1954 Congress added a phrase to the Pledge of Allegiance to the Flag so that it now contains the words "one Nation under God, indivisible, with liberty and justice for all." In 1952 Congress enacted legislation calling upon the President each year to proclaim a National Day of Prayer. Since 1865 the words "IN GOD WE TRUST" have been impressed on our coins.

Countless similar examples could be listed, but there is no need to belabor the obvious.

Keywords: *Court, God, House of Representatives, National anthem, Pledge of Allegiance, Prayer, Religion, Senate*

Justice William Brennan, concurring
Abington School District v. Schempp,
374 U.S. 203, 241–242 (1963)

... the American experiment in free public education available to all children has been guided in large measure by the dramatic evolution of the religious diversity among the population which our public schools serve. The interaction of these two important forces in our national life has placed in bold relief certain positive values in the consistent application to public institutions generally, and public schools particularly, of the constitutional

decree against official involvements of religion which might produce the evils the Framers meant the Establishment Clause to forestall. The public schools are supported entirely, in most communities, by public funds—funds exacted not only from parents, nor alone from those who hold particular religious views, nor indeed from those who subscribe to any creed at all. It is implicit in the history and character of American public education that the public schools serve a uniquely public function: the training of American citizens in an atmosphere free of parochial, divisive, or separatist influences of any sort—an atmosphere in which children may assimilate a heritage common to all American groups and religions.

Keywords: *Establishment Clause, Framers, Heritage, History, Public education, Public finance, Religion, Religious diversity*

Justice Tom Clark
United States v. Seeger,
380 U.S. 163, 165–166 (1965)

We have concluded that Congress, in using the expression "Supreme Being" rather than the designation "God," was merely clarifying the meaning of religious training and belief so as to embrace all religions and to exclude essentially political, sociological, or philosophical views. We believe that under this construction, the test of belief "in a relation to a Supreme being" is whether a given belief that is sincere and meaningful occupies a place in the life of its possessor parallel to that filled by the orthodox belief in God of one who clearly qualifies for the exemption. Where such beliefs have parallel positions in the lives of their respective holders we cannot say that one is "in a relation to a Supreme being" and the other is not.

Keywords: *Belief, Congress, God, Religions, Religious training, Supreme being*

Justice Hugo Black, concurring
Epperson v. Arkansas,
393 U.S. 97, 109–110 (1968)

I am by no means sure that this case presents a genuinely justiciable case or controversy. Although . . . the statute alleged to be unconstitutional, was passed by the voters of Arkansas in 1928, we are informed that there has never been even a single attempt by the State to enforce it. And the pallid, unenthusiastic, even apologetic defense of the Act presented by the State in this Court indicates that the State would make no attempt to enforce the law should it remain on the books for the next century. Now, nearly 40 years after the law has slumbered on the books as though dead, a teacher alleging fear that the State might arouse from its lethargy and try to punish her has asked for a declaratory judgment holding the law unconstitutional. She was subsequently joined by a parent who alleged his interest in seeing that his two then school-age sons "be informed of all scientific theories and hypotheses. . . ." But whether this Arkansas teacher is still a teacher, fearful of punishment under the Act, we do not know. It may be, as has been published in the daily press, that she has long since given up her job as a teacher and moved to a distant city, thereby escaping the dangers she had imagined might befall her under this lifeless Arkansas Act. And there is not one iota of concrete evidence to show that the parent-intervenor's sons have not been or will not be taught about evolution. The textbook adopted for use in biology classes in Little Rock includes an entire chapter dealing with evolution. There is no evidence that this chapter is not being freely taught in the schools that use the textbook and no evidence that the intervenor's sons, who were 15 and 17 years old when this suit was brought three years ago, are still in high school or yet to take biology.

Keywords: *Constitutionality, Education, Evolution, Judicial review, Justiciable case or controversy, Punishment, Religion, Science, Textbooks*

Justice William Brennan, concurring
Walz v. Tax Commission,
397 U.S. 664, 681 (1970)

The existence from the beginning of the Nation's life of a practice, such as tax exemptions for religious organizations, is not conclusive of its constitutionality. But such practice is a fact of considerable import in the interpretation of abstract constitutional language. On its face, the Establishment Clause is reasonably susceptible of different interpretations regarding the exemptions. This Court's interpretation of the clause, accordingly, is appropriately influenced by the reading it has received in the practices of the Nation.

Keywords: *Constitutional interpretation, Establishment Clause, Religious organizations, Tax exemptions*

Justice John Marshall Harlan, concurring
Welsh v. United States,
398 U.S. 333, 354 (1970)
Unless we are to assume an Alice-in-Wonderland world where words have no meaning, I think it fair to say that Congress' choice of language cannot fail to convey to the discerning reader the very policy choice that the prevailing opinion today completely obliterates: that between conventional religions that usually have an organized and formal structure and dogma and a cohesive group identity, even when nontheistic, and cults that represent schools of thought and in the usual case are without formal structure or are, at most, loose and informal associations of individuals who share common ethical, moral, or intellectual views.
Keywords: Associations, Congressional language, Cults, First Amendment, Group identity, Nontheistic, Religion, Statutory interpretation

Chief Justice Warren Burger
Tilton v. Richardson,
403 U.S. 672, 685–686 (1971)
There are generally significant differences between the religious aspects of church-related institutions of higher learning and parochial elementary and secondary schools. . . . College students are less impressionable and less susceptible to religious indoctrination. . . . Furthermore, by their very nature, college and postgraduate courses tend to limit the opportunities for sectarian influence by virtue of their own disciplines.
Keywords: College, College students, Establishment Clause, Higher educa-tion, Parochial education, Postgradu-ate education, Religious indoctrina-tion, Sectarian, Secular education

Chief Justice Warren Burger
Tilton v. Richardson,
403 U.S. 672, 687 (1971)
Since religious indoctrination is not a substantial purpose of these church-related colleges, there is less likelihood than in primary and secondary schools that religion will permeate the area of secular education. This reduces the risk that government aid will in fact serve to support religious activities. Correspondingly the necessity for intensive government surveillance is diminished and the resulting entanglements between government and religion lessened. Such inspection as may be necessary to ascertain that the facilities are devoted to secular education is minimal. . . .
Keywords: Church-related colleges, College students, Establishment Clause, Higher education, Parochial education, Primary education, Reli-gious indoctrination, Secondary edu-cation, Secular education

Chief Justice Warren Burger
Wisconsin v. Yoder,
406 U.S. 205, 218 (1972)
The impact of the compulsory-attendance law on respondents' practice of the Amish religion is not only severe, but inescapable, for the Wisconsin law affirmatively compels them, under threat of criminal sanction, to perform acts undeniably at odds with fundamental tenets of their religious beliefs. . . . they must either abandon belief and be assimilated into society

at large, or be forced to migrate to some other and more tolerant region.

Keywords: *Assimilation, Compulsory-attendance, Criminality, Religion*

Justice William Rehnquist, dissenting
Wooley v. Maynard,
430 U.S. 705, 722 (1977)
The logic of the Court's opinion leads to startling, and I believe totally unacceptable, results. For example, the mottoes "In God We Trust" and "E Pluribus Unum" appear on the coin and currency of the United States. I cannot imagine that the statutes proscribing defacement of United States currency impinge upon the First Amendment rights of an atheist. The fact that an atheist carries and uses United States currency does not, in any meaningful sense, convey any affirmation of belief on his part in the motto "In God We Trust." Similarly, there is no affirmation of belief involved in the display of state license tags upon the private automobiles involved here.

Keywords: *Atheism, Belief, Currency, First Amendment, Free religion, License plates*

Justice William Brennan, concurring
McDaniel v. Paty,
435 U.S. 618, 641 (1978)
The State's goal of preventing sectarian bickering and strife may not be accomplished by regulating religious speech and political association. The Establishment Clause does not license government to treat religion and those who teach or practice it, simply by virtue of their status as such, as subversive of American ideals and therefore subject to

unique disabilities. Government may not inquire into the religious beliefs and motivations of officeholders—it may not remove them from office merely for making public statements regarding religion, or question whether their legislative actions stem from religious conviction.

Keywords: *Beliefs, Legislation, Officeholders, Political association, Religion, Speech*

Justice Byron White
Committee for Public Education & Religious Liberty v. Regan,
444 U.S. 646, 662 (1980)
. . . Establishment Clause cases are not easy; they stir deep feelings; and we are divided among ourselves, perhaps reflecting the different views on this subject of the people of this country. What is certain is that our decisions have tended to avoid categorical imperatives and absolutist approaches at either end of the range of possible outcomes. This course sacrifices clarity and predictability for flexibility, but this promises to be the case until the continuing interaction between the courts and the States—the former charged with interpreting and upholding the Constitution and the latter seeking to provide education for their youth—produces a single, more encompassing construction of the Establishment Clause.

Keywords: *Absolutist approaches, Diversity, Education, Establishment Clause, Federalism, States*

Chief Justice Warren Burger
United States v. Lee,
455 U.S. 252, 260 (1982)
If, for example, a religious adherent be-

lieves war is a sin, and if a certain percentage of the federal budget can be identified as devoted to war-related activities, such individuals would have a similarly valid claim to be exempt from paying that percentage of the income tax. The tax system could not function if denominations were allowed to challenge the tax system because tax payments were spent in a manner that violates their religious belief.
Keywords: *Budget, Income tax, Religious adherent, Sin, Taxation, War*

Justice William Brennan, dissenting
Marsh v. Chambers,
463 U.S. 783, 808 (1983)

Legislative prayer clearly violates the principles of neutrality and separation that are embedded within the Establishment Clause. . . . It intrudes on the right to conscience by forcing some legislators either to participate in a "prayer opportunity," with which they are in basic disagreement, or to make their disagreement a matter of public comment by declining to participate. It forces all residents of the State to support a religious exercise that may be contrary to their own beliefs. It requires the State to commit itself on fundamental theological issues. It has the potential for degrading religion by allowing a religious call to worship to be intermeshed with a secular call to order. And it injects religion into the political sphere by creating the potential that each and every selection of a chaplain, or consideration of a particular prayer, or even reconsideration of the practice itself, will provoke a political battle along religious lines and ultimately alienate some religiously identified group of citizens.

Keywords: *Beliefs, Chaplain, Establishment Clause, Legislative power, Legislative prayer, Religion, States, Theology, Worship*

Justice John Paul Stevens, dissenting
Marsh v. Chambers,
463 U.S. 783, 822–823 (1983)

In a democratically elected legislature, the religious beliefs of the chaplain tend to reflect the faith of the majority of the lawmakers' constituents. Prayers may be said by a Catholic priest in the Massachusetts Legislature and by a Presbyterian minister in the Nebraska Legislature, but I would not expect to find a Jehovah's Witness or a disciple of Mary Baker Eddy or the Reverend Moon serving as the official chaplain in any state legislature. Regardless of the motivation of the majority that exercises the power to appoint the chaplain, it seems plain to me that the designation of a member of one religious faith to serve as the sole official chaplain of a state legislature for a period of 16 years constitutes the preference of one faith over another in violation of the Establishment Clause of the First Amendment.

Keywords: *Chaplain, Constituency, Democracy, Establishment Clause, Faith, First Amendment, Legislative power, Legislature motivation, Prayer*

Justice William Brennan, dissenting
Lynch v. Donnelly,
465 U.S. 668, 710–711 (1984)

When government decides to recognize Christmas Day as a public holiday, it does no more than accommodate the calendar of public activities to the plain fact that many Americans will expect on that day to spend time visiting with their families, attending religious services, and perhaps enjoying some respite from preholiday activities. The Free Exercise Clause, of course, does not necessarily compel the government to provide this accommodation, but neither is the Establishment Clause offended by such a step. Because it is clear that the celebration of Christmas has both secular and sectarian elements, it may well be that by taking note of the holiday, the government is simply seeking to serve the same kinds of wholly secular goals—for instance, promoting goodwill and a common day of rest. . . . If public officials go further and participate in the secular celebration of Christmas—by, for example, decorating public places with such secular images as wreaths, garlands, or Santa Claus figures—they move closer to the limits of their constitutional power but nevertheless remain within the boundaries set by the Establishment Clause. But when those officials participate in or appear to endorse the distinctively religious elements of this otherwise secular event, they encroach upon First Amendment freedoms. For it is at that point that the government brings to the forefront the theological content of the holiday, and places the prestige, power, and financial support of a civil authority in the service of a particular faith.

Keywords: *Christmas, Establishment Clause, Faith, Free Exercise Clause, Government, Pubic officials, Religion, Secular*

Justice Sandra Day O'Connor, concurring
Wallace v. Jaffree,
472 U.S. 38, 73 (1985)
It is difficult to discern a serious threat to religious liberty from a room of silent, thoughtful schoolchildren.

Keywords: *Education, First Amendment, Free Exercise Clause, Liberty, Pray, Religion, School*

Chief Justice Warren Burger, dissenting
Wallace v. Jaffree,
472 U.S. 38, 84–85 (1985)
Some who trouble to read the opinions in these cases will find it ironic—perhaps even bizarre—that on the very day we heard arguments in the cases, the Court's session opened with an invocation for Divine protection. Across the park a few hundred yards away, the House of Representatives and the Senate regularly open each session with a prayer. These legislative prayers are not just one minute in duration, but are extended, thoughtful invocations and prayers for Divine guidance. They are given, as they have been since 1789, by clergy appointed as official chaplains and paid from the Treasury of the United States. Congress has also provided chapels in the Capitol, at public expense, where Members and others may pause for prayer, meditation—or a moment of silence. Inevitably some wag is bound to say that the Court's holding today reflects a belief that the historic practice of the Congress and this Court is justified because members of the Judiciary and Congress are more in need of Divine guidance than are schoolchildren. Still others will say that all this controversy

is "much ado about nothing," since no power on earth—including this Court and Congress—can stop any teacher from opening the schoolday with a moment of silence for pupils to meditate, to plan their day—or to pray if they voluntarily elect to do so.

Keywords: *Congress, Education, Establishment Clause, History, Invocations, Judicial prayer, Legislative prayer, Prayer, Public funding, Religion, School Prayer, Students, Teachers, Voluntary prayer*

Justice William Rehnquist, dissenting
Wallace v. Jaffree,
472 U.S. 38, 113 (1985)

George Washington himself, at the request of the very Congress which passed the Bill of Rights, proclaimed a day of "public thanksgiving and prayer, to be observed by acknowledging with grateful hearts the many and signal favors of Almighty God." History must judge whether it was the Father of his Country in 1789, or a majority of the Court today, which has strayed from the meaning of the Establishment Clause.

Keywords: *Bill of Rights, Congress, Establishment Clause, George Washington, God, Judicial authority, Prayer, Religion, Thanksgiving*

Justice Lewis Powell, concurring
Edwards v. Aguillard,
482 U.S. 578, 599 (1987)

A religious purpose alone is not enough to invalidate an act of a state legislature. The religious purpose must predominate.

Keywords: *Establishment Clause, Religion, State legislatures*

Justice Lewis Powell, concurring
Edwards v. Aguillard,
482 U.S. 578, 606–608 (1987)

As a matter of history, schoolchildren can and should properly be informed of all aspects of this Nation's religious heritage. I would see no constitutional problem if schoolchildren were taught the nature of the Founding Fathers' religious beliefs and how these beliefs affected the attitudes of the times and the structure of our government. Courses in comparative religion of course are customary and constitutionally appropriate. In fact, since religion permeates our history, a familiarity with the nature of religious beliefs is necessary to understand many historical as well as contemporary events. In addition, it is worth noting that the Establishment Clause does not prohibit per se the educational use of religious documents in public school education. Although this Court has recognized that the Bible is "an instrument of religion," it also has made clear that the Bible "may constitutionally be used in an appropriate study of history, civilization, ethics, comparative religion, or the like." The book is, in fact, "the world's all-time best seller" with undoubted literary and historic value apart from its religious content. The Establishment Clause is properly understood to prohibit the use of the Bible and other religious documents in public school education only when the purpose of the use is to advance a particular religious belief.

Keywords: *Beliefs, Bible, Civilization, Comparative religion, Education, Establishment Clause, Ethics, Founding Fathers, Heritage, History, Public* school, Religion, Religious documents, Schoolchildren

Justice Antonin Scalia, dissenting
Edwards v. Aguillard,
482 U.S. 578, 615 (1987)
Our cases in no way imply that the Establishment Clause forbids legislators merely to act upon their religious convictions. We surely would not strike down a law providing money to feed the hungry or shelter the homeless if it could be demonstrated that, but for the religious beliefs of the legislators, the funds would not have been approved. Also, political activism by the religiously motivated is part of our heritage. Notwithstanding the majority's implication to the contrary, we do not presume that the sole purpose of a law is to advance religion merely because it was supported strongly by organized religions or by adherents of particular faiths. To do so would deprive religious men and women of their right to participate in the political process. Today's religious activism may give us the Balanced Treatment Act, but yesterday's resulted in the abolition of slavery, and tomorrow's may bring relief for famine victims.
Keywords: Establishment Clause, Faiths, Heritage, Judicial review, Legislators, Political activism, Political process, Religion

Justice Antonin Scalia, dissenting
Lee v. Weisman,
505 U.S. 577, 631–632 (1992)
In holding that the Establishment Clause prohibits invocations and benedictions at public school graduation ceremonies, the Court—with nary a mention that it is doing so—lays waste a tradition that is as old as public school graduation ceremonies themselves, and that is a component of an even more longstanding American tradition of nonsectarian prayer to God at public celebrations generally. As its instrument of destruction, the bulldozer of its social engineering, the Court invents a boundless, and boundlessly manipulable, test of psychological coercion, which promises to do for the Establishment Clause what the Durham rule did for the insanity defense.
Keywords: Benedictions, Establishment Clause, Graduations, History, Invocations, Public schools, Sectarian, Social engineering

Justice Antonin Scalia, concurring
Lamb's Chapel v. Center Moriches Union Free School District,
508 U.S. 385, 399 (1993)
For my part, I agree with the long list of constitutional scholars who have criticized *Lemon* [v. *Kurtzman* (1971)] and bemoaned the strange Establishment Clause geometry of crooked lines and wavering shapes its intermittent use has produced.
Keywords: Constitutionality, Criticism, Establishment Clause

Chief Justice William Rehnquist
Zobrest v. Catalina Foothills School District,
509 U.S. 1, 13 (1993)
... the task of a sign-language interpreter seems to us quite different from that of a teacher or guidance counselor. ... the Establishment Clause lays down no ab-

solute bar to the placing of a public employee in a sectarian school. Such a flat rule, smacking of antiquated notions of "taint," would indeed exalt form over substance. Nothing in this record suggests that a sign-language interpreter would do more than accurately interpret whatever material is presented to the class as a whole. In fact, ethical guidelines require interpreters to "transmit everything that is said in exactly the same way it was intended." James' parents have chosen of their own free will to place him in a pervasively sectarian environment. The sign-language interpreter they have requested will neither add to nor subtract from that environment, and hence the provision of such assistance is not barred by the Establishment Clause.

Keywords: *Education, Establishment Clause, Guidance counselor, Interpreter, Sectarian schools, Sign-language, Teacher*

10. Liberty, Freedom, Happiness

This chapter provides evidence of how the Court conceptualizes personal freedoms and liberties. Some would argue that this is, in fact, a study of the implementation of the Ninth Amendment.

Justice William Johnson, dissenting
Shanks v. Dupont,
28 U.S. 242, 258 (1830)
... a government cannot be too liberal in extending to individuals the right of using their talents and seeking their fortunes wherever their judgments may lead them. ...
Keywords: *Fortunes, Government, Judgment, Talents*

Justice Joseph Story
The Amistad,
40 U.S. 518, 596–597 (1841)
When the *Amistad* arrived, she was in possession of the negroes, asserting their freedom; and in no sense could they possibly intend to import themselves here, as slaves, or for sale as slaves.
Keywords: *Freedom, Slavery*

Justice Robert Grier
Phalen v. Virginia,
49 U.S. 163, 168 (1850)
Experience has shown that the common forms of gambling are innocuous when placed in contrast with the widespread pestilence of lotteries. The former are confined to a few persons and places, but the latter infests the whole community; it enters every dwelling; it reaches every class; it preys upon the hard earnings of the poor; it plunders the ignorant and simple.
Keywords: *Experience, Gambling, Lotteries*

Justice Peter Daniel, dissenting
Barber v. Barber,
62 U.S. 582, 602 (1858)
It is not in accordance with the design and operation of a Government having its origin in causes and necessities, political, general, and external, that it should assume to regulate the domestic relations of society; should, with a kind of inquisitorial authority, enter the habitations and even into the chambers and nurseries of private families, and inquire into and pronounce upon the morals and habits and affections or antipathies of the members of every household.
Keywords: *Domestic Relations, Families, Government intrusion, Habits, Morals, Privacy*

Justice Stephen Field
Cummings v. Missouri,
71 U.S. 277, 320 (1866)
The deprivation of any rights, civil or political, previously enjoyed, may be punishment, the circumstances attending and the causes of the deprivation determining this fact.
Keywords: *Civil rights, Liberties, Political rights, Punishment*

Justice Samuel Miller, dissenting
Ex parte Garland,
71 U.S. 333, 395 (1866)
The Constitution of the United States provides as a qualification for the offices of President and Vice-President that the person elected must be a native-born citizen. Is this a punishment to all those naturalized citizens who can never attain that qualification? The constitutions of nearly all the States require as a qualification for voting that the voter shall be a white male citizen. Is this a punishment for all the blacks who can never become white?

Keywords: *Native-born citizens, Naturalized citizens, Oaths, President, Qualifications, State constitutions, Vice president*

Justice Joseph Bradley, dissenting
Blyew v. United States,
80 U.S. 581, 599 (1871)
To deprive a whole class of the community of this right, to refuse their evidence and their sworn complaints, is to brand them with a badge of slavery; is to expose them to wanton insults and fiendish assaults; is to leave their lives, their families, and their property unprotected by law. It gives unrestricted license and impunity to vindictive outlaws and felons to rush upon these helpless people and kill and slay them at will, as was done in this case. To say that actions or prosecutions intended for the redress of such outrages are not "causes affecting the persons" who are the victims of them, is to take, it seems to me, a view of the law too narrow, too technical, and too forgetful of the liberal objects it had in view.

If, in such a raid as I have supposed, a colored person is merely wounded or maimed, but is still capable of making complaint, and on appearing to do so, has the doors of justice shut in his face on the ground that he is a colored person, and cannot testify against a white citizen, it seems to me almost a stultification of the law to say that the case is not within its scope.

Keywords: *Citizens, Justice, Outlaws, Prosecutions, Race, Rule of law, Slavery, Victims, Witnesses*

Justice Joseph Bradley, dissenting
Blyew v. United States,
80 U.S. 581, 601 (1871)
Slavery, when it existed, extended its influence in every direction, depressing and disfranchising the slave and his race in every possible way. Hence, in order to give full effect to the National will in abolishing slavery, it was necessary in some way to counteract these various disabilities and the effects flowing from them. Merely striking off the fetters of the slave, without removing the incidents and consequences of slavery, would hardly have been a boon to the colored race.

Keywords: *Abolition, Race, Slavery*

Justice Stephen Field, dissenting
In re Slaughter-House Cases,
83 U.S. 36, 91 (1872)
The abolition of slavery and involuntary servitude was intended to make every one born in this country a freeman, and as such to give to him the right to pursue the ordinary avocations of life without other restraint than such as affects all oth-

ers, and to enjoy equally with them the fruits of his labor. A prohibition to him to pursue certain callings, open to others of the same age, condition, and sex, or to reside in places where others are permitted to live, would so far deprive him of the rights of a freeman, and would place him, as respects others, in a condition of servitude. A person allowed to pursue only one trade or calling, and only in one locality of the country, would not be, in the strict sense of the term, in a condition of slavery, but probably none would deny that he would be in a condition of servitude. He certainly would not possess the liberties nor enjoy the privileges of a freeman. The compulsion which would force him to labor even for his own benefit only in one direction, or in one place, would be almost as oppressive and nearly as great an invasion of his liberty as the compulsion which would force him to labor for the benefit or pleasure of another, and would equally constitute an element of servitude.

Keywords: *Abolition, Employment, Freeman, Involuntary servitude, Labor, Liberty, Privileges, Servitude, Slavery*

Justice Joseph Bradley, concurring
Bradwell v. Illinois,
83 U.S. 130, 141 (1872)

Man is, or should be, woman's protector and defender. The natural and proper timidity and delicacy which belongs to the female sex evidently unfits it for many of the occupations of civil life. The constitution of the family organization, which is founded in the divine ordinance, as well as in the nature of things, indicates the domestic sphere as that which properly belongs to the domain and functions of womanhood. The harmony, not to say identity, of interests and views which belong, or should belong, to our family institution is repugnant to the idea of a woman adopting a distinct and independent career from that of her husband. The paramount destiny and mission of woman are to fulfil the noble and benign offices of wife and mother. This is the law of the Creator.

Keywords: *Careers, Civil life, Divine ordinance, Family law, Family organization, Gender equality, Man, Womanhood*

Justice Stephen Field, dissenting
Munn v. Illinois,
94 U.S. 113, 142 (1876)

By the term "liberty," as used in the provision, something more is meant than mere freedom from physical restraint or the bounds of a prison. It means freedom to go where one may choose, and to act in such manner, not inconsistent with the equal rights of others, as his judgment may dictate for the promotion of his happiness; that is, to pursue such callings and avocations as may be most suitable to develop his capacities, and give to them their highest enjoyment.

Keywords: *Freedom, Liberty, Physical restraint, Prison*

Justice Henry Brown
Plessy v. Ferguson,
163 U.S. 537, 551 (1896)

The argument . . . assumes social prejudices may be overcome by legislation, and that equal rights cannot be secured to the negro except by an enforced commingling of the two races. We cannot accept this proposition. If the two races are to meet upon terms of social equality, it must be the result of natural affinities, a mutual appreciation of each other's merits and a voluntary consent of individuals.

Keywords: Equal rights, Legislation, Race, Social equality, Social prejudices

Justice Oliver Wendell Holmes
Davis v. Mills,
194 U.S. 451, 457 (1904)
Constitutions are intended to preserve practical and substantial rights, not to maintain theories. It is pretty safe to assume that when the law may deprive a man of all the benefits of what once was his, it may deprive him of technical title as well.

Keywords: Constitutions, Law, Practical rights, Substantial rights

Justice Charles Evans Hughes
Chicago, B. & Q.R. Co. v. McGuire,
219 U.S. 549, 567 (1911)
. . . freedom of contract is a qualified and not an absolute right. There is no absolute freedom to do as one wills or to contract as one chooses. The guaranty of liberty does not withdraw from legislative supervision that wide department of activity which consists of the making of contracts, or deny to government the power to provide restrictive safeguards. Liberty implies the absence of arbitrary restraint, not immunity from reasonable regulations and prohibitions imposed in the interests of the community.

Keywords: Arbitrary restraint, Community interests, Contracts, Freedom of contract, Immunity, Legislative supervision, Liberty, Regulations, Safeguards

Justice Charles Evans Hughes
Truax v. Raich,
239 U.S. 33, 41 (1915)
It requires no argument to show that the right to work for a living in the common occupations of the community is of the very essence of the personal freedom and opportunity that it was the purpose of the amendments to secure.

Keywords: Community, Occupations, Personal freedom, Right to work

Justice William Day
United States v. Doremus,
249 U.S. 86, 93–94 (1919)
Every tax is in some measure regulatory. To some extent it interposes an economic impediment to the activity taxed as compared with others not taxed. But a tax is not any the less a tax because it has a regulatory effect.

Keywords: Activity, Economic impediment, Regulatory, Tax

Justice James McReynolds
Meyer v. Nebraska,
262 U.S. 390, 399 (1923)
Without doubt, it [liberty in the Fourteenth Amendment] denotes not merely freedom from bodily restraint but also the right of the individual to contract, to engage in any of the common occupations of life, to acquire useful knowledge, to marry, establish a home and bring up children, to worship God according to the dictates of his own conscience, and generally to enjoy those privileges long

recognized at common law as essential to the orderly pursuit of happiness by free men.

Keywords: *Bodily restraint, Children, Common law, Conscience, Contract, Family, Fourteenth Amendment, Freedom, Freemen, Knowledge, Liberty, Marriage, Occupations, Privileges, Pursuit of happiness, Worship*

Justice James McReynolds
Pierce v. Society of Sisters of the Holy Names of Jesus and Mary,
268 U.S. 510, 535 (1925)
The fundamental theory of liberty upon which all governments in this Union repose excludes any general power of the State to standardize its children by forcing them to accept instruction from public teachers only. The child is not the mere creature of the State; those who nurture him and direct his destiny have the right, coupled with the high duty, to recognize and prepare him for additional obligations.

Keywords: *Children, Liberty, Public school teachers, State*

Justice Oliver Wendell Holmes
Buck v. Bell,
274 U.S. 200, 207 (1927)
We have seen more than once that the public welfare may call upon the best citizens for their lives. It would be strange if it could not call upon those who already sap the strength of the State for these lesser sacrifices, often not felt to be such by those concerned, in order to prevent our being swamped with incompetence. It is better for all the world, if instead of waiting to execute degenerate

offspring for crime, or to let them starve for their imbecility, society can prevent those who are manifestly unfit from continuing their kind.

Keywords: *Citizens, Degenerate offspring, Imbecility, Incompetence, Mental illness, Procreation, Public welfare, Society, State*

Justice George Sutherland
Jones v. Securities and Exchange Commission,
298 U.S. 1, 26 (1936)
The citizen, when interrogated about his private affairs, has a right before answering to know why the inquiry is made; and if the purpose disclosed is not a legitimate one, he may not be compelled to answer.

Keywords: *Citizen, Interrogation, Private affairs*

Justice George Sutherland, dissenting
Associated Press v. National Labor Review Board,
301 U.S. 103, 135 (1937)
No one can read the long history which records the stern and often bloody struggles by which these cardinal rights were secured, without realizing how necessary it is to preserve them against any infringement, however slight.

Keywords: *Cardinal rights, History, Infringement*

Justice George Sutherland, dissenting
Associated Press v. National Labor Review Board,
301 U.S. 103, 137 (1937)
Freedom is not a mere intellectual abstraction; and it is not merely a word to

adorn an oration upon occasions of patriotic rejoicing. It is an intensely practical reality, capable of concrete enjoyment in a multitude of ways day by day.
Keywords: Freedom, Intellectual abstraction, Patriotism

Justice George Sutherland, dissenting
Associated Press v. National Labor Review Board,
301 U.S. 103, 141 (1937)
. . . the saddest epitaph which can be carved in memory of a vanished liberty is that it was lost because its possessors failed to stretch forth a saving hand while yet there was time.
Keyword: Liberty

Justice Harlan Fiske Stone, dissenting
Minersville School District v. Gobitis,
310 U.S. 586, 604 (1940)
The guaranties of civil liberty are but guaranties of freedom of the human mind and spirit and of reasonable freedom and opportunity to express them.
Keywords: Civil liberty, Expression, Freedom, Mind, Spirit

Chief Justice Charles Evans Hughes
Cox v. New Hampshire,
312 U.S. 569, 574 (1941)
Civil liberties, as guaranteed by the Constitution, imply the existence of an organized society maintaining public order without which liberty itself would be lost in the excesses of unrestrained abuses.
Keywords: Civil liberties, Liberties, Public order, Organized society, Unrestrained abuses

Justice Frank Murphy, dissenting
Goldman v. United States,
316 U.S. 129, 138 (1942)
The conditions of modern life have greatly expanded the range and character of those activities which require protection from intrusive action by government officials if men and women are to enjoy the full benefit of that privacy which the Fourth Amendment was intended to provide. It is our duty to see that this historic provision receives a construction sufficiently liberal and elastic to make it serve the needs and manners of each succeeding generation. Otherwise, it may become obsolete, incapable of providing the people of this land adequate protection. To this end we must give mind not merely to the exact words of the amendment, but also to its historic purpose, its high political character, and its modern social and legal implications.
Keywords: Constitutional construction, Constitutional interpretation, Fourth Amendment, Intrusive act, Modern life, Political character, Privacy

Justice William Douglas
Skinner v. Oklahoma ex rel Williamson,
316 U.S. 535, 541 (1942)
We are dealing here with legislation which involves one of the basic civil rights of man. Marriage and procreation are fundamental to the very existence and survival of the race. There is no redemption for the individual whom the law touches. Any experiment [of compulsory sterilization] which the State conducts is to his irreparable injury. He is forever deprived of a basic liberty.

Keywords: *Civil rights, Legislation, Marriage, Procreation, Race, Sterilization*

Justice Felix Frankfurter
McNabb v. United States,
318 U.S. 332, 347 (1943)
The history of liberty has largely been the history of observance of procedural safeguards.
Keywords: *History, Liberty, Procedure*

Justice Stanley Reed, dissenting
Martin v. Struthers,
319 U.S. 141, 157 (1943)
The First Amendment does not compel a pedestrian to pause on the street to listen to the argument supporting another's views of religion or politics. Once the door is opened, the visitor may not insert a foot and insist on a hearing. He certainly may not enter the home. To knock or ring, however, comes close to such invasions. To prohibit such a call leaves open distribution of the notice on the street or at the home without signal to announce its deposit. Such assurance of privacy falls far short of an abridgment of freedom of the press.
Keywords: *First Amendment, Free press, Pedestrian, Politics, Privacy, Religion*

Justice Hugo Black
Marsh v. Alabama,
326 U.S. 501, 506 (1946)
Ownership does not always mean absolute dominion. The more an owner, for his advantage, opens up his property for use by the public in general, the more do his rights become circumscribed by the statutory and constitutional rights of those who use it. Thus, the owners of privately held bridges, ferries, turnpikes and railroads may not operate them as freely as a farmer does his farm. Since these facilities are built and operated primarily to benefit the public and since their operation is essentially a public function, it is subject to state regulation.
Keywords: *Constitutional rights, Ownership, Property, Public benefit, Public function, State regulation, Statutory rights*

Justice Frank Murphy, concurring
Duncan v. Kahanamoku,
327 U.S. 304, 330 (1946)
From time immemorial despots have used real or imagined threats to the public welfare as an excuse for needlessly abrogating human rights.
Keywords: *Despotism, History, Human rights, Liberty, Public welfare*

Justice Felix Frankfurter, concurring
Adamson v. California,
332 U.S. 46, 62 (1947)
It is not invidious to single out Miller, Davis, Bradley, Waite, Matthews, Gray, Fuller, Holmes, Brandeis, Stone and Cardozo (to speak only of the dead) as judges who were alert in safeguarding and promoting the interests of liberty and human dignity through law. But they were also judges mindful of the relation of our federal system to a progressively democratic society and therefore duly regardful of the scope of authority that was left to the states even after the Civil War.
Keywords: *Democratic society, Federal System, Human dignity, Judges, Liberty, Scope of authority, States*

Justice Hugo Black, dissenting
Adamson v. California,
332 U.S. 46, 89 (1947)
I cannot consider the Bill of Rights to be an outworn 18th century "strait jacket." . . . Its provisions may be thought outdated abstractions by some. And it is true that they were designed to meet ancient evils. But they are the same kind of human evils that have emerged from century to century wherever excessive power is sought by the few at the expense of the many. In my judgment the people of no nation can lose their liberty so long as a Bill of Rights like ours survives and its basic purposes are conscientiously interpreted, enforced and respected so as to afford continuous protection against old, as well as new, devices and practices which might thwart those purposes.
Keywords: *Ancient evils, Bill of Rights, History, Human evils, Liberty, Power*

Justice Hugo Black, dissenting
H.P. Hood & Sons v. DuMond,
336 U.S. 525, 562 (1949)
The Due Process Clause and Commerce Clause have been used like Siamese twins in a never ending stream of challenges to government regulation.
Keywords: *Commerce Clause, Constitutional adjudication, Due Process Clause, Governmental regulations*

Justice Felix Frankfurter, dissenting
United States v. Rabinowitz,
339 U.S. 56, 69 (1950)
It is a fair summary of history to say that the safeguards of liberty have frequently been forged in controversies involving not very nice people.

Keywords: *History, Liberty, Safeguards*

Justice William Douglas, dissenting
United States v. Wunderlich,
342 U.S. 98, 101 (1951)
Law has reached its finest moments when it has freed man from the unlimited discretion of some ruler, some civil or military official, some bureaucrat. Where discretion is absolute, man has always suffered. At times it has been his property that has been invaded; at times, his privacy; at times, his liberty of movement; at times, his freedom of thought; at times, his life. Absolute discretion is a ruthless master. It is more destructive of freedom than any of man's other inventions.
Keywords: *Bureaucrat, Despot, Discretion, Freedom, Freedom of thought, Liberty, Privacy, Property*

Justice William Douglas, concurring
United States v. Rumely,
345 U.S. 41, 58 (1953)
If the lady from Toledo can be required to disclose what she read yesterday and what she will read tomorrow, fear will take the place of freedom in the libraries, book stores, and homes of the land.
Keywords: *Fear, Freedom, Liberty, Privacy*

Justice William Douglas, dissenting
Barsky v. Board of Regents,
347 U.S. 442, 472 (1954)
The right to work, I had assumed, was the most precious liberty that man possesses. Man has indeed as much right to work as he has to live, to be free, to own

property. The American ideal was stated by Emerson in his essay on politics, "A man has a right to be employed, to be trusted, to be loved, to be revered." It does many men little good to stay alive and free and propertied, if they cannot work. To work means to eat. It also means to live. For many it would be better to work in jail, than to sit idle on the curb. The great values of freedom are in the opportunities afforded man to press to new horizons, to pit his strength against the forces of nature, to match skills with his fellow man.

Keywords: Freedom, Liberty, Right to work, Values

Chief Justice Earl Warren
Bolling v. Sharpe,
347 U.S. 497, 499–500 (1954)
Although the Court has not assumed to define "liberty" with any great precision, that term is not confined to mere freedom from bodily restraint. Liberty under law extends to the full range of conduct which the individual is free to pursue, and it cannot be restricted except for a proper governmental objective.

Keywords: Bodily restraint, Conduct, Freedom, Governmental objective, Liberty

Justice Felix Frankfurter, concurring
Griffin v. Illinois,
351 U.S. 12, 23 (1956)
Law addresses itself to actualities. It does not face actuality to suggest that Illinois affords every convicted person, financially competent or not, the opportunity to take an appeal, and that it is not Illinois that is responsible for

disparity in material circumstances. Of course a State need not equalize economic conditions. A man of means may be able to afford the retention of an expensive, able counsel not within reach of a poor man's purse. Those are contingencies of life which are hardly within the power, let alone the duty, of a State to correct or cushion. But when a State deems it wise and just that convictions be susceptible to review by an appellate court, it cannot by force of its exactions draw a line which precludes convicted indigent persons, forsooth erroneously convicted, from securing such a review merely by disabling them from bringing to the notice of an appellate tribunal errors of the trial court which would upset the conviction were practical opportunity for review not foreclosed.

Keywords: Appellate review, Conviction, Counsel, Financial wherewithal, Indigence, Law, Life, States

Chief Justice Earl Warren
Rathbun v. United States,
355 U.S. 107, 111 (1957)
Common experience tells us that a call to a particular telephone number may cause the bell to ring in more than one ordinarily used instrument. Each party to a telephone conversation takes the risk that the other party may have an extension telephone and may allow another to overhear the conversation. When such takes place there has been no violation of any privacy of which the parties may complain.

Keywords: Privacy, Telephone

Justice William Douglas, concurring
Gibson v. Florida Legislative Committee,
372 U.S. 539, 565 (1963)
In my view, government is not only powerless to legislate with respect to membership in a lawful organization; it is also precluded from probing the intimacies of spiritual and intellectual relationships in the myriad of such societies and groups that exist in this country, regardless of the legislative purpose sought to be served.
Keywords: *Associations, Groups, Legislation, Legislative intent, Organizations, Rights*

Justice William Douglas
Griswold v. Connecticut,
381 U.S. 479, 484 (1965)
. . . specific guarantees in the Bill of Rights have penumbras, formed by emanations from those guarantees that help give them life and substance. Various guarantees create zones of privacy.
Keywords: *Bill of Rights, Emanations, Penumbras, Privacy, Rights*

Justice Hugo Black, dissenting
Griswold v. Connecticut,
381 U.S. 479, 509–510 (1965)
"Privacy" is a broad, abstract and ambiguous concept which can easily be shrunken in meaning but which can also easily be interpreted as a constitutional ban against many things other than searches and seizures. . . . I get nowhere in this case by talk about a constitutional "right to privacy" as an emanation from one or more constitutional provisions. I like my privacy as well as the next one, but I am nevertheless compelled to ad-

mit that government has a right to invade it unless prohibited by some specific constitutional provision.
Keywords: *Constitutional rights, Privacy, Searches, Seizures*

Justice Hugo Black
Afroyim v. Rusk,
387 U.S. 253, 267–268 (1967)
Citizenship is no light trifle to be jeopardized any moment Congress decides to do so under the name of one of its general or implied grants of power. In some instances, loss of citizenship can mean that a man is left without the protection of citizenship in any country in the world—as a man without a country. Citizenship in this Nation is a part of a cooperative affair. Its citizenry is the country and the country is its citizenry. The very nature of our free government makes it completely incongruous to have a rule of law under which a group of citizens temporarily in office can deprive another group of citizens of their citizenship.
Keywords: *Citizenship, Congress, Democracy, Freedom, Implied powers, International affairs, Rule of law*

Justice William Douglas, dissenting
Warden v. Hayden,
387 U.S. 294, 323–324 (1967)
Privacy involves the choice of the individual to disclose or to reveal what he believes, what he thinks, what he possesses. The article may be a non-descript work of art, a manuscript of a book, a personal account book, a diary, invoices, personal clothing, jewelry, or whatnot. Those who wrote the Bill of Rights believed that every individual needs both

to communicate with others and to keep his affairs to himself. That dual aspect of privacy means that the individual should have the freedom to select for himself the time and circumstances when he will share his secrets with others and decide the extent of that sharing. This is his prerogative not the States.' The Framers, who were as knowledgeable as we, knew what police surveillance meant and how the practice of rummaging through one's personal effects could destroy freedom.
Keywords: *Bill of Rights, Framers, Freedom, Liberty, Police surveillance, Privacy*

Justice John Marshall Harlan, concurring
Terry v. Ohio,
392 U.S. 1, 32 (1968)
Any person, including a policeman, is at liberty to avoid a person he considers dangerous.
Keywords: *Danger, Liberty, Police*

Justice Hugo Black, dissenting
Tinker v. Des Moines Independent School District,
393 U.S. 503, 524 (1969)
Uncontrolled and uncontrollable liberty is an enemy to domestic peace.
Keywords: *Domestic peace, Liberty*

Justice Abe Fortas, dissenting
Street v. New York,
394 U.S. 576, 616 (1969)
If a state statute provided that it is a misdemeanor to burn one's shirt or trousers or shoes on the public thoroughfare, it could hardly be asserted that the citizen's constitutional right is violated. If the arsonist asserted that he was burning his shirt or trousers or shoes as a protest against the Government's fiscal policies, for example, it is hardly possible that his claim to First Amendment shelter would prevail against the State's claim of a right to avert danger to the public and to avoid obstruction to traffic as a result of the fire. This is because action, even if clearly for serious protest purposes, is not entitled to the pervasive protection that is given to speech alone.
Keywords: *Constitutional rights, Criminality, First Amendment, Free speech, Police power, States, Statutes*

Justice Abe Fortas, dissenting
Street v. New York,
394 U.S. 576, 618 (1969)
One may not justify burning a house, even if it is his own, on the ground, however sincere, that he does so as a protest. One may not justify breaking the windows of a government building on that basis. Protest does not exonerate lawlessness. And the prohibition against flag burning on the public thoroughfare being valid, the misdemeanor is not excused merely because it is an act of flamboyant protest.
Keywords: *First Amendment, Flag burning, Free speech, Lawlessness, Protest*

Justice William Douglas
Wisconsin v. Constantineau,
400 U.S. 433, 437 (1971)
Where a person's good name, reputation, honor, or integrity is at stake because of what the government is doing to him, notice and an opportunity to be heard are essential.
Keywords: *Good name, Governmental intrusion, Honor, Integrity, Privacy, Reputation*

Justice John Marshall Harlan
Boddie v. Connecticut,
401 U.S. 371, 376 (1971)
Without a prior judicial imprimatur, individuals may freely enter into and rescind commercial contracts, for example, but we are unaware of any jurisdiction where private citizens may covenant for or dissolve marriages without state approval. Even where all substantive requirements are concededly met, we know of no instance where two consenting adults may divorce and mutually liberate themselves from the constraints of legal obligations that go with marriage, and more fundamentally the prohibition against remarriage, without invoking the State's judicial machinery.
Keywords: *Contracts, Divorce, Judiciary, Legal obligations, Marriage, Remarriage, State*

Justice William Douglas
Eisenstadt v. Baird,
405 U.S. 438, 453 (1972)
It is true that in *Griswold* the right of privacy in question inhered in the marital relationship. Yet the marital couple is not an independent entity with a mind and heart of its own, but an association of two individuals each with a separate intellectual and emotional make-up. If the right of privacy means anything, it is the right of an individual, married or single, to be free from unwarranted governmental intrusion into matters so fundamentally affecting a person as the decision whether to bear or beget a child.
Keywords: *Family, Governmental intrusion, Marital relationship, Privacy, Rights, Sexual relations*

Justice Potter Stewart
Lynch v. Household Finance Corp.,
405 U.S. 538, 552 (1972)
. . . the dichotomy between personal liberties and property rights is a false one. Property does not have rights. People have rights. The right to enjoy property without unlawful deprivation, no less than the right to speak or the right to travel, is, in truth, a "personal" right, whether the "property" in question be a welfare check, a home or a savings account. In fact, a fundamental interdependence exists between the personal right to liberty and the personal right to property. Neither could have meaning without the other. That rights in property are basic civil rights has long been recognized.
Keywords: *Civil rights, Deprivation, Freedom, Personal liberties, Property rights*

Justice Lewis Powell
United States v. United States District Court,
407 U.S. 297, 314 (1972)
History abundantly documents the tendency of Government—however benevolent and benign its motives—to view with suspicion those who most fervently dispute its policies. Fourth Amendment protection becomes the more necessary when the targets of official surveillance may be those suspected of unorthodoxy in their political beliefs. The danger to political dissent is acute where the Government attempts to act under so vague a concept as the power to protect "domestic security."
Keywords: *Domestic security, Fourth Amendment, Governmental intrusion,*

History, Liberties, Political beliefs, Political dissent, Privacy, Surveillance

Justice Lewis Powell, dissenting
Rosario v. Rockefeller,
410 U.S. 752, 766 (1973)
Deferment of a right . . . can be tantamount to its denial.
Keyword: *Rights*

Justice Byron White, concurring
Smith v. Goguen,
415 U.S. 566, 584–585 (1974)
It should not be beyond the reasonable comprehension of anyone who would conform his conduct to the law to realize that sewing a flag on the seat of his pants is contemptuous of the flag.
Keywords: *Conduct, Desecration, Flag*

Justice William Douglas, dissenting
DeFunis v. Odegaard,
416 U.S. 312, 337 (1974)
There is no constitutional right for any race to be preferred. The years of slavery did more than retard the progress of blacks. Even a greater wrong was done the whites by creating arrogance instead of humility and by encouraging the growth of the fiction of a superior race. There is no superior person by constitutional standards.
Keywords: *Constitutional rights, Race, Slavery*

Justice William Douglas, dissenting
Jackson v. Metropolitan Edison Co.,
419 U.S. 345, 361 (1974)
I agree that doctors, lawyers, and grocers are not transformed into state actors simply because they provide arguably essential goods and services and are regulated by the State.
Keywords: *Police power, Private sector, Public interest, Regulations, States*

Justice Thurgood Marshall, dissenting
Jackson v. Metropolitan Edison Co.,
419 U.S. 345, 372 (1974)
Private parties performing functions affecting the public interest can often make a persuasive claim to be free of the constitutional requirements applicable to governmental institutions because of the value of preserving a private sector in which the opportunity for individual choice is maximized.
Keywords: *Freedom, Liberty, Private sector, Privacy, Public interest*

Per Curiam
Buckley v. Valeo,
424 U.S. 1, 68 (1976)
It is undoubtedly true that public disclosure of contributions to candidates and political parties will deter some individuals who otherwise might contribute. In some instances, disclosure may even expose contributors to harassment or retaliation. These are not insignificant burdens on individual rights, and they must be weighed carefully against the interests which Congress has sought to promote by this legislation.
Keywords: *Candidates, Congressional intent, Contributions, Electoral*

process, Political parties, Privacy, Rights

Chief Justice Warren Burger, concurring in part, dissenting in part
Buckley v. Valeo,
424 U.S. 1, 237 (1976)
The public right to know ought not be absolute when its exercise reveals private political convictions. Secrecy, like privacy, is not per se criminal. On the contrary, secrecy and privacy as to political preferences and convictions are fundamental in a free society. For example, one of the great political reforms was the advent of the secret ballot as a universal practice.
Keywords: *Freedom, Political beliefs, Political preferences, Privacy, Public interest, Secrecy*

Justice William Brennan, dissenting
Paul v. Davis,
424 U.S. 693, 734–735 (1976)
. . . the analysis has a hollow ring in light of the Court's acceptance of the truth of the allegation that the "active shoplifter" label would "seriously impair future employment opportunities." This is clear recognition that an official "badge of infamy" affects tangible interests of the defamed individual and not merely an abstract interest in how people view him; for the "badge of infamy" has serious consequences in its impact on no less than the opportunities open to him to enjoy life, liberty, and the pursuit of happiness. It is inexplicable how the Court can say that a person's status is "altered" when the State suspends him from school, revokes his driver's license, fires him from a job, or denies him the right

to purchase a drink of alcohol, but is in no way "altered" when it officially pins upon him the brand of a criminal, particularly since the Court recognizes how deleterious will be the consequences that inevitably flow from its official act. Our precedents clearly mandate that a person's interest in his good name and reputation is cognizable as a "liberty" interest within the meaning of the Due Process Clause, and the Court has simply failed to distinguish those precedents in any rational manner in holding that no invasion of a "liberty" interest was effected in the official stigmatizing of respondent as a criminal without any "process" whatsoever. . . . I have always thought that one of this Court's most important roles is to provide a formidable bulwark against governmental violation of the constitutional safeguards securing in our free society the legitimate expectations of every person to innate human dignity and sense of worth. It is a regrettable abdication of that role and a saddening denigration of our majestic Bill of Rights when the Court tolerates arbitrary and capricious official conduct branding an individual as a criminal without compliance with constitutional procedures designed to ensure the fair and impartial ascertainment of criminal culpability. Today's decision must surely be a short-lived aberration.
Keywords: *Arbitrary and capricious, Badge of infamy, Bill of Rights, Criminality, Defamation, Dignity, Due process, Fairness, Freedom, Governmental intrusion, Invasion of privacy, Liberty, Official act, Pursuit of happiness*

Justice Harry Blackmun
Castaneda v. Partida,
430 U.S. 482, 499 (1977)
Because of the many facets of human motivation, it would be unwise to presume as a matter of law that human beings of one definable group will not discriminate against other members of that group.
Keywords: *Discrimination, Human motivations, Group identity*

Justice William Rehnquist, dissenting
Carey v. Population Services International,
431 U.S. 678, 717 (1978)
Those who valiantly but vainly defended the heights of Bunker Hill in 1775 made it possible that men such as James Madison might later sit in the first Congress and draft the Bill of Rights to the Constitution. The post-Civil War Congresses which drafted the Civil War amendments to the Constitution could not have accomplished their task without the blood of brave men on both sides which was shed at Shiloh, Gettysburg, and Cold Harbor. If those responsible for these Amendments, by feats of valor or efforts of draftsmanship, could have lived to know that their efforts had enshrined in the Constitution the right of commercial vendors of contraceptives to peddle them to unmarried minors through such means as window displays and vending machines located in the men's room of truck stops, notwithstanding the considered judgment of the New York Legislature to the contrary, it is not difficult to imagine their reaction.

Keywords: *Advertising, Civil War amendments, Commercial vendors, Contraception, History, Marriage, Minors*

Justice Lewis Powell
Ambach v. Norwick,
441 U.S. 68, 75 (1979)
The distinction between citizens and aliens, though ordinarily irrelevant to private activity, is fundamental to the definition and government of a State. The assumption of citizenship status denotes an association with the polity which, in a democratic republic, exercises the powers of governance. The form of this association is important; an oath of allegiance or similar ceremony cannot substitute for the unequivocal legal bond citizenship represents. It is because of this special significance of citizenship that governmental entities, when exercising the functions of government, have wider latitude in limiting the participation of noncitizens.
Keywords: *Aliens, Citizenship, Democratic republic, Governance, Governmental entities, Noncitizens, Oath of allegiance, Polity, Private activity, States*

Justice William Brennan
Carey v. Brown,
447 U.S. 455, 471 (1980)
The State's interest in protecting the wellbeing, tranquility, and privacy of the home is certainly of the highest order in a free and civilized society.
Keywords: *Civilization, Liberty, Privacy, Societal interests, State interest*

Justice Potter Stewart
Harris v. McRae,
448 U.S. 297, 316 (1980)
. . . regardless of whether the freedom of a woman to choose to terminate her pregnancy for health reasons lies at the core or the periphery of the due process liberty recognized in *Wade,* it simply does not follow that a woman's freedom of choice carries with it a constitutional entitlement to the financial resources to avail herself of the full range of protected choices.
Keywords: Abortion, Choice, Constitutional entitlement, Due process, Financial resources, Freedom, Health, Liberty, Pregnancy, Woman

Justice Potter Stewart
Harris v. McRae,
448 U.S. 297, 325 (1980)
Abortion is inherently different from other medical procedures, because no other procedure involves the purposeful termination of a potential life.
Keywords: Abortion, Medical procedures, Potential life

Justice Thurgood Marshall, dissenting
Harris v. McRae,
448 U.S. 297, 338 (1980)
The Court's opinion studiously avoids recognizing the undeniable fact that for women eligible for Medicaid—poor women—denial of a Medicaid-funded abortion is equivalent to denial of legal abortion altogether. By definition, these women do not have the money to pay for an abortion themselves. If abortion is medically necessary and a funded abortion is unavailable, they must resort to back-alley butchers, attempt to induce an abortion themselves by crude and dangerous methods, or suffer the serious medical consequences of attempting to carry the fetus to term. Because legal abortion is not a realistic option for such women, the predictable result of the Hyde Amendment will be a significant increase in the number of poor women who will die or suffer significant health damage because of an inability to procure necessary medical services.
Keywords: Abortion, Health, Medicaid, Money, Medically necessary, Poor women

Justice Harry Blackmun
Santosky v. Kramer,
455 U.S. 745, 753 (1982)
The fundamental liberty interest of natural parents in the care, custody, and management of their child does not evaporate simply because they have not been model parents or have lost temporary custody of their child to the State.
Keywords: Children, Custody, Fundamental liberty, Parents, States

Justice William Rehnquist
Schall v. Martin,
467 U.S. 253, 265 (1984)
Children, by definition, are not assumed to have the capacity to take care of themselves. They are assumed to be subject to the control of their parents, and if parental control falters, the State must play its part as parens patriae.
Keywords: Children, Parens patriae, Parents, States

Justice Harry Blackmun
Thornburgh v. American College of
Obstetricians & Gynecologists,
476 U.S. 747, 772 (1986)
Our cases long have recognized that the Constitution embodies a promise that a certain private sphere of individual liberty will be kept largely beyond the reach of government. That promise extends to women as well as to men. Few decisions are more personal and intimate, more properly private, or more basic to individual dignity and autonomy, than a woman's decision—with the guidance of her physician and within the limits specified in *Roe*—whether to end her pregnancy. A woman's right to make that choice freely is fundamental. Any other result, in our view, would protect inadequately a central part of the sphere of liberty that our law guarantees equally to all.
Keywords: Abortion, Choice, Government intrusion, Liberty, Pregnancy, Roe

Justice John Paul Stevens, concurring
Thornburgh v. American College of
Obstetricians & Gynecologists,
476 U.S. 747, 781 (1986)
Acceptance of the fundamental premises that underlie the decision in *Roe v. Wade*, as well as the application of those premises in that case, places the primary responsibility for decision in matters of childbearing squarely in the private sector of our society. The majority remains free to preach the evils of birth control and abortion and to persuade others to make correct decisions while the individual faced with the reality of a diffi-

cult choice having serious and personal consequences of major importance to her own future—perhaps to the salvation of her own immortal soul—remains free to seek and to obtain sympathetic guidance from those who share her own value preferences.
Keywords: Abortion, Birth control, Childbearing, Private sector, Soul, Roe, Values

Justice John Paul Stevens, concurring
Thornburgh v. American College of
Obstetricians & Gynecologists,
476 U.S. 747, 781–782 (1986)
In the final analysis, the holding in *Roe v. Wade* presumes that it is far better to permit some individuals to make incorrect decisions than to deny all individuals the right to make decisions that have a profound effect upon their destiny. Arguably a very primitive society would have been protected from evil by a rule against eating apples; a majority familiar with Adam's experience might favor such a rule. But the lawmakers who placed a special premium on the protection of individual liberty have recognized that certain values are more important than the will of a transient majority.
Keywords: Lawmakers, Liberty, Rights, Roe, Values

Justice Byron White, dissenting
Thornburgh v. American College of
Obstetricians & Gynecologists,
476 U.S. 747, 790 (1986)
Fundamental liberties and interests are most clearly present when the Constitution provides specific textual recognition of their existence and importance.

Thus, the Court is on relatively firm ground when it deems certain of the liberties set forth in the Bill of Rights to be fundamental and therefore finds them incorporated in the Fourteenth Amendment's guarantee that no State may deprive any person of liberty without due process of law. When the Court ventures further and defines as "fundamental" liberties that are nowhere mentioned in the Constitution (or that are present only in the so-called "penumbras" of specifically enumerated rights), it must, of necessity, act with more caution, lest it open itself to the accusation that, in the name of identifying constitutional principles to which the people have consented in framing their Constitution, the Court has done nothing more than impose its own controversial choices of value upon the people.

Keywords: Bill of Rights, Constitutional principles, Due process, Enumerated rights, Fourteenth Amendment, Framers, Fundamental liberties, Incorporation, Judicial authority, Judicial legitimacy, Judicial will, Penumbras, States

Justice William Brennan
Houston v. Hill,
482 U.S. 451, 471–472 (1987)
We are mindful that the preservation of liberty depends in part upon the maintenance of social order.
Keywords: Liberty, Social order

Justice William Brennan, dissenting
California v. Greenwood,
486 U.S. 35, 45–46 (1988)
Scrutiny of another's trash is contrary to commonly accepted notions of civilized behavior. I suspect, therefore, that members of our society will be shocked to learn that the Court, the ultimate guarantor of liberty, deems unreasonable our expectation that the aspects of our private lives that are concealed safely in a trash bag will not become public.
Keywords: Civilized behavior, Liberty, Society, Trash

Justice Anthony Kennedy
Treasury Employees v. Von Raab,
489 U.S. 656, 679 (1989)
We hold that the suspicionless testing of employees who apply for promotion to positions directly involving the interdiction of illegal drugs, or to positions that require the incumbent to carry a firearm, is reasonable. The Government's compelling interests in preventing the promotion of drug users to positions where they might endanger the integrity of our Nation's borders or the life of the citizenry outweigh the privacy interests of those who seek promotion to these positions, who enjoy a diminished expectation of privacy by virtue of the special, and obvious, physical and ethical demands of those positions.
Keywords: Compelling interest, Drug testing, Firearms, Illegal drugs, Privacy, Probable cause, Public employees, Public interest

Justice William Brennan, dissenting
Michael H. v. Gerald D.,
491 U.S. 110, 141 (1989)
In construing the Fourteenth Amendment to offer shelter only to those interests specifically protected by historical practice,

moreover, the plurality ignores the kind of society in which our Constitution exists. We are not an assimilative, homogeneous society, but a facilitative, pluralistic one, in which we must be willing to abide someone else's unfamiliar or even repellent practice because the same tolerant impulse protects our own idiosyncrasies. Even if we can agree, therefore, that "family" and "parenthood" are part of the good life, it is absurd to assume that we can agree on the content of those terms and destructive to pretend that we do. In a community such as ours, "liberty" must include the freedom not to conform. The plurality today squashes this freedom by requiring specific approval from history before protecting anything in the name of liberty.

Keywords: *Conformity, Fourteenth Amendment, Freedom, Historical practice, Judicial interpretation, Liberty, Society*

Justice Anthony Kennedy
Patterson v. McLean Credit Union,
491 U.S. 164, 188 (1989)

The law now reflects society's consensus that discrimination based on the color of one's skin is a profound wrong of tragic dimension. Neither our words nor our decisions should be interpreted as signaling one inch of retreat from Congress' policy to forbid discrimination in the private, as well as the public, sphere. Nevertheless, in the area of private discrimination, to which the ordinance of the Constitution does not directly extend, our role is limited to interpreting what Congress may do and has done.

Keywords: *Congressional power, Discrimination, Judicial authority, Policy, Private discrimination*

Justice William Brennan
Texas v. Johnson,
491 U.S. 397, 419–420 (1989)

The way to preserve the flag's special role is not to punish those who feel differently about these matters. It is to persuade them that they are wrong. . . . And, precisely because it is our flag that is involved, one's response to the flag-burner may exploit the uniquely persuasive power of the flag itself. We can imagine no more appropriate response to burning a flag than waving one's own, no better way to counter a flag-burner's message than by saluting the flag that burns, no surer means of preserving the dignity even of the flag that burned than by—as one witness here did—according its remains a respectful burial. We do not consecrate the flag by punishing its desecration, for in doing so we dilute the freedom that this cherished emblem represents.

Keywords: *Desecration, Dignity, Emblem, Flag, Flag-burning, Freedom, Message*

Justice Anthony Kennedy, concurring in part, dissenting in part
Hodgson v. Minnesota,
497 U.S. 417, 501 (1990)

It is true that, for all too many young women, the prospect of two parents, perhaps even one parent, sustaining her with support that is compassionate and committed is an illusion. Statistics on drug and alcohol abuse by parents and documentations of child neglect and mistreatment are but fragments of the evidence showing the tragic reality that becomes day-to-day life for thousands of minors. But the Court errs in serious degree when it commands its own solution to the cruel consequences of individual misconduct, parental failure, and social ills. The legislative authority is entitled to attempt to meet these wrongs by taking reasonable measures to recognize and promote the primacy of the family tie, a concept which this Court now seems intent on declaring a constitutional irrelevance.

Keywords: *Alcohol abuse, Child neglect, Drugs, Evidence, Family, Legislative authority, Minors, Parental failure, Parents, Social ills, Statistics, Women*

Justice Harry Blackmun
International Union, UAW v. Johnson Controls, Inc.,
499 U.S. 187, 206 (1991)
Decisions about the welfare of future children must be left to the parents who conceive, bear, support, and raise them rather than to the employers who hire those parents.

Keywords: *Child rearing, Children, Health and welfare, Employers, Parents*

Justice Anthony Kennedy
Edmonson v. Leesville Concrete Co.,
500 U.S. 614, 630–631 (1991)
If our society is to continue to progress as a multiracial democracy, it must recognize that the automatic invocation of race stereotypes retards that progress, and causes continued hurt and injury.

Keywords: *Democracy, Multiracial society, Race, Stereotypes*

Justice Antonin Scalia, concurring
Barnes v. Glen Theatre, Inc.,
501 U.S. 560, 574–575 (1991)
The dissent confidently asserts that the purpose of restricting nudity in public places in general is to protect nonconsenting parties from offense; and argues that, since only consenting, admission-paying patrons see respondents dance, that purpose cannot apply, and the only remaining purpose must relate to the communicative elements of the performance. Perhaps the dissenters believe that "offense to others" ought to be the only reason for restricting nudity in public places generally, but there is no basis for thinking that our society has ever shared that Thoreauvian "you-may-do-what-you-like-so-long-as-it-does-not-injure-someone-else" beau ideal—much less for thinking that it was written into the Constitution.

Keywords: *Communicative elements, Dance, Nudity, Performance, Public places, Restrictions*

Justice Sandra Day O'Connor
Planned Parenthood of Southeastern Pennsylvania v. Casey,
505 U.S. 833, 844 (1992)
Liberty finds no refuge in a jurisprudence of doubt.

Keywords: *Jurisprudence, Liberty, Philosophy*

Justice Antonin Scalia, dissenting
Romer v. Evans,
517 U.S. 620, 644 (1996)
The Court's opinion contains grim, disapproving hints that Coloradans have been guilty of "animus" or "animosity"

toward homosexuality, as though that has been established as Unamerican. Of course it is our moral heritage that one should not hate any human being or class of human beings. But I had thought that one could consider certain conduct reprehensible—murder, for example, or polygamy, or cruelty to animals—and could exhibit even "animus" toward such conduct. Surely that is the only sort of "animus" at issue here: moral disapproval of homosexual conduct. . . .

Keywords: *Conduct, Heritage, Homosexuality, Morality, States*

Justice John Paul Stevens, concurring
Washington v. Glucksberg,
117 S. Ct. 2302, 2305 (1997)

A State, like Washington, that has authorized the death penalty and thereby has concluded that the sanctity of human life does not require that it always be preserved, must acknowledge that there are situations in which an interest in hastening death is legitimate. Indeed, not only is that interest sometimes legitimate, I am also convinced that there are times when it is entitled to constitutional protection.

Keywords: *Constitutional protection, Constitutional rights, Death, Death penalty, Human life, Right to die*

Justice David Souter, concurring
Washington v. Glucksberg,
117 S. Ct. 2258, 2293 (1997)

One must bear in mind that the nature of the right claimed, if recognized as one constitutionally required, would differ in no essential way from other constitutional rights guaranteed by enumeration or derived from some more definite tex-

tual source than "due process." An unenumerated right should not therefore be recognized, with the effect of displacing the legislative ordering of things, without the assurance that its recognition would prove as durable as the recognition of those other rights differently derived. To recognize a right of lesser promise would simply create a constitutional regime too uncertain to bring with it the expectation of finality that is one of this Court's central obligations in making constitutional decisions.

Keywords: *Constitutional regime, Constitutional rights, Due process, Enumerated rights, Unenumerated rights*

Chief Justice William Rehnquist, dissenting
Saenz v. Roe,
526 U.S. ___, ___ (1999)

. . . I cannot see how the right to become a citizen of another State is a necessary "component" of the right to travel, or why the Court tries to marry these separate and distinct rights. A person is no longer "traveling" in any sense of the word when he finishes his journey to a State which he plans to make his home. Indeed, under the Court's logic, the protections of the Privileges or Immunities Clause recognized in this case come into play only when an individual stops traveling with the intent to remain and become a citizen of a new State. The right to travel and the right to become a citizen are distinct, their relationship is not reciprocal, and one is not a "component" of the other.

Keywords: *Citizenship, Privileges and Immunities Clause, Right to travel, State*

Justice Stephen Breyer, dissenting
College Savings Bank v. Florida Prepaid Postsecondary Education Expense Board,
527 U.S. ___, ___ (1999)
Federalism helps to protect liberty not simply in our modern sense of helping the individual remain free of restraints imposed by a distant government, but more directly by promoting the sharing among citizens of governmental decisionmaking authority.
Keywords: *Citizens, Federalism, Governmental decision making, Individual, Liberty*

Justice Antonin Scalia, dissenting
Chicago v. Morales,
527 U.S. ___, ___ (1999)
The citizens of Chicago were once free to drive about the city at whatever speed they wished. At some point Chicagoans (or perhaps Illinoisans) decided this would not do, and imposed prophylactic speed limits designed to assure safe operation by the average (or perhaps even subaverage) driver with the average (or perhaps even subaverage) vehicle. This infringed upon the "freedom" of all citizens, but was not unconstitutional. Similarly, the citizens of Chicago were once free to stand around and gawk at the scene of an accident. At some point Chicagoans discovered that this obstructed traffic and caused more accidents. They did not make the practice unlawful, but they did authorize police officers to order the crowd to disperse, and imposed penalties for refusal to obey such an order. Again, this prophylactic measure infringed upon the "freedom" of all citizens, but was not unconstitu-

tional. Until the ordinance that is before us today was adopted, the citizens of Chicago were free to stand about in public places with no apparent purpose— to engage, that is, in conduct that appeared to be loitering. In recent years, however, the city has been afflicted with criminal street gangs. As reflected in the record before us, these gangs congregated in public places to deal in drugs, and to terrorize the neighborhoods by demonstrating control over their "turf." Many residents of the inner city felt that they were prisoners in their own homes. Once again, Chicagoans decided that to eliminate the problem it was worth restricting some of the freedom that they once enjoyed. The means they took was similar to the second, and more mild, example given above rather than the first: Loitering was not made unlawful, but when a group of people occupied a public place without an apparent purpose and in the company of a known gang member, police officers were authorized to order them to disperse, and the failure to obey such an order was made unlawful. The minor limitation upon the free state of nature that this prophylactic arrangement imposed upon all Chicagoans seemed to them (and it seems to me) a small price to pay for liberation of their streets. The majority today invalidates this perfectly reasonable measure by ignoring our rules governing facial challenges, by elevating loitering to a constitutionally guaranteed right, and by discerning vagueness where, according to our usual standards, none exists.
Keywords: *Citizens, Constitutional*

rights, *Freedom, Law, Liberation, Loitering, Police, Safety, Street gangs*

Justice Clarence Thomas, dissenting
Chicago v. Morales,
527 U.S. ___, ___ (1999)
By focusing exclusively on the imagined "rights" of the two percent, the Court today has denied our most vulnerable citizens the very thing that Justice Stevens elevates above all else—the "freedom of movement." And that is a shame.
Keywords: *Citizens, Freedom of movement, Rights*

11. The Arrest . . . The Trial . . . The Punishment

How the United States treats its most despicable citizens (criminals) can be considered a direct reflection of the validity of its system based on liberty and freedom for all. In this chapter you will find the constant struggle for which social philosophy controls the reins of the criminal justice system.

Justice William Day
Weeks v. United States,
232 U.S. 383, 393 (1914)
The efforts of the courts and their officials to bring the guilty to punishment . . . are not to be aided by the sacrifice of those great principles established by years of endeavor and suffering which have resulted in their embodiment in the fundamental law of the land.
Keywords: *Fundamental law, Guilt, Principles, Punishment*

Justice Harlan Fiske Stone
McGuire v. United States,
273 U.S. 95, 99 (1927)
A criminal prosecution is more than a game in which the government may be checkmated and the game lost merely because its officers have not played according to rule.
Keywords: *Criminal prosecution*

Justice Louis Brandeis, dissenting
Olmstead v. United States,
277 U.S. 438, 474 (1928)
The progress of science in furnishing the government with means of espionage is not likely to stop with wiretapping. Ways may some day be developed by which the government, without removing papers from secret drawers, can reproduce them in court, and by which it will be enabled to expose to a jury the most intimate occurrences of the home. Advances in the psychic and related sciences may bring means of exploring unexpressed beliefs, thoughts and emotions. . . . Can it be that the Constitution affords no protection against such invasions of individual security?
Keywords: *Beliefs, Emotions, Espionage, Individual security, Jury, Science, Thoughts, Wiretap*

Justice Oliver Wendell Holmes
McBoyle v. United States,
283 U.S. 25, 27 (1931)
Although it is not likely that a criminal will carefully consider the text of the law before he murders or steals, it is reasonable that a fair warning should be given to the world in language that the common world will understand, of what the law intends to do is a certain line is passed. To make the warning fair, so far as possible the line should be clear.

Keywords: Criminal, Fair warning, Statutory language

Justice George Sutherland
Powell v. Alabama,
287 U.S. 45, 68–69 (1932)
The right to be heard would be, in many cases, of little avail if it did not comprehend the right to be heard by counsel. Even the intelligent and educated layman has small and sometimes no skill in the science of law. If charged with crime, he is incapable, generally, of determining for himself whether the indictment is good or bad. He is unfamiliar with the rules of evidence. Left without the aid of counsel he may be put on trial without a proper charge, and convicted upon incompetent evidence, or evidence irrelevant to the issue or otherwise inadmissible. He lacks both the skill and knowledge adequately to prepare his defense, even though he have a perfect one. He requires the guiding hand of counsel at every step in the proceedings against him. Without it, though he may be not guilty, he faces the danger of conviction because he does not know how to establish his innocence.
Keywords: Conviction, Counsel, Crime, Defense, Evidence, Guilt, Indictment, Innocence, Right to be heard, Science of law, Trial

Chief Justice Charles Evans Hughes
Sorrells v. United States,
287 U.S. 435, 450 (1932)
Where defendant has been duly indicted for an offense found to be within the statute, and the proper authorities seek to proceed with the prosecution, the court cannot refuse to try the case in the constitutional method because it desires to let the defendant go free.
Keywords: Constitutional method, Defendant, Indictment, Judiciary, Prosecution

Justice Benjamin Cardozo
Snyder v. Massachusetts,
291 U.S. 97, 122 (1934)
Privileges so fundamental as to be inherent in every concept of a fair trial that could be acceptable to the thought of reasonable men will be kept inviolate and inviolable, however crushing may be the pressure of incriminating proof. But justice, though due to the accused, is due to the accuser also. The concept of fairness must not be strained till it is narrowed to a filament. We are to keep the balance true.
Keywords: Accused, Fair trial, Justice, Proof

Justice Owen Roberts
Hansen v. Haff,
291 U.S. 559, 562–563 (1934)
People not of good moral character, like others, travel from place to place and change their residence. But to say that because they indulge in illegal or immoral acts, they travel for that purpose, is to emphasize that which is incidental and ignore what is of primary significance.
Keywords: Moral character, Travel

Chief Justice Charles Evans Hughes
United States v. Wood,
299 U.S. 123, 145 (1936)
Impartiality is not a technical conception. It is a state of mind.
Keywords: Impartial, State of mind

Justice Owen Roberts
United States v. Norris,
300 U.S. 564, 574 (1937)
Perjury is an obstruction of justice; its perpetration well may affect the dearest concerns of the parties before a tribunal. Deliberate material falsification under oath constitutes the crime of perjury, and the crime is complete when a witness's statement has once been made. It is argued that to allow retraction of perjured testimony promotes the discovery of the truth and, if made before the proceeding is concluded, can do no harm to the parties. The argument overlooks the tendency of such a view to encourage false swearing in the belief that if the falsity be not discovered before the end of the hearing it will have its intended effect, but, if discovered, the witness may purge himself of crime by resuming his role as witness and substituting the truth for his previous falsehood. It ignores the fact that the oath administered to the witness calls on him freely to disclose the truth in the first instance and not to put the court and the parties to the disadvantage, hindrance, and delay of ultimately extracting the truth by cross-examination, by extraneous investigation or other collateral means.
Keywords: *Crime, Cross-examination, Falsehood, Material falsification, Oath, Obstruction of justice, Perjury, Testimony, Tribunal, Truth, Witness*

Justice Benjamin Cardozo
Palko v. Connecticut,
302 U.S. 319, 328 (1937)
The state is not attempting to wear the accused out by a multitude of cases with accumulated trials. It asks no more than this, that the case against him shall go on until there shall be a trial free from the corrosion of substantial legal error. This is not cruelty at all, nor even vexation in any immoderate degree.
Keywords: *Accused, Legal error, Retrial, Trials*

Justice George Sutherland, dissenting
Nardone v. United States,
302 U.S. 379, 387 (1938)
My abhorrence of the odious practices of the town gossip, the peeping Tom, and the private eavesdropper is quite as strong as that of any of my brethren. But to put the sworn officers of the law, engaged in the detection and apprehension of organized gangs of criminals, in the same category, is to lose all sense of proportion.
Keywords: *Criminal degree, Crime, Gangs, Law enforcement, Surveillance*

Justice Hugo Black
Johnson v. Zerbst,
304 U.S. 458, 465 (1938)
The purpose of the constitutional guaranty of a right to counsel is to protect an accused from conviction resulting from his own ignorance of his legal and constitutional rights, and the guaranty would be nullified by a determination that an accused's ignorant failure to claim his rights removes the protection of the constitution.
Keywords: *Accused, Constitutional rights, Conviction, Legal rights, Right to counsel*

Justice Hugo Black
Chambers v. Florida,
309 U.S. 227, 241 (1940)

Today, as in ages past, we are not without tragic proof that the exalted power of some governments to punish manufactured crime dictatorially is the handmaid of tyranny. Under our constitutional system, courts stand against any winds that blow as havens of refuge for those who might otherwise suffer because they are helpless, weak, outnumbered, or because they are non-conforming victims of prejudice and public excitement.

Keywords: *Constitutional system, Crime, Dictatorship, Government, Prejudice, Public excitement, Tyranny, Victims*

Justice Stanley Reed
Edwards v. United States,
312 U.S. 473, 482 (1941)

The refusal to permit the accused to prove his defense may prove trivial when the facts are developed. Procedural errors often are. But procedure is the skeleton which forms and supports the whole structure of a case. The lack of a bone mars the symmetry of the body. The parties must be given an opportunity to plead and prove their contentions or else the impression of the judge arising from sources outside the record dominates results. The requirement that allegations must be supported by evidence tested by cross-examination protects against falsehood. The opportunity to assert rights through pleading and testimony is essential to their successful protection. Infringement of that opportunity is forbidden.

Keywords: *Accused, Allegations, Cross-examination, Defense, Evidence, Falsehood, Pleading, Procedural errors, Testimony*

Justice Felix Frankfurter, dissenting
Glasser v. United States,
315 U.S. 60, 89 (1942)

The fact that Glasser is an attorney, of course, does not mean that he is not entitled to the protection which is afforded all persons by the Sixth Amendment. But the fact that he is an attorney with special experience in criminal cases, and not a helpless illiterate, may be—as we believe it to be here—extremely relevant in determining whether he was denied such protection.

Keywords: *Attorney, Constitutional protection, Criminal cases, Sixth Amendment*

Justice Felix Frankfurter
Adams v. United States ex rel McCann,
317 U.S. 269, 276 (1943)

The Constitution does not compel an accused who admits his guilt to stand trial against his own wishes.

Keywords: *Accused, Guilt, Trial*

Chief Justice Harlan Fiske Stone
Viereck v. United States,
318 U.S. 236, 243 (1943)

The unambiguous words of a statute which imposes criminal penalties are not to be altered by judicial construction so as to punish one not otherwise within its reach, however deserving of punishment his conduct may seem.

Keywords: *Conduct, Criminal penalties, Judicial construction, Punishment, Statute*

Justice Felix Frankfurter
McNabb v. United States,
318 U.S. 332, 343 (1943)

A democratic society, in which respect for the dignity of all men is central, naturally guards against the misuse of the law enforcement process. Zeal in tracking down crime is not in itself an assurance of soberness of judgment. Disinterestedness in law enforcement does not alone prevent disregard of cherished liberties. Experience has therefore counseled that safeguards must be provided against the dangers of the overzealous as well as the despotic.

Keywords: *Crime, Democracy, Despotism, Dignity, Law enforcement, Liberty*

Justice Robert Jackson, dissenting
Bowles v. United States,
319 U.S. 33, 37 (1943)

. . . for some reason, the prosecution denied Bowles the right to inspect his Selective Service file and kept it out of evidence. What the file may reveal I do not know. I strongly suspect he will be no better off for seeing it. Yet the prosecuting attorneys presumably knew what was in the file and they withheld it from him. My experience indicates that it would be more reasonable to assume that they illegally suppressed the file to help their case than to assume such behavior was purposeless. I see no reason why the strong inferences that usually arise from suppression, destruction, or failure to produce evidence in control of a litigating party should not apply here.

Keywords: *Evidence, Litigating, Prosecution, Suppression*

Justice Hugo Black, concurring
Tot v. United States,
319 U.S. 463, 472 (1943)

. . . a verdict against a defendant must be preceded by the introduction of some evidence which tends to prove the elements of the crime charged.

Keywords: *Defendant, Elements of crime, Evidence, Verdict*

Justice Hugo Black, dissenting
Boone v. Lightner,
319 U.S. 561, 578 (1943)

The Court emphasizes that Boone is a member of the bar. But, for the duration of the war, he is primarily a soldier, with a job to do which Congress intended should overshadow personal interests, whether his or those of others who seek a personal judgment against him. It is difficult for me to believe that he could adequately have prepared for this trial without a leave of many weeks. The purpose of the [Soldiers' and Sailors' Civil Relief] Act is to prevent soldiers and sailors from being harassed by civil litigation "in order to enable such persons to devote their entire energy to the defense needs of the nation." He is required to devote himself to serious business, and should not be asked either to attempt to convince his superior officers of the importance of his private affairs or to spend his time hunting for lawyers.

Keywords: *Civil litigation, Lawyer, Legal bar, Private affair, Soldier, Superior officers, Trial, War*

Justice Robert Jackson, dissenting
Ashcraft v. Tennessee,
322 U.S. 143, 162 (1944)
If the constitutional admissibility of a confession is no longer to be measured by the mental state of the individual confessor but by a general doctrine dependent on the clock, it should be capable of statement in definite terms. If thirty-six hours is more than is permissible, what about 24? Or 12? Or 6? Or 1? All are "inherently coercive." Of course questions of law like this often turn on matters of degree. But are not the states entitled to know, if this court is able to state, what the considerations are which make any particular degree decisive? How else may state courts apply our tests?
Keywords: *Confession, Confessor, Constitutional admissibility, Judicial tests, Mental state, State courts*

Justice Hugo Black
Robinson v. United States,
324 U.S. 282, 286 (1945)
It is for Congress and not for us to decide whether it is wise public policy to inflict the death penalty at all.
Keywords: *Criminal law, Criminal procedure, Criminology, Death penalty, Legislative branch, Public policy*

Justice Wiley Rutledge, dissenting
Robinson v. United States,
324 U.S. 282, 292 (1945)
This case involves the law's extreme penalty. That penalty should not rest on doubtful command or vague and uncertain conditions. The words used here, for its imposition, are too general and unprecise, the purposes Congress had in using them too obscure and contradictory, the consequences of applying them are too capricious, whether for the victim or for the kidnapper, to permit their giving foundation for exercise of the power of life and death over the citizen, though he be a convicted criminal. Other penalties might be rectified with time, if wrong. This one cannot be.
Keywords: *Criminal law, Criminal procedure, Death penalty, Statutory interpretation*

Justice Wiley Rutledge, dissenting in part
Malinski v. New York,
324 U.S. 401, 428 (1945)
A man once broken in will does not readily, if ever, recover from the breaking. No change in circumstances can wholly wipe out its effects upon himself or upon others. Thereafter he acts with knowledge that the damage has been done. Others do likewise. He is suspect by his own mouth and must continue so, whether he repudiates or confirms the confession. If he repudiates, he incurs the additional suspicion of lying, and his credibility as a witness in his own behalf is impaired, if not destroyed. If he confirms, he does so with the knowledge he has already confessed and any other course will bring upon him the suspicions and the burden of proof they entail.
Keywords: *Burden of proof, Confession, Credibility, Lying, Witness*

Justice Frank Murphy, dissenting in part
Malinski v. New York,
324 U.S. 401, 434 (1945)
Those clothed with authority in court rooms of this nation have the duty to conduct and supervise proceedings so that an accused person may be adjudged solely according to the dictates of justice and reason. This duty is an especially high one in capital cases. Instead of an attitude of indifference and carelessness in such matters, judges and officers of the court should take the initiative to create an atmosphere free from undue passion and emotionalism. This necessarily requires the exclusion of attacks or appeals made by counsel tending to reflect upon the race, creed or color of the defendant. Here the defendants' very lives were at stake and it was of the utmost importance that the trial be conducted in surroundings free from poisonous and dangerous irrelevancies that might inflame the jury to the detriment of the defendants. Brazen appeals relating to their race or faith had no relevance whatever to the grave issue facing the jury and could only be designed to influence the jury unfairly; and subtle and indirect attacks were even more dangerous and effective. Statements of this character are the direct antithesis of every principle of American justice and fair play. They alone are enough to cast grave doubts upon the validity of the entire proceedings.
Keywords: *Accused, Capital cases, Character, Counsel, Creed, Defendant, Emotionalism, Fair play, Faith, Judicial authority, Jury, Justice, Race, Trial, Undue passion*

Justice William Douglas, dissenting
Cramer v. United States,
325 U.S. 1, 66 (1945)
Certainly a person who takes the stand in defense of a treason charge against him will not be presumed to commit perjury when he makes admissions against self-interest. Admissions against self-interest have indeed always been considered as the highest character of evidence.
Keywords: *Constitutional history, Defense, Evidence, Political history, Perjury, Self-interest, Treason*

Justice William Douglas
Screws v. United States,
325 U.S. 91, 108–109 (1945)
The fact that a prisoner is assaulted, injured, or even murdered by state officials does not necessarily mean that he is deprived of any right protected or secured by the constitution or laws of the United States.
Keywords: *Color of law, Constitutional rights, Criminal procedure, Fourteenth Amendment, Police, Prisoner, State officials*

Justice Frank Murphy, dissenting
Screws v. United States,
325 U.S. 91, 160–161 (1945)
We are told local authorities cannot be relied upon for courageous and prompt action, that often they have personal or political reasons for refusing to prosecute. If it be significantly true that crimes against local law cannot be locally prosecuted, it is an ominous sign indeed. In any event, the cure is a reinvigoration of State responsibility. It is not an undue incursion of remote federal authority into

local duties with consequent debilitation of local responsibility.

Keywords: *Federalism, Local authorities, Prosecution, Prosecutorial discretion, State responsibility*

Justice Hugo Black, dissenting
Williams v. North Carolina,
325 U.S. 226, 261–262 (1945)
Anglo-American law has, until today, steadfastly maintained the principle that before an accused can be convicted of crime, he must be proven guilty beyond a reasonable doubt. These petitioners have been sentenced to prison because they were unable to prove their innocence to the satisfaction of the state of North Carolina. They have been convicted under a statute so uncertain in its application that not even the most learned member of the bar could have advised them in advance as to whether their conduct would violate the law.

Keywords: *Accused, Burden of proof, Conduct, Criminal procedure, Guilt, Innocence, Reasonable doubt, Statutory ambiguity, Statutory intent*

Justice Hugo Black
In re Michael,
326 U.S. 224, 227–228 (1945)
All perjured relevant testimony is at war with justice, since it may produce a judgment not resting on truth. Therefore it cannot be denied that it tends to defeat the sole ultimate objective of a trial. It need not necessarily, however, obstruct or halt the judicial process. For the function of trial is to sift the truth from a mass of contradictory evidence, and to do so

the fact-finding tribunal must hear both truthful and false witnesses.

Keywords: *Evidence, Fact-finding, Judicial process, Justice, Testimony, Trial, Tribunal, Truth, Witnesses*

Justice Felix Frankfurter, dissenting
Thiel v. Southern Pacific Co.,
328 U.S. 217, 230 (1946)
. . . American society is happily not so fragmentized that those who get paid by the day adopt a different social outlook, have a different sense of justice, and a different conception of a juror's responsibility than their fellow workers paid by the week.

Keywords: *Juror, Justice, Society*

Justice Felix Frankfurter, dissenting
Fisher v. United States,
328 U.S. 463, 477 (1946)
A shocking crime puts law to its severest test.

Keywords: *Crime, Law*

Justice Harold Burton, dissenting
Louisiana ex rel Francis v. Resweber,
329 U.S. 459, 476 (1947)
If the state officials deliberately and intentionally had placed the relator in the electric chair five times and, each time, had applied electric current to his body in a manner not sufficient, until the final time, to kill him, such a form of torture would rival that of burning at the stake. Although the failure of the first attempt, in the present case, was unintended, the reapplication of the electric current will be intentional. How many deliberate and intentional reapplications of electric current does it take to produce a cruel, un-

usual and unconstitutional punishment?
Keywords: *Capital punishment, Cruel and unusual punishment, Death penalty, Eighth Amendment, Electric chair, Punishment, State officials, Torture*

Justice Felix Frankfurter, dissenting
Harris v. United States,
331 U.S. 145, 157 (1947)
A decision [on a Fourth Amendment controversy] may turn on whether one gives that Amendment a place second to none in the Bill of Rights, or considers it on the whole a kind of nuisance, a serious impediment in the war against crime.
Keywords: *Bill of Rights, Constitutional balance, Crime, Fourth Amendment*

Justice Felix Frankfurter, dissenting
Harris v. United States,
331 U.S. 145, 172 (1947)
Stooping to questionable methods neither enhances that respect for law which is the most potent element in law enforcement, nor, in the long run, do such methods promote successful prosecution. In this country police testimony is often rejected by juries precisely because of a widely entertained belief that illegal methods are used to secure testimony. Thus, dubious police methods defeat the very ends of justice by which such methods are justified.
Keywords: *Juries, Justice, Law enforcement, Police methods, Police testimony, Prosecution, Testimony*

Justice Frank Murphy, dissenting
Harris v. United States,
331 U.S. 145, 183 (1947)
The Court today has resurrected and approved, in effect, the use of the odious general warrant or writ of assistance, presumably outlawed forever from our society by the fourth amendment. A warrant of arrest, without more, is now sufficient to justify an unlimited search of a man's home from cellar to garret for evidence of any crime, provided only that he is arrested in his home. Probable cause for the search need not be shown; an oath or affirmation is unnecessary; no description of the place to be searched or the things to be seized need be given; and the magistrate's judgment that these requirements have been satisfied is now dispensed with. In short, all the restrictions put upon the issuance and execution of search warrants by the fourth amendment are now dead letters as to those who are arrested in their homes.
Keywords: *Affirmation, Arrest, Arrest warrant, Crime, Evidence, Fourth Amendment, Magistrate's judgment, Oath, Probable cause, Search, Search Warrant, Seizure, Warrant, Writ of assistance*

Justice Robert Jackson, dissenting
Harris v. United States,
331 U.S. 145, 195 (1947)
I do not criticize the officers involved in this case, because this court's decisions afford them no clear guidance.
Keywords: *Judicial guidance, Law enforcement*

Justice Robert Jackson
United States v. Bayer,
331 U.S. 532, 540–541 (1947)
... after an accused has once let the cat out of the bag by confessing, no matter what

the inducement, he is never thereafter free of the psychological and practical disadvantages of having confessed. He can never get the cat back in the bag. The secret is out for good. In such a sense, a later confession always may be looked upon as fruit of the first. But this Court has never gone so far as to hold that making a confession under circumstances which preclude its use, perpetually disables the confessor from making a usable one after those conditions have been removed.

Keywords: *Accused, Confession, Confessor*

Justice Robert Jackson, dissenting
Price v. Johnston,
334 U.S. 266, 297 (1948)
Perjury has few terrors for a man already sentenced to 65 years' imprisonment for a crime of violence. Even such honor as exists among thieves is not too precious to be sacrificed for a chance at liberty.

Keywords: *Imprisonment, Liberty, Perjury, Violent crime*

Justice William Douglas
McDonald v. United States,
335 U.S. 451, 456 (1948)
Power is a heady thing; and history shows that the police acting on their own cannot be trusted.

Keywords: *History, Police, Power, Trust*

Justice Wiley Rutledge, dissenting
Michelson v. United States,
335 U.S. 469, 489 (1948)
General bad character, much less general bad reputation, has not yet become a criminal offense in our scheme. Our whole tradition is that a man can be punished by criminal sanctions only for specific acts defined beforehand to be criminal, not for general misconduct or bearing a reputation for such misconduct.

Keywords: *Character, Criminal, Criminal offense, Criminal sanctions, Misconduct, Reputation*

Justice William Douglas, concurring
United States v. Carignan,
342 U.S. 36, 46 (1951)
What happens behind doors that are opened and closed at the sole discretion of the police is a black chapter in every country—the free as well as the despotic, the modern as well as the ancient.

Keywords: *Despot, Police*

Justice Hugo Black, dissenting
Gallegos v. Nebraska,
342 U.S. 55, 73–74 (1951)
Americans justly complain when their fellow citizens in certain European countries are pounced upon at will by state police, held in jail incommunicado, and later convicted of crime on confessions obtained during such incarceration. Yet in part upon just such a confession, this court today affirms Nebraska's conviction of a citizen of Mexico who can neither read nor understand English.

Keywords: *Confessions, Crime, Incarceration, Jail, Literacy, State police*

Justice Felix Frankfurter
Rochin v. California,
342 U.S. 165, 172 (1952)
. . . we are compelled to conclude that the proceedings by which this conviction was obtained do more than offend

some fastidious squeamishness or private sentimentalism about combatting crime too energetically. This is conduct that shocks the conscience. Illegally breaking into the privacy of the petitioner, the struggle to open his mouth and remove what was there, the forcible extraction of his stomach's contents—this course of proceeding by agents of government to obtain evidence is bound to offend even hardened sensibilities. They are methods too close to the rack and the screw to permit of constitutional differentiation.
Keywords: *Conviction, Crime, Privacy, Search and seizure, Shocks the conscience*

Justice Robert Jackson
Morissette v. United States,
342 U.S. 246, 250–251 (1952)
The contention that an injury can amount to a crime only when inflicted by intention is no provincial or transient notion. It is as universal and persistent in mature systems of law as belief in freedom of human will and a consequent ability and duty of the normal individual to choose between good and evil. A relation between some mental element and punishment for a harmful act is almost as instinctive as the child's familiar exculpatory "But I didn't mean to," and has afforded the rational basis for a tardy and unfinished substitution of deterrence and reformation in place of retaliation and vengeance as the motivation for public prosecution.
Keywords: *Crime, Deterrence, Human will, Motivation, Public prosecution, Reformation, Retaliation, Vengeance*

Justice Robert Jackson
On Lee v. United States,
343 U.S. 747, 756 (1952)
Society can ill afford to throw away the evidence produced by the falling out, jealousies, and quarrels of those who live by outwitting the law. Certainly no one would foreclose the turning of state's evidence by denizens of the underworld.
Keyword: *Evidence*

Justice Felix Frankfurter, dissenting
On Lee v. United States,
343 U.S. 747, 758 (1952)
To approve legally what we disapprove morally, on the ground of practical convenience, is to yield to a short-sighted view of practicality. It derives from a preoccupation with what is episodic and a disregard of long-run consequences.
Keywords: *Judicial approval, Morality, Practicality*

Justice Tom Clark
Breithaupt v. Abram,
352 U.S. 432, 439 (1957)
Modern community living requires modern scientific methods of crime detection lest the public go unprotected. The increasing slaughter on our highways, most of which should be avoidable, now reaches the astounding figures only heard of on the battlefield. The States, through safety measures, modern scientific methods, and strict enforcement of traffic laws, are using all reasonable means to make automobile driving less dangerous.
Keywords: *Automobiles, Crime detection, Driving, Highway, Law enforcement, Police power, Safety, Science, States, Traffic laws*

Justice William Douglas, dissenting
Breithaupt v. Abram,
352 U.S. 432, 444 (1957)
. . . if the decencies of a civilized state are the test, it is repulsive to me for the police to insert needles into an unconscious person in order to get the evidence necessary to convict him, whether they find the person unconscious, give him a pill which puts him to sleep, or use force to subdue him. The indignity to the individual is the same in one case as in the other, for in each is his body invaded and assaulted by the police who are supposed to be the citizen's protector.
Keywords: *Civilized state, Conviction, Evidence, Indignity, Police*

Justice Hugo Black
Schware v. Board of Bar Examiners of New Mexico,
353 U.S. 232, 241 (1957)
The mere fact that a man has been arrested has very little, if any, probative value in showing that he has engaged in any misconduct.
Keywords: *Arrest, Misconduct, Probative value*

Justice Hugo Black
Reid v. Covert,
354 U.S. 1, 5–6 (1957)
The United States is entirely a creature of the Constitution. Its power and authority have no other source. It can only act in accordance with all the limitations imposed by the Constitution. When the Government reaches out to punish a citizen who is abroad, the shield which the Bill of Rights and other parts of the Constitution provide to protect his life and liberty

should not be stripped away just because he happens to be in another land.
Keywords: *Authority, Bill of Rights, Liberty, Power, Punishment*

Justice Felix Frankfurter
Mallory v. United States,
354 U.S. 449, 456 (1957)
It is not the function of the police to arrest, as it were, at large and to use an interrogating process at police headquarters in order to determine whom they should charge before a committing magistrate on "probable cause."
Keywords: *Arrest, Interrogation, Magistrate, Police, Probable cause*

Justice Hugo Black
Green v. United States,
355 U.S. 184, 187–188 (1957)
The underlying idea [of the Double Jeopardy Clause], one that is deeply ingrained in at least the Anglo-American system of jurisprudence, is that the state with all its resources and power should not be allowed to make repeated attempts to convict an individual for an alleged offense, thereby subjecting him to embarrassment, expense and ordeal and compelling him to live in a continuing state of anxiety and insecurity, as well as enhancing the possibility that even though innocent he may be found guilty.
Keywords: *Alleged offense, Conviction, Double jeopardy, Guilt, Innocence, Jurisprudence*

Justice William Douglas, dissenting
Crooker v. California,
357 U.S. 433, 446–447 (1958)
No matter how well educated, and how

well trained in the law an accused may be, he is sorely in need of legal advice once he is arrested for an offense that may exact his life. The innocent as well as the guilty may be caught in a web of circumstantial evidence that is difficult to break. A man may be guilty of indiscretions but not of the crime. He may be implicated by ambiguous circumstances difficult to explain away. He desperately needs a lawyer to help extricate him if he's innocent.

Keywords: Accused, Arrest, Circumstantial evidence, Guilt, Innocence, Lawyer, Legal advice, Legal counsel, Legal training

Justice Potter Stewart
Robinson v. California,
370 U.S. 660, 668 (1962)
It is unlikely that any State at this moment in history would attempt to make it a criminal offense for a person to be mentally ill, or a leper, or to be afflicted with a venereal disease. A State might determine that the general health and welfare require that the victims of these and other human afflictions be dealt with by compulsory treatment, involving quarantine, confinement, or sequestration. But, in the light of contemporary human knowledge, a law which made a criminal offense of such a disease would doubtless be universally thought to be an infliction of cruel and unusual punishment in violation of the Eighth and Fourteenth Amendments.

Keywords: Compulsory treatment, Confinement, Criminal offense, Cruel and unusual punishment, Disease, Eighth Amendment, Fourteenth Amendment, Health and welfare, History, Mentally ill, Quarantine, Sequestration, State, Victims

Justice Tom Clark, dissenting
Edwards v. South Carolina,
372 U.S. 229, 244 (1963)
. . . to say that the police may not intervene until the riot has occurred is like keeping out the doctor until the patient dies.

Keywords: Police, Riot

Justice Hugo Black
Gideon v. Wainwright,
372 U.S. 335, 344 (1963)
Governments, both state and federal, quite properly spend vast sums of money to establish machinery to try defendants accused of crime. Lawyers to prosecute are everywhere deemed essential to protect the public's interest in an orderly society. Similarly, there are few defendants charged with crime, few indeed, who fail to hire the best lawyers they can get to prepare and present their defenses. That government hires lawyers to prosecute and defendants who have the money hire lawyers to defend are the strongest indications of the widespread belief that lawyers in criminal courts are necessities, not luxuries. The right of one charged with crime to counsel may not be deemed fundamental and essential to fair trials in some countries, but it is in ours.

Keywords: Accusation, Constitutional rights, Counsel, Crime, Criminal Courts, Defendants, Defense, Fair trial, Government, Lawyers, Orderly society, Prosecution, Public's interest

Justice Byron White, dissenting
Massiah v. United States,
377 U.S. 201, 209 (1964)
It is only a sterile syllogism—an unsound one, besides—to say that because [the accused] had a right to counsel's aid before and during the trial, his out-of-court conversations and admissions must be excluded if obtained without counsel's consent or presence.
Keywords: *Accused, Counsel, Out-of-court conversations, Right to counsel, Trial*

Justice Arthur Goldberg
Escobedo v. Illinois,
378 U.S. 478, 490 (1964)
No system worth preserving should have to fear that if an accused is permitted to consult with a lawyer, he will become aware of, and exercise, these rights. If the exercise of constitutional rights will thwart the effectiveness of a system of law enforcement, then there is something very wrong with that system.
Keywords: *Accused, Constitutional rights, Counsel, Law enforcement, Lawyer*

Chief Justice Earl Warren, concurring
Estes v. Texas,
381 U.S. 532, 575 (1965)
It is argued that television not only entertains but also educates the public. But the function of a trial is not to provide an educational experience; and there is a serious danger that any attempt to use a trial as an educational tool will both divert it from its proper purpose and lead to suspicions concerning the integrity of the trial process.

Keywords: *Education, Educational experience, Educational tool, Entertainment, Public, Television, Trial, Trial process*

Justice John Marshall Harlan, concurring
Estes v. Texas,
381 U.S. 532, 592 (1965)
Courtroom television introduces into the conduct of a criminal trial the element of professional "showmanship," an extraneous influence whose subtle capacities for serious mischief in a case of this sort will not be underestimated by any lawyer experienced in the elusive imponderables of the trial arena. In the context of a trial of intense public interest, there is certainly a strong possibility that the timid or reluctant witness, for whom a court appearance even at its traditional best is a harrowing affair, will become more timid or reluctant when he finds that he will also be appearing before a "hidden audience" of unknown but large dimensions. There is certainly a strong possibility that the "cocky" witness having a thirst for the limelight will become more "cocky" under the influence of television. And who can say that the juror who is gratified by having been chosen for a front-line case, an ambitious prosecutor, a publicity-minded defense counsel, and even a conscientious judge will not stray, albeit unconsciously, from doing what "comes naturally" into pluming themselves for a satisfactory television "performance"?
Keywords: *Court appearance, Courtroom television, Criminal trial, Defense counsel, Judge, Juror, Lawyer, Prosecutor, Public interest, Television, Trial Arena, Witness*

Justice Abe Fortas
Kent v. United States,
383 U.S. 541, 555–556 (1966)
While there can be no doubt of the original laudable purpose of juvenile courts, studies and critiques in recent years raise serious questions as to whether actual performance measures well enough against theoretical purpose to make tolerable the immunity of the process from the reach of constitutional guarantees applicable to adults.... There is evidence, in fact, that there may be grounds for concern that the child receives the worst of both worlds, that he gets neither the protections accorded to adults nor the solicitous care and regenerative treatment postulated for children.
Keywords: *Children, Constitutional guarantees, Constitutional protection, Juvenile courts*

Justice Byron White, dissenting
Miranda v. Arizona,
384 U.S. 436, 542–543 (1966)
In some unknown number of cases the Court's rule will return a killer, a rapist or other criminal to the streets and to the environment which produced him, to repeat his crime whenever it pleases him. As a consequence, there will not be a gain, but loss, in human dignity. The real concern is not the unfortunate consequences of this new decision on the criminal law as an abstract, disembodied series of authoritative proscriptions, but the impact on those who rely on the public authority for protection and who without it can only engage in violent self-help with guns, knives and the help of their neighbors similarly inclined. There is, of course, a saving factor: the next victims are uncertain, unnamed and unrepresented in this case.
Keywords: *Crime, Criminal law, Human dignity, Protection, Public authority, Victims, Violent self-help*

Justice Potter Stewart
Hoffa v. United States,
385 U.S. 293, 310 (1966)
There is no constitutional right to be arrested. The police are not required to guess at their peril the precise moment at which they have probable cause to arrest a suspect, risking a violation of the Fourth Amendment if they act too soon, and a violation of the Sixth Amendment if they wait too long.
Keywords: *Arrest, Constitutional right, Fourth Amendment, Police, Probable cause, Sixth Amendment, Suspect*

Justice Hugo Black
Chapman v. California,
386 U.S. 18, 22 (1967)
... there may be some constitutional errors which in the setting of a particular case are so unimportant and insignificant that they may, consistent with the Federal constitution, be deemed harmless, not requiring the automatic reversal of the conviction.
Keywords: *Constitutional errors, Conviction, Reversal*

Justice Abe Fortas
In re Gault,
387 U.S. 1, 28 (1967)
Under our constitution, the condition of being a boy does not justify a kangaroo court.
Keywords: *Juvenile legal system*

Justice Potter Stewart, dissenting
In re Gault,
387 U.S. 1, 78–79 (1967)
Juvenile proceedings are not criminal trials. They are not civil trials. They are simply not adversary proceedings. Whether treating with a delinquent child, a neglected child, a defective child, or a dependent child, a juvenile proceeding's whole purpose and mission is the very opposite of the mission and purpose of a prosecution in a criminal court. The object of the one is correction of a condition. The object of the other is conviction and punishment for a criminal act.
Keywords: *Criminal trials, Civil trials, Delinquency, Juvenile justice, Punishment*

Justice William Douglas, dissenting
Warden v. Hayden,
387 U.S. 294, 321 (1967)
The right of privacy protected by the Fourth Amendment relates in part of course to the precincts of the home or the office. But it does not make them sanctuaries where the law can never reach. There are such places in the world. A mosque in Fez, Morocco, that I have visited, is by custom a sanctuary where any refugee may hide, safe from police intrusion. We have no such sanctuaries here. A policeman in "hot pursuit" or an officer with a search warrant can enter any house, any room, any building, any office. The privacy of those places is of course protected against invasion except in limited situations.
Keywords: *Fourth Amendment, Police officer, Privacy, Search warrant*

Justice William Douglas, concurring
Berger v. New York,
388 U.S. 41, 65 (1967)
If a statute were to authorize placing a policeman in every home or office where it was shown that there was probable cause to believe that evidence of crime would be obtained, there is little doubt that it would be struck down as a bald invasion of privacy, far worse than the general warrants prohibited by the Fourth Amendment. I can see no difference between such a statute and one authorizing electronic surveillance, which, in effect, places an invisible policeman in the home. If anything, the latter is more offensive because the homeowner is completely unaware of the invasion of privacy.
Keywords: *Crime, Electronic surveillance, Evidence, Fourth Amendment, Policeman, Privacy, Probable cause, Statute, Warrants*

Justice Hugo Black, dissenting
Berger v. New York,
388 U.S. 41, 73 (1967)
However obnoxious eavesdroppers may be they are assuredly not engaged in a more "ignoble" or "dirty business" than are bribers, thieves, burglars, robbers, rapists, kidnapers, and murderers, not to speak of others. And it cannot be denied that to deal with such specimens of our society, eavesdroppers are not merely useful, they are frequently a necessity. I realize that some may say, "Well, let the prosecuting officers use more scientific measures than eavesdropping." It is always easy to hint at mysterious means available just around the corner to catch outlaws. But crimes, unspeakably horrid

crimes, are with us in this country, and we cannot afford to dispense with any known method of detecting and correcting them unless it is forbidden by the Constitution or deemed inadvisable by legislative policy—neither of which I believe to be true about eavesdropping.

Keywords: *Crimes, Eavesdroppers, Legislative policy, Outlaws, Prosecutors, Science*

Justice William Brennan
United States v. Wade,
388 U.S. 218, 238 (1967)

In our view counsel can hardly impede legitimate law enforcement; on the contrary . . . law enforcement may be assisted by preventing the infiltration of taint in the prosecution's identification evidence. That result cannot help the guilty avoid conviction but can only help assure that the right man has been brought to justice.

Keywords: *Conviction, Counsel, Evidence, Exculpatory evidence, Guilt, Justice, Law enforcement, Prosecution*

Justice Byron White, dissenting
United States v. Wade,
388 U.S. 218, 256–258 (1967)

Law enforcement officers have the obligation to convict the guilty and to make sure they do not convict the innocent. They must be dedicated to making the criminal trial a procedure for the ascertainment of the true facts surrounding the commission of the crime. To this extent, our so-called adversary system is not adversary at all; nor should it be. But defense counsel has no comparable obligation to ascertain or present the truth.

Our system assigns him a different mission. He must be and is interested in preventing the conviction of the innocent, but, absent a voluntary plea of guilty, we also insist that he defend his client whether he is innocent or guilty. The State has the obligation to present the evidence. Defense counsel need present nothing, even if he knows what the truth is. He need not furnish any witnesses to the police, or reveal any confidences of his client, or furnish any other information to help the prosecution's case. If he can confuse a witness, even a truthful one, or make him appear at a disadvantage, unsure or indecisive, that will be his normal course. Our interest in not convicting the innocent permits counsel to put the State to its proof, to put the State's case in the worst possible light, regardless of what he thinks or knows to be the truth. Undoubtedly there are some limits which defense counsel must observe but more often than not, defense counsel will cross-examine a prosecution witness, and impeach him if he can, even if he thinks the witness is telling the truth, just as he will attempt to destroy a witness who he thinks is lying. In this respect, as part of our modified adversary system and as part of the duty imposed on the most honorable defense counsel, we countenance or require conduct which in many instances has little, if any, relation to the search for truth.

Keywords: *Adversary system, Conduct, Conviction, Criminal trial, Cross-examination, Defense counsel, Evidence, Guilt, Impeach, Innocence, Law enforcement, Plea, Police, Proof, Truth, Witnesses*

Justice Potter Stewart
Katz v. United States,
389 U.S. 347, 351 (1967)
. . . the Fourth Amendment protects people, not places. What a person knowingly exposes to the public, even in his own home or office, is not a subject of Fourth Amendment protection. But what he seeks to preserve as private, even in an area accessible to the public, may be constitutionally protected.
Keywords: *Fourth Amendment, Privacy*

Justice Potter Stewart
Witherspoon v. Illinois,
391 U.S. 510, 522 (1968)
. . . a sentence of death cannot be carried out if the jury that imposed or recommended it was chosen by excluding veniremen for cause simply because they voiced general objections to the death penalty or expressed conscientious or religious scruples against its infliction.
Keywords: *Capital punishment, Death penalty, Jury, Veniremen*

Chief Justice Earl Warren
Terry v. Ohio,
392 U.S. 1, 23–25 (1968)
Certainly it would be unreasonable to require that police officers take unnecessary risks in the performance of their duties. American criminals have a long tradition of armed violence, and every year in this country many law enforcement officers are killed in the line of duty, and thousands more are wounded. Virtually all of these deaths and a substantial portion of the injuries are inflicted with guns and knives. In view of these facts, we cannot blind ourselves to the need for law enforcement officers to protect themselves and other prospective victims of violence in situations where they may lack probable cause for an arrest. When an officer is justified in believing that the individual whose suspicious behavior he is investigating at close range is armed and presently dangerous to the officer or to others, it would appear to be clearly unreasonable to deny the officer the power to take necessary measures to determine whether the person is in fact carrying a weapon and to neutralize the threat of physical harm. We must still consider, however, the nature and quality of the intrusion on individual rights which must be accepted if police officers are to be conceded the right to search for weapons in situations where probable cause to arrest for crime is lacking. Even a limited search of the outer clothing for weapons constitutes a severe, though brief, intrusion upon cherished personal security, and it must surely be an annoying, frightening, and perhaps humiliating experience.
Keywords: *Arrest, Crime, Criminals, Duty, Law enforcement, Personal security, Police, Probable cause, Rights, Risks, Search, Suspicious behavior, Victims, Violence, Weapons*

Justice Byron White, concurring
Terry v. Ohio,
392 U.S. 1, 34 (1968)
There is nothing in the Constitution which prevents a policeman from addressing questions to anyone on the streets. Absent special circumstances, the person approached may not be detained

or frisked but may refuse to cooperate and go on his way. However, given the proper circumstances . . . it seems to me the person may be briefly detained against his will while pertinent questions are directed to him. Of course, the person stopped is not obliged to answer, answers may not be compelled, and refusal to answer furnishes no basis for an arrest, although it may alert the officer to the need for continued observation.

Keywords: *Arrest, Detained, Frisked, Law enforcement, Police, Questioning, Search*

Justice William Douglas, dissenting
Terry v. Ohio,
392 U.S. 1, 38–39 (1968)

To give the police greater power than a magistrate is to take a long step down the totalitarian path. Perhaps such a step is desirable to cope with modern forms of lawlessness. But if it is taken, it should be the deliberate choice of the people through a constitutional amendment. Until the Fourth Amendment, which is closely allied with the Fifth, is rewritten, the person and the effects of the individual are beyond the reach of all government agencies until there are reasonable grounds to believe (probable cause) that a criminal venture has been launched or is about to be launched. There have been powerful hydraulic pressures throughout our history that bear heavily on the Court to water down constitutional guarantees and give the police the upper hand. That hydraulic pressure has probably never been greater than it is today. Yet if the individual is no longer to be sovereign, if the police

can pick him up whenever they do not like the cut of his jib, if they can "seize" and "search" him in their discretion, we enter a new regime. The decision to enter it should be made only after a full debate by the people of this country.

Keywords: *Constitutional democracy, Constitutional guarantees, Constitutional history, Criminality, Fifth Amendment, Fourth Amendment, Law enforcement, Lawlessness, Magistrate, Police, Probable cause, Self-government, Search, Seizure, Sovereignty, Totalitarian*

Justice Thurgood Marshall
Powell v. Texas,
392 U.S. 514, 535–536 (1968)

We cannot cast aside the centuries-long evolution of the collection of interlocking and overlapping concepts which the common law has utilized to assess the moral accountability of an individual for his antisocial deeds. The doctrines of *actus reus, mens rea*, insanity, mistake, justification, and duress have historically provided the tools for a constantly shifting adjustment of the tension between the evolving aims of the criminal law and changing religious, moral, philosophical, and medical views of the nature of man.

Keywords: *Antisocial deeds, Common Law, Criminal law, History, Moral accountability, Nature of man*

Justice William Brennan
In re Winship,
397 U.S. 358, 364 (1970)

. . . use of the reasonable-doubt standard is indispensable to command the respect and confidence of the community in applications of the criminal law. It is critical that the moral force of the criminal law not be diluted by a standard of proof that leaves people in doubt whether innocent men are being condemned. It is also important in our free society that every individual going about his ordinary affairs have confidence that his government cannot adjudge him guilty of a criminal offense without convincing a proper factfinder of his guilt with utmost certainty.

Keywords: *Burden of proof, Criminal law, Criminal offense, Fact-finder, Free society, Guilt, Reasonable doubt, Standard of proof*

Chief Justice Warren Burger, dissenting
In re Winship,
397 U.S. 358, 376 (1970)
What the juvenile court system needs is not more but less of the trappings of legal procedure and judicial formalism; the juvenile court system requires breathing room and flexibility in order to survive, if it can survive the repeated assaults from this Court.

Keywords: *Judicial formalism, Juvenile court system, Legal procedure*

Justice Byron White
Brady v. United States,
397 U.S. 742, 756–757 (1970)
Often the decision to plead guilty is heavily influenced by the defendant's appraisal of the prosecution's case against him and by the apparent likelihood of securing leniency should a guilty plea be offered and accepted. Considerations like these frequently present imponderable questions for which there are no certain answers; judgments may be made that in the light of later events seem improvident, although they were perfectly sensible at the time. The rule that a plea must be intelligently made to be valid does not require that a plea be vulnerable to later attack if the defendant did not correctly assess every relevant factor entering into his decision. A defendant is not entitled to withdraw his plea merely because he discovers long after the plea has been accepted that his calculus misapprehended the quality of the State's case or the likely penalties attached to alternative courses of action.

Keywords: *Defendant, Guilt, Penalties, Plea, Prosecution*

Justice Byron White
United States v. White,
401 U.S. 745, 752 (1971)
Inescapably, one contemplating illegal activities must realize and risk that his companions may be reporting to the police. If he sufficiently doubts their trustworthiness, the association will very probably end or never materialize. But if he has doubts, or allays them, or risks what doubt he has, the risk is his. In terms of what his course will be, what he will or will not do or say, we are unpersuaded that he would distinguish between probable informers on the one hand and probable informers with transmitters on the other. Given the possibility or probability that one of his colleagues is cooperating with the police, it is only speculation to assert that the defendant's utterances would be substantially different or his sense of security any less if he also thought it possible

that the suspected colleague is wired for sound.

Keywords: *Defendant, Illegal activities, Informers, Police, Wired*

Justice Potter Stewart, dissenting
Perez v. United States,
402 U.S. 146, 158 (1971)

Because I am unable to discern any rational distinction between loan sharking and other local crime, I cannot escape the conclusion that this statute was beyond the power of Congress to enact. The definition and prosecution of local, intrastate crimes are reserved to the States under the Ninth and Tenth Amendments.

Keywords: *Congressional power, Intrastate crimes, Loan-sharking, Ninth Amendment, Statute, Tenth Amendment*

Chief Justice Warren Burger
Bivens v. Six Unknown Named Agents of the Federal Bureau of Narcotics,
403 U.S. 388, 419 (1971)

I submit that society has at least as much right to expect rationally graded responses from judges in place of the universal "capital punishment" we inflict on all evidence when police error is shown in its acquisition.

Keywords: *Evidence, Judicial authority, Police error, Society*

Justice William Douglas, concurring
United States v. Marion,
404 U.S. 307, 330–331 (1971)

The anxiety and concern attendant on public accusation may weigh more heavily upon an individual who has not yet been formally indicted or arrested for, to him, exoneration by a jury of his peers may be only a vague possibility lurking in the distant future. Indeed, the protection underlying the right to a speedy trial may be denied when a citizen is damned by clandestine innuendo and never given the chance promptly to defend himself in a court of law. Those who are accused of crime but never tried may lose their jobs or their positions of responsibility, or become outcasts in their communities.

Keywords: *Accused, Arrest, Citizen, Court of law, Crime, Exoneration, Indictment, Jury, Outcasts, Public accusation, Right to a speedy trial*

Justice William Douglas
Papachristou v. Jacksonville,
405 U.S. 156, 171 (1972)

A presumption that people who might walk or loaf or loiter or stroll or frequent houses where liquor is sold, or who are supported by their wives or who look suspicious to the police are to become future criminals is too precarious for a rule of law. The implicit presumption in these generalized vagrancy standards—that crime is being nipped in the bud—is too extravagant to deserve extended treatment. Of course, vagrancy statutes are useful to the police. Of course, they are nets making easy the roundup of so-called undesirables. But the rule of law implies equality and justice in its application. Vagrancy laws of the Jacksonville type teach that the scales of justice are so tipped that even-handed administration of the law is not possible. The rule of law, evenly applied to minorities as well as majorities, to the poor as well as the rich, is the great mucilage that holds society together.

Keywords: *Criminality, Law enforcement, Police, Roundup, Rule of law, Undesirables, Vagrancy*

Justice Lewis Powell, concurring
Argersinger v. Hamlin,
407 U.S. 25, 55 (1972)
To avoid these equal protection problems and to preserve a range of sentencing options as prescribed by law, most judges are likely to appoint counsel for indigents in all but the most minor offenses where jail sentences are extremely rare. It is doubtful that the States possess the necessary resources to meet this sudden expansion of the right to counsel.

Keywords: *Counsel, Equal protection, Indigents, Jail sentences, Minor Offenses, Right to counsel, Sentencing options, State resources*

Justice Lewis Powell
Barker v. Wingo,
407 U.S. 514, 521 (1972)
Delay is not an uncommon defense tactic. As the time between the commission of the crime and trial lengthens, witnesses may become unavailable or their memories may fade. If the witnesses support the prosecution, its case will be weakened, sometimes seriously so. And it is the prosecution which carries the burden of proof.

Keywords: *Burden of proof, Criminal commission, Defense tactic, Prosecution, Trial, Witness*

Justice Potter Stewart, concurring
Furman v. Georgia,
408 U.S. 238, 308 (1972)
The instinct for retribution is part of the nature of man, and channeling that instinct in the administration of criminal justice serves an important purpose in promoting the stability of a society governed by law. When people begin to believe that organized society is unwilling or unable to impose upon criminal offenders the punishment they "deserve," then there are sown the seeds of anarchy—of self-help, vigilante justice, and lynch law.

Keywords: *Anarchy, Criminal justice, Criminal offender, Lynch law, Nature of man, Organized society, Punishment, Retribution, Society, Vigilante justice*

Justice Harry Blackmun, dissenting
Furman v. Georgia,
408 U.S. 238, 405–406 (1972)
Cases such as these provide for me an excruciating agony of the spirit. I yield to no one in the depth of my distaste, antipathy, and indeed, abhorrence, for the death penalty, with all its aspects of physical distress and fear and moral judgment exercised by finite minds. That distaste is buttressed by a belief that capital punishment serves no useful purpose that can be demonstrated. For me, it violates childhood's training and life experiences, and is not compatible with the philosophical convictions I have been able to develop. It is antagonistic to any sense of "reverence for life." Were I a legislator, I would vote against the death penalty. . . .

Keywords: *Capital punishment, Death penalty, Life experiences, Moral judgment, Philosophical convictions, Reverence for life*

Justice Potter Stewart
United States v. Dionisio,
410 U.S. 1, 17–18 (1973)
The grand jury may not always serve its historic role as a protective bulwark standing solidly between the ordinary citizen and an overzealous prosecutor, but if it is even to approach the proper performance of its constitutional mission, it must be free to pursue its investigations unhindered by external influence or supervision so long as it foes not trench upon the legitimate rights of any witness called before it.
Keywords: *Constitutional mission, Grand jury, Investigations, Prosecution, Witness*

Justice Potter Stewart, dissenting
United States v. Russell,
411 U.S. 423, 449–450 (1973)
It is the Government's duty to prevent crime not to promote it. Here, the Government's agent asked that the illegal drug be produced for him, solved his quarry's practical problems with the assurance that he could provide the one essential ingredient that was difficult to obtain, furnished that element as he had promised, and bought the finished product from the respondent—all so that the respondent could be prosecuted for producing and selling the very drug for which the agent had asked and for which he had provided the necessary component. Under the objective approach that I would follow, this respondent was entrapped, regardless of his predisposition or "innocence."
Keywords: *Crime, Drug, Entrapped, Innocence, Prosecuted*

Justice Harry Blackmun
Gosa v. Mayden,
413 U.S. 665, 685 (1973)
Wholesale invalidation of convictions rendered years ago could well mean that convicted persons would be freed without retrial, for witnesses . . . no longer may be readily available, memories may have added, records may be incomplete or missing, and physical evidence may have disappeared. Society must not be made to tolerate a result of that kind when there is no significant question concerning the accuracy of the process by which judgment was rendered or, in other words, when essential justice is not involved.
Keywords: *Convictions, Essential justice, Memories, Physical evidence, Process, Retrial, Society, Witness*

Justice Lewis Powell
United States v. Calandra,
414 U.S. 338, 349 (1974)
Because the grand jury does not finally adjudicate guilt or innocence, it has traditionally been allowed to pursue its investigative and accusatorial functions unimpeded by the evidentiary and procedural restrictions applicable to a criminal trial. Permitting witnesses to invoke the exclusionary rule before a grand jury would precipitate adjudication of issues hitherto reserved for trial on the merits and would delay and disrupt grand jury proceedings. Suppression hearings would halt the orderly progress of an investigation and might necessitate extended litigation of issues only tangentially related to the grand jury's primary objective.

Keywords: *Accusatorial function, Adjudication, Criminal trial, Evidentiary restrictions, Exclusionary Rule, Grand jury, Guilt, Innocence, Investigative function, Procedural restrictions, Suppression hearings, Witnesses*

Justice Potter Stewart
Fuller v. Oregon,
417 U.S. 40, 53–54 (1974)
We live in a society where the distribution of legal assistance, like the distribution of all goods and services, is generally regulated by the dynamics of private enterprise. A defendant in a criminal case who is just above the line separating the indigent from the nonindigent must borrow money, sell off his meager assets, or call upon his family or friends in order to hire a lawyer. We cannot say that the Constitution requires that those only slightly poorer must remain forever immune from any obligation to shoulder the expenses of their legal defense, even when they are able to pay without hardship.
Keywords: *Criminal case, Defendant, Indigency, Lawyer, Legal assistance, Legal defense, Legal expenses, Legal fees, Private enterprise, Society*

Justice William Rehnquist
Hampton v. United States,
425 U.S. 484, 490 (1976)
If the police engage in illegal activity in concert with a defendant beyond the scope of their duties the remedy lies, not in freeing the equally culpable defendant, but in prosecuting the police under the applicable provisions of state or federal law.

Keywords: *Culpable defendant, Defendant, Illegal activity, Police, Prosecution*

Justice Potter Stewart
Gregg v. Georgia,
428 U.S. 153, 187 (1976)
. . . we are concerned here only with the imposition of capital punishment for the crime of murder, and when a life has been taken deliberately by the offender, we cannot say that the punishment is invariably disproportionate to the crime. It is an extreme sanction, suitable to the most extreme of crimes.
Keywords: *Capital punishment, Murder, Punishment*

Justice Potter Stewart
Gregg v. Georgia,
428 U.S. 153, 199 (1976)
Nothing in any of our cases suggests that the decision to afford an individual defendant mercy violates the Constitution.
Keywords: *Defendant, Mercy*

Justice Thurgood Marshall, dissenting
Gregg v. Georgia,
428 U.S. 153, 240 (1976)
. . . society's judgment that the murderer "deserves" death must be respected not simply because the preservation of order requires it, but because it is appropriate that society make the judgment and carry it out. It is this latter notion, in particular, that I consider to be fundamentally at odds with the Eighth Amendment. The mere fact that the community demands the murderer's life in return for the evil he has done cannot sustain the death penalty . . . "the Eighth Amend-

ment demands more than that a challenged punishment be acceptable to contemporary society."

Keywords: *Community, Death penalty, Eighth Amendment, Murderer, Preservation of order, Punishment*

Justice Potter Stewart
Brewer v. Williams,
430 U.S. 387, 406 (1977)

The pressures on state executive and judicial officers charged with the administration of the criminal law are great, especially when the crime is murder and the victim a small child. But it is precisely the predictability of those pressures that makes imperative a resolute loyalty to the guarantees that the Constitution extends to us all.

Keywords: *Constitutional guarantees, Crime, Criminal law, Judicial officers, Murder, State executive, Victim*

Chief Justice Warren Burger, dissenting
Brewer v. Williams,
430 U.S. 387, 415–416 (1977)

The result in this case ought to be intolerable in any society which purports to call itself an organized society. It continues the Court—by the narrowest margin—on the much-criticized course of punishing the public for the mistakes and misdeeds of law enforcement officers, instead of punishing the officer directly, if in fact he is guilty of wrongdoing. It mechanically and blindly keeps reliable evidence from juries whether the claimed constitutional violation involves gross police misconduct or honest human error.

Keywords: *Evidence, Gross police misconduct, Guilt, Human error, Juries, Law enforcement officers, Organized society, Wrongdoing*

Justice Byron White, dissenting
Ingraham v. Wright,
430 U.S. 651, 689 (1977)

. . . if a prisoner is beaten mercilessly for a breach of discipline, he is entitled to the protection of the Eighth Amendment, while a schoolchild who commits the same breach of discipline and is similarly beaten is simply not covered.

Keywords: *Breach of discipline, Corporal punishment, Eighth Amendment, Prisoner, Schoolchild*

Justice Byron White, dissenting
Ingraham v. Wright,
430 U.S. 651, 691 (1977)

By holding that the Eighth Amendment protects only criminals, the majority adopts the view that one is entitled to the protections afforded by the Eighth Amendment only if he is punished for acts that are sufficiently opprobrious for society to make them "criminal." This is a curious holding in view of the fact that the more culpable the offender the more likely it is that the punishment will not be disproportionate to the offense, and consequently, the less likely it is that the punishment will be cruel and unusual. Conversely, a public school student who is spanked for a mere breach of discipline may sometimes have a strong argument that the punishment does not fit the offense, depending upon the severity of the beating, and therefore that it is cruel and unusual. Yet the majority would afford the student no protection no matter how inhumane and barbaric the punishment inflicted on him might be.

Keywords: *Barbaric, Breach of discipline, Constitutional protections, Criminals, Cruel and unusual punishment, Culpable, Eighth Amendment, Inhumane, Offense, Public school, Punishment*

Justice Byron White
Coker v. Georgia,
433 U.S. 584, 598 (1977)

Rape is without doubt deserving of serious punishment; but in terms of moral depravity and of the injury to the person and to the public, it does not compare with murder, which does involve the unjustified taking of human life. Although it may be accompanied by another crime, rape by definition does not include the death or even the serious injury to another person. The murderer kills; the rapist, if no more than that, does not. Life is over for the victim of the murderers; for the rape victim, life may not be nearly so happy as it was, but it is not over and normally is not beyond repair.

Keywords: *Crime, Death, Human life, Moral depravity, Murder, Punishment, Rape, Serious injury, Victim*

Justice William Rehnquist, dissenting
California v. Minjares,
443 U.S. 916, 919 (1979)

I do not claim to be an expert in comparative law, but I feel morally certain that the United States is the only nation in the world in which the most relevant, most competent evidence as to the guilt or innocence of the accused is mechanically excluded because of the manner in which it may have been obtained.

Keywords: *Accused, Comparative law, Evidence, Exclusionary rule, Guilt, Innocence*

Justice John Paul Stevens
Martinez v. California,
444 U.S. 277, 281 (1980)

. . . the basic risk that repeat offenses may occur is always present in any parole system. A legislative decision that has an incremental impact on the probability that death will result in any given situation—such as setting the speed limit at 55–miles-per-hour instead of 45—cannot be characterized as state action depriving a person of life just because it may set in motion a chain of events that ultimately leads to the random death of an innocent bystander.

Keywords: *Chain of events, Innocent bystander, Legislative decisions, Offenses, Parole, Random death, State action*

Justice Lewis Powell, dissenting
Rummel v. Estelle,
445 U.S. 263, 288 (1980)

A statute that levied a mandatory life sentence for overtime parking might well deter vehicular lawlessness, but it would offend our felt sense of justice. The Court concedes today that the principle of disproportionality plays a role in the review of sentences imposing the death penalty, but suggests that the principle may be less applicable when a noncapital sentence is challenged. Such a limitation finds no support in the history of Eighth Amendment jurisprudence.

Keywords: *Death penalty, Eighth Amendment, Justice, Life sentence, Mandatory sentencing, Noncapital sentence, Principle of disproportionality, Sentencing, Statute*

Justice Harry Blackmun, concurring
Rawlings v. Kentucky,
448 U.S. 98, 112 (1980)
Not every concept of ownership or possession is "arcane." Not every interest in property exists only in the desiccated atmosphere of ancient maxims and dusty books.
Keywords: *Ancient maxims, Ownership, Possession, Property*

Justice John Paul Stevens, dissenting
Rosales-Lopez v. United States,
451 U.S. 182, 197 (1981)
Even when there are no "special circumstances" connected with an alleged criminal transaction indicating an unusual risk of racial or other group bias, a member of the Nazi party should not be allowed to sit in judgment on a Jewish defendant.
Keywords: *Alleged criminal transaction, Defendant, Group bias, Race*

Chief Justice Warren Burger, dissenting
Globe Newspaper Co. v. Superior Court,
457 U.S. 596, 612 (1982)
Historically our society has gone to great lengths to protect minors charged with crime, particularly by prohibiting the release of the names of offenders, barring the press and public from juvenile proceedings, and sealing the records of those proceedings. Yet today the Court holds unconstitutional a state statute designed to protect not the accused, but the minor victims of sex crimes. In doing so, it advances a disturbing paradox. Although states are permitted, for example, to mandate the closure of all proceedings in order to protect a 17–year-old charged with rape, they are not permitted to require the closing of part of criminal proceedings in order to protect an innocent child who has been raped or otherwise sexually abused.
Keywords: *Accused, Children, Crime, History, Juvenile proceedings, Minors, Minor victims, Offenders, Press, Sex crimes, Sexually abused, Society*

Chief Justice Warren Burger
Hudson v. Palmer,
468 U.S. 517, 527–528 (1984)
A right of privacy in traditional Fourth Amendment terms is fundamentally incompatible with the close and continual surveillance of inmates and their cells required to ensure institutional security and internal order. We are satisfied that society would insist that the prisoner's expectation of privacy always yield to what must be considered the paramount interest in institutional security. We believe that it is accepted by our society that "loss of freedom of choice and privacy are inherent incidents of confinement."
Keywords: *Fourth Amendment, Inmates, Institutional security, Internal order, Prisoner, Privacy, Surveillance*

Justice Harry Blackmun, concurring
New Jersey v. T.L.O.,
469 U.S. 325, 353 (1985)
. . . immediate action obviously would not be possible if a teacher were required

to secure a warrant before searching a student. Nor would it be possible if a teacher could not conduct a necessary search until the teacher thought there was probable cause for the search. A teacher has neither the training nor the day-to-day experience in the complexities of probable cause that a law enforcement officer possesses, and is ill-equipped to make a quick judgment about the existence of probable cause. The time required for a teacher to ask the questions or make the observations that are necessary to turn reasonable grounds into probable cause is time during which the teacher, and other students, are diverted from the essential task of education. A teacher's focus is, and should be, on teaching and helping students, rather than on developing evidence against a particular troublemaker.

Keywords: Education, Evidence, Law enforcement officers, Probable cause, Search warrant, Students, Teachers

Justice Lewis Powell
Wayte v. United States,
470 U.S. 598, 607–608 (1985)
. . . the decision to prosecute is particularly ill-suited to judicial review. Such factors as the strength of the case, the prosecution's general deterrence value, the Government's enforcement priorities, and the case's relationship to the Government's overall enforcement plan are not readily susceptible to the kind of analysis the courts are competent to undertake. Judicial supervision in this area, moreover, entails systemic costs of particular concern. Examining the basis of a prosecution delays the criminal proceed-

ing, threatens to chill law enforcement by subjecting the prosecutor's motives and decisionmaking to outside inquiry, and may undermine prosecutorial effectiveness by revealing the Government's enforcement policy. All of these are substantial concerns that make the courts properly hesitant to examine the decision whether to prosecute.

Keywords: Criminal proceeding, Deterrence, Enforcement priorities, Judicial analysis, Judicial review, Judicial supervision, Law enforcement, Prosecutorial decisions, Prosecutorial effectiveness

Justice Sandra Day O'Connor, dissenting
Tennessee v. Garner,
471 U.S. 1, 26 (1985)
Although the Court has recognized that the requirements of the Fourth Amendment must respond to the reality of social and technological change, fidelity to the notion of constitutional—as opposed to purely judicial—limits on governmental action requires us to impose a heavy burden on those who claim that practices accepted when the Fourth Amendment was adopted are now constitutionally impermissible.

Keywords: Constitutional limitations, Fourth Amendment, Judicial limitations, Technology

Justice John Paul Stevens, dissenting
California v. Carney,
471 U.S. 386, 407–408 (1985)
Although it may not be a castle, a motor home is usually the functional equivalent of a hotel room, a vacation and retirement home, or a hunting and fishing

cabin. These places may be as Spartan as a humble cottage when compared to the most majestic mansion, but the highest and most legitimate expectations of privacy associated with these temporary abodes should command the respect of this Court.

Keywords: *Motor home, Privacy*

Justice William Brennan, dissenting
Glass v. Louisiana,
471 U.S. 1080, 1094 (1985)
. . . there is an ever-more urgent question whether electrocution in fact is a "humane" method for extinguishing human life or is, instead, nothing less than the contemporary technological equivalent of burning people at the stake.

Keywords: *Capital punishment, Death penalty, Eighth Amendment, Electrocution, Humanity*

Justice Byron White, dissenting
Booth v. Maryland,
482 U.S. 496, 516–517 (1987)
The Court's judgment is based on the premises that the harm that a murderer causes a victim's family does not in general reflect on his blameworthiness, and that only evidence going to blameworthiness is relevant to the capital sentencing decision. Many if not most jurors, however, will look less favorably on a capital defendant when they appreciate the full extent of the harm he caused, including the harm to the victim's family. There is nothing aberrant in a juror's inclination to hold a murderer accountable not only for his internal disposition in committing the crime but also for the full extent of the harm he caused; many if not

most persons would also agree, for example, that someone who drove his car recklessly through a stoplight and unintentionally killed a pedestrian merits significantly more punishment than someone who drove his car recklessly through the same stoplight at a time when no pedestrian was there to be hit. . . . if punishment can be enhanced in noncapital cases on the basis of the harm caused, irrespective of the offender's specific intention to cause such harm, I fail to see why the same approach is unconstitutional in death cases. If anything, I would think that victim impact statements are particularly appropriate evidence in capital sentencing hearings: the State has a legitimate interest in counteracting the mitigating evidence which the defendant is entitled to put in, see, by reminding the sentencer that just as the murderer should be considered as an individual, so too the victim is an individual whose death represents a unique loss to society and in particular to his family.

Keywords: *Blameworthiness, Capital defendant, Capital sentencing, Defendant, Evidence, Family, Harm, Jurors, Mitigating evidence, Murderer, Noncapital cases, Punishment, Sentencer, Victim impact statement, Victim's family*

Justice Antonin Scalia, dissenting
Booth v. Maryland,
482 U.S. 496, 520 (1987)
Recent years have seen an outpouring of popular concern for what has come to be known as "victims' rights"—a phrase that describes what its proponents feel is the failure of courts of justice to take

into account in their sentencing decisions not only the factors mitigating the defendant's moral guilt, but also the amount of harm he has caused to innocent members of society. Many citizens have found one-sided and hence unjust the criminal trial in which a parade of witnesses comes forth to testify to the pressures beyond normal human experience that drove the defendant to commit his crime, with no one to lay before the sentencing authority the full reality of human suffering the defendant has produced—which (and not moral guilt alone) is one of the reasons society deems his act worthy of the prescribed penalty. Perhaps these sentiments do not sufficiently temper justice with mercy, but that is a question to be decided through the democratic processes of a free people, and not by the decrees of this Court.

Keywords: Citizens, Courts of justice, Criminal trial, Defendant, Harm, Democratic process, Free people, Human experience, Human suffering, Judicial decrees, Justice, Mercy, Moral guilt, Penalty, Sentencing authority, Sentencing decisions, Society, Testify, Victims' rights, Witnesses

Justice John Paul Stevens, dissenting
Michigan Department of State Police v. Sitz,
496 U.S. 444, 465 (1990)
These fears are not, as the Court would have it, solely the lot of the guilty. To be law abiding is not necessarily to be spotless, and even the most virtuous can be unlucky. Unwanted attention from the local police need not be less discomforting simply because one's secrets are not the stuff of criminal prosecutions. More-over, those who have found—by reason of prejudice or misfortune—that encounters with the police may become adversarial or unpleasant without good cause will have grounds for worrying at any stop designed to elicit signs of suspicious behavior. Being stopped by the police is distressing even when it should not be terrifying, and what begins mildly may by happenstance turn severe.

Keywords: Checkpoints, Criminals, Guilt, Innocent, Police, Prosecution, Suspicious behavior

Justice John Paul Stevens, dissenting
Michigan Department of State Police v. Sitz,
496 U.S. 444, 468–469 (1990)
. . . I believe the Court is quite wrong in blithely asserting that a sobriety checkpoint is no more intrusive than a permanent checkpoint. In my opinion, unannounced investigatory seizures are, particularly when they take place at night, the hallmark of regimes far different from ours; the surprise intrusion upon individual liberty is not minimal. On that issue, my difference with the Court may amount to nothing less than a difference in our respective evaluations of the importance of individual liberty, a serious, albeit inevitable, source of constitutional disagreement.

Keywords: Checkpoints, Constitutional interpretation, Investigations, Liberty, Seizures, Sobriety

Justice Anthony Kennedy
McCleskey v. Zant,
499 U.S. 467, 491 (1991)
Our federal system recognizes the independent power of a State to articulate

societal norms through criminal law; but the power of a State to pass laws means little if the State cannot enforce them.

Keywords: *Criminal law, Federalism, Federal system, Law enforcement, Societal norms, State independence*

Justice Anton Scalia, dissenting
Riverside v. McLaughlin,
500 U.S. 44, 71 (1991)

One hears the complaint, nowadays, that the Fourth Amendment has become constitutional law for the guilty; that it benefits the career criminal (through the exclusionary rule) often and directly, but the ordinary citizen remotely if at all. By failing to protect the innocent arrestee, today's opinion reinforces that view. The common law rule of prompt hearing had as its primary beneficiaries the innocent—not those whose fully justified convictions must be overturned to scold the police; nor those who avoid conviction because the evidence, while convincing, does not establish guilt beyond a reasonable doubt; but those so blameless that there was not even good reason to arrest them. While in recent years we have invented novel applications of the Fourth Amendment to release the unquestionably guilty, we today repudiate one of its core applications so that the presumptively innocent may be left in jail. Hereafter a law-abiding citizen wrongfully arrested may be compelled to await the grace of a Dickensian bureaucratic machine, as it churns its cycle for up to two days— never once given the opportunity to show a judge that there is absolutely

no reason to hold him, that a mistake has been made. In my view, this is the image of a system of justice that has lost its ancient sense of priority, a system that few Americans would recognize as our own.

Keywords: *Arrestee, Citizens, Common law, Constitutional law, Criminal, Evidence, Exclusionary rule, Fourth Amendment, Guilt, Innocent, Judicial legitimacy, Police, Reasonable doubt*

Chief Justice William Rehnquist
Payne v. Tennessee,
501 U.S. 808, 825 (1991)

Victim impact evidence is simply another form or method of informing the sentencing authority about the specific harm caused by the crime in question, evidence of a general type long considered by sentencing authorities.

Keywords: *Evidence, Harm, Sentencing, Sentencing authority, Victim impact evidence*

Justice Harry Blackmun, concurring
Hudson v. McMillian,
503 U.S. 1, 13–14 (1992)

The Court today appropriately puts to rest a seriously misguided view that pain inflicted by an excessive use of force is actionable under the Eighth Amendment only when coupled with "significant injury," e.g., injury that requires medical attention or leaves permanent marks. Indeed, were we to hold to the contrary, we might place various kinds of state-sponsored torture and abuse—of the kind ingeniously designed to cause pain but without a telltale "significant injury"—entirely beyond the pale of the Constitution. In other words, the Constitutional prohibition of "cruel and unusual punishments" then might not constrain prison officials from lashing prisoners with leather straps, whipping them with rubber hoses, beating them with naked fists, shocking them with electric currents, asphyxiating them short of death, intentionally exposing them to undue heat or cold, or forcibly injecting them with psychosis-inducing drugs. These techniques, commonly thought to be practiced only outside this Nation's borders, are hardly unknown within this Nation's prisons.

Keywords: *Constitutional prohibition, Cruel and unusual punishment, Eighth Amendment, Excessive use of force, Prison, State-sponsored torture*

Justice Antonin Scalia, dissenting
Georgia v. McCollum,
505 U.S. 42, 70 (1992)
Today's decision gives the lie once again to the belief that an activist, "evolutionary" constitutional jurisprudence always evolves in the direction of greater individual rights. In the interest of promoting the supposedly greater good of race relations in the society as a whole (make no mistake that that is what underlies all of this), we use the Constitution to destroy the ages-old right of criminal defendants to exercise peremptory challenges as they wish, to secure a jury that they consider fair.

Keywords: *Constitutional jurisprudence, Constitutional manipulation, Criminal defendants, Individual rights, Jury, Peremptory challenges, Race relations, Society*

Chief Justice William Rehnquist
Wisconsin v. Mitchell,
508 U.S. 476, 489 (1993)
The First Amendment . . . does not prohibit the evidentiary use of speech to establish the elements of a crime or to prove motive or intent. Evidence of a defendant's previous declarations or statements is commonly admitted in criminal trials subject to evidentiary rules dealing with relevancy, reliability, and the like.

Keywords: *Elements of crime, Evidence, First Amendment, Intent, Motive, Speech*

Justice Antonin Scalia, concurring
Callins v. Collins,
510 U.S. 1127, 1128 (1994)
Convictions in opposition to the death penalty are often passionate and deeply held. That would be no excuse for reading them into a Constitution that does not contain them, even if they represented the convictions of a majority of Americans. Much less is there any excuse for using that course to thrust a minority's views upon the people. JUSTICE BLACKMUN begins his statement by describing with poignancy the death of a convicted murderer by lethal injection. He chooses, as the case in which to make that statement, one of the less brutal of the murders that regularly come before us—the murder of a man ripped by a bullet suddenly and unexpectedly, with no opportunity to prepare himself and his affairs, and left to bleed to death on the floor of a tavern. The death-by-injection which JUSTICE BLACKMUN describes looks pretty desirable next to

that. It looks even better next to some of the other cases currently before us which JUSTICE BLACKMUN did not select as the vehicle for his announcement that the death penalty is always unconstitutional—for example, the case of the 11–year-old girl raped by four men and then killed by stuffing her panties down her throat. . . . How enviable a quiet death by lethal injection compared with that! If the people conclude that such more brutal deaths may be deterred by capital punishment; indeed, if they merely conclude that justice requires such brutal deaths to be avenged by capital punishment; the creation of false, untextual and unhistorical contradictions within "the Court's Eighth Amendment jurisprudence" should not prevent them.

Keywords: *Capital punishment, Constitutional limitations, Death penalty, Deterrence, Eighth Amendment, History, Judicial process, Justice, Lethal injection*

Justice Harry Blackmun, dissenting
Callins v. Collins,
510 U.S. 1127, 1130 (1994)
From this date forward, I no longer shall tinker with the machinery of death. For more than 20 years I have endeavored—indeed, I have struggled—along with a majority of this Court, to develop procedural and substantive rules that would lend more than the mere appearance of fairness to the death penalty endeavor. Rather than continue to coddle the Court's delusion that the desired level of fairness has been achieved and the need for regulation eviscerated, I feel morally and intellectually obligated simply to concede that the death penalty experiment has failed. It is virtually self-evident to me now that no combination of procedural rules or substantive regulations ever can save the death penalty from its inherent constitutional deficiencies.

Keywords: *Capital punishment, Constitutional deficiencies, Death penalty, Fairness, Procedural rules, Regulations, Substantive rules*

Justice Antonin Scalia, concurring
Minnesota v. Carter,
525 U.S. ___, ___ (1998)
The dissent may be correct that a person invited into someone else's house to engage in a common business (even common monkey-business, so to speak) ought to be protected against government searches of the room in which that business is conducted; and that persons invited in to deliver milk or pizza (whom the dissent dismisses as "classroom hypotheticals" as opposed, presumably, to flesh-and-blood hypotheticals) ought not to be protected against government searches of the rooms that they occupy. I am not sure of the answer to those policy questions. But I am sure that the answer is not remotely contained in the Constitution, which means that it is left—as many, indeed most, important questions are left—to the judgment of state and federal legislators. We go beyond our proper role as judges in a democratic society when we restrict the people's power to govern themselves over the full range of policy choices that the Constitution has left available to them.

Keywords: *Business, Democratic society, Governmental searches, Legislators, Self-government*

Justice Sandra Day O'Connor, dissenting
Swidler & Berlin v. United States,
524 U.S. 399, 416 (1998)
Where the exoneration of an innocent criminal defendant or a compelling law enforcement interest is at stake, the harm of precluding critical evidence that is unavailable by any other means outweighs the potential disincentive to forthright communication. In my view, the cost of silence warrants a narrow exception to the rule that the attorney-client privilege survives the death of the client.
Keywords: *Attorney-client confidentiality, Criminal law, Evidence, Law enforcement*

Justice Antonin Scalia, concurring in part, dissenting in part
Neder v. United States,
119 S. Ct. 1827, 1844–1845 (1999)
The Constitutionally required step that was omitted here is distinctive, in that the basis for it is precisely that, absent voluntary waiver of the jury right, *the Constitution does not trust judges to make determinations of criminal guilt.* Perhaps the Court is so enamoured of judges in general, and federal judges in particular, that it forgets that they (we) are officers of the Government, and hence proper objects of that healthy suspicion of the power of government which possessed the Framers and is embodied in the Constitution. Who knows?—20 years of appointments of federal judges by oppressive administrations might produce judges willing to enforce oppressive criminal laws, and to interpret criminal laws oppressively—at least in the view of the citizens in some vicinages where criminal prosecutions must be brought. And so the people reserved the function of determining criminal guilt to themselves, sitting as jurors. It is not within the power of us Justices to cancel that reservation—neither by permitting trial judges to determine the guilt of a defendant who has not waived the jury right, nor (when a trial judge has done so anyway) by reviewing the facts ourselves and pronouncing the defendant without-a-doubt guilty.
Keywords: *Constitutional limitations, Criminal guilt, Criminal prosecutions, Framers, Governmental power, Judicial trust, Jury, Oppressive government, Waiver*

12. The Global Community

This chapter explores how international events impact America's institutions. The Supreme Court has been fairly consistent when it comes to the judicial review of the military, war and the war powers, treaties, immigration, and deportation. Moreover, this section also deals with the unique constitutional nature of insurrections, civil war, and Indian affairs. This chapter along with chapter 2 provides the most complete analysis of the powers of the presidency.

Chief Justice John Marshall
Ex parte Bollman,
8 U.S. 75, 126 (1807)
If war be actually levied, ... all those who perform any part, however minute, or however remote from the scene of action, and who are actually leagued in the general conspiracy, are to be considered as traitors.
Keywords: *Traitors, War*

Justice Joseph Story, dissenting
Brown v. United States,
12 U.S. 110, 149 (1814)
By the constitution, the executive is charged with the faithful execution of the laws; and the language of the act declaring war authorizes him to carry it into effect. In what manner, and to what extent, shall he carry it into effect? What are the legitimate objects of the warfare which he is to wage? There is no act of the legislature defining the powers, objects or mode

of warfare: by what rule, then, must he be governed? I think the only rational answer is by the law of nations as applied to a state of war. Whatever act is legitimate, whatever act is approved by the law, or hostilities among civilized nations, such he may, in his discretion, adopt and exercise; for with him the sovereignty of the nation rests as to the execution of the laws. If any of such acts are disapproved by the legislature, it is in their power to narrow and limit the extent to which the rights of war shall be exercised; but until such limit is assigned, the executive must have all the right of modern warfare vested in him, to be exercised in his sound discretion, or he can have none. Upon what principle, I would ask, can he have an implied authority to adopt one and not another? The best manner of annoying, injuring and pressing the enemy, must, from the nature of things, vary under different circumstances; and the executive is responsible to the nation for the faithful discharge of his duty, under all the changes of hostilities.
Keywords: *Chief executive, Civilized nations, Constitutional language, Executive discretion, Faithful discharge, Hostilities, Law of nations, Legislative disapproval, Sovereignty, War, Warfare*

Chief Justice John Marshall
Foster v. Neilson,
27 U.S. 253, 307 (1829)
In a controversy between two nations

concerning national boundary, it is scarcely possible that the courts of either should refuse to abide by the measures adopted by its own government. There being no common tribunal to decide between them, each determines for itself on its own rights, and if they cannot adjust their differences peaceably, the right remains with the strongest. The judiciary is not that department of the government, to which the assertion of its interests against foreign powers is confided; and its duty commonly is to decide upon individual rights, according to those principles which the political departments of the nation have established.

Keywords: *Boundaries, Common tribunal, Foreign powers, Individual rights, International controversy, Judicial limitations, Political departments*

Chief Justice Roger Taney
Dred Scott v. Sandford,
60 U.S. 393, 403–404 (1856)

The situation of this population was altogether unlike that of the Indian race. The latter, it is true, formed no part of the colonial communities, and never amalgamated with them in social connections or in government. But although they were uncivilized, they were yet a free and independent people, associated together in nations or tribes, and governed by their own laws. Many of these political communities were situated in territories to which the white race claimed the ultimate right of dominion. But that claim was acknowledged to be subject to the right of the Indians to occupy it as long as they thought proper, and neither the English nor colonial Governments claimed or exercised any dominion over the tribe or nation by whom it was occupied, nor claimed the right to the possession of the territory, until the tribe or nation consented to cede it. These Indian Governments were regarded and treated as foreign Governments, as much so as if an ocean had separated the red man from the white; and their freedom has constantly been acknowledged, from the time of the first emigration to the English colonies to the present day, by the different Governments which succeeded each other. Treaties have been negotiated with them, and their alliance sought for in war; and the people who compose these Indian political communities have always been treated as foreigners not living under our Government. It is true that the course of events has brought the Indian tribes within the limits of the United States under subjection to the white race; and it has been found necessary, for their sake as well as our own, to regard them as in a state of pupilage, and to legislate to a certain extent over them and the territory they occupy. But they may, without doubt, like the subjects of any other foreign Government, be naturalized by the authority of Congress, and become citizens of a State, and of the United States; and if an individual should leave his nation or tribe, and take up his abode among the white population, he would be entitled to all the rights and privileges which would belong to an emigrant from any other foreign people.

Keywords: *Citizenship, Colonial community, Foreign governments, Indian* race, Political communities, Right of dominion, Rights and privileges, Social connections, Territories, White race

Justice Robert Grier
The Prize Cases,
67 U.S. 635, 670 (1863)
Whether the President in fulfilling his duties, as Commander-in-chief, in suppressing an insurrection, has met with such armed hostile resistance, and a civil war of such alarming proportions as will compel him to accord to them the character of belligerents, is a question to be decided by *him*, and this Court must be governed by the decisions and acts of the political department of the Government to which this power was entrusted.
Keywords: *Belligerents, Civil war, Commander-in-chief, Hostile resistance, Insurrection, Judicial authority, Judicial limitations, Political departments, President*

Justice Samuel Nelson, dissenting
The Prize Cases,
67 U.S. 635, 698 (1863)
I am compelled to the conclusion that no civil war existed between this Government and the States in insurrection till recognized by the Act of Congress 13th of July 1861; that the President does not possess the power under the Constitution to declare war or recognize its existence within the meaning of the law of nations, which carries with it belligerent rights, and thus change the country and all its citizens from a state of peace to a state of war; that this power belongs exclusively to the Congress of the United States. . . .

Keywords: *Belligerent rights, Civil war, Congressional authority, Declaration of war, Insurrection, International law, Presidential authority, Presidential limitations, States*

Justice Samuel Miller
Chy Lung v. Freeman,
92 U.S. 275, 279 (1875)
If (the United States) should get into a difficulty which would lead to war, or to suspension of intercourse, would California alone suffer, or all the union?
Keywords: *States, Union, War*

Chief Justice Morrison Waite
Young v. United States,
97 U.S. 39, 67 (1877)
Property captured during the war was not taken by way of punishment for the treason of the owner, any more than the life of a soldier slain in battle was taken to punish him. He was killed because engaged in war, and exposed to its dangers. So property was captured because it had become involved in the war, and its removal from the enemy was necessary in order to lessen their warlike power. It was not taken because of its ownership, but because of its character.
Keywords: *Capture, Property, Punishment, Ownership, Treason, War*

Justice Stephen Field
Dow v. Johnson,
100 U.S. 158, 169 (1879)
. . . the military should always be kept in subjection to the laws of the country to which it belongs, and that he is no friend to the republic who advocates the contrary. The established principle of every free

people is, that the law shall alone govern; and to it the military must always yield.

Keywords: *Free people, Military, Republic*

Justice Samuel Miller
Edye v. Robertson,
112 U.S. 580, 599 (1884)

. . . we are of opinion that, so far as a treaty made by the United States with any foreign nation can become the subject of judicial cognizance in the courts of this country, it is subject to such acts as congress may pass for its enforcement, modification, or repeal.

Keywords: *Congressional oversight, Judicial cognizance, Treaty*

Justice Horace Gray
Jones v. Meehan,
175 U.S. 1, 11 (1899)

. . . the negotiations for the treaty are conducted, on the part of the United States, an enlightened and powerful nation, by representatives skilled in diplomacy, masters of a written language, understanding the modes and forms of creating the various technical estates known to their law, and assisted by an interpreter employed by themselves; that the treaty is drawn up by them and in their own language; that the Indians, on the other hand, are a weak and dependent people, who have no written language and are wholly unfamiliar with all the forms of legal expression, and whose only knowledge of the terms in which the treaty is framed is that imparted to them by the interpreter employed by the United States; and that the treaty must therefore be construed, not according to

the technical meaning of its words to learned lawyers, but in the sense in which they would naturally be understood by the Indians.

Keywords: *Diplomacy, Executive branch, Native Americans, Treaties, Treaty language*

Chief Justice Edward Douglas White
Arver v. United States,
245 U.S. 366, 390 (1918)

. . . as we are unable to conceive upon what theory the exaction by government from the citizen of the performance of his supreme and noble duty of contributing to the defense of the rights and honor of the nation as the result of a war declared by the great representative body of the people can be said to be the imposition of involuntary servitude in violation of the prohibitions of the Thirteenth Amendment, we are constrained to the conclusion that the contention to that effect is refuted by its mere statement.

Keywords: *Involuntary servitude, National defense, Representative body, Thirteenth Amendment, War*

Justice Frank Murphy, dissenting
Creek Nation v. United States,
318 U.S. 629, 641 (1943)

As a people our dealings with the Indian tribes have been too often marked by injustice, neglect, and even ruthless disregard of their interests and necessities. As a nation we have incurred moral and political responsibilities toward them and their descendants, which have been requited in some measure by treaties and statutes framed for the protection and advancement of their interests. Those enactments should always be read in the light of this high and noble purpose, in a manner that will give full scope and effect to the humane and liberal policy that has been adopted by the Congress to rectify past wrongs.

Keywords: Congressional intent, History, Humanity, Indian tribes, Public policy, Statutes, Treaties

Chief Justice Harlan Fiske Stone
Hirabayashi v. United States,
320 U.S. 81, 99 (1943)

Whatever views we may entertain regarding the loyalty to this country of the citizens of Japanese ancestry, we cannot reject as unfounded the judgment of the military authorities and of Congress that there were disloyal members of that population, whose number and strength could not be precisely and quickly ascertained. We cannot say that the war-making branches of the government did not have ground for believing that in a critical hour such persons could not readily be isolated and separately dealt with, and constituted a menace to the national defense and safety, which demanded that prompt and adequate measures be taken to guard against it.

Keywords: Ancestry, Citizens, Congressional powers, Loyalty, Military authorities, National defense, War-making branches

Justice William Douglas, concurring
Hirabayashi v. United States,
320 U.S. 81, 107–108 (1943)

. . . I think it important to emphasize that we are dealing here with a problem of loyalty not assimilation. Loyalty is a matter of mind and of heart not of race. That indeed is the history of America. Moreover, guilt is personal under our constitutional system. Detention for reasonable cause is one thing. Detention on account of ancestry is another.

Keywords: Ancestry, Assimilation, Detention, Guilt, History, Loyalty, Race

Justice Wiley Rutledge, concurring
Falbo v. United States,
320 U.S. 549, 557 (1944)

Experience demonstrates that in time of war individual liberties cannot always be entrusted safely to uncontrolled administrative discretion.

Keywords: Administrative discretion, Experience, History, Individual liberties, War

Justice Hugo Black
Korematsu v. United States,
323 U.S. 214, 219–220 (1944)

. . . hardships are part of war, and war is an aggregation of hardships. All citizens alike, both in and out of uniform, feel the impact of war in greater or lesser measure. Citizenship has its responsibilities as well as its privileges, and in time of war the burden is always heavier. Compulsory exclusion of large groups of citizens from their homes, except under circumstances of direst emergency and peril, is inconsistent with our basic governmental institutions. But when under conditions of modern warfare our shores are threatened by hostile forces, the power to protect must be commensurate with the threatened danger.

Keywords: Citizens, Compulsory exclusion, Danger, Emergency, Govern-

mental institutions, Hardships, Hostile forces, Privileges, Responsibilities, War

Justice Felix Frankfurter, concurring
Korematsu v. United States,
323 U.S. 214, 224 (1944)
. . . the validity of action under the war power must be judged wholly in the context of war. That action is not to be stigmatized as lawless because like action in times of peace would be lawless.
Keywords: *Governmental actions, War power*

Justice Frank Murphy, dissenting
Korematsu v. United States,
323 U.S. 214, 234 (1944)
. . . it is essential that there be definite limits to military discretion, especially where martial law has not been declared. Individuals must not be left impoverished of their constitutional rights on a plea of military necessity that has neither substance nor support. . . .
Keywords: *Citizens, Constitutional rights, Martial law, Military discretion, Military necessity*

Justice Frank Murphy, dissenting
Korematsu v. United States,
323 U.S. 214, 242 (1944)
All residents of this nation are kin in some way by blood or culture to a foreign land. Yet they are primarily and necessarily a part of the new and distinct civilization of the United States. They must accordingly be treated at all times as the heirs of the American experiment and as entitled to all the rights and freedoms guaranteed by the Constitution.

Keywords: *American experiment, Citizens, Civilization, Constitutional guarantees, Constitutional rights, Culture, Freedoms*

Justice Robert Jackson, dissenting
Korematsu v. United States,
323 U.S. 214, 245–246 (1944)
Much is said of the danger to liberty from the Army program for deporting and detaining these citizens of Japanese extraction. But a judicial construction of the due process clause that will sustain this order is a far more subtle blow to liberty than the promulgation of the order itself. A military order, however unconstitutional, is not apt to last longer than the military emergency. Even during that period a succeeding commander may revoke it all. But once a judicial opinion rationalizes such an order to show that it conforms to the Constitution, or rather rationalizes the Constitution to show that the Constitution sanctions such an order, the Court for all time has validated the principle of racial discrimination in criminal procedure and of transplanting American citizens. The principle then lies about like a loaded weapon ready for the hand of any authority that can bring forward a plausible claim of an urgent need. Every repetition imbeds that principle more deeply in our law and thinking and expands it to new purposes.
Keywords: *Citizens, Criminal procedure, Danger, Deportation, Detention, Due process, Judicial construction, Judicial rationalization, Liberty, Military emergency, Military order, Racial discrimination, Unconstitutional principles*

Chief Justice Harlan Fiske Stone
Mexico v. Hoffman,
324 U.S. 30, 35 (1945)
. . . courts should not so act as to embarrass the executive arm in its conduct of foreign affairs.
Keywords: *Executive branch, Foreign affairs, Judicial limitations, Separation of powers*

Justice William Douglas
Bridges v. Wixon,
326 U.S. 135, 154 (1945)
Though deportation is not technically a criminal proceeding, it visits a great hardship on the individual and deprives him of the right to stay and live and work in this land of freedom. That deportation is a penalty—at times a most serious one—cannot be doubted. Meticulous care must be exercised lest the procedure by which he is deprived of that liberty not meet the essential standards of fairness.
Keywords: *Criminal proceeding, Deportation, Freedom, Liberty, Penalty, Standards of fairness*

Justice Robert Jackson, concurring
Northwestern Band of Shoshone Indians v. United States,
324 U.S. 335, 355 (1945)
Nothing is gained by dwelling upon the unhappy conflicts that have prevailed between the Shoshones and the whites—conflicts which sometimes leaves one in doubt which side could make the better claim to be civilized. The generation of Indians who suffered the privations, indignities, and brutalities of the westward

march of the whites have gone to the happy hunting ground, and nothing that we can do can square the account with them. Whatever survives is a moral obligation resting on the descendants of the whites to do for the descendants of the Indians what in the conditions of this twentieth century is the decent thing.
Keywords: *Brutalities, Decency, History, Indignities, Moral obligation, Native Americans*

Justice Frank Murphy, dissenting
In re Yamashita,
327 U.S. 1, 28–29 (1946)
The effect in this instance, unfortunately, will be magnified infinitely, for here we are dealing with the rights of man on an international level. To subject an enemy belligerent to an unfair trial, to charge him with an unrecognized crime, or to vent on him our retributive emotions only antagonizes the enemy nation and hinders the reconciliation necessary to a peaceful world.
Keywords: *Belligerent, Enemy, Enemy nation, Fair trial, International law, Peaceful world, Retributive emotions, Rights of man, Unrecognized crime*

Justice Frank Murphy, dissenting
Haupt v. United States,
330 U.S. 631, 648 (1947)
An overt act of treason, however, should rest upon something more substantial than a reasonable doubt. Treason is different from ordinary crimes, possessing unique and difficult standards of proof which confine it within narrow spheres.

It has such serious connotations that its substance cannot be left to conjecture.
Keywords: *Crimes, Overt act, Reasonable doubt, Treason*

Justice Robert Jackson
Chicago & Southern Air Lines v.
Waterman Steamship Corp.,
333 U.S. 103, 111 (1948)
The President, both as Commander-in-chief and as the Nation's organ for foreign affairs, has available intelligence services whose reports neither are nor ought to be published to the world. It would be intolerable that courts, without the relevant information, should review and perhaps nullify actions of the Executive taken on information properly held secret. Nor can courts sit in camera in order to be taken into executive confidences. But even if courts could require full disclosure, the very nature of executive decisions as to foreign policy is political, not judicial. Such decisions are wholly confided by our Constitution to the political departments of the government, Executive and Legislative. They are delicate, complex, and involve large elements of prophecy. They are and should be undertaken only by those directly responsible to the people whose welfare they advance or imperil. They are decisions of a kind for which the Judiciary has neither aptitude, facilities nor responsibility and have long been held to belong in the domain of political power not subject to judicial intrusion or inquiry.
Keywords: *Commander-in-chief, Executive, Executive confidences, Executive decisions, Foreign affairs, In camera, Intelligence, Judicial authority, Judicial review, Political departments, President, Secrecy*

Justice Robert Jackson, concurring
Woods v. Cloyd W. Miller Co.,
333 U.S. 138, 146 (1948)
No one will question that [the war] power is the most dangerous one to free government in the whole catalogue of powers. It usually is invoked in haste and excitement when calm legislative consideration of constitutional limitation is difficult. It is executed in a time of patriotic fervor that makes moderation unpopular. And, worst of all, it is interpreted by the Judges under the influence of the same passions and pressures. Always, as in this case, the Government urges hasty decision to forestall some emergency or serve some purpose and pleads that paralysis will result if its claims to power are denied or their confirmation delayed.
Keywords: *Constitutional limitations, Emergency, Free government, Legislative deliberation, Patriotism, War power*

Justice Robert Jackson, dissenting
Knauff v. Shaughnessy,
338 U.S. 537, 551–552 (1950)
Congress will have to use more explicit language than any yet cited before I will agree that it has authorized an administrative officer to break up the family of an American citizen or force him to keep his wife by becoming an exile. Likewise, it will have to be much more explicit before I can agree that it authorized a finding of serious misconduct against the wife of an American citizen without no-

tice of charges, evidence of guilt and a chance to meet it.

Keywords: *Citizen, Congress, Congressional intent, Exile, Family*

Justice Stanley Reed
Carlson v. Landon,
342 U.S. 524, 537 (1952)
Deportation is not a criminal proceeding and has never been held to be punishment.
Keywords: *Criminal proceeding, Deportation, Punishment*

Justice Felix Frankfurter, concurring
Harisiades v. Shaughnessy,
342 U.S. 580, 597 (1952)
. . . whether immigration laws have been crude and cruel, whether they may have reflected xenophobia in general or anti-semitism or anti-catholicism, the responsibility belongs to Congress.
Keywords: *Congressional responsibilities, Immigration, Xenophobia*

Justice Robert Jackson, concurring
Youngstown Sheet & Tube Company v. Sawyer,
343 U.S. 579, 645 (1952)
We should not use this occasion to circumscribe, much less to contract, the lawful role of the President as Commander-in-Chief. I should indulge the widest latitude of interpretation to sustain his exclusive function to command the instruments of national force, at least when turned against the outside world for security of our society. But, when it is turned inward, not because of rebellion but because of a lawful economic struggle between industry and labor, it should have no such indulgence.

Keywords: *Commander-in-chief, Economic struggle, Executive authority, Executive limitations, Judicial review, National force, President, Rebellion, Security, Separation of powers*

Justice William Douglas
Kawakita v. United States,
343 U.S. 717, 736 (1952)
An American citizen owes allegiance to the United States wherever he may reside.
Keywords: *Allegiance, Citizen*

Chief Justice Earl Warren, dissenting
Perez v. Brownell,
356 U.S. 44, 64 (1958)
Citizenship *is* man's basic right for it is nothing less than the right to have rights. Remove this priceless possession and there remains a stateless person, disgraced and degraded in the eyes of his countrymen. He has no lawful claim to protection from any nation, and no nation may assert rights on his behalf. His very existence is at the sufferance of the state within whose borders he happens to be.
Keywords: *Basic right, Citizenship*

Justice Potter Stewart, concurring
New York Times Co. v. United States,
403 U.S. 713, 728 (1971)
Yet it is elementary that the successful conduct of international diplomacy and the maintenance of an effective national defense require both confidentiality and secrecy. Other nations can hardly deal with this Nation in an atmosphere of mutual trust unless they can be assured that their confidences will be kept. And within our own ex-

ecutive departments, the development of considered and intelligent international policies would be impossible if those charged with their formulation could not communicate with each other freely, frankly, and in confidence. In the area of basic national defense the frequent need for absolute secrecy is, of course, self-evident.

Key Words: *Communication, Confidentiality, Diplomacy, International affairs, National defense, Secrecy, Trust*

Justice Potter Stewart
Greer v. Spock,
424 U.S. 828, 840 (1976)
. . . nothing in the Constitution . . . disables a military commander from acting to avert what he perceives to be a clear danger to the loyalty, discipline, or morale of troops on the base under his command.

Keywords: *Loyalty, Military commander, Military discipline, Troop morale*

Chief Justice Warren Burger
Central Intelligence Agency v. Sims,
471 U.S. 159, 180 (1985)
The national interest sometimes makes it advisable, or even imperative, not to disclose information that may lead to the identity of intelligence sources.

Keywords: *Intelligence, National interest, Secrecy*

Chief Justice William Rehnquist
Goldman v. Weinberger,
475 U.S. 503, 509–510 (1986)
The desirability of dress regulations in the military is decided by the appropriate military officials, and they are under no constitutional mandate to abandon their considered professional judgment. . . . The First Amendment does not require the military to accommodate such religious practices in the face of its view that they would detract from the uniformity sought by the dress regulations.

Keywords: *Constitutional mandate, Dress codes, First Amendment, Military, Military officials, Religious practice, Uniformity*

Justice Sandra Day O'Connor, dissenting
Goldman v. Weinberger,
475 U.S. 503, 533 (1986)
Napoleon may have been correct to assert that, in the military sphere, morale is to all other factors as three is to one, but contradicted assertions of necessity by the military do not on the scales of justice bear a similarly disproportionate weight to sincere religious beliefs of the individual.

Keywords: *Justice, Military, Religious beliefs*

Chief Justice William Rehnquist
United States v. Verdugo-Urquidez,
494 U.S. 259, 275 (1990)
Some who violate our laws may live outside our borders under a regime quite different from that which obtains in this country. Situations threatening to important American interests may arise halfway around the globe, situations which in the view of the political branches of our Government require an American response with armed force. If there are to be restrictions on searches and seizures which oc-

cur incident to such American action, they must be imposed by the political branches through diplomatic understanding, treaty, or legislation.

Keywords: American interests, Armed forces, Criminals, Diplomacy, Legislation, Political branches, Searches and seizures, Treaties

Justice John Paul Stevens, concurring
United States v. Balsys,
524 U.S. 666, 701 (1998)
. . . I do not believe our Bill of Rights was intended to have any effect on the conduct of foreign proceedings.

Keywords: Bill of Rights, Foreign affairs

13. Everything Else

This final chapter proves that the Supreme Court is eventually forced to decide every constitutional/legal/social controversy sometime. Here you will find passages about various substantive legal areas—family law, wills, torts, etc. Of course this mixed bag chapter cannot include every subject area, but the student of the Court will certainly appreciate the breadth and scope of the cases and controversies that find themselves resolved one-at-a-time by nine-citizens-at-a-time.

Justice William Johnson, dissenting
Shanks v. Dupont,
28 U.S. 242, 262 (1830)
If the moral government of our maker and our parents is to be deduced from gratuitous benefits bestowed on us, why may not the government that has shielded our infancy claim from us a debt of gratitude to be repaid after manhood?
Keywords: *Debt of gratitude, Moral government*

Justice Samuel Miller, dissenting
Ex parte Garland,
71 U.S. 333, 385–386 (1866)
That fidelity to the government under which he lives, a true and loyal attachment to it, and a sincere desire for its preservation, are among the most essential qualifications which should be required in a lawyer, seems to me to be too clear for argument. The history of the

Anglo-Saxon race shows that, for ages past, the members of the legal profession have been powerful for good or evil to the government. They are, by the nature of their duties, the moulders of public sentiment on questions of government, and are every day engaged in aiding in the construction and enforcement of the laws. From among their numbers are necessarily selected the judges who expound the laws and the Constitution. To suffer treasonable sentiments to spread here unchecked, is to permit the stream on which the life of the nation depends to be poisoned at its source.
Keywords: *Constitutional authority, History, Lawyer, Legal construction, Legal profession, Loyalty, Public opinion, Public sentiment, Treason*

Justice Samuel Miller, dissenting
Ex parte Garland,
71 U.S. 333, 392 (1866)
A person proposing to appear in the court as an attorney is asked to take a certain oath. There is no charge made against him that he has been guilty of any of the crimes mentioned in that oath. There is no prosecution. There is not even an implication of guilt by reason of tendering him the oath, for it is required of the man who has lost everything in defence of the government, and whose loyalty is written in the honorable scars which cover his body, the same as of the guiltiest traitor in the land. His refusal

to take the oath subjects him to no prosecution. His taking it clears him of no
guilt, and acquits him of no charge.
Keywords: *Attorney, Crimes, Guilt,*
Oath, Prosecution

Justice Stephen Field
Maynard v. Hill,
125 U.S. 190, 211 (1888)
Other contracts may be modified, restricted, or enlarged, or entirely released
upon consent of the parties. Not so with
marriage. Once the relation is formed, the
law steps in and holds the parties to various obligations and liabilities. It is an
institution, in the maintenance and pu-
rity of which the public is deeply interested, for it is the foundation of the family and of society, without which there
would be neither civilization nor
progress.
Keywords: *Civilization, Contracts,*
Family, Marriage, Public interest, So-
ciety

Justice Horace Gray
Atherton v. Atherton,
181 U.S. 155, 163 (1901)
A husband without a wife, or a wife without a husband, is unknown to the law.
Keywords: *Husband, Legal recogni-*
tion, Wife

Justice David Brewer
United States v. Detroit Timber &
Lumber Co.,
200 U.S. 321, 337 (1906)
. . . the headnote is not the work of the
court, nor does it state its decision,—
though a different rule, it is true, is prescribed by statute in some states. It is sim-

ply the work of the reporter, gives his
understanding of the decision, and is
prepared for the convenience of the profession in the examination of the reports.
Keywords: *Headnotes, Judicial deci-*
sions, Legal reporter, Legal profession

**Justice Oliver Wendell Holmes, dissent-
ing**
Haddock v. Haddock,
201 U.S. 562, 628 (1906)
I do not suppose that civilization will
come to an end whichever way this case
is decided.
Keywords: *Civilization, Judicial review*

Justice Oliver Wendell Holmes, dissenting
Adkins v. Children's Hospital of District
of Columbia,
261 U.S. 525, 567–568 (1923)
The end, to remove conditions leading
to ill health, immorality and the deterio-
ration of the race, no one would deny to
be within the scope of constitutional legislation. The means are means that have
the approval of Congress, of many States,
and of those governments from which
we have learned our greatest lessons.
When so many intelligent persons, who
have studied the matter more than any
of us can, have thought that the means
are effective and are worth the price it
seems to me impossible to deny that the
belief reasonably may be held by reasonable men. If the law encountered no other
objection than that the means bore no
relation to the end or that they cost too
much I do not suppose that anyone
would venture to say that it was bad.
Keywords: *Constitutional legislation,*
Ends/means, Health, Morality, Race

Justice Louis Brandeis
Southwestern Bell Telephone Co. v. Public Service Commission,
262 U.S. 276, 310 (1923)
Value is a word of many meanings.
Keywords: *Definitions, Value*

Justice George Sutherland
Village of Euclid, Ohio v. Ambler Reality Co.,
272 U.S. 365, 388 (1926)
A nuisance may be merely a right thing in the wrong place, like a pig in the parlor instead of the barnyard.
Keywords: *Nuisance*

Justice Hugo Black
Federal Trade Commission v. Standard Education Society,
302 U.S. 112, 116 (1938)
The fact that a false statement may be obviously false to those who are trained and experienced does not change its character, nor take away its power to deceive others less experienced. There is no duty resting upon a citizen to suspect the honesty of those with whom he transacts business. Laws are made to protect the trusting as well as the suspicious. The best element of business has long since decided that honesty should govern competitive enterprises, and that the rule of caveat emptor should not be relied upon to reward fraud and deception.
Keywords: *Business, Caveat emptor, Competition, Deception, Falsehood, Fraud, Honesty, Legal purposes*

Justice Robert Jackson
Spies v. United States,
317 U.S. 492, 497 (1943)
The difference between willful failure to pay a tax when due, which is made a misdemeanor, and willful attempt to defeat and evade one, which is made a felony, is not easy to detect or define. Both must be willful, and willful, as we have said, is a word of many meanings, its construction often being influenced by its context.
Keywords: *Legal Terminology, Statutory construction, Willful*

Justice Wiley Rutledge
Prince v. Massachusetts,
321 U.S. 158, 166 (1944)
It is cardinal with us that the custody, care and nurture of the child reside first in the parents, whose primary function and freedom include preparation for the obligations the state can neither supply nor hinder.
Keywords: *Children, Custody, Parents, States*

Justice Wiley Rutledge
Thomas v. Collins,
323 U.S. 516, 535 (1945)
. . . whether words intended and designed to fall short of invitation would miss that mark is a question both of intent and of effect. No speaker, in such circumstances, safely could assume that anything he might say upon the general subject would not be understood by some as an invitation. In short, the supposedly clear-cut distinction between discussion, laudation, general advocacy, and solicitation puts the speaker in these circumstances wholly at the mercy of the varied understanding of his hearers and consequently of whatever inference may be drawn as to his intent and meaning.

Keywords: *Discussion, Hearers, Inferences, Intent, Meaning, Speakers*

Justice Hugo Black, dissenting
Williams v. North Carolina,
325 U.S. 226, 274 (1945)
Implicit in the majority of the opinions rendered by this and other courts, which, whether designedly or not, have set up obstacles to the procurement of divorces, is the assumption that divorces are an unmitigated evil, and that the law can and should force unwilling persons to live with each other. Others approach the problem as one which can best be met by moral, ethical and religious teachings. Which viewpoint is correct is not our concern. I am confident, however, that today's decision will no more aid in the solution of the problem than the Dred Scott decision aided in settling controversies over slavery.
Keywords: *Divorce, Ethical, Judicial solutions, Morality, Public policy, Religious*

Justice William Douglas
Cleveland v. United States,
329 U.S. 14, 19 (1946)
The establishment or maintenance of polygamous households is a notorious example of promiscuity.
Keywords: *Households, Polygamy, Promiscuity*

Justice Frank Murphy, dissenting
Cleveland v. United States,
329 U.S. 14, 25–26 (1946)
There are four fundamental forms of marriage: (1) monogamy; (2) polygyny, or one man with several wives; (3) polyandry, or one woman with several husbands; and (4) group marriage. The term "polygamy" covers both polygyny and polyandry. Thus we are dealing here with polygyny, one of the basic forms of marriage. Historically, its use has far exceeded that of any other form. It was quite common among ancient civilizations and was referred to many times by the writers of the Old Testament; even today it is to be found frequently among certain pagan and non-Christian peoples of the world. We must recognize, then, that polygyny, like other forms of marriage, is basically a cultural institution rooted deeply in the religious beliefs and social mores of those societies in which it appears. It is equally true that the beliefs and mores of the dominant culture of the contemporary world condemn the practice as immoral and substitute monogamy in its place. To those beliefs and mores I subscribe, but that does not alter the fact that polygyny is a form of marriage built upon a set of social and moral principles. It must be recognized and treated as such.
Keywords: *Ancient civilizations, Cultural institution, Group marriage, History, Marriage, Monogamy, Morality, Polyandry, Polygamy, Polygyny, Religious beliefs, Social mores*

Justice Felix Frankfurter, concurring
Hurd v. Hodge,
334 U.S. 24, 36 (1948)
Equity is rooted in conscience.
Keywords: *Conscience, Equity, Fairness, Principle*

Justice Felix Frankfurter
Goesaert v. Cleary,
335 U.S. 464, 465–466 (1948)

Michigan could, beyond question, forbid all women from working behind a bar. This is so despite the vast changes in the social and legal position of women. The fact that women may now have achieved the virtues that men have long claimed as their prerogatives and now indulge in vices that men have long practiced, does not preclude the states from drawing a sharp line between the sexes, certainly in such matters as the regulation of the liquor traffic.

Keywords: *Employment, Legal status, Liquor traffic, Social status, States, Vices, Virtues, Women*

Justice Felix Frankfurter, dubitante
Radio Corp. v. United States,
341 U.S. 412, 425 (1951)

One of the more important sources of the retardation or regression of civilization is man's tendency to use new inventions indiscriminately or too hurriedly without adequate reflection of long-range consequences.

Keywords: *Civilization, Consequences, Inventions*

Justice Robert Jackson, dissenting
Dalehite v. United States,
346 U.S. 15, 51–52 (1953)

This is a day of synthetic living, when to an ever-increasing extent our population is dependent upon mass producers for its food and drink, its cures and complexions, its apparel and gadgets. These no longer are natural or simple products but complex ones whose composition and qualities are often secret. Such a dependent society must exact greater care than in more simple days and must require from manufacturers or producers increased integrity and caution as the only protection of its safety and well-being. Purchasers cannot try out drugs to determine whether they kill or cure. Consumers cannot test the youngster's cowboy suit or the wife's sweater to see if they are apt to burst into fatal flames. Carriers, by land or by sea, cannot experiment with the combustibility of goods in transit. Where experiment or research is necessary to determine the presence or the degree of danger, the product must not be tried out on the public, nor must the public be expected to possess the facilities or the technical knowledge to learn for itself of inherent but latent dangers. The claim that a hazard was not foreseen is not available to one who did not use foresight appropriate to his enterprise.

Keywords: *Consumers, Contemporary culture, Danger, Experimentation, Foreseeability, Hazards, Mass production, Research, Safety, Society, Technology*

Chief Justice Earl Warren
Brown v. Board of Education,
347 U.S. 483, 493 (1954)

Today, education is perhaps the most important function of state and local governments. Compulsory school attendance laws and the great expenditures for education both demonstrate our recognition of the importance of education to our democratic society. It is required in the performance of our most basic public responsibilities, even service in the armed forces. It is the very foundation of good citizenship. Today it is a principal instrument in awakening the child to cultural values, in preparing him for later professional training, and in helping him to adjust normally to his environment. In these days, it is doubtful that any child may reasonably be expected to succeed in life if he is denied the opportunity of an education. Such an opportunity, where the state has undertaken to provide it, is a right which must be made available to all on equal terms.

Keywords: Children, Citizenship, Compulsory school attendance, Democratic society, Education, Equality, Local government, Opportunities, Public funding, Public responsibilities, State government

Justice Felix Frankfurter, concurring
Schware v. Board of Bar Examiners of New Mexico,
353 U.S. 232, 247 (1957)
Certainly since the time of Edward I, through all the vicissitudes of seven centuries of Anglo-American history, the legal profession has played a role all its own. The bar has not enjoyed prerogatives; it has been entrusted with anxious responsibilities. One does not have to inhale the self-adulatory bombast of after-dinner speeches to affirm that all the interests of man that are comprised under the constitutional guarantees given to "life, liberty and property" are in the professional keeping of lawyers. It is a fair characterization of the lawyer's responsibility in our society that he stands "as a shield," to quote Devlin, J., in defense of right and to ward off wrong. From a profession charged with such responsibilities there must be exacted those qualities of truth-speaking, of a high sense of honor, of granite discretion, of the strictest observance of fiduciary responsibility, that have, throughout the centuries, been compendiously described as "moral character."

Keywords: Discretion, Fiduciary responsibility, History, Honor, Legal profession, Legal responsibilities, Moral character, Society, Truth

Justice William Brennan
Roth v. United States,
354 U.S. 476, 487 (1957)
. . . sex and obscenity are not synonymous. Obscene material is material which deals with sex in a manner appealing to prurient interest. The portrayal of sex, e.g., in art, literature and scientific works, is not itself sufficient reason to deny material the constitutional protection of freedom of speech and press. Sex, a great and mysterious motive force in human life, has indisputably been a subject of absorbing interest to mankind through the ages; it is one of the vital problems of human interest and public concern.

Keywords: Constitutional protection, Free press, Free speech, Human interest, Obscenity, Prurient interest, Public concern, Sex

Justice Hugo Black, dissenting
In re Anastaplo,
366 U.S. 82, 114–116 (1961)
. . . this record shows that Anastaplo has many of the qualities that are needed in

the American Bar. It shows, not only that Anastaplo has followed a high moral, ethical and patriotic course in all of the activities of his life, but also that he combines these more common virtues with the uncommon virtue of courage to stand by his principles at any cost. It is such men as these who have most greatly honored the profession of the law—men like Malsherbes, who, at the cost of his own life and the lives of his family, sprang unafraid to the defense of Louis XVI against the fanatical leaders of the Revolutionary government of France—men like Charles Evans Hughes, Sr., later Mr. Chief Justice Hughes, who stood up for the constitutional rights of socialists to be socialists and public officials despite the threats and clamorous protests of self-proclaimed superpatriots—men like Charles Evans Hughes, Jr., and John W. Davis, who, while against everything for which the Communists stood, strongly advised the Congress in 1948 that it would be unconstitutional to pass the law then proposed to outlaw the Communist Party—men like Lord Erskine, James Otis, Clarence Darrow, and the multitude of others who have dared to speak in defense of causes and clients without regard to personal danger to themselves. The legal profession will lose much of its nobility and its glory if it is not constantly replenished with lawyers like these. To force the Bar to become a group of thoroughly orthodox, time-serving, government-fearing individuals is to humiliate and degrade it.

Keywords: *Courage, Ethics, Legal profession, Morality, Orthodoxy, Patriotism, Principled, Virtue*

Justice William Douglas
Levy v. Louisiana,
391 U.S. 68, 72 (1968)
Legitimacy or illegitimacy of birth has no relation to the nature of the wrong allegedly inflicted on the mother. These children, though illegitimate, were dependent on her; she cared for them and nurtured them; they were indeed hers in the biological and in the spiritual sense; in her death they suffered wrong in the sense that any dependent would.

Keywords: *Birth, Dependency, Illegitimacy, Parent*

Justice Hugo Black, dissenting
Tinker v. Des Moines Independent School District,
393 U.S. 503, 518 (1969)
. . . if the time has come when pupils of state-supported schools, kindergartens, grammar schools, or high schools, can defy and flout orders of school officials to keep their minds on their own schoolwork, it is the beginning of a new revolutionary era of permissiveness in this country fostered by the judiciary.

Keywords: *Behavior, Education, Judicial legitimacy, Public policy, Schools, Students*

Justice Hugo Black, dissenting
Tinker v. Des Moines Independent School District,
393 U.S. 503, 525–526 (1969)
This case . . . wholly without constitutional reasons in my judgment, subjects all the public schools in the country to the whims and caprices of their loudest-mouthed, but maybe not their brightest, students. I, for one, am not fully persuaded that

school pupils are wise enough, even with this Court's expert help from Washington, to run the 23,390 public school systems in our 50 States. I wish, therefore, wholly to disclaim any purpose on my part to hold that the Federal constitution compels the teachers, parents, and elected school officials to surrender control of the American public school system to public school students.

Keywords: *Belligerence, Constitutional legitimacy, Dissent, Education, Judicial authority, Judicial review, Judicial wisdom, Parents, Schools, Students, Teachers*

Chief Justice Warren Burger
Lemon v. Kurtzman,
403 U.S. 602, 624 (1971)
A certain momentum develops in constitutional theory and it can be a "downhill thrust" easily set in motion but difficult to retard or stop. Development by momentum is not invariably bad; indeed, it is the way the common law has grown, but it is a force to be recognized and reckoned with. The dangers are increased by the difficulty of perceiving in advance exactly where the "verge" of the precipice lies.

Keywords: *Common law, Constitutional theory, Slippery slope*

Justice Byron White
Lindsey v. Normet,
405 U.S. 56, 74 (1972)
We do not denigrate the importance of decent, safe and sanitary housing. But the Constitution does not provide judicial remedies for every social and economic ill. We are unable to perceive in

that document any constitutional guarantee of access to dwellings of a particular quality or any recognition of the right of a tenant to occupy the real property of his landlord beyond the term of his lease, without the payment of rent. Absent constitutional mandate, the assurance of adequate housing and the definition of landlord-tenant relationships are legislative, not judicial, functions.

Keywords: *Access to dwellings, Constitutional limitations, Economic ill, Housing, Judicial limitations, Judicial remedies, Landlord-tenant relationship, Legislative function, Real property, Social ill*

Justice Lewis Powell
Weber v. Aetna Casualty & Surety Co.,
406 U.S. 164, 175–176 (1972)
The status of illegitimacy has expressed through the ages society's condemnation of irresponsible liaisons beyond the bonds of marriage. But visiting this condemnation on the head of an infant is illogical and unjust. Moreover, imposing disabilities on the illegitimate child is contrary to the basic concept of our system that legal burdens should bear some relationship to individual responsibility or wrongdoing. Obviously, no child is responsible for his birth and penalizing the illegitimate child is an ineffectual—as well as an unjust—way of deterring the parent. Courts are powerless to prevent the social opprobrium suffered by these hapless children, but the Equal Protection Clause does enable us to strike down discriminatory laws relating to status of birth where—as in this case—the classification is justified by no legitimate state interest, compelling or otherwise.

Keywords: *Birth, Children, Classification, Discrimination, Equal protection, Illegitimacy, Infants, Legal burdens, Marriage, Morality, State interest*

Justice William Douglas, dissenting
Flood v. Kuhn,
407 U.S. 258, 286 (1972)
This Court's decision in *Federal Baseball* [*Club* v. *National League* (1922)] is a derelict in the stream of the law that we, its creator, should remove. Only a romantic view of a rather dismal business account over the last 50 years would keep that derelict in midstream.
Keywords: *Baseball, Business, Judicial romanticism*

Justice William Douglas, dissenting
Flood v. Kuhn,
407 U.S. 258, 287 (1972)
An industry so dependent on radio and television as is baseball and gleaning vast interstate revenues would be hard put to say with the Court in *Federal Baseball* case that baseball was only a local exhibition, not trade or commerce. . . . Baseball is today big business that is packaged with beer, with broadcasting, and with other industries. The beneficiaries of the *Federal Baseball* decision are not the Babe Ruths, Ty Cobbs, and Lou Gehrigs.
Keywords: *Baseball, Business, Commerce, Industry, Interstate revenues, Local exhibition, Trade*

Justice Harry Blackmun, concurring
Lau v. Nichols,
414 U.S. 563, 571–572 (1974)
Against the possibility that the Court's judgment may be interpreted too broadly, I stress the fact that the children with whom we are concerned here number about 1,800. This is a very substantial group that is being deprived of any meaningful schooling because the children cannot understand the language of the classroom. We may only guess as to why they have had no exposure to English in their preschool years. Earlier generations of American ethnic groups have overcome the language barrier by earnest parental endeavor or by the hard fact of being pushed out of the family or community nest and into the realities of broader experience.
Keywords: *Children, Community, English, Ethnic groups, Family, History, Language, School*

Justice Harry Blackmun
Planned Parenthood of Missouri v. Danforth,
428 U.S. 52, 69–70 (1976)
We are not unaware of the deep and proper concern and interest that a devoted and protective husband has in his wife's pregnancy and in the growth and development of the fetus she is carrying. Neither has this Court failed to appreciate the importance of the marital relationship in our society. Moreover, we recognize that the decision whether to undergo or to forego an abortion may have profound effects on the future of any marriage, effects that are both physical and mental, and possibly deleterious. Notwithstanding these factors, we cannot hold that the State has the constitutional authority to give the spouse unilaterally the ability to pro-

hibit the wife from terminating her pregnancy, when the State itself lacks that right.
Keywords: *Abortion, Constitutional authority, Fetus, Husband, Marital relationship, Marriage, Pregnancy, Society, Spouse, States, Wife*

Justice Byron White, concurring
Nixon v. Administrator of General Services,
433 U.S. 425, 490–491 (1977)
. . . I would question whether a mere historical interest in purely private communications would be a sufficient predicate for taking them for public use. Historical considerations are normally sufficient grounds for condemning property; but whatever may be true of the great bulk of the materials in the event they are declared to be Mr. Nixon's property, I doubt that the Government is entitled to his purely private communications merely because it wants to preserve them and offers compensation.
Keywords: *Compensation, Historical interest, Private communications, Property, Public use, Takings*

Justice William Rehnquist, dissenting
In re Primus,
436 U.S. 412, 440 (1978)
. . . the Court tells its own tale of two lawyers: One tale ends happily for the lawyer and one does not. If we were given the latitude of novelists in deciding between happy and unhappy endings for the heroes and villains of our tales, I might well join in the Court's disposition of both cases. But under our federal system it is for the States to decide which lawyers shall be admitted to the Bar and remain there; this Court may interfere only if the State's decision is rendered impermissible by the United States Constitution. We can, of course, develop a jurisprudence of epithets and slogans in this area, in which "ambulance chasers" suffer one fate and "civil liberties lawyers" another.
Keywords: *Fates, Federal system, Jurisprudence, Lawyers, States*

Justice Harry Blackmun, dissenting
World-wide Volkswagen Corporation v. Woodson,
444 U.S. 286, 318 (1980)
It has been said that we are a nation on wheels. What we are concerned with here is the automobile and its peripatetic character. One need only examine our national network of interstate highways, or make an appearance on one of them, or observe the variety of license plate present not only on those highways but in any metropolitan area, to realize that any automobile is likely to wander from its place of licensure or from its place of distribution and retail sale. Miles per gallon on the highway (as well as in the city) and mileage per tankful are familiar allegations in manufacturers' advertisements today. To expect that any new automobile will remain in the vicinity of its retail sale—like the 1914 electric drive car by the proverbial "little old lady"—is to blink at reality.
Keywords: *Advertising, Automobiles, Cities, Highways, Miles per gallon, Travel*

Justice Sandra Day O'Connor, dissenting
Goldman v. Weinberger,
475 U.S. 503, 531 (1986)
A citizen pursuing even the most noble

cause must remain within the bounds of the law. So, too, the Government may, even in pursuing its most compelling interests, be subject to specific restraints in doing so.

Keywords: *Citizen, Ends/means, Governmental restraints, Individual restraints*

Justice John Paul Stevens, concurring in part, dissenting in part
Patterson v. McLean Credit Union,
491 U.S. 164, 221 (1989)
A contract is not just a piece of paper. Just as a single word is the skin of a living thought, so is a contract evidence of a vital, ongoing relationship between human beings.

Keywords: *Contracts, Human interaction*

Justice Antonin Scalia, concurring
Cruzan v. Director, Missouri Department of Health,
497 U.S. 261, 292–293 (1990)
The various opinions in this case portray quite clearly the difficult, indeed agonizing, questions that are presented by the constantly increasing power of science to keep the human body alive for longer than any reasonable person would want to inhabit it. The States have begun to grapple with these problems through legislation. I am concerned, from the tenor of today's opinions, that we are poised to confuse that enterprise as successfully as we have confused the enterprise of legislating concerning abortion—requiring it to be conducted against a background of federal constitutional imperatives that are unknown because they are being newly crafted from Term to Term. That would be a great misfortune.

Keywords: *Constitutional imperatives, Human body, Legislation, Novel concepts, Science, States*

Justice John Paul Stevens, dissenting
Lucas v. South Carolina Coastal Council,
505 U.S. 1003, 1069 (1992)
Arresting the development of the common law is not only a departure from our prior decisions; it is also profoundly unwise. The human condition is one of constant learning and evolution—both moral and practical. Legislatures implement that new learning; in doing so, they must often revise the definition of property and the rights of property owners. Thus, when the Nation came to understand that slavery was morally wrong and mandated the emancipation of all slaves, it, in effect, redefined "property."

Keywords: *Common law, Legal development, Legislatures, Morality, Ownership, Precedents, Property, Slavery*

Justice Harry Blackmun
Daubert v. Merrell Dow Pharmaceuticals, Inc.,
509 U.S. 579, 596–597 (1993)
It is true that open debate is an essential part of both legal and scientific analyses. Yet there are important differences between the quest for truth in the courtroom and the quest for truth in the laboratory. Scientific conclusions are subject to perpetual revision. Law, on the other hand, must resolve disputes finally and quickly. The scientific project is advanced by broad and wide-ranging consideration of a mul-

titude of hypotheses, for those that are incorrect will eventually be shown to be so, and that in itself is an advance. Conjectures that are probably wrong are of little use, however, in the project of reaching a quick, final, and binding legal judgment—often of great consequence—about a particular set of events in the past. We recognize that, in practice, a gatekeeping role for the judge, no matter how flexible, inevitably on occasion will prevent the jury from learning of authentic insights and innovations. That, nevertheless, is the balance that is struck by Rules of Evidence designed not for the exhaustive search for cosmic understanding, but for the particularized resolution of legal disputes.

Keywords: *Judges, Laboratory, Rules of evidence, Science*

Chief Justice William Rehnquist
United States v. Lopez,
514 U.S. 549, 567 (1995)
The possession of a gun in a local school zone is in no sense an economic activity that might, through repetition elsewhere, substantially affect any sort of interstate commerce. Respondent was a local student at a local school; there is no indication that he had recently moved in interstate commerce, and there is no requirement that his possession of the firearm have any concrete tie to interstate commerce.

Keywords: *Economic activity, Federalism, Firearms, Interstate commerce, Schools, States' rights, Students*

Justice Stephen Breyer, dissenting
United States v. Lopez,
514 U.S. 549, 625 (1995)
. . . in today's economic world, gun-re-

lated violence near the classroom makes a significant difference to our economic, as well as our social, well-being.

Keywords: *Economic activity, Education, Gun violence, Public policy, Schools*

Justice Antonin Scalia, dissenting
Romer v. Evans,
517 U.S. 620, 652–653 (1996)
When the Court takes sides in the culture wars, it tends to be with the knights rather than the villeins—and more specifically with the Templars, reflecting the views and values of the lawyer class from which the Court's Members are drawn. How that class feels about homosexuality will be evident to anyone who wishes to interview job applicants at virtually any of the Nation's law schools. The interviewer may refuse to offer a job because the applicant is a Republican; because he is an adulterer; because he went to the wrong prep school or belongs to the wrong country club; because he eats snails; because he is a womanizer; because she wears real-animal fur; or even because he hates the Chicago Cubs. But if the interviewer should wish not to be an associate or partner of an applicant because he disapproves of the applicant's homosexuality, then he will have violated the pledge which the Association of American Law Schools requires all its member-schools to exact from job interviewers: "assurance of the employer's willingness" to hire homosexuals. This law-school view of what "prejudices" must be stamped out may be contrasted with the more plebeian attitudes that apparently still prevail in the United

States Congress, which has been unresponsive to repeated attempts to extend to homosexuals the protections of federal civil rights laws . . . .

Key Words: *Civil rights, Culture, Employment, Homosexuality, Law schools, Lawyers*

Justice Antonin Scalia
Oncale v. Sundowner Offshore Services, Inc.,
523 U.S. 75, 81–82 (1998)
A professional football player's working environment is not severely or pervasively abusive, for example, if the coach smacks him on the buttocks as he heads onto the field—even if the same behavior would reasonably be experienced as abusive by the coach's secretary (male or female) back at the office. The real social impact of workplace behavior often depends on a constellation of surrounding circumstances, expectations, and relationships which are not fully captured by a simple recitation of the words used or the physical acts performed. Common sense, and an appropriate sensitivity to social context, will enable courts and juries to distinguish between simple teasing or roughhousing among members of the same sex, and conduct which a reasonable person in the plaintiff's position would find severely hostile or abusive.

Keywords: *Common sense, Conduct, Same sex, Sexual harassment, Social impact, Workplace behavior*

Justice Clarence Thomas, dissenting
Burlington Industries Inc. v. Ellerth,
524 U.S. 742, 769–770 (1998)
If a supervisor creates a hostile work environment, however, he does not act for the employer. As the Court concedes, a supervisor's creation of a hostile work environment is neither within the scope of his employment, nor part of his apparent authority. Indeed, a hostile work environment is antithetical to the interest of the employer. In such circumstances, an employer should be liable only if it has been negligent. That is, liability should attach only if the employer either knew, or in the exercise of reasonable care should have known, about the hostile work environment and failed to take remedial action. Sexual harassment is simply not something that employers can wholly prevent without taking extraordinary measures—constant video and audio surveillance, for example—that would revolutionize the workplace in a manner incompatible with a free society.

Keywords: *Employment law, Hostile workplace, Sexual harassment, Vicarious liability*

Justice Antonin Scalia, dissenting
Holloway v. United States,
526 U.S. ___, ___ (1999)
Conditional intent is no more embraced by the unmodified word "intent" than a sea lion is embraced by the unmodified word "lion."

Keywords: *Definitions, Intent*

Justice Anthony Kennedy, dissenting
Davis v. Monroe County Board of Education,
526 U.S. ___, ___ (1999)
In the final analysis, this case is about federalism. Yet the majority's decision today says not one word about the federal balance. Preserving our federal system is a

legitimate end in itself. It is, too, the means to other ends. It ensures that essential choices can be made by a government more proximate to the people than the vast apparatus of federal power. Defining the appropriate role of schools in teaching and supervising children who are beginning to explore their own sexuality and learning how to express it to others is one of the most complex and sensitive issues our schools face. Such decisions are best made by parents and by the teachers and school administrators who can counsel with them. The delicacy and immense significance of teaching children about sexuality should cause the Court to act with great restraint before it displaces state and local governments.

Keywords: Children, Ends/means, Federalism, Federal power, Parents, School administrators, Schools, Sexuality, States, Teachers, Teaching

Appendix A

The Constitution of the United States of America

Preamble

We the People of the United States, in Order to form a more perfect Union, establish Justice, insure domestic Tranquillity, provide for the common defence, promote the general Welfare, and secure the Blessings of Liberty to ourselves and our Posterity, do ordain and establish this Constitution for the United States of America.

Article I

Section 1

All legislative Powers herein granted shall be vested in a Congress of the United States, which shall consist of a Senate and House of Representatives.

Section 2

The House of Representatives shall be composed of Members chosen every second Year by the People of the several States, and the Electors in each State shall have the Qualifications requisite for Electors of the most numerous Branch of the State Legislature.

No Person shall be a Representative who shall not have attained to the age of twenty five Years, and been seven Years a Citizen of the United States, and who shall not, when elected, be an Inhabitant of that State in which he shall be chosen. Representatives and direct Taxes shall be apportioned among the several States which may be included within this Union, according to their respective Numbers, which shall be determined by adding to the whole Number of free Persons, including those bound to Service for a Term of Years, and excluding Indians not taxed, three fifths of all other Persons. The actual Enumeration shall be made within three Years after the first Meeting of the Congress of the United States, and within every subsequent Term of ten Years, in such Manner as they shall by Law direct. The Number of Representatives shall not exceed one for every thirty Thousand, but each State shall have at Least one Representative; and until such enumeration shall be made, the State of New Hampshire shall be entitled to chuse three, Massachusetts eight, Rhode-Island and Providence Plantations one, Connecticut five, New-York six, New Jersey four, Pennsylvania eight, Delaware one, Maryland six, Virginia ten, North Carolina five, South Carolina five, and Georgia three.

When vacancies happen in the Representation from any State, the Executive Authority thereof shall issue Writs of Election to fill such Vacancies.

The House of Representatives shall chuse their Speaker and other Officers; and shall have the sole Power of Impeachment.

Section 3

The Senate of the United States shall be composed of two Senators from each State, chosen by the Legislature thereof, for six Years; and each Senator shall have one Vote.

Immediately after they shall be assembled in Consequence of the first Election, they shall be divided as equally as may be into three Classes. The Seats of the Senators of the first Class shall be vacated at the Expiration of the second Year, of the second Class at the Expiration of the fourth Year, and of the third Class at the Expiration of the sixth Year, so that one third may be chosen every second Year; and if Vacancies happen by Resignation, or otherwise, during the Recess of the Legislature of any State, the Executive thereof may make temporary Appointments until the next Meeting of the Legislature, which shall then fill such Vacancies.

No Person shall be a Senator who shall not have attained to the Age of thirty Years, and been nine Years a Citizen of the United States, and who shall not, when elected, be an Inhabitant of that State for which he shall be chosen.

The Vice President of the United States shall be President of the Senate but shall have no Vote, unless they be equally divided.

The Senate shall chuse their other Officers, and also a President pro tempore, in the Absence of the Vice President, or when he shall exercise the Office of President of the United States.

The Senate shall have the sole Power to try all Impeachments. When sitting for that Purpose, they shall be on Oath or Affirmation. When the President of the United States is tried the Chief Justice shall preside: And no Person shall be convicted without the Concurrence of two thirds of the Members present.

Judgment in Cases of Impeachment shall not extend further than to removal from Office, and disqualification to hold and enjoy any Office of honor, Trust or Profit under the United States: but the Party convicted shall nevertheless be liable and subject to Indictment, Trial, Judgment and Punishment, according to Law.

Section 4

The Times, Places and Manner of holding Elections for Senators and Representatives, shall be prescribed in each State by the Legislature thereof; but the Congress may at any time by Law make or alter such Regulations, except as to the Places of chusing Senators.

The Congress shall assemble at least once in every Year, and such Meeting shall be on the first Monday in December, unless they shall by Law appoint a different Day.

Section 5

Each House shall be the Judge of the Elections, Returns and Qualifications of its own Members, and a Majority of each shall constitute a Quorum to do Business; but a smaller Number may adjourn from day to day, and may be authorized to compel the Attendance of absent Members, in such Manner, and under such Penalties as each House may provide.

Each House may determine the Rules of its Proceedings, punish its Members for disorderly Behaviour, and, with the Concurrence of two thirds, expel a Member.

Each House shall keep a Journal of its Proceedings, and from time to time publish the same, excepting such Parts as may in their Judgment require Secrecy; and the Yeas and Nays of the Members of either House on any question shall, at the Desire of one fifth of those Present, be entered on the Journal.

Neither House, during the Session of Congress, shall, without the Consent of the other, adjourn for more than three days, nor to any other Place than that in which the two Houses shall be sitting.

Section 6

The Senators and Representatives shall receive a Compensation for their Services, to be ascertained by Law, and paid out of the Treasury of the United States. They shall in all Cases, except Treason, Felony and Breach of the Peace, be privileged from Arrest during their Attendance at the Session of their respective Houses, and in going to and returning from the same; and for any Speech or Debate in either House, they shall not be questioned in any other Place.

No Senator or Representative shall, during the Time for which he was elected, be appointed to any civil Office under the Authority of the United States, which shall have been created, or the Emoluments whereof shall have been encreased during such time; and no Person holding any Office under the United States, shall be a Member of either House during his Continuance in Office.

Section 7

All Bills for raising Revenue shall originate in the House of Representatives; but the Senate may propose or concur with amendments as on other Bills.

Every Bill which shall have passed the House of Representatives and the Senate, shall, before it become a law, be presented to the President of the United States: If he approve he shall sign it, but if not he shall return it, with his Objections to that House in which it shall have originated, who shall enter the Objections at large on their Journal, and proceed to reconsider it. If after such Reconsideration two thirds of that House shall agree to pass the Bill, it shall be sent, together with the Objections, to the other House, by which it shall likewise be reconsidered, and if approved by two thirds of that House, it shall become a Law. But in all such Cases the Votes of both Houses shall be determined by Yeas and Nays, and the Names of the Persons voting for and against the Bill shall be entered on the Journal of each House respectively. If any Bill shall not be returned by the President within ten Days (Sundays excepted) after it shall have been presented to him, the Same shall be a Law, in like Manner as if he had signed it, unless the Congress by their Adjournment prevent its Return, in which Case it shall not be a Law.

Every Order, Resolution, or Vote to which the Concurrence of the Senate and House of Representatives may be necessary (except on a question of Adjournment) shall be presented to the President of the United States; and before the Same shall take Effect, shall be approved by him, or being disapproved by him, shall be repassed by two thirds of the Senate and House of Representatives, according to the Rules and Limitations prescribed in the Case of a Bill.

Section 8

The Congress shall have Power To lay and collect Taxes, Duties, Imposts and Excises, to pay the Debts and provide for the common Defence and general Welfare of the United States; but all Duties, Imposts and Excises shall be uniform throughout the United States;

To borrow Money on the credit of the United States;

To regulate Commerce with foreign Nations, and among the several States, and with the Indian Tribes;

To establish an uniform Rule of Naturalization, and uniform Laws on the subject of Bankruptcies throughout the United States;

To coin Money, regulate the Value thereof, and of foreign Coin, and fix the Standard of Weights and Measures;

To provide for the Punishment of counterfeiting the Securities and current Coin of the United States;

To establish Post Offices and post Roads;

To promote the Progress of Science and useful Arts, by securing for limited Times to Authors and Inventors the exclusive Right to their respective Writings and Discoveries;

To constitute Tribunals inferior to the supreme Court;

To define and punish Piracies and Felonies committed on the high Seas, and Offences against the Law of Nations;

To declare War, grant Letters of Marque and Reprisal, and make Rules concerning Captures on Land and Water;

To raise and support Armies, but no Appropriation of Money to that Use shall be for a longer Term than two Years;

To provide and maintain a Navy;

To make Rules for the Government and Regulation of the land and naval Forces;

To provide for calling forth the Militia to execute the Laws of the Union, suppress Insurrections and repeal Invasions;

To provide for organizing, arming, and disciplining, the Militia, and for governing such Part of them as may be employed in the Service of the United States, reserving to the States respectively, the Appointment of the Officers, and the Authority of training the Militia according to the discipline prescribed by Congress;

To exercise exclusive Legislation in all

Cases whatsoever, over such District (not exceeding ten Miles square) as may, by Cession of Particular States, and the Acceptance of Congress, become the Seat of the Government of the United States, and to exercise like Authority over all Places purchased by the Consent of the Legislature of the State in which the Same shall be, for the Erection of Forts, Magazines, Arsenals, dock-Yards and other needful Buildings;_And

To make all Laws which shall be necessary and proper for carrying into Execution the foregoing Powers and all other Powers vested by this Constitution in the Government of the United States, or in any Department or Officer thereof.

Section 9

The Migration or Importation of such Persons as any of the States now existing shall think proper to admit, shall not be prohibited by the Congress prior to the Year one thousand eight hundred and eight, but a Tax or duty may be imposed on such Importation, not exceeding ten dollars for each Person.

The Privilege of the Writ of Habeas Corpus shall not be suspended, unless when in Cases or Rebellion or Invasion the public Safety may require it.

No Bill of Attainder or ex post facto Law shall be passed.

No Capitation, or other direct, Tax shall be laid, unless in Proportion to the Census of Enumeration herein before directed to be taken.

No Tax or Duty shall be laid on Articles exported from any State.

No Preference shall be given by any Regulation of Commerce or Revenue to the Ports of one State over those of another: nor shall Vessels bound to, or from, one State, be obliged to enter, clear or pay Duties in another.

No Money shall be drawn from the Treasury, but in Consequence of Appropriations made by Law; and a regular Statement and Account of the Receipts and Expenditures of all public Money shall be published from time to time.

No Title of Nobility shall be granted by the United States: And no Person holding any Office of Profit or Trust under them, shall, without the Consent of the Congress, accept of any present, Emolument, Office, or Title, of any kind whatever, from any King, Prince or foreign State.

Section 10

No State shall enter into any Treaty, Alliance, or Confederation; grant Letters of Marque and Reprisal; coin Money; emit Bills of Credit; make any Thing but gold and silver Coin a Tender in Payment of Debts; pass any Bill of Attainder, ex post facto Law, or Law impairing the Obligation of Contracts, or grant any Title of Nobility.

No State shall, without the Consent of the Congress, lay any Imposts or Duties on Imports or Exports, except what may be absolutely necessary for executing it's inspection Laws: and the net Produce of all Duties and Imposts, laid by any State on Imports or Exports, shall be for the Use of the Treasury of the United States; and all such Laws shall be subject to the Revision and Controul of the Congress.

No State shall, without the Consent of Congress, lay any Duty of Tonnage, keep Troops, or Ships of War in time of Peace, enter into any Agreement or Compact with another State, or with a foreign Power, or engage in War, unless actually invaded, or in such imminent Danger as will not admit of delay.

Article II

Section 1

The executive Power shall be vested in a President of the United States of America. He shall hold his Office during the Term of four Years, and, together with the Vice President, chosen for the same Term, be elected, as follows:

Each State shall appoint, in such Manner as the Legislature thereof may direct, a Number of Electors, equal to the whole Number of Senators and Representatives to which the State may be entitled in the Congress: but no Senator or Representative, or Person holding an Office of Trust or Profit under the United States, shall be appointed an Elector.

The Electors shall meet in their respective States, and vote by Ballot for two Persons, of whom one at least shall not be an Inhabitant of the same State with themselves. And they shall make a List of all the Persons voted for, and of the Number of Votes for each; which List they shall sign and certify, and transmit sealed to the Seat of the Government of the United States, directed to the President of the Senate. The President of the Senate shall, in the Presence of the Senate and House of Representatives, open all the Certificates, and the Votes shall then be counted. The Person having the greatest Number of Votes shall be the President, if such Number be a Majority of the whole Number of Electors appointed; and if there be more than one who have such Majority, and have an equal Number of Votes, then the House of Representatives shall immediately chuse by Ballot one of them for President; and if no Person have a Majority, then from the five highest on the List the said House shall in like Manner chuse the President. But in chusing the President, the Votes shall be taken by States, the Representatives from each State having one Vote; a quorum for this Purpose shall consist of a Member or Members from two thirds of the States, and a Majority of all the States shall be necessary to a Choice. In every Case, after the Choice of the President, the Person having the greatest Number of Votes of the Electors shall be the Vice President. But if there should remain two or more who have equal Votes, the Senate shall chuse from them by Ballot the Vice President.

The Congress may determine the Time of chusing the Electors, and the Day on which they shall give their Votes; which Day shall be the same throughout the United States.

No Person except a natural born Citizen, or a Citizen of the United States, at the time of the Adoption of this Constitution, shall be eligible to the Office of President; neither shall any person be eligible to that Office who shall not have attained to the Age of thirty five Years, and been fourteen Years a Resident within the United States.

In Case of the Removal of the President from Office, or of his Death, Resignation, or Inability to discharge the Powers and Duties of the said Office, the Same shall devolve on the Vice President, and the Congress may by Law provide for the Case of Removal, Death, Resignation or Inability, both of the President and Vice President, declaring what Officer shall then act as President, and such Officer shall act accordingly, until the Disability be removed, or a President shall be elected.

The President shall, at stated Times, receive for his Services, a Compensation, which shall neither be encreased nor diminished during the Period for which he shall have been elected, and he shall not receive within that Period any other Emolument from the United States, or any of them.

Before he enter on the Execution of his Office, he shall take the following Oath or Affirmation:—"I do solemnly swear (or affirm) that I will faithfully execute the Office of President of the United States, and will to the best of my Ability, preserve, protect and defend the Constitution of the United States."

Section 2

The President shall be Commander in Chief of the Army and Navy of the United States, and of the Militia of the several States, when called into the actual Service of the United States; he may require the Opinion, in writing, of the principal Officer in each of the executive Departments, upon any Subject relating to the Duties of their respective Offices, and he shall have Power to Grant Reprieves and Pardons for Offences against the United States, except in Cases of Impeachment.

He shall have Power, by and with the Advice and Consent of the Senate, to make Treaties, provided two thirds of the Senators present concur; and he shall nominate, and by and with the Advice and Consent of the Senate, shall appoint Ambassadors, other public Ministers and Consuls, Judges of the supreme Court, and all other Officers of the United States, whose Appointments are not herein otherwise provided for, and which shall be established by Law: but the Congress may by Law vest the Appointment of such inferior Officers, as they think proper, in the President alone, in the Courts of Law, or in the Heads of Departments.

The President shall have Power to fill up all Vacancies that may happen during the Recess of the Senate, by granting Commissions which shall expire at the End of their next Session.

Section 3

He shall from time to time give to the Congress Information on the State of the Union, and recommend to their Consideration such Measures as he shall judge necessary and expedient; he may, on extraordinary Occasions, convene both Houses, or either of them, and in Case of Disagreement between them, with Respect to the Time of Adjournment, he may adjourn them to such Time as he shall think proper; he shall receive Ambassadors and other public Ministers; he shall take Care that the Laws be faithfully executed, and shall Commission all the Officers of the United States.

Section 4

The President, Vice President and all Civil Officers of the United States, shall be removed from Office on Impeachment for and Conviction of, Treason, Bribery, or other high Crimes and Misdemeanors.

Article III

Section 1

The judicial Power of the United States, shall be vested in one supreme Court, and in such inferior Courts as the Congress may from time to time ordain and establish. The Judges, both of the supreme and inferior Courts, shall hold their Offices during good Behaviour, and shall, at stated Times, receive for their Services, a Compensation, which shall not be diminished during their Continuance in Office.

Section 2

The judicial Power shall extend to all Cases, in Law and Equity, arising under this Constitution, the Laws of the United States, and Treaties made, or which shall be made, under their Authority;_to all Cases affecting Ambassadors, other public ministers and Consuls;_to all Cases of admiralty and maritime Jurisdiction;_to Controversies to which the United States shall be a Party;_to Controversies between two or more States;_between a State and Citizens of another State;_between Citizens of different States;_between Citizens of the same State claiming Lands under Grants of different States, and between a State, or the Citizens thereof, and foreign States, Citizens or Subjects.

In all Cases affecting Ambassadors, other public Ministers and Consuls, and those in which a State shall be Party, the supreme Court shall have original Jurisdiction. In all the other Cases before mentioned, the supreme Court shall have appellate Jurisdiction, both as to Law and Fact, with such Exceptions, and under such Regulations as the Congress shall make.

The Trial of all Crimes, except in Cases of Impeachment, shall be by Jury; and such Trial shall be held in the State where the said Crimes shall have been committed; but when not committed within any State, the Trial shall be at such Place or Places as the Congress may by Law have directed.

Section 3

Treason against the United States, shall consist only in levying War against them, or in adhering to their Enemies, giving them Aid and Comfort. No Person shall be convicted of Treason unless on the Testimony of two Witnesses to the same overt Act, or on Confession in open Court.

The Congress shall have Power to declare the Punishment of Treason, but no Attainder of Treason shall work Corruption of Blood, or Forfeiture except during the Life of the Person attainted.

Article IV

Section 1

Full Faith and Credit shall be given in each State to the public Acts, Records, and judicial Proceedings of every other State. And the Congress may by general Laws prescribe the Manner in which such Acts, Records and Proceedings shall be proved, and the Effect thereof.

Section 2

The Citizens of each State shall be entitled to all Privileges and Immunities of Citizens in the several States.

A Person charged in any State with Treason, Felony, or other Crime, who shall flee from Justice, and be found in another State, shall on Demand of the executive Authority of the State from which he fled, be delivered up, to be removed to the State having Jurisdiction of the Crime.

No Person held to Service or Labour in one State, under the Laws thereof, escaping into another, shall, in Consequence of any Law or Regulation therein, be discharged from such Service or Labour, but shall be delivered up on Claim of the Party to whom such Service or Labour may be due.

Section 3

New States may be admitted by the Congress into this Union; but no new State shall be formed or erected within the Jurisdiction of any other State; nor any State be formed by the Junction of two or more States, or Parts of States, without the Consent of the Legislatures of the States concerned as well as of the Congress.

The Congress shall have Power to dispose of and make all needful Rules and Regulations respecting the Territory or other Property belonging to the United States; and nothing in this Constitution shall be so construed as to Prejudice any Claims of the United States, or of any particular State.

Section 4

The United States shall guarantee to every State in this Union a Republican Form of Government, and shall protect each of them against Invasion; and on Application of the Legislature, or of the Executive (when the Legislature cannot be convened) against domestic Violence.

Article V

The Congress, whenever two thirds of both Houses shall deem it necessary, shall propose Amendments to this Constitution, or, on the Application of the Legislatures of two thirds of the several States, shall call a Convention for proposing Amendments, which, in either Case, shall be valid to all Intents and Purposes, as Part of this Constitution, when ratified by the Legislatures of three fourths of the several States, or by Conventions in three fourths thereof, as the one or the other Mode of Ratification may be proposed by the Congress; Provided that no Amendment which may be made prior to the Year One thousand eight hundred and eight shall in any Manner affect the first and fourth Clauses in the Ninth Section of the first Article; and that no State, without its Consent, shall be deprived of its equal Suffrage in the Senate.

Article VI

All Debts contracted and Engagements entered into, before the Adoption of this Constitution, shall be as valid against the United States under this Constitution, as under the Confederation.

This Constitution, and the Laws of the United States which shall be made in Pursuance thereof; and all Treaties made, or which shall be made, under the Authority of the United States, shall be the supreme Law of the Land; and the Judges in every State shall be bound thereby, any Thing in the Constitution or Laws of any state to the Contrary notwithstanding.

The Senators and Representatives before mentioned, and the Members of the several State Legislatures, and all executive and judicial Officers, both of the United States and of the several States, shall be bound by Oath or Affirmation, to support this Constitution; but no religious Test shall ever be required as a Qualification to any Office or public Trust under the United States.

Article VII

The Ratification of the Conventions of nine States, shall be sufficient for the Establishment of this Constitution between the States so ratifying the same.

Amendment I

Congress shall make no law respecting an establishment of religion, or prohibiting the free exercise thereof; or abridging the freedom of speech, or of the press; or the right of the people peaceably to assemble, and to petition the Government for a redress of grievances.

Amendment II

A well regulated Militia, being necessary to the security of a free State, the right of the people to keep and bear Arms, shall not be infringed.

Amendment III

No Soldier shall, in time of peace be quartered in any house, without the consent of the Owner, nor in time of war, but in a manner to be prescribed by law.

Amendment IV

The right of the people to be secure in their persons, houses, papers, and effects, against unreasonable searches and seizures, shall not be violated, and no Warrants shall issue, but upon probable cause, supported by Oath or affirmation, and particularly describing the place to be searched, and the persons or things to be seized.

Amendment V

No person shall be held to answer for a capital, or otherwise infamous crime, unless on a presentment or indictment of a Grand Jury, except in cases arising in the land or naval forces, or in the Militia, when in actual service in time of War or public danger; nor shall any person be subject for the same offence to be twice put in jeopardy of life or limb; nor shall be compelled in any criminal case to be a witness against himself, nor be deprived of life, liberty, or property, without due process of law; nor shall private property be taken for public use, without just compensation.

Amendment VI

In all criminal prosecutions, the accused shall enjoy the right to a speedy and public trial, by an impartial jury of the State and district wherein the crime shall have been committed, which district shall have been previously ascertained by law, and to be informed of the nature and cause of the accusation; to be confronted with the witnesses against him; to have compulsory process for obtaining witnesses in his favor, and to have the Assistance of Counsel for his defence.

Amendment VII

In Suits at common law, where the value in controversy shall exceed twenty dollars, the right of trial by jury shall be preserved, and no fact tried by a jury, shall be otherwise re-examined in any Court of the United States, than according to the rules of the common law.

Amendment VIII

Excessive bail shall not be required, nor excessive fines imposed, nor cruel and unusual punishments inflicted.

Amendment IX

The enumeration in the Constitution, of certain rights, shall not be construed to deny or disparage others retained by the people.

Amendment X

The powers not delegated to the United States by the Constitution, nor prohibited by it to the States, are reserved to the States respectively, or to the people.

Amendment XI

The Judicial power of the United States shall not be construed to extend to any suit in law or equity, commenced or prosecuted against one on the United States by Citizens of another State, or by Citizens or Subjects of any Foreign State.

Amendment XII

The Electors shall meet in their respective states and vote by ballot for President and Vice-President, one of whom, at least, shall not be an inhabitant of the same state with themselves; they shall name in their ballots the person voted for as President, and in distinct ballots the person voted for as Vice-President, and they shall make distinct lists of all persons voted for as President, and of all persons voted for as Vice-President, and of the number of votes for each, which lists they shall sign and certify, and transmit sealed to the seat of the government of the United States, directed to the President of the Senate;—The President of the Senate shall, in the presence of the Senate and House of Representatives, open all the certificates and the votes shall then be counted;—The person having the greatest Number of votes for President, shall be the President, if such number be a majority of the whole number of Electors appointed; and if no person have such majority, then from the persons having the highest numbers not exceeding three on the list of those voted for as President, the House of Representatives shall choose immediately, by ballot, the President. But in choosing the President, the votes shall be taken by states, the representation from each state having one vote; a quorum for this purpose shall consist of a member or members from two-thirds of the states, and a majority of all the states shall be necessary to a choice. And if the House of Representatives shall not choose a President

whenever the right of choice shall devolve upon them, before the fourth day of March next following, then the Vice-President shall act as President, as in the case of the death or other constitutional disability of the President—The person having the greatest number of votes as Vice-President, shall be the Vice-President, if such number be a majority of the whole number of Electors appointed, and if no person have a majority, then from the two highest numbers on the list, the Senate shall choose the Vice-President; a quorum for the purpose shall consist of two-thirds of the whole number of Senators, and a majority of the whole number shall be necessary to a choice. But no person constitutionally ineligible to the office of President shall be eligible to that of Vice-President of the United States.

Amendment XIII

Section 1

Neither slavery nor involuntary servitude, except as a punishment for crime whereof the party shall have been duly convicted, shall exist within the United States, or any place subject to their jurisdiction.

Section 2

Congress shall have power to enforce this article by appropriate legislation.

Amendment XIV.

Section 1

All persons born or naturalized in the United States and subject to the jurisdiction thereof, are citizens of the United States and of the State wherein they reside. No State shall make or enforce any law which shall abridge the privileges or immunities of citizens of the United States; nor shall any State deprive any person of life, liberty, or property, without due process of law; nor deny to any person within its jurisdiction the equal protection of the laws.

Section 2

Representatives shall be apportioned among the several States according to their respective numbers, counting the whole number of persons in each State, excluding Indians not taxed. But when the right to vote at any election for the choice of electors for President and Vice President of the United States, Representatives in Congress, the Executive and Judicial officers of a State, or the members of the Legislature thereof, is denied to any of the male inhabitants of such State, being twenty-one years of age, and citizens of the United States, or in any way abridged, except for participation in rebellion, or other crime, the basis of representation therein shall be reduced in the proportion which the number of such male citizens shall bear to the whole number of male citizens twenty-one years of age in such State.

Section 3

No person shall be a Senator or Representative in Congress, or elector of President and Vice President, or hold any office, civil or military, under the United States, or under any State, who, having previously taken an oath, as a member of Congress, or as an officer of the United States, or as a member of any State legislature, or as an executive or judicial officer of any State, to support the Constitution of the United States, shall have engaged in insurrection or rebellion against the same, or given aid or comfort to the enemies thereof. But Congress may by a vote of two-thirds of each House, remove such disability.

Section 4

The validity of the public debt of the United States, authorized by law, including debts incurred for payment of pensions and bounties for services in suppressing insurrection or rebellion, shall not be questioned. But neither the United States nor any State shall assume or pay any debt or obligation incurred in aid of insurrection or rebellion against the United States, or any claim for the loss or emancipation of any slave; but all such debts, obligations and claims shall be held illegal and void.

Section 5

The Congress shall have power to enforce, by appropriate legislation, the provisions of this article.

Amendment XV

Section 1

The right of citizens of the United States to vote shall not be denied or abridged by the United States or by any State on account of race, color, or previous condition of servitude.

Section 2

The Congress shall have power to enforce this article by appropriate legislation.

Amendment XVI

The Congress shall have power to lay and collect taxes on incomes, from whatever source derived, without apportionment among the several States, and without regard to any census or enumeration.

Amendment XVII

The Senate of the United States shall be composed of two Senators from each State, elected by the people thereof, for six years; and each Senator shall have one vote. The electors in each State shall have the qualifications requisite for electors of the most numerous branch of the State legislatures.

When vacancies happen in the representation of any State in the Senate, the executive authority of such State shall issue writs of election to fill such vacancies: Provided, That the legislature of any State may empower the executive thereof to make temporary appointments until the people fill the vacancies by election as the legislature may direct.

This amendment shall not be so con-

strued as to affect the election or term of any Senator chosen before it becomes valid as part of the Constitution.

Amendment XVIII

Section 1

After one year from the ratification of this article the manufacture, sale, or transportation of intoxicating liquors within, the importation thereof into, or the exportation thereof from the United States and all territory subject to the jurisdiction thereof for beverage purposes is hereby prohibited.

Section 2

The Congress and the several States shall have concurrent power to enforce this article by appropriate legislation.

Section 3

This article shall be inoperative unless it shall have been ratified as an amendment to the Constitution by the legislatures of the several States, as provided in the Constitution, within seven years from the date of the submission hereof to the States by the Congress.

Amendment XIX

The right of citizens of the United States to vote shall not be denied or abridged by the United States or by any State on account of sex. Congress shall have power to enforce this article by appropriate legislation.

Amendment XX

Section 1

The terms of the President and Vice President shall end at noon on the 20th day of January, and the terms of Senators and Representatives at noon on the 3d day of January, of the years in which such terms would have ended if this article had not been ratified; and the terms of their successors shall then begin.

Section 2

The Congress shall assemble at least once in every year, and such meeting shall begin at noon on the 3d day of January, unless they shall by law appoint a different day.

Section 3

If, at the time fixed for the beginning of the term of the President, the President elect shall have died, the Vice President elect shall become President. If a President shall not have been chosen before the time fixed for the beginning of his term, or if the President elect shall have failed to qualify, then the Vice President elect shall act as President until a President shall have qualified; and the Congress may by law provide for the case wherein neither a President elect nor a Vice President elect shall have qualified, declaring who shall then act as President, or the manner in which one who is to act shall be selected, and such person shall act accordingly until a President or Vice President shall have qualified.

Section 4

The Congress may by law provide for the case of the death of any of the persons from whom the House of Representatives may choose a President whenever the right of choice shall have devolved upon them, and for the case of the death of any of the persons from whom the Senate may choose a Vice President whenever the right of choice shall have devolved upon them.

Section 5

Sections 1 and 2 shall take effect on the 15th day of October following the ratification of this article.

Section 6

This article shall be inoperative unless it shall have been ratified as an amendment to the Constitution by the legislatures of three-fourths of the several States within seven years from the date of its submission.

Amendment XXI

Section 1

The eighteenth article of amendment to the Constitution of the United States is hereby repealed.

Section 2

The transportation or importation into any State, Territory, or possession of the United States for delivery or use therein of intoxicating liquors, in violation of the laws thereof, is hereby prohibited.

Section 3

This article shall be inoperative unless it shall have been ratified as an amendment to the Constitution by conventions in the several States, as provided in the Constitution, within seven years from the date of the submission hereof to the States by the Congress.

Amendment XXII

Section 1

No person shall be elected to the office of the President more than twice, and no person who has held the office of President, or acted as President, for more than two years of a term to which some other person was elected President shall be elected to the office of the President more than once. But this Article shall not apply to any person holding the office of President, when this Article was proposed by the Congress, and shall not prevent any person who may be holding the office of President, or acting as President, during the term within which this Article becomes operative from holding the office of President or acting as President during the remainder of such term.

Section 2

This article shall be inoperative unless it shall have been ratified as an amendment to the Constitution by the legislatures of three-fourths of the several States within seven years from the date of its submission to the States by the Congress.

Amendment XXIII

Section 1

The District constituting the seat of Government of the United States shall appoint in such manner as the Congress may direct: A number of electors of President and Vice President equal to the whole number of Senators and Representatives in Congress to which the District would be entitled if it were a State, but in no event more than the least populous State; they shall be in addition to those appointed by the States, but they shall be considered, for the purposes of the election of President and Vice President, to be electors appointed by a State; and they shall meet in the District and perform such duties as provided by the twelfth article of amendment.

Section 2

The Congress shall have power to enforce this article by appropriate legislation.

Amendment XXIV

Section 1

The right of citizens of the United States to vote in any primary or other election for President or Vice President, for electors for President or Vice President, or for Senator or Representative in Congress, shall not be denied or abridged by the United States or any State by reason of failure to pay any poll tax or other tax.

Section 2

The Congress shall have power to enforce this article by appropriate legislation.

Amendment XXV

Section 1

In case of the removal of the President from office or of his death or resignation, the Vice President shall become President.

Section 2

Whenever there is a vacancy in the office of the Vice President, the President shall nominate a Vice President who shall take office upon confirmation by a majority vote of both Houses of Congress.

Section 3

Whenever the President transmits to the President pro tempore of the Senate and the Speaker of the House of Representatives has written declaration that he is unable to discharge the powers and duties of his office, and until he transmits to them a written declaration to the contrary, such powers and duties shall be discharged by the Vice President as Acting President.

Section 4

Whenever the Vice President and a majority of either the principal officers of the executive departments or of such other body as Congress may by law provide, transmit to the President pro tempore of the Senate and the Speaker of the House of Representatives their written declaration that the President is unable to discharge the powers and duties of his office, the Vice President shall immediately assume the powers and duties of the office as Acting President.

Thereafter, when the President transmits to the President pro tempore of the Senate and the Speaker of the House of Representatives has written declaration that no inability exists, he shall resume the powers and duties of his office unless the Vice President and a majority of either the principal officers of the executive department or of such other body as Congress may by law provide, transmit within four days to the President pro tempore of the Senate and the Speaker of the House of Representatives their written declaration that the President is unable to discharge the powers and duties of his office. Thereupon Congress shall decide the issue, assembling within forty-eight hours for that purpose if not in session. If the Congress, within twenty-one days after receipt of the latter written declaration, or, if Congress is not in session, within twenty-one days after Congress is required to assemble, determines by two-thirds vote of both Houses that the President is unable to discharge the powers and duties of his office, the Vice President shall continue to discharge the same as Acting President; otherwise, the President shall resume the powers and duties of his office.

Amendment XXVI

Section 1

The right of citizens of the United States, who are eighteen years of age or older, to vote shall not be denied or abridged by the United States or by any State on account of age.

Section 2

The Congress shall have power to enforce this article by appropriate legislation.

Amendment XXVII

No law varying the compensation for the services of the Senators and Representatives shall take effect, until an election of Representatives shall have intervened.

Appendix B

Table of Cases with Case Summaries

A.L.A. Schechter Poultry Corp. v.
United States,
295 U.S. 495 (1935)
[105]
Schechter was convicted of federal laws pertaining to the slaughtering and selling of poultry. Schechter challenged on the grounds that the federal laws were an unconstitutional delegation of congressional authority, that through the laws Congress was in effect regulating intrastate commerce, and that the laws violated Schecter's due process rights guaranteed in the Fifth Amendment. The Supreme Court reversed the conviction.

Abington School District v. Schempp,
374 U.S. 203 (1963)
[158]
Pennsylvania law required that bible verses were read, without comment, at the beginning of each school day. With written parental permission any student could be excused from participation. The Schempp family challenged the law. The Court found that the law violated both the Establishment Clause and the Free Exercise Clause.

Ableman v. Booth,
62 U.S. 506 (1858)
[76–77]
Booth was charged with aiding and abetting a fugitive slave, as regulated by an act of Congress. He was turned over to the federal marshal, Ableman, who was to deliver him to jail. Booth filed a writ of habeas corpus with the state court challenging the constitutionality of the fugitive slave law. A justice on the Wisconsin supreme court ruled in favor of Booth and ordered his release. Ableman appealed to the full court; the ruling was upheld. Ableman then appealed to the U.S. Supreme Court questioning whether the state court had supremacy over the federal court and federal laws. The state judgment was reversed.

Abrams v. United States,
250 U.S. 616 (1919)
[129–130]
Abrams and other defendants were convicted of conspiring to violate the Espionage Act of Congress. With the United States at war with Germany, the defendants conspired to utter, print, write and publish disloyal materials with the intention to bring scorn upon the United States and weaken its military capabilities. The defendants challenged the convictions on the grounds that they violated First Amendment rights of free speech and press. The Supreme Court upheld the convictions.

Adams v. United States ex rel McCann, 317 U.S. 269 (1943)

[193]

McCann, indicted for mail fraud, opted to represent himself without a jury trial. He was convicted of the charges. McCann retained counsel for his appeal. The Circuit Court of Appeals ruled that a nonlawyer, charged with a felony, could not waive rights to a jury trial. The Supreme Court reversed the circuit court judgment.

Adamson v. California, 332 U.S. 46 (1947)

[173–174]

Adamson was convicted of first-degree murder and sentenced to death. At his trial, the defendant did not testify on his behalf. A state law stated that failure to testify on one's behalf could be commented upon by court and by counsel and to be considered by court and jury. On appeal, Adamson claimed that he did not testify because he was concerned that his prior convictions would be disclosed and negative inferences would be drawn from them. The Supreme Court upheld the conviction.

Adderley v. Florida, 385 U.S. 39 (1966)

[138]

Peaceful protesters on public property were arrested and convicted of trespass. They challenged on the grounds that the arrests violated their First and Fourteenth Amendment rights. The Supreme Court upheld the convictions.

Adkins v. Children's Hospital 261 U.S. 525 (1923)

[62–63, 236]

The Children's Hospital employed a large number of women in various capacities at an agreed upon wage rate, which was below the minimum wage devised by a District of Columbia board pursuant to a congressional act. The board attempted to enforce its rules and the hospital challenged the constitutionality of the law. The Supreme Court ruled that the minimum-wage law violated due process and freedom to contract.

Adler v. Board of Education, 342 U.S. 485 (1952)

[86–87]

New York law made ineligible for employment in any public school any member of any organization advocating the overthrow of the government by force, violence or any unlawful means. Adler challenged the due process constitutionality of the law. The Supreme Court upheld the law stating that public education needed loyal teachers and there was no constitutional right to employment.

Afroyim v. Rusk, 387 U.S. 253 (1967)

[176]

Afroyim, a naturalized U.S. citizen, went to Israel and voted in an Israeli election. The State Department refused to renew his passport stating that Afroyim had lost his citizenship pursuant to the Nationality Act of 1940, which provided that a United States citizen loses citizenship if he votes in a foreign political election. He challenged congressional power to strip a citizen of citizenship. The Supreme Court invalidated the law on Fourteenth Amendment grounds.

Akron v. Akron Center for Reproductive Health, Inc.,
462 U.S. 416 (1983)
[47–48, 108–109]
Among other requirements, an Akron, Ohio ordinance required second and third trimester abortions to be performed in a hospital, that parental consent for underage mothers be secured by physicians, that the implications and alternatives to abortion are explained to the mothers, and that a 24-hour waiting period be instituted. The Supreme Court ruled that these requirements were unconstitutional.

Alden v. Maine,
527 U.S. ___ (1999)
[73–74,112]
Maine probation officers sued the state of Maine for violation of the overtime provisions of federal law. The state argued that, based on the grounds of state sovereign immunity, they could not be sued without its consent. The Supreme Court found in favor of the state.

Aldridge v. Williams,
44 U.S. 9 (1845)
[24]
Aldridge and others were importers challenging import duties created by federal regulations and statute. The circuit court ruled for Williams–port collector. The Supreme Court affirmed.

Ambach v. Norwick,
441 U.S. 68 (1979)
[94, 181]
New York law prohibited teacher certification to noncitizens, unless the individual applied for citizenship. Norwick was married to an American citizen, but did not seek citizenship. Norwick challenged the law on Equal Protection grounds. The Supreme Court disagreed, ruling that states have a legitimate interest in educational goals.

American Communications Association v. Douds,
339 U.S. 382 (1950)
[9]
The case challenged a statute that imposed restrictions and limited benefits to labor organizations that failed to file noncommunist loyalty statements. The Supreme Court ruled that in a legitimate effort to prevent "political strikes" Congress could require anticommunist requirements.

American Federation of Labor v. American Sash & Door Co.,
335 U.S. 538 (1949)
[36]
The Supreme Court upheld an Arizona constitutional amendment prohibiting discrimination against nonunion employees.

American Party of Texas v. White,
415 U.S. 767 (1974)
[93]
Minor political parties in Texas challenged state electoral laws as violations of their First and Fourteenth Amendment rights. They argued that the laws favored major political parties and discriminated against minor parties. Except for the absentee-ballot provision of the laws, the Supreme Court rejected the minor parties' contentions.

Anderson v. Dunn,
19 U.S. 204 (1821)
[75, 76]

Anderson, a member of the House of Representatives, was adjudged guilty by the House for a breach of privileges (bribery). Dunn, the Sergeant at Arms, was ordered to take Anderson into custody. Anderson challenged the legislative arrest. The Supreme Court upheld the congressional power as justified to control the actions of its members.

Anniston Mfg. Co. v. Davis,
301 U.S. 337 (1937)
[63]

Anniston challenged the procedural aspects of a federal statute imposing taxes. The Supreme Court ruled against Anniston stating that if administrative remedies and hearings in a statute were fair and allowed for judicial review, the statute met the demands of due process.

Apex Hosiery Co. v. Leader,
310 U.S. 469 (1940)
[8]

Corporation sued labor organization for damages sustained as a result of a strike. The Supreme Court ruled in favor of the union stating that the actions of the union did not violate the interstate commerce provisions of the Sherman Act.

Argersinger v. Hamlin,
407 U.S. 25 (1972)
[211]

Argersinger, an indigent, was arrested for carrying a concealed weapon. He was not represented by counsel at trial and was convicted of the charges. He challenged the state's refusal to provide counsel. Florida argued that the right of counsel applied only to nonpetty offenses. The Supreme Court disagreed.

Arizonans for Official English v. Arizona,
520 U.S. 43 (1997)
[111–112]

State law required that English be its official language for its business and communication and that any challenges to the law would be decided exclusively by the state judiciary. State employee Maria Kelly Yniguez challenged the law stating that, read broadly, the law forced her to stop speaking Spanish or face disciplinary consequences. The Supreme Court found the case moot and did not rule on the merits of the controversy.

Arver v. United States,
245 U.S. 366 (1918)
[227]

The case challenged a law allowing the president to call for a draft. The Supreme Court ruled that the draft was not equivalent to involuntary servitude as prohibited by the Thirteenth Amendment.

Ashcraft v. Tennessee,
322 U.S. 143 (1944)
[195]

Ashcraft was charged with hiring Ware to murder his wife. They were tried jointly and convicted. Both challenged the convictions on the grounds that the confessions were coerced and were the sole basis for their convictions. The Supreme Court vacated the convictions and remanded the cases on the grounds that Ashcraft's confession was coerced and

Ware's conviction was directly related to Ashcraft's confession.

Ashwander v. Tennessee Valley Authority, 297 U.S. 288 (1936)
[31]
The T.V.A. contracted with the Alabama Power Company. Preferred stockholders sued stating that the contract was injurious to the company and that it was beyond federal powers. The Supreme Court upheld the contract.

Associated Press v. National Labor Review Board, 301 U.S. 103 (1937)
[171–172]
Associated Press dismissed an employee. A labor organization challenged the dismissal claiming that it was in retaliation for attempts at unionizing. Associated Press was ordered to cease and desist from its practices. They challenged the constitutionality of the decree and the statute. The Supreme Court found that the dismissal was directly related to the union efforts and as such a violation of the statute.

Atherton v. Atherton, 181 U.S. 155 (1901)
[236]
Husband (Peter) and wife (Mary) lived in Kentucky. Due to Peter's cruel treatment, Mary and child fled to her family in New York. Peter remained in Kentucky and subsequently obtained a divorce there. New York State did not recognize the Kentucky divorce decree. Peter challenged as a violation of the Full Faith and Credit provision of the federal constitution. The Supreme Court agreed with the husband.

Bailey v. Drexel Furniture Co., 259 U.S. 20 (1922)
[81]
Drexel was a furniture manufacturer. Bailey, United States collector of internal revenue, notified Drexel that it owed back taxes for employing a fourteen-year-old boy. Drexel paid under protest. The Supreme Court ruled that the Child Labor Tax Law was invalid because it crossed the line between legitimate taxation and a penalty.

Bain Peanut Co. of Texas v. Pinson, 282 U.S. 499 (1931)
[30]
Bain Peanut was sued in Comanche County, Texas. Its principal office was in Tarrant County, Texas. Bain challenged the action on Fourteenth Amendment grounds. The Supreme Court found that Bain Peanut could be sued in other counties.

Baker v. Carr, 369 U.S. 186 (1962)
[67, 88, 106]
Tennessee voters challenged a state apportionment law claiming that their votes were debased. The lower court denied relief and an appeal was brought to the Supreme Court. The Court ruled that the voters had an Equal Protection Clause case and the judiciary had the power to hear and resolve the case.

Baldwin v. G.A.F. Seelig, Inc., 294 U.S. 511 (1935)
[82–83]
Seelig was a milk dealer in New York City, but bought its milk from a Vermont corporation. The legal question was whether

a New York State law regulating the distribution of milk could regulate Seelig's interstate commerce. The Supreme Court found that the state could regulate some aspects of interstate commerce.

Baldwin v. Montana Fish & Game Commission,
436 U.S. 371 (1978)
[123]
Hunters contested a Montana elk-hunting law that imposed larger licensing fees on nonstate residents than in-state residents. The district court denied relief and the Supreme Court affirmed, stating that hunting access does not fall under privileges and immunities rights. Moreover, since in-state residents already contributed resources to the preservation of elk, it was not a violation of equal protection for nonstate residents to pay a higher hunting fee.

Baltimore & Ohio Railroad Co. v. Baugh,
149 U.S. 368 (1893)
[27]
Baugh, a fireman on a locomotive, was injured, he claimed, from the negligence of the engineer. He sued to recover for his injuries. The jury was instructed to find for Baugh if the injury was due to negligence or carelessness of an employer over an employee. The jury found for Baugh. The Supreme Court reversed, ruling that Baugh knew the peril and with this knowledge voluntarily rode with the engineer on the engine. As such, he assumed the risk.

Bank of United States v. Deveaux,
9 U.S. 61 (1809)
[54]
Georgia law taxed the Savannah branch of the Bank of the United States. The Bank refused to pay the tax and state officials entered the office and confiscated the amount due. The Bank sued, as a body corporate, for trespass. The Supreme Court ruled that an incorporated entity had standing to sue.

Barber v. Barber,
62 U.S. 582 (1858)
[167]
Husband (Hiram) and wife (Huldad) were married and lived in New York. He left for Wisconsin and obtained a divorce decree. In a New York State decree, Hiram was ordered to pay support and maintenance. He challenged on jurisdictional grounds. The Supreme Court ruled in favor of the wife.

Barker v. Wingo,
407 U.S. 514 (1972)
[211]
Barker was arrested for murder. The state delayed his trial for five years as it sought to convict an accomplice. After several trials, the accomplice was convicted and subsequently agreed to serve as a witness for the prosecution against Barker. was convicted. He challenged on the grounds that his right to a speedy trial was denied. The Supreme Court upheld the conviction.

Barnes v. Glen Theatre, Inc.,
501 U.S. 560 (1991)
[15–16, 149, 186]
Two Indiana nude-dancing businesses sued the state seeking to enjoin its public indecency law. They argued that the law's prohibition against total nudity in public places violated the First

Amendment. The Supreme Court upheld the law.

Barron v. City of Baltimore,
32 U.S. 243 (1833)
[76]
Barron claimed that the city diverted the flow of waterways as a consequence of construction which resulted in damages to his wharf. He sued on Fifth Amendment grounds. The Court ruled that Fifth Amendment issues involved only federal issues, not state disputes.

Barsky v. Board of Regents,
347 U.S. 442 (1954)
[174–175]
New York law authorized disciplinary actions against any physicians convicted of a crime. Barsky's license was suspended for his conviction for failing to abide by a congressional subpoena. He challenged the conviction on the grounds that the law was vague. The Supreme Court ruled that the law was not arbitrary or capricious.

Baumgartner v. United States,
322 U.S. 665 (1944)
[133]
The federal government sought to have Baumgartner's certificate of naturalization revoked because he failed, years before, to renounce his former allegiance and swear support to the U.S. Constitution. The Supreme Court ruled for Baumgartner.

Beal v. Doe,
432 U.S. 438 (1977)
[44]
Medicaid-eligible individuals were denied financial assistance for abortions because they failed to provide standard documentation that the procedure was a medical necessity. They challenged the state law on equal protection grounds. The Supreme Court upheld the state requirements.

Beauharnais v. Illinois,
343 U.S. 250 (1952)
[135]
Beauharnais, president of the White Circle League, organized the circulation of a prosegregation leaflet. It called for an uprising of whites. State law prohibited the publishing, selling, or exhibition in public places of derogatory racial materials that could lead to breach of peace or riots. The Court ruled that the law was not a violation of First Amendment freedoms stating that false and defamatory speech is not protected speech.

Bell v. United States,
349 U.S. 81 (1955)
[10–11]
Bell pled guilty to two counts of transporting women across state lines for illicit purposes. He challenged the conviction on the grounds that it was one act (two women, but the same trip in the same vehicle) and he should not be punished twice. The Supreme Court agreed, reversing the conviction.

Bell v. Wolfish,
441 U.S. 520 (1979)
[42, 123]
Prison inmates challenged prison rules regarding double-bunking, prohibition of receiving hard-cover books, and personal and property searches on the

grounds that these governmental actions violated the Fourth and Fifth Amendments. The Supreme Court ruled in favor of the prison practices.

Bennis v. Michigan,
516 U.S. 442 (1996)
[73]
Husband was arrested for engaging in sexual activity with a prostitute. The state seized the car in which the police observed the illegal activity. The wife, co-owner of the automobile, was unaware of the activity. She sued the state for compensation under the Fifth and Fourteenth Amendments. The Supreme Court ruled in favor of the seizure.

Benton v. Maryland,
395 U.S. 784 (1969)
[119]
Benton was tried for burglary and larceny. He was convicted of burglary. Pursuant to the holding in a subsequent but unrelated case, the conviction was overturned and remanded. He was again charged with both crimes, but this time convicted of both crimes. He challenged on double-jeopardy grounds. The Supreme Court extended double-jeopardy protections to the states, overturning and remanding Benton's convictions.

Berger v. New York,
388 U.S. 41 (1967)
[205–206]
Berger was convicted of conspiracy to bribe a public official. The evidence was obtained by electronic eavesdropping. The Supreme Court held that the state law was too broad and thus violated the

Fourth and Fourteenth Amendments. The conviction was reversed.

Bigelow v. RKO Radio Pictures,
327 U.S. 251 (1946)
[85]
Bigelow sued on the grounds that RKO conspired to distribute movies first to theatres owned by RKO. The Supreme Court ruled that there was sufficient evidence to allow Bigelow's suit to proceed.

Bishop v. Woods,
426 U.S. 341 (1976)
[70–71]
Police officer's employment was terminated without a pretermination hearing. He challenged the procedure on due process grounds. The Supreme Court upheld the procedure.

Bivens v. Six Unknown Named Agents of the Federal Bureau of Narcotics,
403 U.S. 388 (1971)
[210]
Bivens argued that federal agents entered his apartment and arrested him for alleged narcotics violations. The agents also engaged in a comprehensive search of the premises. Bivens was arrested without a warrant and without probable cause. Bivens sought financial compensation from each agent for violating his constitutional rights. The Supreme Court ruled that Bivens was entitled to a trial that could provide him with a financial remedy.

Blyew v. United States,
80 U.S. 581 (1871)
[26, 168]
White defendants were convicted of

murdering an elderly black woman. The convictions were challenged on jurisdictional grounds and whether black witnesses could testify at the trial. The Supreme Court reversed the convictions.

Boddie v. Connecticut,
401 U.S. 371 (1971)
[178]
Welfare recipients challenged, on due process grounds, a state law requiring certain court fees for bringing an action for divorce. The Supreme Court ruled that because obtaining a divorce can be achieved only by state action, financial requirements cannot put such access beyond the means of citizens.

Bolling v. Sharpe,
347 U.S. 497 (1954)
[175]
The case challenged, on Fifth Amendment grounds, public-school desegregation in the District of Columbia. The Supreme Court ruled that, like the states, the federal government is prohibited from maintaining racially segregated public schools.

Boone v. Lightner,
319 U.S. 561 (1943)
[194]
Boone's mother-in-law established a trust for his children, naming Boone as trustee. While Boone was in the military, the state required him to account for his execution of the trust. Boone requested a delay until his military service expired. The state rejected his petition. The Supreme Court upheld the state decision.

Booth v. Maryland,
482 U.S. 496 (1987)
[218–219]
Defendants were convicted of murder and robbery. The prosecution requested the death penalty. State law required the use of a victim impact statement (VIS) in the presentence report. Booth moved to have the VIS suppressed as unduly inflammatory. The state denied his motion and the jury subsequently sentenced Booth to death. Booth challenged the VIS as prohibited by the Eighth Amendment. The Supreme Court agreed and reversed the sentence and remanded for further proceedings.

Bowers v. Hardwick,
478 U.S. 186 (1986)
[42, 126]
Hardwick was charged with violating state sodomy laws. He was accused of committing the act with another, consenting male in the bedroom of his own house. Hardwick challenged the law as violating several provisions of the federal constitution. The Supreme Court ruled that the Constitution does not grant homosexuals the right to engage in sodomy nor does it deny the state the right to criminalize the act.

Bowles v. United States,
319 U.S. 33 (1943)
[194]
Bowles was convicted of violating provisions of the Selective Service Act. He argued that he was entitled to an exemption as a conscientious objector and that he was denied the right to prepare an adequate defense because he was unable

to inspect his entire file. The Supreme Court upheld the conviction.

Boyd v. United States,
116 U.S. 616 (1886)
[60–61]
Dr. Boyd was convicted of illegally dispensing morphine. The question was whether the prescriptions were issued in the course of his professional practice. He challenged the jury charge. The Supreme Court upheld the conviction.

Boykin v. Alabama,
395 U.S. 238 (1969)
[89]
Boykin pled guilty to five counts of robbery. The jury sentenced him to death. He challenged the validity of the plea because the judge never asked him relevant questions to determine the validity and voluntariness of the plea. The Supreme Court, finding a violation of due process, overturned the conviction.

Bradenburg v. Ohio,
395 U.S. 444 (1969)
[139]
A leader of the Ku Klux Klan was convicted of advocating the use the criminal activity to accomplish Klan political goals. He challenged the state law on First and Fourteenth Amendment grounds. The Supreme Court ruled that punishment for advocacy alone was unconstitutional and reversed the conviction.

Bradwell v. Illinois,
83 U.S. 130 (1872)
[169]
Myra Bradwell petitioned the state to be granted a license to practice law. The state refused her application, in part because of the custom of the day that married women could not enter into a contract. She challenged on Fourteenth Amendment grounds (Privileges and Immunities Clause). The Supreme Court found that the right to practice law had no relationship to the rights of citizenship protected in the Privileges and Immunities Clause and thus found in favor of the state.

Brady v. United States,
397 U.S. 742 (1970)
[209]
Brady pled guilty to kidnapping. He challenged the conviction based on his assertion that his counsel pressured him to plead guilty and that the plea was induced by representations of leniency. The Supreme Court upheld the conviction.

Branzburg v. Hayes,
408 U.S. 665 (1972)
[141]
Reporter Branzburg published an article in a newspaper detailing his observations about two local residents who synthesized marijuana from hashish. The story included a photograph of the hashish. The reporter was subpoenaed to appear before the local grand jury to disclose who the residents were as reported in the story. The reporter refused to testify on First Amendment grounds. The Supreme Court ruled that reporters were not immune from testifying before a grand jury.

Braunfeld v. Brown,
366 U.S. 599 (1961)
[156]
Pennsylvania state law prohibited retail sales on Sundays. Retailers who

were observers of the orthodox Jewish faith closed their stores from nightfall Friday to nightfall Saturday. They challenged the law on First Amendment (Establishment Clause) and Fourteenth Amendment (Equal Protection Clause) grounds. The Supreme Court upheld the state law.

Breithaupt v. Abram,
352 U.S. 432 (1957)
[200, 201]
Breithaupt was convicted of involuntary manslaughter. He challenged on the grounds that a blood test was conducted without his permission. The Supreme Court upheld the conviction and concluded that the blood test did not violate Breithaupt's due-process rights.

Brewer v. Williams,
430 U.S. 387 (1977)
[214]
Escaped mental patient Williams was convicted of murdering a ten-year-old female. Statements that were instrumental in his conviction were solicited by police prior to Williams' discussion with his attorneys. He challenged the conviction. The Supreme Court agreed that Williams' rights were denied, and the conviction was reversed.

Bridges v. California,
314 U.S. 252 (1942)
[33, 64–65, 133]
Petitioners were convicted of contempt of court and fined as a result of publishing in newspapers comments about pending court cases. They challenged on First Amendment grounds and the Su-

preme Court ruled that the convictions were unconstitutional.

Bridges v. Wixon,
326 U.S. 135 (1945)
[230]
Deportation proceedings were initiated against Bridges, an alien. It was alleged that he was affiliated with the Communist Party of the United States, which advocated the overthrow of the United States government. The finding for deportation was overruled by the Supreme Court.

Briscoe v. Bank of Kentucky,
36 U.S. 257 (1837)
[57–58]
The Supreme Court was asked, among other issues, whether notes issued by a state-chartered bank were bills of credit and thus unconstitutional. The Supreme Court found no constitutional violations.

Broadrick v. Oklahoma,
413 U.S. 601 (1973)
[143]
State civil servants were restricted by state law as to the amount of political activity they could engage in. Three state employees challenged the law on vagueness and overbreadth grounds. The Supreme Court upheld the state law.

Brockett v. Spokane Arcades, Inc.,
472 U.S. 491 (1985)
[48]
Washington state law prohibited the showing of lewd films in a business setting. The law was challenged on First Amendment grounds. The Supreme Court upheld the state law.

Brown v. Board of Education,
347 U.S. 483 (1954)
[239–240]
The Supreme Court found that "separate but equal" in segregated public schools was inherently unconstitutional (a violation of the Equal Protection Clause of the Fourteenth Amendment).

Brown v. Board of Education,
349 U.S. 294 (1955)
[38, 66]
The Supreme Court established judicial guidelines for local courts in desegregating public schools.

Brown v. Glines,
444 U.S. 348 (1980)
[146]
United States Air Force rules required that its members be granted approval prior to circulating petitions on its military bases and to members of Congress. Glines was disciplined for violating these rules. The Supreme Court upheld the military rules.

Brown v. Maryland,
25 U.S. 419 (1827)
[57]
The question the Supreme Court was to decide was whether a state can constitutionally require an importer to take out a state license for such importing. The Court found the state law unconstitutional.

Brown v. United States,
12 U.S. 110 (1814)
[244]
A United States ship, chartered to a United States company conducting trade with Great Britain, was stopped under an embargo but later released. Part of its cargo was sold to an American citizen. The United States then filed suit claiming the cargo as a war prize. The Supreme Court reversed the confiscation.

Buchanan v. Warley,
245 U.S. 60 (1917)
[115]
A contract between a white person and a colored person would have been nullified by a city ordinance. The Supreme Court found that the ordinance violated the Fourteenth Amendment.

Buck v. Bell,
274 U.S. 200 (1927)
[171]
State law allowed for the sterilization of "mental defectives." The state police power authorizing the procedure to be performed on Carrie Buck was challenged. The Supreme Court upheld the law.

Buckley v. Valeo,
424 U.S. 1 (1976)
[70, 93–94, 144, 179–180]
Federal law limited financial contributions to political candidates for federal elective office and limited the amounts that these candidates could spend in seeking office. Several individuals challenged the law on a variety of constitutional grounds. The Supreme Court ruled, in part, that the contributions provisions were constitutional but the expenditures provisions violated the First Amendment.

Burlington Industries Inc. v. Ellerth,
524 U.S. 742 (1998)
[247]
Ellerth quit her job with Burlington because she had allegedly been subjected to constant sexual harassment by a supervisor, a mid-level manager. Ellerth refused his advances but suffered no job-related retaliation. She did not lodge any complaints with officials at Burlington. The Supreme Court upheld Ellerth's right to sue for constructive discharge but also gave Burlington the right to an affirmative defense.

Burnet v. Coronado Oil & Gas Co.,
285 U.S. 393 (1932)
[30]
Oklahoma leased some of its land to Coronado for oil and gas production. The IRS assessed income taxes on the corporation, but the Court of Appeals ruled that the lease was an instrumentality of the state dedicated to benefiting its public schools. A tax on the lease would hinder this function, which was required by federal law. The Supreme Court affirmed this ruling.

Calder v. Bull,
3 U.S. 386 (1798)
[54, 101]
Heirs to a will challenged state legislative authority overruling a state court ruling of a probate matter. The Supreme Court upheld the legislative authority.

California v. Carney,
471 U.S. 386 (1985)
[217–218]
Law enforcement officials following up on information about drug activities in a motor home searched it without a search warrant and found marijuana. Carney was subsequently convicted. He challenged on Fourth Amendment grounds. The Supreme Court upheld the conviction stating that a mobile "home" did not have the same protections as a stationary home.

California v. Greenwood,
486 U.S. 35 (1988)
[184]
Police obtained evidence of narcotics trafficking in Greenwood's trash. A search warrant was then obtained to search his house, where additional evidence was discovered. The Supreme Court ruled that discarded garbage did not enjoy Fourth Amendment protections.

California v. Minjares,
443 U.S. 916 (1979)
[215]
The opinion was a dissent from a denial of stay. The dissent believed that the case posed an opportunity to further evaluate the exclusionary doctrine.

Callins v. Collins,
510 U.S. 1127 (1994)
[221–222]
Callins, a convicted murderer, is sentenced to death by lethal injection. Petition for writ of certiorari denied.

Cantwell v. Connecticut,
310 U.S. 296 (1940)
[152]
Some Jehovah's Witnesses were convicted pursuant to a breach-of-peace

state law prohibiting solicitation of money for religious causes without prior approval from the appropriate public official. The Supreme Court reversed the convictions on First Amendment grounds.

Carey v. Brown,
447 U.S. 455 (1980)
[181]

Appellants were convicted of picketing the home of the Mayor of Chicago, protesting his stance on a political issue. They challenged the statute proscribing this activity. The Supreme Court found the statute unconstitutional on equal protection and First Amendment grounds.

Carey v. Population Services International,
431 U.S. 678 (1978)
[181]

New York State law outlawed the distribution, advertising, or selling of contraceptives. Appellees challenged the statute. The Supreme Court found the statute unconstitutional on First Amendment grounds.

Carlson v. Landon,
342 U.S. 524 (1952)
[232]

The question in this case is whether the United States Attorney General, as the executive head of the Immigration and Naturalization Service, can hold without bail, at his discretion, pending the results of a deportation hearing, active alien communists who advocate the overthrow by force of the U.S. government. The Supreme Court ruled in the negative.

Carter v. Carter Coal Co.,
298 U.S. 238 (1936)
[63]

Federal law regulated maximum hours and minimum wages in coal mines. Failure to abide by these regulations resulted in a tax levy. Stockholders sued the company to enjoin it from paying the tax or abiding by the regulations of the law. The Supreme Court found the federal law an unconstitutional expansion of congressional authority of the Commerce Clause.

Castaneda v. Partida,
430 U.S. 482 (1977)
[181]

A Mexican American convicted of a crime challenged the state's underrepresentation of Mexican Americans on county grand juries. The Supreme Court found that the lack of representation was discriminatory and as such a violation of equal protection guarantees.

Central Intelligence Agency v. Sims,
471 U.S. 159 (1985)
[233]

Sims requested information from the C.I.A. under the federal Freedom of Information Act. The C.I.A. provided some of the requested information but declined to provide all of it, citing national security reasons. Sims challenged. The Supreme Court ruled that the C.I.A. was required to supply some of the withheld information.

Chambers v. Florida,
309 U.S. 227 (1940)
[193]

Four young black men were convicted

of robbing and murdering an elderly white man. They were sentenced to death. They challenged the excessive nature of their police interrogations as violations of their due process protections. The Supreme Court reversed the convictions.

Champlin Refining Co. v. Corporation Commission,
286 U.S. 210 (1932)
[7]
Champlain was engaged in interstate and intrastate production and refining of crude oil. It alleged that state laws violated its due process and equal protection rights. The Supreme Court found the state law too vague and indefinite to be constitutional.

Chandler v. Florida,
449 U.S. 560 (1981)
[146–147]
Appellants, who had objected to the allowed television coverage of their trial, were convicted by the jury. They challenged the convictions on the grounds that the forced television coverage denied them a fair and impartial jury and trial. The Supreme Court upheld the convictions.

Chandler v. Miller,
520 U.S. 305 (1997)
[111]
Georgia law required candidates for certain state electoral offices to take a drug test and to make the results public. Libertarian Party candidate challenged the law on First, Fourth, and Fourteenth Amendment grounds. The Supreme

Court found the law to be unconstitutional.

Chapman v. California,
386 U.S. 18 (1967)
[204]
Petitioners were convicted of crimes after a criminal trial in which the prosecutor made extensive comments about the defendants' failure to testify. The convictions were challenged under the Fifth and Fourteenth Amendments. The Supreme Court reversed the convictions.

Chapman v. Houston Welfare Rights Org.,
441 U.S. 600 (1979)
[45]
Petitioners sued their respective states for state decisions depriving them of federal welfare benefits. The Supreme Court ruled that the lower courts did not have jurisdiction to decide the cases.

Chas. C. Steward Machine Co. v. Davis,
301 U.S. 548 (1937)
[83]
Steward Machine challenged federal tax on employers of eight or more employees. The Supreme Court upheld the law.

Cherokee Nation v. Georgia,
30 U.S. 1 (1831)
[23–24]
The Cherokee Nation sought an injunction against the state for the execution of all state laws against the Indian nation arguing that they were a foreign nation under the federal Constitution. The Supreme Court ruled in favor of the state.

Chicago & Southern Air Lines v.
Waterman Steamship Corp.,
333 U.S. 103 (1948)
[231]
Waterman was denied approval, pursuant to federal law, of the ability to engage in overseas and foreign air transportation rights. Approval was granted to Chicago & Southern. The Supreme Court dismissed Waterman's petition for judicial review.

Chicago v. Morales,
527 U.S. ___ (1999)
[16, 100, 128, 188–189]
City ordinance prohibited loitering of gang members and other individuals with gang members. Morales challenged his conviction on First and Fourteenth Amendment grounds. The Supreme Court ruled that the ordinance gave too much discretion to the police and too little notice to citizens and was thus unconstitutional.

Chicago, B&Q.R. Co. v. McGuire,
219 U.S. 549 (1911)
[170]
McGuire, while a railroad brakeman, was injured as a result of negligence on the part of the railroad. He sued for and received damages for his injuries. The railroad challenged the state law that precluded them from utilizing a certain means of defense. The Supreme Court upheld the law.

Chicot County Drainage District v. Baxter
State Bank,
308 U.S. 371 (1940)
[32–33]
Bank defaulted on bonds due Chicot. The

Supreme Court decided that the case should be dismissed.

Chy Lung v. Freeman,
92 U.S. 275 (1875)
[226]
Immigrant was held pending immigration examination, payment, and assurances. The Supreme Court found that the relevant law provided too much discretion to the appropriate public official.

Citizens' Savings & Loan Association v.
Topeka,
87 U.S. 655 (1874)
[79]
Association sued city for interest on bonds. The bonds were issued pursuant to state law for the creation and maintenance of bridges. Association argued that the law allowed Topeka to incur debt without any restrictions on the power to do so. The Supreme Court found in favor of Topeka.

Civil Rights Cases,
109 U.S. 3 (1883)
[5, 79]
This was a challenge to the constitutionality of the federal Civil Rights Act of 1875, which, in part, prevented racial discrimination in public accommodations. The Supreme Court found the Act unconstitutional.

Cleveland v. United States,
329 U.S. 14 (1946)
[238]
Mormons were convicted of violating the Mann Act. They challenged the statute's intent ("for any other immoral pur-

poses") as it related to their practicing polygamy. The Supreme Court upheld the convictions.

Clinton v. City of New York,
524 U.S. 417 (1998)
[52, 73]
The case involved the constitutionality of the line-item veto as passed by Congress and exercised by President Clinton. The Supreme Court ruled that the federal law violated the Presentment Clause of the Constitution.

Cohen v. California,
403 U.S. 15 (1971)
[140]
Appellant was convicted of disturbing the peace by wearing a jacket with offensive speech on it. The Supreme Court reversed the conviction as contrary to the rights and guarantees expressed in the First and Fourteenth Amendments.

Cohens v. Virginia,
19 U.S. 264 (1821)
[23, 55–56]
This case involved the right to sell lottery tickets contrary to state law but permissible under federal law. The Supreme Court upheld the conviction.

Coker v. Georgia,
433 U.S. 584 (1977)
[215]
Coker was convicted of rape and sentenced to death as allowed by state law because the rape was committed in the course of committing another felony and because he had a prior conviction for another capital-felony crime. He challenged

the sentence on Eighth Amendment grounds. The Supreme Court reversed the sentence and remanded the case.

Colegrove v. Green,
328 U.S. 549 (1946)
[65]
Illinois voters challenged state official involvement in federal congressional district elections. The Supreme Court affirmed the lower court's dismissal of the case.

Coleman v. Miller,
307 U.S. 433 (1939)
[32]
The case involved Kansas state legislative resolutions rejecting and then endorsing (with the aid of the lieutenant governor) a federal constitutional amendment. The state Senate passed another resolution calling for the state attorney general to represent the state. The state supreme court rejected the request and this decision was affirmed by the Supreme Court.

College Savings Bank v. Florida Prepaid Postsecondary Education Expense Board,
527 U.S. ___ (1999)
[16, 188]
Bank is a New Jersey-chartered bank selling certificates of deposit designed to finance the costs of college education. They own a patent on the process. Board is an arm of the state of Florida and allegedly infringed on Bank's patent. Bank sought to sue the state. The Supreme Court ruled that the state sovereign immunity doctrine prevented the suit, without the permission of the state.

Columbus Board of Education v. Penick, 443 U.S. 449 (1979)

[46, 124]

Class action sued Board for the perpetuation of racial segregation in the school system. Trial court found the school board's actions directly caused the continuation of the racial practices. It ordered the Board to amend its practices. The Supreme Court affirmed the order.

Commissioner of Internal Revenue v. Scottish American Investment Co., 323 U.S. 119 (1944)

[34]

Foreign-investment trusts were found to have offices in the United States and as such could be taxed as resident foreign corporations. The Supreme Court found in favor of the commissioner.

Committee for Public Education & Religious Liberty v. Regan, 444 U.S. 646 (1980)

[161]

State funding was allocated to nonpublic schools performing state-mandated functions. The expenditures for religious schools were challenged on First and Fourteenth Amendment grounds. The Supreme Court found the funding did not violate the Establishment Clause.

Consolidated Edison Co. v. Public Service Commission, 447 U.S. 530 (1980)

[146]

New York State regulation prohibited appellant from inserting in its monthly bills materials discussing issues of public policy. It was challenged as a violation of free speech protections. The Supreme Court found the regulation unconstitutional.

Coolidge v. New Hampshire, 403 U.S. 443 (1971)

[69]

The Supreme Court ruled that the state attorney general, acting as a justice of the peace, could not be considered a neutral and detached magistrate as required when issuing search warrants. In this case such action was determined to violate the Fourth Amendment.

Coopage v. Kansas, 236 U.S. 1 (1915)

[114]

Coopage tried to coerce an employee under the threat of termination to sign a statement calling for the withdrawal of the union. Such action violated state law and Coopage was convicted of the crime. The Supreme Court found the conviction violated Coopage's due process protections, and the conviction was reversed.

Cox Broadcasting Corp. v. Cohn, 420 U.S. 469 (1975)

[144]

Reporter broadcast the name of a deceased rape victim in violation of state statute. Victim's relative sued. The Supreme Court ruled that the statute did not violate the First and Fourteenth Amendments.

Cox v. New Hampshire,
312 U.S. 569 (1941)
[144, 172]
Jehovah's Witnesses were convicted of assembly without a special license pursuant to state law. They challenged under the First and Fourteenth Amendments. The Supreme Court ruled that local control over the use of streets did not necessarily violate the First Amendment.

Coyle v. Smith,
221 U.S. 559 (1911)
[104]
State law authorized Oklahoma to relocate its capitol. This was challenged as violating the federal laws admitting the state into the union. The Supreme Court ruled that for the state to be on equal footing with the other states it had the right to relocate its capitol.

Craig v. Boren,
429 U.S. 190 (1976)
[122]
Craig, a male between the ages of 18 and 21, was prevented by state law from purchasing 3.2% beer. Women that age were allowed to make the beer purchase. Craig sued for gender-based discrimination. The Supreme Court found the law violated the Equal Protection Clause.

Craig v. Harney,
331 U.S. 367 (1947)
[133]

Newspaper publisher, writer, and reporter were convicted of contempt of court for publishing an article critical of a local judge involved in a pending criminal trial. The Supreme Court reversed the convictions.

Cramer v. United States,
325 U.S. 1 (1945)
[196]

Cramer, a German-born but naturalized United States citizen, was convicted of treason because of his affiliation with convicted saboteurs. The Supreme Court reversed the conviction.

Creek Nation v. United States,
318 U.S. 629 (1943)
[227–228]
Pursuant to treaties, Indian nation granted land rights to railroads, which agreed to pay fixed annual sums to the federal government for the benefit of the tribes. The tribes argued that the railroads failed to comply with the provisions of the treaties and sued the United States. The Supreme Court found that the United States was not liable for the purported actions of others.

Crooker v. California,
357 U.S. 433 (1958)
[201–202]
Petitioner was interrogated about a murder for fourteen hours and subsequently confessed. He was convicted and sentenced to death. He challenged the conviction stating that the confession was coerced. The Supreme Court did not find any compelling constitutional violations and affirmed the conviction.

Cruzan v. Director, Missouri Department of Health,
497 U.S. 261 (1990)
[99, 109–110, 127, 245]
Petitioner, as a result of severe injuries, was in a vegetative state. Her parents requested the termination of artificial life support, but the hospital refused. The state trial court authorized the termination. The state supreme court reversed and the Supreme Court affirmed this decision.

Cummings v. Missouri,
71 U.S. 277 (1866)
[167]
Roman Catholic priest was convicted of teaching and preaching without first taking a loyalty oath as required by state constitution. The Supreme Court reversed the conviction.

Cunningham v. Neagle,
135 U.S. 1 (1890)
[27]
Neagle, a deputy United States marshal in the act of protecting Supreme Court Justice Stephen Field from an assassin, killed the would-be assassin. He was arrested for murder under state law. The Supreme Court affirmed the decision to release Neagle.

Dalehite v. United States,
346 U.S. 15 (1953)
[239]
This tort action against the U.S. government for death resulting from an explosion caused by negligence resulted in a finding against the government. The Court of Appeals reversed the verdict and the Supreme Court affirmed.

Dallas v. Stanglin,
490 U.S. 19 (1989)
[148]
City ordinance allowed for the licensing of dance halls reserved for children between the ages fourteen and eighteen. Respondent challenged the ordinance as a violation of both the First (association rights) and Fourteenth Amendments (equal protection). The Supreme Court ruled in favor of the ordinance.

Dandridge v. Williams,
397 U.S. 471 (1970)
[107]
AFDC recipients sued Maryland for its regulations regarding welfare administration. In finding for the state, the Supreme Court stated that it was not within its power to second-guess state officials' decisions regarding the allocation of public funds as long as the process passed constitutional muster.

Daniels v. Williams,
474 U.S. 327 (1986)
[71]
Prison inmate petitioner sued for injuries sustained from slipping on a pillow on a stairway. The Supreme Court affirmed the motion for summary judgment against the petitioner asserting that due process claims are not triggered by negligence.

Daubert v. Merrell Dow Pharmaceuticals, Inc.,
509 U.S. 579 (1993)
[245–246]
It was alleged that a prescription drug

caused severe birth defects. At the trial conflicting scientific evidence was presented, and the court found that some of the evidence did not meet generally accepted standards. The Court of Appeals affirmed citing case law. The Supreme Court vacated the lower courts' ruling, stating the guide to the admissibility of federal evidence was statutory.

Davis v Mills,
194 U.S. 451 (1904)
[170]

This case involved the application and limitations of procedural rules relative to civil litigation between parties residing in different states.

Davis v. Monroe County Board of Education,
526 U.S.___(1999)
[52–53, 247–248]

Fifth-grade girl was a victim of a five-month barrage of physical and verbal sexual harassment from a male student. Some of the harassment took place in front of several teachers who failed to stop the harasser. The girl did complain to school officials, who failed to act. The girl sued the school district for Title IX violations. The Supreme Court ruled against the school district.

Day-Brite Lighting, Inc. v. Missouri,
342 U.S. 421 (1952)
[86]

Day-Brite refused to let employee leave during lunch break to vote, but did allow the employee to leave before the end of the workday. Day-Brite withheld a salary for the final period of time employee was away from employment. State law prevented employers from withholding employee salary when employee leaves work to vote in a public election. The Supreme Court upheld the state law.

DeFunis v. Odegaard,
416 U.S. 312 (1974)
[43, 179]

This case involved state law-school admission policy allegedly grounded in racially discriminatory practices. The Supreme Court found that the controversy was moot and vacated the case.

DeJonge v. Oregon,
299 U.S. 353 (1937)
[131]

Appellant was convicted of criminal syndicalism, which, among other things, included assisting in conducting a Communist Party meeting. The Supreme Court found the state law related to this one issue an unconstitutional violation of the Due Process Clause of the Fourteenth Amendment.

Den ex dem Murray v. Hoboken Land & Improvement Co.,
59 U.S. 272 (1856)
[113]

This case explored the constitutional implications of what constitutes judicial power as defined in Article III of the federal constitution. More specifically, the Supreme Court tried to decide whether an executive department official (in this case the solicitor of the treasury) acting under federal law could exercise judicial power without infringing due-process guarantees.

Dennis v. United States,
341 U.S. 494 (1951)
[37]
United States Communist Party members were convicted of violating federal law prohibiting the teaching and advocacy of overthrowing the United States government by force and violence. They challenged on First and Fifth Amendment grounds. The Supreme Court upheld the convictions.

Department of Commerce v. United States House of Representatives,
525 U.S. ___ (1999)
[52]
Census Bureau planned to conduct the 2000 Decennial Census using statistical sampling. This was challenged as violating the Actual Enumeration Clause of the Constitution. The Supreme Court agreed that this plan was unconstitutional.

DeShaney v. Winnebago County Department of Social Services,
489 U.S. 189 (1989)
[98]
Petitioner, a child, was subject to repeated beatings by his father. When Social Services learned of the treatment, they tried to protect the boy but did not remove him from his father's custody. The father subsequently beat the boy so severely that the result was permanent brain damage. The mother sued respondents for violating the minor's due process protections. The Supreme Court affirmed a summary judgment for the Department.

Diaz v. Gonzalez,
261 U.S. 102 (1923)
[29]
Widowed mother sold her land, children challenged to nullify the sale. The Supreme Court upheld the sale.

Douglas v. California,
372 U.S. 353 (1963)
[40, 118]
Indigent petitioners were convicted of state crimes. On their only right to appeal they applied for the appointment of counsel. The intermediate-level appellate court denied their request. Their convictions were affirmed. The Supreme Court ruled that on the one-and-only right to an appeal, indigents had the right to counsel.

Douglas v. Jeannette,
319 U.S. 157 (1943)
[153]
Jehovah's Witnesses were threatened with prosecution for selling merchandise without a license and without paying a fee as required by a local ordinance. This case hinged on whether a federal court has jurisdiction to determine the constitutional validity of the ordinance. The Supreme Court affirmed the decision directing the case against appellants be dismissed.

Dow v. Johnson,
100 U.S. 158 (1879)
[226–227]
During the Civil War the New Orleans region was seized by Union forces and General Dow was put in charge. He declared martial law. Johnson, a resident

of the area, sued Dow for wantonly abusing his powers. The question is whether a military officer can be held liable to a civil action for injuries resulting from acts ordered by him as an officer of the military when in enemy country when the acts in question were not justified by the necessities of war. The Supreme Court found for Dow.

Dred Scott v. Sandford,
60 U.S. 393 (1856)
[4–5, 25, 58–59, 76, 102, 225—226]
Scott, a Negro slave belonging to Emerson, was taken by Emerson to Missouri and sold to Sandford. Scott sued for his freedom. The question was whether a Negro slave was considered property and thus not entitled to the privileges and immunities of citizens. The Supreme Court ruled against Scott.

Dun & Bradstreet, Inc. v. Greenmoss Builders,
472 U.S. 749 (1985)
[147]
Petitioner, a credit reporting agency, provided erroneous information that Greenmoss had filed for bankruptcy. Greenmoss sued for defamation. The Supreme Court found for petitioner.

Duncan v. Kahanamoku,
327 U.S. 304 (1946)
[173]
Civilians were convicted of crimes by military tribunals. The Supreme Court ruled that the military tribunals lacked sufficient authority.

Duncan v. Louisiana,
391 U.S. 145 (1968)
[119]
Appellant was convicted of battery. Under state law the potential punishment was up to two years' imprisonment. Duncan was sentenced to sixty days. Prior to the trial he had requested a jury trial, but his request was denied because the state constitution allowed jury trials only for capital crimes or when imprisonment with hard labor could be imposed. The Supreme Court reversed the conviction and remanded the case.

Edmonson v. Leesville Concrete Co.,
500 U.S. 614 (1991)
[186]
Edmonson sued Leesville for negligence. During jury selection Leesville used peremptory challenges to remove black persons from the potential jury. Edmonson asked the trial court to question Leesville's action. It refused. The Supreme Court reversed.

Edwards v. Aguillard,
482 U.S. 578 (1987)
[164–165]
State law required that when creationism is taught in public schools, evolution must also be taught and vice versa. Appellants challenged the law on Establishment Clause grounds. The Supreme Court agreed that the law was unconstitutional.

Edwards v. South Carolina,
372 U.S. 229 (1963)
[202]
Petitioners were arrested for peaceably

protesting what they believed to be the state's racially discriminatory policies. The Supreme Court reversed the convictions as a violation of the First and Fourteenth Amendments.

Edwards v. United States,
312 U.S. 473 (1941)
[193]
Petitioner was granted immunity by the S.E.C. and testified as to fraudulent behavior. He was then convicted of fraud by the attorney general. The conviction was reversed.

Edye v. Robertson,
112 U.S. 580 (1884)
[227]
This case involved the regulation of immigration, and the power to do so resides with Congress. Moreover, taxes levied on immigration need not be uniform to be constitutional.

Eisenstadt v. Baird,
405 U.S. 438 (1972)
[178]
Baird was convicted of distributing contraceptives in violation of state law. The Supreme Court ruled that the law violated the Equal Protection Clause because it enforced dissimilar treatment between married and unmarried persons.

Endicott Johnson Corp. v. Perkins,
317 U.S. 501 (1943)
[18]
Petitioner was subpoenaed for violations of federal-minimum wage laws. Endicott challenged the secretary of labor's power

to issue the subpoena. The Supreme Court ruled that Congress could enact the subpoena provision.

Engel v. Vitale,
370 U.S. 421 (1962)
[156–158]
Board of Education required school principal to enforce the recitation of a prayer by all students at the beginning of each school day. Parents challenged the state-approved prayer. The Supreme Court ruled that the prayer requirement was inconsistent with the Establishment Clause.

Epperson v. Arkansas,
393 U.S. 97 (1968)
[41, 106–107, 159]
State law prevented the teaching of evolution. Public-school teacher challenged the law. The Supreme Court ruled that the law violated the First and Fourteenth Amendments.

Erznoznik v. Jacksonville,
422 U.S. 205 (1975)
[144]
City ordinance prevented the showing of any nudity at drive-in movies where the screen was viewable from a public place. Drive-in movie manager challenged the ordinance after his arrest for its violation. The Supreme Court found the ordinance unconstitutional.

Escobedo v. Illinois,
378 U.S. 478 (1964)
[203]
Petitioner was interrogated about a murder. He was not informed of his

rights nor was his attorney allowed to consult with him. He was convicted of the crime. The Supreme Court reversed the conviction.

Estes v. Texas,
381 U.S. 532 (1965)
[136–137, 203]
Estes was indicted for a crime. Extreme pretrial publicity had an impact on potential jurors. Over the objections of Estes much of the trial was broadcast on television. Petitioner challenged his conviction. The Supreme Court ruled that broadcasting the trial over the express objections of the defendant violated his rights to a fair trial. The conviction was set aside.

Evans v. Abney,
396 U.S. 435 (1970)
[119]
Conveyed property was left in trust for the creation of a public park for the exclusive use of white people. The trust was challenged as an abridgment of the Fourteenth Amendment. The Supreme Court affirmed the termination of the trust and the return of the property to the heirs.

Everson v. Board of Education of Ewing TP,
330 U.S. 1 (1947)
[155]
Public funds were used to transport children to parochial schools. The law was challenged by a school-district taxpayer. The Supreme Court ruled that the funding did not violate the Constitution.

Ex parte Bollman,
8 U.S. 75 (1807)
[224]
The case concerned the appellate jurisdiction of the Supreme Court in the issuance of a writ of habeas corpus. The Supreme Court determined that Congress had provided them with the power.

Ex parte Clarke,
100 U.S. 399 (1879)
[103]
City councilman (and precinct election judge) was convicted of malfeasance concerning an election. The Supreme Court denied the writ of habeas corpus.

Ex parte Garland,
71 U.S. 333 (1866)
[5, 168, 235–236]
Federal law required attorneys to take a loyalty oath before practicing law in a federal court. Petitioner did take the oath. Garland subsequently took part in the Civil War on the side of the Confederacy. Following the rebellion Garland received a full presidential pardon for his actions during the war. The case involved his petition to practice law again. The Supreme Court approved his request.

Ex parte McCardle,
74 U.S. 506 (1868)
[26]
Mississippi newspaper editor McCardle was arrested and placed in military custody on charges of publishing "incendiary and libelous articles." Under an 1867 law, McCardle filed a writ of habeas corpus; on appeal the Supreme Court granted jurisdiction. Overriding a presi-

dential veto in 1868, Congress repealed the 1867 law granting the Court appellant jurisdiction of habeas corpus cases.

Ex parte Milligan,
71 U.S. 2 (1866)
[59, 77]
Milligan, a civilian, was convicted by a military commission for crimes against the United States during the Civil War and sentenced to death. He challenged the military court's jurisdiction. The Supreme Court upheld the conviction.

Ex parte Mitsuye Endo,
323 U.S. 283 (1944)
[84]
Petitioner was an American citizen of Japanese ancestry. Because of her racial heritage she was interned pursuant to a presidential executive order during the Second World War. She sought a writ of habeas corpus. The Supreme Court approved the petition.

Ex parte Siebold,
100 U.S. 371 (1879)
[60]
Petitioners were precinct election judges who were convicted of malfeasance in the discharge of their duties. They filed petitions for writs of habeas corpus. The Supreme Court denied their request.

Ex parte Virginia,
100 U.S. 339 (1879)
[103]
Virginia judge was arrested for failure to accept blacks as grand and petit jurors. The judge and the state filed writs of habeas corpus for his release. The Supreme Court denied the petitions.

Falbo v. United States,
320 U.S. 549 (1944)
[228]
Falbo was classified by draft board as a conscientious objector and ordered to report for an assignment of national importance. He willfully failed to obey the order and was indicted for violating the law. The Supreme Court upheld the indictment.

Federal Communications Commission v. Pacifica Foundation,
438 U.S. 726 (1978)
[145–146]
Radio station was cited but not sanctioned for broadcasting obscene and vulgar language (they replayed the George Carlin monologue "Filthy Words"). The ruling was challenged as constituting censorship. The Supreme Court found that the F.C.C. did not violate First Amendment protections.

Federal Communications Commission v. Pottsville Broadcasting Co.,
309 U.S. 134 (1940)
[33]
The case involved the authority of Congress to delegate to the F.C.C. and the judiciary the power to regulate radio broadcasting. The Supreme Court ruled in favor of the congressional authority.

Federal Election Commission v. Massachusetts Citizens for Life, Inc.,
479 U.S. 238 (1986)
[147–148]
Federal election law prohibited corpo-

rations from using their general treasury funds to make expenditures of any kind to any federal election campaign. Appellee, a nonprofit, nonstock, right-to-life organization, was charged with violating the federal statute. The court of appeals held that the law, as applied, was unconstitutional. The Supreme Court affirmed.

Federal Energy Regulatory Commission v. Mississippi,
456 U.S. 742 (1982)
[108]
Federal public utility statute required certain state compliance. Mississippi challenged on Commerce Clause and Tenth Amendment grounds. The Supreme Court upheld the federal law.

Federal Trade Commission v. Bunte Brothers Inc.,
312 U.S. 349 (1941)
[8, 64]
The F.T.C. found Bunte engaged in unfair methods of competition. Since the dispute involved intrastate commerce, the Supreme Court ruled against the use of power by the F.T.C.

Federal Trade Commission v. Standard Education Society,
302 U.S. 112 (1938)
[237]
The F.T.C. found Standard to be engaged in unfair, false, deceptive, and misleading practices and issued a cease-and-desist order. The order was challenged based upon the validity of the testimony used by the F.T.C. The Supreme Court upheld the order by the F.T.C.

Federal Trade Commission v. Ticor Title Insurance Co.,
504 U.S. 621 (1992)
[110]
The F.T.C. charged six title insurance companies with horizontal price fixing. Several states had previously set rates. Thus the insurance companies asserted immunity from the antitrust proceedings. The F.T.C. rejected the claim. The Supreme Court upheld the F.T.C..

Federation of Labor v. McAdory,
325 U.S. 450 (1945)
[35, 65]
Labor unions brought suit against county officials charged with enforcing state law regulating unions having members who were employed by the state. The petitioners argued that the law was unconstitutional on several grounds. The Supreme Court dismissed the case, in effect upholding the state law.

Fisher v. United States,
328 U.S. 463 (1946)
[197]
Fisher was convicted of murder and sentenced to death. He challenged, stating the trial judge refused to instruct the jury to take into account the possibility of his insanity. The Supreme Court affirmed the conviction.

Flast v. Cohen,
392 U.S. 83 (1968)
[41]
Taxpayers alleged that federal funds were used to finance the purchase of educational materials in parochial schools, constituting a violation of the Establishment Clause

of the First Amendment. The district court ruled that the appellants lacked standing. The Supreme Court reversed and allowed the suit to proceed.

Flood v. Kuhn,
407 U.S. 258 (1972)
[243]
Professional baseball player was traded to another team without his knowledge or consent. He challenged on antitrust grounds. The Supreme Court ruled against the player.

Florida Bar v. Went For It, Inc.,
515 U.S. 618 (1995)
[151]
Lawyer referral service and an individual attorney challenged state law, on First and Fourteenth Amendment grounds, that prohibited attorneys from soliciting victims of accidents or disasters by direct mail for thirty days after the incident. The Supreme Court upheld the state law.

Follett v. McCormick,
321 U.S. 573 (1944)
[153–154]
Jehovah's Witness was convicted of violating a town ordinance regulating the selling of books. The Supreme Court found this license tax, which was required to engage in First Amendment privileges to be unconstitutional.

Fong Yue Ting v. United States,
149 U.S. 698 (1893)
[61]
Chinese laborers were arrested for not having certificates of residence pursuant to federal law and rules. The arrests were challenged on due-process grounds. The Supreme Court affirmed the arrests.

Ford v. Wainwright,
477 U.S. 399 (1986)
[126]
Petitioner was convicted of murder and sentenced to death. During his incarceration awaiting execution he began to exhibit signs of mental illness. Pursuant to state law he was examined by psychiatrists. Additional evidence was offered by petitioner's counsel but refused by the state. Petitioner was denied a new evidentiary hearing. The Supreme Court ruled in favor of the right to a new hearing.

Foster v. Neilson,
27 U.S. 253 (1829)
[224–225]
The case involved a dispute over the ownership of property that had been sold several times. The Supreme Court ruled in favor of Neilson.

Francis v. Southern Pacific Co.,
333 U.S. 445 (1948)
[35–36]
Minor children sued for damages related to the death of their father, a passenger on Southern Pacific's train. The trial judge allowed the jury to decide only on the question of wanton negligence and not ordinary negligence. The jury found for Southern. The Supreme Court affirmed the verdict.

Friedman v. Rogers,
440 U.S. 1 (1979)
[146]
State law prohibited the practice of optometry under a trade name. The law

was challenged on First and Fourteenth Amendment grounds. The Supreme Court found the law constitutional.

Frost & Frost Trucking Co. v. Railroad Commission,
271 U.S. 583 (1926)
[104]
Private carrier was ordered by the state to suspend activities pending receipt of a certificate of public conveyance and necessity pursuant to state law. The order was challenged as a violation of the Fourteenth Amendment. The Supreme Court found the law unconstitutional.

Fuller v. Oregon,
417 U.S. 40 (1974)
[213]
Fuller pled guilty to a crime. As a condition to his probationary sentence he was ordered to pay the attorney and investigator hired by the state to provide him with a defense because of his indigency. He challenged. The Supreme Court found in favor of the state.

Fullilove v. Klutznick,
448 U.S. 448 (1980)
[13–14, 125]
Federal law required that a percentage of local public works using federal funds are to be awarded to minority-group members. The law was challenged as a violation of the Fourteenth Amendment. The Supreme Court upheld the law.

Furman v. Georgia,
408 U.S. 238 (1972)
[211]
The Supreme Court ruled that, as they stood at the time, state statutes impos-

ing and carrying out death penalties were an unconstitutional violation of the Eighth Amendment.

Gallegos v. Nebraska,
342 U.S. 55 (1951)
[199]
Following twenty-five days of interrogation and confinement, non-English-speaking petitioner pled guilty to homicide. He was convicted of manslaughter. He challenged asserting that he was mistreated. The Supreme Court affirmed his conviction.

Garcia v. San Antonio Metropolitan Transit Authority,
469 U.S. 528 (1985)
[109]
State mass transit authority received substantial funds from federal sources. A federal agency ruled that the Authority was not immune from federal minimum wage and overtime requirements. The Authority challenged the finding. The Supreme Court ruled in favor of the federal agency.

Garrison v. Louisiana,
379 U.S. 64 (1964)
[136]
District attorney was convicted of accusing state judges of laziness and inefficiency. The Supreme Court overturned the conviction.

Georgia v. McCollum,
505 U.S. 42 (1992)
[221]
White man was charged with assaulting two African Americans. The trial judge denied prosecution's motion to deny the

defense the use of racially motivated peremptory challenges in the selection of the trial. The state supreme court affirmed the decision. The Supreme Court reversed this ruling and remanded the case.

Gibbons v. Ogden,
22 U.S. 1 (1824)
[56–57]
Under New York State law, Robert Livingston and Robert Fulton were granted an exclusive right to operate steamboats in New York waters. They assigned the New York–New Jersey portion of their monopoly to Aaron Gibbon. Thomas Gibbons, a former partner of Ogden, operated, without consent, two steamboats in the area assigned to Ogden. Ogden obtained an injunction. The Supreme Court invalidated the New York law because it infringed upon congressional power to regulate interstate commerce.

Gibson v. Florida Legislative Committee,
372 U.S. 539 (1963)
[176]
President of Miami branch of the N.A.A.C.P. was convicted of refusing to disclose membership list to state legislature investigating communist infiltration. The Supreme Court ruled that the conviction violated the First and Fourteenth Amendments and as such reversed the conviction.

Gideon v. Wainwright,
372 U.S. 335 (1963)
[202]
Indigent man was denied the right to have counsel appointed to him when he was arrested for a noncapital case. The Supreme Court ruled that this denial was an infringement of Gideon's constitutional rights.

Gilligan v. Morgan,
413 U.S. 1 (1973)
[43]
Respondents argued that the Governor's action deploying the National Guard to quell civil disorder on the college campus violated students' rights to free speech and assembly. The Supreme Court ruled that the case was moot and that the separation of powers precluded the Court from resolving the controversy.

Ginsberg v. New York,
390 U.S. 629 (1968)
[106]
Appellant was convicted of selling pornography to a minor. The Supreme Court affirmed the conviction.

Gitlow v. New York,
268 U.S. 652 (1925)
[130]
Gitlow was convicted of criminal anarchy. The Supreme Court found the statute did not violate the Fourteenth Amendment and upheld the conviction.

Glass v. Louisiana,
471 U.S. 1080 (1985)
[218]
This was a petition for a rehearing to determine whether electrocution as a means of execution violated the Eighth Amendment. The petition was denied.

Glasser v. United States,
315 U.S. 60 (1942)
[193]
Petitioners were convicted of conspiracy
to defraud the United States. They challenged on a variety of grounds including the validity of the indictment, the
gender composition of the jury, and the
use of evidence and testimony. The Supreme Court reversed the convictions
and remanded the case.

Glidden Co. v. Zdanok,
370 U.S. 530 (1962)
[39]
The case involved the differences between Article I and Article III courts. The
Supreme Court affirmed the Court of
Appeals' decision that Article I courts
and their nonlife-tenured judges were
constitutional.

Globe Newspaper Co. v. Superior Court,
457 U.S. 596 (1982)
[216]
Because the victims of sexual offenses were
minors, the trial court excluded the press
and public from defendant's trial. A newspaper publisher challenged. The defendant was acquitted. The Supreme Court
overturned the mandatory exclusion law.

Goesaert v. Cleary,
335 U.S. 464 (1948)
[9, 239]
State law prohibited women from being
employed as bartenders unless they were
related to the owner. The law was challenged on equal protection grounds. The
Supreme Court affirmed the right of the
state to create and enforce such laws.

Goldman v. United States,
316 U.S. 129 (1942)
[172]
Petitioners were convicted of conspiracy
to commit bribery. Goldman challenged
the admissibility of evidence relative to
notes taken during a telephone conversation. The Supreme Court affirmed the
convictions.

Goldman v. Weinberger,
475 U.S. 503 (1986)
[233,244–245]
Ordained rabbi/officer in the United
States Air Force was ordered not to wear
his yarmulke while on duty and in uniform. He challenged on free religion
grounds. The Supreme Court affirmed
the military order.

Gompers v. Buck's Stove & Range Co.,
221 U.S. 418 (1911)
[28–29]
Petitioners were convicted of contempt
for violating their injunction on boycott-
ing Buck's. The Supreme Court reversed
the conviction.

Gompers v. United States,
233 U.S. 604 (1914)
[90]
The case challenged the statutory construction of contempt. The Supreme
Court found the statute's time-frame provisions too vague and expansive.

Gordon v. Lance,
403 U.S. 1 (1971)
[90]
State constitution and state law precluded state subdivisions from incur-

ring bond debt or to raising taxes beyond those set by their constitution without the super-majority approval of voters. County board of education proposed the issuance of general obligation bonds. The vote in favor was over 51%, but below the required 60%. The proposal failed. Those in favor challenged the constitutionality of the super-majority requirement. The Supreme Court ruled that the requirement was constitutional.

Gosa v. Mayden,
413 U.S. 665 (1973)
[212]
Petitioners were court-martialed and convicted of separate and unrelated crimes. They challenged on the grounds that military tribunals could be instituted only for service-connected crimes per the Supreme Court's ruling in *O'Callahan* v. *Parker*, 395 U.S. 258. The Supreme Court reaffirmed the service-connected rule.

Gravel v. United States,
408 U.S. 606 (1972)
[12–13, 90–91]
United States senator read into the public record classified documents. A federal grand jury investigated the allegation that the senator also arranged for private publication of the classified material. They subpoenaed the senator's aide. The subpoena was challenged as violating the Speech and Debate Clause. The Court of Appeals ruled that the aide could not be interviewed relative to the legislative actions of the senator. The Supreme Court vacated the case, affirming the Court of Appeals' ruling that the aide could be questioned about the efforts for private publication since this had no relationship to legislative activities.

Gray v. Sanders,
372 U.S. 368 (1963)
[88]
Appellee challenged the method the state would use to count votes in a primary election for federal and statewide seats. The Supreme Court ruled that the method violated the Equal Protection Clause.

Grayned v. Rockford,
408 U.S. 104 (1972)
[42]
Appellant was convicted on violating an antipicketing ordinance and an antinoise ordinance for his part in demonstrating in front of a high school. The Supreme Court found the antipicketing ordinance was unconstitutional; they also upheld the conviction per the antinoise ordinance.

Green v. United States,
355 U.S. 184 (1957)
[201]
Petitioner was indicted for first-and second-degree murder. The jury convicted him on the second-degree charge but was silent on the first-degree indictment. The conviction was reversed and remanded. On retrial the new jury convicted Green on the first-degree murder charge. He challenged on double-jeopardy grounds. The Supreme Court reversed the conviction and remanded it, ruling that it did violate the Fifth Amendment.

Greer v. Spock,
424 U.S. 828 (1976)
[233]
The military base allowed limited civilian access, prohibited political speeches and demonstrations and the distribution of literature without the prior approval of the base commander. Respondents' requests were rejected. They challenged on First and Fifth Amendment grounds. The Supreme Court held that the base rules were constitutional.

Gregg v. Georgia,
428 U.S. 153 (1976)
[213–214]
Gregg was convicted of murder and robbery. In a bifurcated process the jury sentenced him to death. He challenged on Eighth and Fourteenth Amendment grounds. The Supreme Court affirmed the sentence.

Griffin v. Illinois,
351 U.S. 12 (1956)
[175]
Petitioners were convicted of armed robbery. On their automatic right to appeal for error they requested a free copy of the certified record. Although they were indigent their request was denied as it was not related to a death-penalty case. The Supreme Court found the petitioners' constitutional rights were violated.

Griswold v. Connecticut,
381 U.S. 479 (1965)
[176]
Pursuant to state law appellants were convicted of prescribing contraceptive devices and materials to married women. They challenged the conviction on Fourteenth Amendment grounds. The Supreme Court reversed the conviction stating the statute violates privacy rights as implicitly guaranteed in the Bill of Rights.

Groves v. Slaughter,
40 U.S. 449 (1841)
[24]
The case involved a contract making slaves subject to sale as merchandise pursuant to the state's constitution. The Supreme Court allowed the contract to be enforced without explicitly ruling on the slave-as-merchandise aspect.

Gulf Oil Corp. v. Gilbert,
330 U.S. 501 (1947)
[35]
Respondent brought action against petitioner in federal court for damages to his warehouse allegedly due to negligence. The question was what state law would be applied and what court had jurisdiction. The Supreme Court ruled that the District Court was within its authority to dismiss the case and remit respondent to the courts in his own community.

H.P. Hood & Sons v. DuMond,
336 U.S. 525 (1949)
[36, 85–86, 174]
The case involved New York's power to regulate the interstate milk business where such regulation advanced local economic interests. The Supreme Court found the state statute unconstitutional.

Haddock v. Haddock,
201 U.S. 562 (1906)
[236]
Husband separated from wife, relocated to Connecticut, and obtained a divorce there. The wife sued for abandonment in New York State. The state court refused to accept the divorce decree as binding. The decision was challenged on the Full Faith and Credit Clause. The Supreme Court ruled that the Connecticut decree was not entitled to enforcement in New York.

Hammer v. Dagenhart,
247 U.S. 251 (1918)
[6]
Father of two minor sons challenged congressional authority to prevent interstate commerce in the products of child labor. The Supreme Court found the federal statute in question to be unconstitutional.

Hampton v. United States,
425 U.S. 484 (1976)
[213]
Petitioner was convicted of federal narcotics offenses. He challenged on the ground of entrapment. The Supreme Court affirmed the conviction.

Hansen v. Haff,
291 U.S. 559 (1934)
[191]
Petitioner, a citizen of Denmark residing and working as a domestic in the United States, was allegedly having an illicit relationship with a married man. Pursuant to federal immigration law prohibiting prostitutes and others engaged in immoral behavior from entering the United States, she was denied reentry into the United States after visiting her home country. The Supreme Court reversed the deportation decision.

Harisiades v. Shaughnessy,
342 U.S. 580 (1952)
[232]
Federal law allowed for the deportation of immigrants involved with the Communist Party. After the petitioners had been granted permanent residence status, they joined the party. They challenged the deportation order on due process grounds. The Supreme Court affirmed the deportation.

Harlow v. Fitzgerald,
457 U.S. 800 (1982)
[20–21]
Presidential aides were accused of and sued for conspiring to violate respondent's constitutional and statutory rights. Petitioners argued that they were entitled to absolute immunity from incidents related to their offices. The Supreme Court reversed the dismissal of the case.

Harper v. Virginia Board of Elections,
383 U.S. 663 (1966)
[118–119]
Virginia residents were required to pay a poll tax in order to exercise their right to vote. They challenged. The Supreme Court found the state law unconstitutional.

Harris v. McRae,
448 U.S. 297 (1980)
[46, 182]
A statutory amendment to the federal

Social Security Act limited the use of federal funds to reimburse the costs of abortions under Medicare. Appellees challenged on due process and free religion grounds. The Supreme Court ruled that the Hyde Amendment did not violate the Constitution.

Harris v. United States,
331 U.S. 145 (1947)
[198]
Petitioner was convicted of violating federal law. He challenged the search warrant that led to his arrest and conviction. The Supreme Court affirmed the conviction.

Harrison v. PPG Industries Inc.,
446 U.S. 578 (1980)
[13]
Pursuant to federal law the E.P.A. imposed new pollution-control standards on PPG. PPG sought a federal-court review of the E.P.A. decision as allowed by the statute. The Court of Appeals dismissed the petition for lack of jurisdiction. The Supreme Court reversed the Court of Appeals' decision and remanded the case.

Haupt v. United States,
330 U.S. 631 (1947)
[230–231]
Petitioner was convicted of treason. He was accused of harboring and aiding other traitors, including his son. The Supreme Court affirmed the conviction.

Hawaii v. Mankichi,
190 U.S. 197 (1903)
[62]
Petitioner was convicted of manslaugh-

ter. He challenged the territory law as being contrary to the United States Constitution. The Supreme Court reversed the conviction and remanded the case.

Helvering v. Davis and Steward Machine Co.,
301 U.S. 619 (1937)
[83]
This case challenged a provision of the Social Security Act, which imposed "old age benefit" taxes on employers. The Supreme Court affirmed the constitutionality of the tax.

Helvering v. Gerhardt,
304 U.S. 405 (1938)
[83–84]
The case concerned issues relative to a federal income tax imposed on state employees. The Supreme Court ruled that the federal government could impose the income tax.

Helvering v. Hallock,
309 U.S. 106 (1940)
[33]
This case involved the taxable status of estate property transferred to a trust. The Supreme Court ruled that the taxation was permissible.

Helvering v. Stockholms Enskilda Bank,
293 U.S. 84 (1934)
[30]
Stockholms, a foreign corporation, received a tax refund with interest. The I.R.S. later recognized its error and assesses a penalty against the corporation for the payment of the interest. The Supreme Court upheld the penalty.

Hennington v. Georgia,
163 U.S. 299 (1896)
[6]
Superintendent of transportation was charged with allowing a freight train to operate on a Sunday, contrary to state law. The train was engaged in interstate travel. He challenged on interstate commerce grounds. The Supreme Court upheld the state regulation.

Hernandez v. Texas,
347 U.S. 475 (1954)
[116]
Petitioner was convicted of murder and sentenced to life imprisonment. He challenged on the grounds that Mexican Americans were systemically excluded from serving on juries in the Texas county where his trial was conducted. The Supreme Court reversed the conviction on equal-protection grounds.

Hines v. Davidowitz,
312 U.S. 52 (1941)
[8]
State law required every alien 18 years old or older to apply for an identification card. This was challenged on equal-protection grounds. The Supreme Court affirmed the overturning of the law.

Hirabayashi v. United States,
320 U.S. 81 (1943)
[228]
Japanese American was convicted of violating a federal law prohibiting individuals from disobeying orders by a military commander in a military area pursuant to a presidential order. He challenged on

Fifth Amendment grounds. The Supreme Court affirmed the conviction.

Hodgson v. Minnesota,
497 U.S. 417 (1990)
[185–186]
State law prohibited abortions to minors without two-parent notification. Although there were some exceptions to this mandatory requirement, the law was challenged on due process and equal-protection grounds. The Supreme Court struck down the state law.

Hoffa v. United States,
385 U.S. 293 (1966)
[204]
Petitioners were convicted of bribing a jury. They challenged this outcome on the grounds that the governmental informant failed to disclose his role to Hoffa (Fourth Amendment challenge) and as a result Hoffa incriminated himself to the informant (the Fifth Amendment challenge). The Supreme Court affirmed the convictions.

Holden v. Hardy,
169 U.S. 366 (1898)
[103–104]
Petitioner was arrested for violating state law regulating work hours in underground mines. He challenged on the privileges and immunities provision in the Fourteenth Amendment. The Supreme Court found the state law constitutional.

Holloway v. United States,
526 U.S. ___ (1999)
[247]
Petitioner was convicted of carjacking

with the intent to cause injury. He challenged the statutory meaning of "conditional intent" as used to convict him. The Supreme Court affirmed the conviction.

Holmes v. Jennison,
39 U.S. 540 (1840)
[58]

This case involved the question of whether a state can be forced by a foreign government to abide by a writ of habeas corpus if the individual in their custody has been accused of crimes against the state. The Supreme Court was unable to decide the issue.

Home Building & Loan Association v. Blaisdell,
290 U.S. 398 (1934)
[82]

Appellant challenged the state law, which provided that during a declared emergency, relief from mortgage foreclosures may be obtained. The basis of the challenge was that the law violated the Contract Clause, the Due Process Clause, and the Equal Protection Clause. The Supreme Court affirmed the constitutionality of the state statute.

Hooven & Allison Co. v. Evatt,
324 U.S. 652 (1945)
[84]

State tax officials assessed fibers purchased overseas by the petitioner. Hooven challenged the state taxation on the grounds that the Constitution prohibited such taxes on imports or exports (Article I, 10, c 12). The Supreme Court nullified the state ruling against the petitioner.

Houston v. Hill,
482 U.S. 451 (1987)
[184]

Pursuant to a municipal ordinance, appellee was arrested for interrupting a police officer engaged in the fulfillment of official duties. He was acquitted and subsequently challenged the constitutionality of the ordinance. The Supreme Court affirmed the lower court finding that the ordinance was overly broad and violated the First Amendment.

Houston v. Moore,
18 U.S. 1 (1820)
[4, 23]

Houston, a member of the state militia, was court-martialed for failing to obey a presidential order to deploy with his militia. He challenged the presidential authority asserting that it usurped the constitutional delegation of Congress. The Supreme Court ruled against Houston.

Hudson v. McMillian,
503 U.S. 1 (1992)
[220–221]

Petitioner, a prison inmate, accused correctional guards of beating him. He also asserted that a supervisor, although not participating in the beating, did not stop it. He sued for damages per his Eighth Amendment rights. The Supreme Court, finding for Hudson, ruled that serious injury need not be the consequence for a party to trigger Eighth Amendment challenges.

Hudson v. Palmer,
468 U.S. 517 (1984)
[216]

Respondent, a prison inmate, accused

prison guards of purposely harassing him and intentionally destroying his personal property during a shakedown. He asserted that this violated his privacy as well as his due process protections. The Supreme Court ruled in favor of the prison stating that an inmate has a diminished right to privacy and has proper recourse to challenge the alleged due process violations.

Hunter v. Erickson,
393 U.S. 385 (1969)
[119]
A city ordinance prohibited discrimination in housing. Later, an amendment to the city charter was enacted that required any ordinance that dealt with the allocation of real property on the basis of racial and civil classifications first had to be passed by a majority of voters. It in effect nullified the city ordinance. The charter amendment was challenged. The Supreme Court struck down the amendment as unconstitutional.

Hurd v. Hodge,
334 U.S. 24 (1948)
[238]
This case involved a restrictive covenant prohibiting the allocation of certain property to minorities under the penalty of a fine. The Supreme Court repudiated the covenant.

Hurtado v. California,
110 U.S. 516 (1884)
[113]
Hurtado was convicted of murder and sentenced to death. He challenged, under the Fourteenth Amendment, the indictment and grand jury portions of the proceedings. The Supreme Court affirmed the conviction.

Hustler Magazine, Inc. v. Falwell,
485 U.S. 46 (1988)
[148]
Respondent, a well-known public figure, sued the petitioner for libel and intentional infliction of emotional distress stemming from a published parody of the respondent. The Supreme Court reversed the verdict against Hustler.

Hyde v. United States,
225 U.S. 347 (1912)
[62]
Petitioner was convicted of conspiracy. On appeal he challenged the jurisdiction of the trial court, as the site the alleged overt act took place was not within the trial county's jurisdiction. The Supreme Court affirmed the conviction.

Illinois Elections Board v. Socialist Workers Party,
440 U.S. 173 (1979)
[94]
State law required new political parties and independent candidates to obtain signatures of 25,000 qualified voters in order to be eligible to appear on statewide ballots. The law also required that subdivisions required signatures from at least 5 percent of those who voted in the previous election. Appellees asserted that the subdivision requirement of 5 percent was actually a greater burden than the 25,000 for statewide office. They argued that this was a violation of the Equal Protection Clause. The Supreme

Court affirmed the overturning of the 5–percent provision.

Immigration and Naturalization Service v. Chadha,
462 U.S. 919 (1983)
[14–15]
Federal immigration law allowed for a one-house legislative veto to invalidate a specific deportation ruling concerning an alien. Chadha's visa expired and he was subject to deportation following a hearing. The decision was then suspended. The House of Representatives then vetoed the suspension decision. Chadha and the I.N.S. challenged on the Separation of Powers doctrine. The Supreme Court for a variety of reasons invalidated the legislative veto and ruled in favor of Chadha.

In re Anastaplo,
366 U.S. 82 (1961)
[240–241]
Petitioner, during his application to practice law, refused to answer questions relative to his participation in the Communist Party. He stated that such inquiries violated his free speech and association protections. Solely on his refusal he was denied admission to the Bar. He challenged. The Supreme Court ruled against petitioner.

In re Debs,
158 U.S. 564 (1895)
[61]
Petitioners were convicted of unlawfully violating an injunction prohibiting a boycott against an interstate railroad company. Writs of habeas corpus were filed. The Supreme Court rejected them.

In re Gault,
387 U.S. 1 (1967)
[88–89, 204–205]
Appellant's minor son was taken into custody for making lewd phone calls. Following a juvenile court hearing he was committed to a state school as a juvenile delinquent. He brought a habeas corpus action challenging the state juvenile justice system. The Supreme Court reversed the confinement finding and remanded the case to the juvenile court to ensure that the minor's right to due process was preserved.

In re Michael,
326 U.S. 224 (1945)
[197]
Petitioner was convicted of contempt in that he provided false and evasive testimony to a grand jury. The Supreme Court reversed the conviction.

In re Primus,
436 U.S. 412 (1978)
[108, 244]
Attorney, working with a branch of the American Civil Liberties Union (A.C.L.U.) informed a woman (who had been sterilized as a condition of receiving public medical assistance) that she could obtain free legal assistance from the A.C.L.U. The state bar initiated disciplinary charges against the petitioner on the ground that such statements unlawfully solicited a client. The Supreme Court ruled that the disciplinary action violated petitioner's First and Fourteenth Amendment rights.

In re Slaughter-House Cases,
83 U.S. 36 (1872)
[78–79, 168–169]

New Orleans granted an exclusive monopoly to two butcher-related companies. Nongranted competitors challenged the city on a variety of issues, some of which were that the monopoly was a violation of the Privileges and Immunities Clause, that the monopolies denied them equal protection of laws, and it deprived them of property without due process. The Supreme Court upheld the monopoly granted to the Slaughter-House Company and Crescent City Live-Stock Landing.

In re Summers,
325 U.S. 561 (1945)
[155]

Petitioner was denied admission to practice law in Illinois. He asserted that the state bar's decision was based solely on his status as a conscientious objector. He challenged on First and Fourteenth Amendment grounds. The Supreme Court ruled against the petitioner.

In re Winship,
397 U.S. 358 (1970)
[89–90, 208–209]

Minor appellant was charged with larceny. Following a family court hearing the boy was placed in a trade school. The family court judge admitted that the evidence may not have proven appellant's guilt beyond a reasonable doubt but that standard was not required for juvenile proceedings. Appellant challenged on Fourteenth Amendment grounds. The Supreme Court ruled that the minor was entitled to due process protections and reversed the family court finding.

In re Yamashita,
327 U.S. 1 (1946)
[230]

Petitioner was commander of Japanese army on the Philippine Islands during WWII. He surrendered and became a prisoner of war. He was charged with a violation of the law of war. He was tried before a military tribunal, adjudged guilty, and sentenced to death. On appeal, he challenged the authority and jurisdiction of the military tribunal. The Supreme Court affirmed the conviction.

Ingraham v. Wright,
430 U.S. 651 (1977)
[122, 214–215]

Petitioners, junior high school students, brought action against public school officials for being subjected to disciplinary corporal punishment. The Supreme Court ruled against the students stating that corporal punishment did not necessarily violate the Eighth Amendment and that a formal hearing to determine punishment was not necessary.

International News Service v. Associated Press,
248 U.S. 215 (1918)
[129]

Associated sued International for taking the results of its news-gathering efforts and using them in their own stories. The Supreme Court upheld the lower court rulings in favor of Associated.

International Union, UAW v. Johnson Controls, Inc.,
499 U.S. 187 (1991)
[186]
Respondent manufactured batteries, which were made, in part, with lead. Lead was known to cause health problems including risks in fetuses. The company unilaterally barred all women, except those documented as infertile, from jobs that exposed them to lead. Petitioners in a class action suit challenged the policy, asserting that it violated Title VII of the Civil Rights Act. The Supreme Court ruled in favor of the petitioners.

Irvine v. California,
347 U.S. 128 (1954)
[116]
Petitioner was convicted of violating state antigambling laws. Prior to petitioner's arrest and without his knowledge, police employed a locksmith to make a copy of his house key. Then, on three occasions, they entered the premises without a search warrant to seize evidence. They were able to obtain such evidence, which subsequently led to arrest and conviction. Petitioner challenged the admissibility of the evidence. The Supreme Court affirmed the conviction but felt that the record demonstrated the police under color of law probably violated petitioner's constitutional rights and that there was a proper legal recourse for it other than overturning the conviction.

Irwin v. Gavit,
268 U.S. 161 (1925)
[30]
Money received by respondent via a will was to be allocated to his minor children. The federal government taxed the money as income. Gavit challenged. The Supreme Court ruled that the income of an estate is equivalent to income as defined under the Constitution and thus taxable.

Jackman v. Rosenbaum Co.,
260 U.S. 22 (1922)
[115]
Pursuant to statute, city ordered the removal of an unsafe wall by a theatre. Theatre owner sued for financial damages sustained for wrongful delay and improper methods in removing the wall. The statute was challenged on Fourteenth Amendment grounds. The Supreme Court found that the law was not unconstitutional.

Jackson v. Metropolitan Edison Co.,
419 U.S. 345 (1974)
[179]
Petitioner brought action against respondent for terminating her electrical service without notice, a hearing, or adequate time to make payment on her obligations. The Supreme Court ruled that although respondent was regulated by the state and that it was granted a partial monopoly by the state, it was not a public entity and thus not required to practice due-process proceedings.

Jacobellis v. Ohio,
378 U.S. 184 (1964)
[41]
Movie theatre manager was convicted under state law of showing an obscene movie. The Supreme Court reversed the conviction.

James Stewart & Co. v. Sadrakula,
309 U.S. 94 (1940)
[63–64]
Subcontractor employee engaged in the construction of post office was killed on the job site. Damages were awarded due to a finding of negligence. The question on appeal was whether state laws relative to workplace safety applied to property just transferred to the federal government. The Supreme Court ruled that in the absence of any direction from Congress, the state law did apply.

Johnson v. Zerbst,
304 U.S. 458 (1938)
[192]
Petitioner, an inmate in a federal penitentiary, filed a writ of habeas corpus on Sixth Amendment grounds (claiming that his right to counsel had never been waived and thus had been violated). The Supreme Court reversed the conviction and remanded the case to determine whether in fact the right to counsel had been violated.

Jones v. Alfred H. Mayer Company,
392 U.S. 409 (1968)
[119]
Petitioner asserts that he was denied the right to purchase a home because he was black. The Supreme Court found in favor of Jones, stating that the Civil Rights Act does apply to private refusals to sell.

Jones v. Meehan,
175 U.S. 1 (1899)
[227]
This case involved title to property involved in a treaty with the Chippewa Indians. The Supreme Court found for Meehan.

Jones v. Opelika,
316 U.S. 584 (1942)
[33–34, 133]
Petitioners, Jehovah's Witnesses, were convicted of selling books without a license, a violation under the city ordinance. They challenged on free-press grounds. The Supreme Court affirmed the conviction.

Jones v. Securities and Exchange Commission,
298 U.S. 1 (1936)
[171]
Petitioner asserted that he had been harassed and that his due process protections were violated when the S.E.C. alleged that he provided false statements and omitted factual information on a required registration for a proposed issue of trust certificates. Based upon the record, the Supreme Court found the Commission exercised arbitrary power and violated petitioner's rights.

Jordan v. De George,
341 U.S. 223 (1951)
[155]
Respondent, a native and citizen of Italy, lived in the United States. He pled guilty to selling alcohol with the intent to defraud the United States by not paying taxes on the sale. He served his prison sentence, and after his release he was again convicted of another offense against the same federal law. While he was serving his prison sentence, deportation proceedings were commenced on

the grounds that he engaged in a crime involving moral turpitude. The hearing concluded that deportation was in order. He challenged. The Supreme Court affirmed the deportation.

Katz v. United States,
389 U.S. 347 (1967)
[207]
Petitioner was convicted of transmitting wagering information via telephone across state lines. Evidence against him was obtained with electronic listening and recording devices, even though a warrant had not been obtained. He challenged. The Supreme Court reversed the conviction.

Kawakita v. United States,
343 U.S. 717 (1952)
[232]
Petitioner, a native-born Japanese American, while in Japan during WWII switched his allegiance from the United State to Japan. He was a civilian employee for a Japanese military materiel manufacturer. He had also been accused of brutally abusing American prisoners of war. Following the conclusion of the war he returned to the United States where he was arrested and convicted of treason. He challenged on citizenship grounds. The Supreme Court affirmed the conviction.

Kendall v. United States ex rel Stokes,
37 U.S. 524 (1838)
[17]
This case involved the status of contracts Stokes and others had with the United States Postal Service. The question involved a separation of powers dispute

(executive–judicial). The Supreme Court affirmed the finding for Stokes.

Kent v. United States,
383 U.S. 541 (1966)
[204]
Minor petitioner was arrested for robbery and rape. The juvenile court waived jurisdiction and petitioner was convicted in district court for housebreaking and robbery. The Supreme Court ruled that because the juvenile court waiver was unconstitutional, the conviction was reversed and remanded.

Keyes v. School District No. 1,
413 U.S. 189 (1973)
[120–121]
Petitioners sought to desegregate one portion of the city's schools. They were granted relief. They then sought to desegregate the entire school district. Relief was not granted. The Supreme Court modified the judicial remedies as provided by the Court of Appeals and remanded the case.

Kirkpatrick v. Preisler,
394 U.S. 526 (1969)
[89]
District Court found that congressional redistricting following the 1960 census used less accurate data than that found in the census report. It rejected the state's redistricting statute. The Supreme Court affirmed this decision.

Knauff v. Shaughnessy,
338 U.S. 537 (1950)
[231–232]
Alien wife of a United States citizen who

served honorably in the military during WWII was denied admission to the United States. The Supreme Court upheld the denial.

Konigsberg v. State Bar of California, 366 U.S. 36 (1961)
[135]
Petitioner sought admission to practice law in the state. He refused to answer questions about his membership in the Communist Party. He was denied admission because of this refusal. The Supreme Court ruled that the denial of admission did not violate the Constitution.

Korematsu v. United States, 323 U.S. 214 (1944)
[228–229]
Japanese American was convicted of violating a military exclusion order issued to prevent Japanese individuals from being in certain places on the West Coast. The government did not dispute petitioner's loyalty to the United States. He challenged asserting that the federal government discriminated against him solely based on his Japanese heritage. The Supreme Court affirmed the conviction.

Kovacs v. Cooper, 336 U.S. 77 (1949)
[66, 134–135]
Appellant was convicted of violating a city ordinance that prohibited the use of a loudspeaker or sound truck to emit loud noise in a public place. He challenged on First and Fourteenth Amendment grounds. The Supreme Court affirmed the conviction.

Ku Klux Cases, 110 U.S. 651 (1884)
[80]
The Supreme Court denied petitioners' writs of habeas corpus following their convictions of conspiracy to threaten with physical harm an African American who wanted to exercise his right and privilege of voting in a federal election.

Lamb's Chapel v. Center Moriches Union Free School District, 508 U.S. 385 (1993)
[165]
Respondent, pursuant to state law, issued rules and regulations for the after-hours use of school property for meetings, including those with a religious purpose. Petitioners who had religious affiliations were denied by the respondent the requisite approval to use the school property. They challenged on free speech grounds. The Supreme Court found for the petitioners.

Lau v. Nichols, 414 U.S. 563 (1974)
[243]
In a class action suit non-English-speaking Chinese students sued the San Francisco school district for relief due to their unequal educational opportunity as guaranteed under the Fourteenth Amendment. The Supreme Court reversed the Court of Appeal and concluded that while there was no constitutional violation there was a statutory rights violation.

Layne & Bowler Corp. v. Western Well Works, Inc.,
261 U.S. 387 (1923)
[29]
The Supreme Court dismissed this patent infringement writ of certiorari.

Lee v. Weisman,
505 U.S. 577 (1992)
[165]
As permitted by state law, petitioner, a middle-school principal, invited a rabbi to offer prayers at respondent's graduation. She sought an injunction, which was granted by the lower court and affirmed by the Supreme Court.

Legal Tender Cases,
79 U.S. 457 (1870)
[59, 60, 77–78]
The case, in part, involved the constitutional authority of Congress to issue legal tender as the primary form of money and thereby altering legally binding private contracts, which required the exchange of gold coin. The Supreme Court ruled that Congress did possess such power.

Lehman v. Shaker Heights,
418 U.S. 298 (1974)
[143–144]
Municipal policy allowed for nonpolitical advertising on the city's public transportation. Petitioner, a candidate for state office, challenged the decision not to allow him to place campaign advertising on the public transit vehicles. The Supreme Court found no violation of the First or Fourteenth Amendments.

Lemon v. Kurtzman,
403 U.S. 602 (1971)
[242]
Two states had laws that allocated public funds to private schools, including parochial schools, if the schools met certain requirements. The Supreme Court found both statutes unconstitutional under the religion clauses of the First Amendment.

Levy v. Louisiana,
391 U.S. 68 (1968)
[241]
Five illegitimate children sued for the wrongful death of their mother. The trial court and the Court of Appeals dismissed the case asserting that surviving children as expressed in the relevant state statute did not include illegitimate children. The Supreme Court reversed, ruling that the case could move forward because such invidious discrimination prohibiting the suit violated the Equal Protection Clause.

License Tax Cases,
72 U.S. 462 (1866)
[25–26]
Federal law prohibited person from engaging in certain trades or businesses without a license. This included selling lottery tickets and selling liquor. The question on appeal was whether the federal license was tantamount to authority to engage in the business even if it is contrary to state law. The Supreme Court answered that the license was not authority.

Lindsey v. Normet,
405 U.S. 56 (1972)
[242]
Appellants, tenants of appellee, refused to pay rent until certain substandard conditions were repaired. Appellee threatened to evict pursuant to state law. Appellants challenged the constitutionality of three provisions of the statute in question. The Supreme Court found two provisions valid while a third violated the Equal Protection Clause of the Fourteenth Amendment.

Loan Association v. Topeka,
87 U.S. 655 (1874)
[26]
The case involved the constitutionality of a municipality issuing a bond for public works and incurring public debt. In this matter the Supreme Court found that the state legislature did not have the authority to allow the municipalities to enter into debt.

Lochner v. New York,
198 U.S. 45 (1905)
[28, 81, 114]
State law regulated the number of hours per week an employee could work in a bakery. The law was challenged vis-à-vis the Contract Clause and the Fourteenth Amendment. The Supreme Court found the state law had no legitimate claim to regulate public health, the health of the employee, or morality and as such found it an unconstitutional use of state police power.

Loughborough v. Blake,
18 U.S. 317 (1820)
[75]
The question before the Court was whether Congress had the right to impose a direct tax on the District of Columbia. The Supreme Court found no constitutional prohibition to such levy.

Louisiana ex rel Francis v. Resweber,
329 U.S. 459 (1947)
[105–106, 197–198]
Petitioner was convicted of murder and sentenced to death by electrocution. He was secured in the electric chair, the switch was thrown, but owing to a malfunction, death did not occur. A new death warrant was issued. Petitioner challenged on Fifth, Eighth, and Fourteenth Amendment grounds. The Supreme Court affirmed the new death warrant.

Lucas v. South Carolina Coastal Council,
505 U.S. 1003 (1992)
[51, 245]
Petitioner purchased beachfront property with the intent to build single-family homes on it. Two years later the state enacted a law that, in effect, prohibited Lucas from building on his property. He challenged on Fifth and Fourteenth Amendment grounds. The Supreme Court found for Lucas and remanded the case.

Luther v. Borden,
48 U.S. 1 (1849)
[25]
It was alleged that Luther was engaged in an insurrection against the state. Borden and others were members of the state militia. Acting on orders, they broke into Luther's house to arrest him. Luther sued for trespass. The Supreme Court affirmed the verdict for Borden.

Lynch v. Donnelly,
465 U.S. 668 (1984)
[162–163]
For decades the city erected a Christmas display that included Santa Claus, a Christmas tree, and a Nativity scene. Respondents challenged on establishment grounds found in the First Amendment. The Supreme Court found for the city.

Lynch v. Household Finance Corp.,
405 U.S. 538 (1972)
[178]
Appellee sued appellant for nonpayment of a promissory note. They also garnished her savings as allowed under state law. Appellant challenged the statutes as violating her equal protection under the law and due process protections. The federal district court dismissed her case on the grounds that they had no jurisdiction over the state court and that the statutes dealt only with personal rights and not property rights. The Supreme Court disagreed finding for appellant, allowing the case to proceed.

Malinski v. New York,
324 U.S. 401 (1945)
[195, 196]
Malinski was convicted of murdering a police officer. The record showed that a confession was coerced. The Supreme Court reversed the conviction.

Mallory v. United States,
354 U.S. 449 (1957)
[201]
Petitioner was convicted of rape and sentenced to death. The record showed that the police violated the Federal Rules of Criminal Procedure in that there was an unnecessary delay in getting Mallory before a magistrate for arraignment. In the delay Mallory, not being advised of his rights, confessed. The Supreme Court reversed the conviction.

Mapp v. Ohio,
367 U.S. 643 (1961)
[66, 67]
Appellant was convicted of possession of pornographic material in violation of state law. Police forced their way into her house with an alleged search warrant to gather incriminating evidence. The admissibility of the evidence was challenged. The Supreme Court reversed the conviction.

Marbury v. Madison,
5 U.S. 137 (1803)
[22, 54]
At the end of the John Adams presidency, Marbury and others were appointed to judicial positions. For political reasons, incoming president Thomas Jefferson disregarded the appointments. Marbury sued John Madison, the secretary of state, seeking to compel him to deliver the appointments. The Judiciary Act of 1789 allowed the Supreme Court original jurisdiction over the matter. The Court ruled that that portion of the law was unconstitutional because original jurisdiction was exclusively defined by the Constitution and could not be amended by legislation.

Marsh v. Alabama,
326 U.S. 501 (1946)
[173]
Company town prohibited the distribution of religious literature. Appellant, a

Jehovah's Witness, was informed of the rule and told to leave the town. She refused and was arrested and convicted. She challenged on free press and religion grounds. The Supreme Court reversed the conviction.

Marsh v. Chambers,
463 U.S. 783 (1983)
[48, 162]

The Nebraska legislature began each session with a prayer from a state-paid chaplain. Respondent challenged the practice as a violation of the Establishment Clause. The Supreme Court ruled that there was no violation of the First Amendment.

Martin v. Hunter's Lessee,
14 U.S. 304 (1816)
[55]

The question before the Court in this case was whether the Supreme Court had appellate jurisdiction over a state's highest court. The Supreme Court ruled that pursuant to the Constitution and federal law it did have the power of judicial review over state courts.

Martin v. Mott,
25 U.S. 19 (1827)
[17]

President ordered state militia into service during the War of 1812. Mott was called up to service. He refused to obey the order, was court-martialed, and convicted. He was fined. Failing to pay the fine, he was imprisoned. He challenged on a variety of grounds. The Supreme Court reversed the lower court and ruled in favor of Mott.

Martin v. Struthers,
319 U.S. 141 (1943)
[9, 173]

Appellant, a Jehovah's Witness, was convicted of violating a city ordinance that prohibited all door-to-door distribution of handbills, circulars, and advertisements. She challenged on free press and religion grounds. The Supreme Court reversed the conviction.

Martinez v. California,
444 U.S. 277 (1980)
[215]

Parolee with a history of sexual offense murdered appellant's 15–year-old daughter. They sued appellee, state officials, for their actions in releasing a dangerous offender. They asserted that such action led to the deprivation of their child's life without due process. State law granted public employees absolute immunity from liability in cases like this. Appellants challenged the constitutionality of the law. The Supreme Court upheld the law.

Maryland v. Baltimore Radio Show,
338 U.S. 912 (1950)
[36]

This was a single opinion relative to the Supreme Court's denial of the petition for writ of certiorari. Respondent was convicted of contempt for broadcasting information about a murder suspect. The Court of Appeals reversed the conviction.

Massachusetts v. Mellon,
262 U.S. 447 (1923)
[81–82]

Federal law was enacted to reduce infant

mortality and to protect the health of mothers and infants. A federal bureau was established to gather information from the states. Federal funds were to be appropriated to the states for their cooperation. The law was challenged as a threat to state sovereignty and a violation of the Due Process Clause. The Supreme Court dismissed the case for lack of jurisdiction.

Massiah v. United States,
377 U.S. 201 (1964)
[203]
Government agents investigating narcotics activity secured the consent of an alleged co-conspirator of the petitioner to install a radio transmitter into the former's car. The statements made by the petitioner were used as evidence that led to conviction of the petitioner. He challenged. The Supreme Court reversed the conviction on the grounds that at the time the statements were made petitioner had already secured the services of an attorney and any statements made should have been made with the assistance of counsel.

Masson v. New Yorker Magazine, Inc.,
501 U.S. 496 (1991)
[149]
Respondent interviewed petitioner for an article that was to appear in the magazine. Petitioner alerted the magazine to several errors prior to publication, but the article was published without correction. He sued for libel. The trial court determined that the issue did not raise a jury question and granted respondent's motion for summary judgment. The Su-

preme Court reversed stating that the case did indeed raise a jury question.

Mathews v. Diaz,
426 U.S. 67 (1976)
[70]
Pursuant to federal law, an alien's eligibility for participation in a federal medical insurance program rested initially on a five-year length of residence in the United States and admission for permanent residence. In a class action appellees challenged the validity of both conditions. The Supreme Court found that they were both constitutional.

Maynard v. Hill,
125 U.S. 190 (1888)
[236]
Husband abandoned wife and children and provided no support. He took up residence in the Oregon Territory, and the wife and children remained in Ohio. The legislative assembly of the territory of Oregon passed an act dissolving his marriage. No prior notice was given to his wife. He remarried. The questions on appeal were whether the legislative assembly had the authority to dissolve the marriage, and, if so, did the divorce preclude the first wife from claims on the husband's property? The Supreme Court answered in the affirmative for both questions.

Mayor, Aldermen and Commonality of New York v. Miln,
36 U.S. 102 (1837)
[57]
Among other things, the state law in questioned required the master of any ship or

vessel entering the port of New York from another country or another state to provide the mayor with a detailed report of all passengers, under penalty of a sizable fine. The law was challenged as violating the enumerated powers of Congress. The Supreme Court upheld the state law.

McBoyle v. United States,
283 U.S. 25 (1931)
[190–191]
Petitioner was convicted under federal law of transporting across state lines an airplane that he knew to be stolen. He challenged the law as to whether it applied to aircraft. The Supreme Court found that the statute's use of the word "vehicle" conjured up in the common mind ground transportation and not airplanes. The conviction was reversed.

McCleskey v. Zant,
499 U.S. 467 (1991)
[219–220]
Petitioner was convicted of murder and sentenced to death. While awaiting trial in the local jail McCleskey boasted to the occupant in the adjacent cell about his role in the murder. The occupant of the cell, unbeknownst to the petitioner, was a police officer who testified as to the statements made by petitioner. McCleskey challenged on the grounds that the state induced him to make the statements without the assistance of counsel. The Supreme Court affirmed the convictions.

McCulloch v. Maryland,
17 U.S. 316 (1819)
[4, 75, 101–102]
In 1816 Congress chartered a U.S. bank which established branches in several states. In 1818 Maryland enacted a law taxing all nonstate-chartered banks operating within the state. The law also established state-mandated procedures for how nonstate-authorized banks could issue bank notes. The state sued James McCulloch, the cashier of the Baltimore branch of the Bank of the United States. After losing in state court, the bank appealed to the Supreme Court. The Supreme Court ruled that although the Constitution does not expressly allow for the creation of a national bank, it falls under the Necessary and Proper Clause.

McDaniel v. Paty,
435 U.S. 618 (1978)
[161]
Appellee, a candidate for delegate to a state constitutional convention, sought to disqualify revival candidate/appellant, who was a Baptist minister. State law prohibited individuals with such religious attachments from serving as delegates. Appellant challenged the constitutionality of the statute. The Supreme Court, finding the statute did violate the First and Fourteenth Amendments, ruled in favor of appellant.

McDonald v. United States,
335 U.S. 451 (1948)
[199]
Petitioners were convicted of operating a numbers game. Police had entered petitioner's boarding room without a search warrant or an arrest warrant. Evidence obtained was used in to convict them. Petitioners challenged. The Supreme Court reversed the conviction.

McGowan v. Maryland,
366 U.S. 420 (1961)
[117]
Appellants, employees of a department store, were convicted of selling certain retail products on a Sunday. State law prohibited the selling of similar products on Sundays. The convictions were challenged on the grounds that they violated the Establishment Clause, the Due Process Clause, and the Equal Protection Clause. The Supreme Court affirmed the convictions.

McGrain v. Daugherty,
273 U.S. 135 (1927)
[6]
Brother of the United States Attorney General was issued a subpoena to appear with documents before a Senate committee investigating alleged malfeasance in the Department of Justice. He failed to appear on two occasions. The Senate issued a warrant for him to be taken into custody and to appear before the committee. The warrant was executed. Daugherty challenged the congressional authority. The Supreme Court upheld the congressional warrant and custody power.

McGrath v. Kristensen,
340 U.S. 162 (1950)
[37]
Respondent, a Danish citizen was visiting the United States temporarily when WWII broke out. His return to Denmark was prevented and he sought and was granted extensions to his temporary visit. A warrant of deportation was issued but withdrawn to allow him, pursuant to federal law, to seek a suspension of the deportation. Relief was denied. He challenged. The Supreme Court affirmed the decision that he was not eligible for naturalization or for the suspension of deportation.

McGuire v. United States,
273 U.S. 95 (1927)
[190]
McGuire was convicted of possessing intoxicating liquor in violation of federal law. Agents acting on a search warrant entered his premises and discovered several gallons of alcohol, which they seized. While on the premises the agents destroyed, without court order, all of the seized liquor save two quarts to be used as evidence against McGuire. To rule on the appeal of the conviction, the Court of Appeals certified two questions to the Supreme Court: (1) Were the officers who destroyed the liquor trespassers? and (2) was the admission into evidence the samples of seized liquor unlawful? The Supreme Court ruled that the first question had no bearing on the criminal trial and appeal. As for the second question, the Court answered in the negative.

McIntyre v. Ohio Elections Commission,
514 U.S. 334 (1995)
[73, 150]
McIntyre distributed pamphlets advocating the rejection of a school tax levy. The pamphlets did not have her name and address on them, which was in violation of state law. Upon her conviction and fine, she challenged the law on First Amendment grounds. The Supreme Court reversed her conviction.

McLaughlin v. Florida,
379 U.S. 184 (1964)
[118]
Appellants, a black man and a white woman, lived together but were not married. They were convicted of violating a state statute that outlawed just that domestic relation. They challenged the statute on equal-protection grounds. The Supreme Court reversed the convictions.

McNabb v. United States,
318 U.S. 332 (1943)
[173, 194]
Petitioners were convicted of murdering a federal officer. The record showed that the investigating officers misused the custody and interrogation process to the detriment of the petitioners. The convictions were challenged and the Supreme Court reversed them.

Meachum v. Fano,
427 U.S. 215 (1976)
[121–122]
Respondents, prison inmates, had been subject to hearings to determine whether they should be transferred from the general prison population to more secure areas. They had been accused of engaging in criminal behavior. Some of the testimony collected during the hearings was done outside the presence of the respondents. Respondents sought an injunction barring their relocation asserting that the hearings violated the Due Process Clause. The Supreme Court ruled in favor of the prison administrators.

Memoirs v. Massachusetts,
383 U.S. 413 (1966)
[41, 137]
Appellee brought civil action against publisher of an allegedly obscene book. The publisher challenged on First and Fourteenth Amendment grounds. The Supreme Court found for the appellant.

Mexico v. Hoffman,
324 U.S. 30 (1945)
[230]
This was an admiralty case involving a ship owned though not possessed by a friendly government. It also involved the jurisdiction of the court in foreign affairs. The Supreme Court affirmed the decision for Hoffman stating that the Mexican government was not immune from the suit.

Meyer v. Nebraska,
262 U.S. 390 (1923)
[170–171]
Meyer was convicted of violating a state law prohibiting the teaching of a foreign language (in this case, German) to a child who had not passed the eighth grade. He challenged on Fourteenth Amendment grounds. The Supreme Court reversed the conviction.

Miami Herald Publishing Co. v. Tornillo,
418 U.S. 241 (1974)
[143]
Appellee was a candidate for state office. Appellant published editorials critical of his candidacy; then it denied appellee the opportunity to reply. He sued citing the state's "right to reply" law. The newspaper challenged the constitutionality of

the law. The Supreme Court held the statutee unconstitutional under the First Amendment's free press guarantees.

Michael H. v. Gerald D., 491 U.S. 110 (1989)
[50, 184–185]
Victoria was born in 1981 to Carole while she was married to and living with appellant. He was listed as the father on the birth certificate. Carole admitted that she had an adulterous relationship with Michael and believed that he was Victoria's father. Blood tests showed over a 98 percent probability that Michael was the father. Michael filed a paternity action and requested visitation rights. Victoria's court-appointed guardian ad litem cross-petitioned that Victoria was entitled to maintain filial relationships with both Michael and Gerald. The trial court granted Gerald's motion for summary judgment on the grounds that state law presumed him to be the father. Michael appealed on procedural and substantive due process. The Supreme Court affirmed the summary judgment for Gerald.

Michael M. v. Superior Court, 450 U.S. 464 (1981)
[125]
Petitioner, a few months shy of his eighteenth birthday, was charged with statutory rape with a woman one year his junior. Prior to the trial he challenged the constitutionality of the statute alleging that it discriminated against men (the young woman was not charged with the same crime although both parties were under 18 years of age). The

Supreme Court upheld the statute.

Michalic v. Cleveland Tankers, Inc., 364 U.S. 325 (1960)
[39]
This case involved a maritime federal law and personal injuries sustained by a member of the crew. The Supreme Court reversed the finding for the respondent and allowed the case to be decided by the jury.

Michelson v. United States, 335 U.S. 469 (1948)
[199]
Petitioner was convicted of bribing a federal agent. He acknowledged the passing of money but asserted it was under threats that amounted to entrapment. The Supreme Court affirmed the conviction.

Michigan Department of State Police v. Sitz, 496 U.S. 444 (1990)
[99, 219]
Police established a highway sobriety checkpoint. The day before the checkpoint was operational, respondents sued for constitutional violations for their potential passage through the checkpoint. The Supreme Court finding for the petitioners ruled that the checkpoint did not violate the Fourth Amendment.

Milk Wagon Drivers Union of Chicago v. Meadowmoor Co. 312 U.S. 287 (1941)
[132]
The state enjoined the union from picketing the company because prior acts of violence had sprung up from the peaceful picketing. The union challenged on

First Amendment grounds. The Supreme Court affirmed the injunction.

Milkovich v. Lorain Journal Co.,
497 U.S. 1 (1990)
[148–149]
Newspaper printed a story alleging that petitioner, a high-school wrestling coach, lied under oath during an investigation regarding an altercation the coach had with another team. Petitioner sued for defamation. The trial court granted summary judgment for the newspaper. Petitioner challenged. The Supreme Court reversed the summary judgment allowing the case to continue.

Miller v. California,
413 U.S. 15 (1973)
[142]
Appellant was convicted of mailing unsolicited pornographic material. He challenged on First Amendment grounds. The Supreme Court vacated the conviction and remanded the case.

Milliken v. Bradley,
418 U.S. 717 (1974)
[121]
Respondents sued on the grounds that the Detroit public schools were racially segregated as a result of actions taken by state and city officials. The district court ordered desegregation plans from the city school district and eighty-five outlying school districts that were not parties to the action. The additional districts challenged. The Supreme Court reversed the judicial order on the additional school districts since there was no record of a relationship between them and the Detroit school district.

Minersville School District v. Gobitis,
310 U.S. 586 (1940)
[152–153, 172]
Jehovah's Witness school children were expelled from public school for refusing to salute the American flag as part of daily school exercises. They challenged on free religion and due process grounds. The Supreme Court ruled in favor of the school district.

Minnesota v. Carter,
525 U.S. ___ (1998)
[222]
A police officer observed narcotics activities through an apartment window-through a gap in closed blinds. Respondents were arrested and convicted. They challenged on Fourth Amendment grounds. The Supreme Court upheld the convictions.

Minor v. Happersett,
88 U.S. 162 (1874)
[79]
Virginia Minor met all the requirements to vote in a federal election except for the fact that she was female. She challenged the state law prohibiting her from voting asserting that it violated the Fourteenth Amendment. The Supreme Court affirmed the state law.

Miranda v. Arizona,
384 U.S. 436 (1966)
[204]
Miranda was arrested and interrogated for several hours without the benefit of

understanding his constitutional rights, including his right to consult with an attorney. He was convicted. Upon his appeal he challenged on Fifth Amendment grounds. The Supreme Court reversed the conviction.

Mississippi University for Women v. Hogan, 458 U.S. 718 (1982)
[126]
The university historically enrolled women only. Respondent, a male nurse, applied for admission to the university's school of nursing and was denied solely because of his gender. He sued on Fourteenth Amendment grounds. The Supreme Court affirmed the lower court ruling that the petitioner's admissions policy violated the Equal Protection Clause of the Fourteenth Amendment.

Missouri ex rel. Gaines v. Canada, 305 U.S. 337 (1938)
[115]
Petitioner, a black man, was denied admission to the state university's law school. He challenged on equal protection grounds. The Supreme Court reversed the lower court and found that the university's admissions policies violated the Equal Protection Clause of the Fourteenth Amendment.

Missouri v. Holland, 252 U.S. 416 (1920)
[62]
A United States-British treaty pertaining to bird migration was put into effect and a federal statute was enacted to enforce the provisions of the treaty. The law was challenged by the state on the grounds

that it interfered with its rights as protected by the Tenth Amendment. The Supreme Court rejected the state's contention, ruling that the migratory bird issue was of national relevance and as such permissible for the national government to regulate.

Missouri v. Jenkins, 495 U.S. 33 (1990)
[50, 51]
The district court found the state had operated a segregated public school system in the Kansas City school district. The court ordered remedies to desegregate the system, including the removal of state barriers to raising new revenue. It also ordered the raising of property taxes. The state challenged the court's authority. The Supreme Court affirmed some of the judicial orders but ruled that the judiciary had virtually no authority to raise taxes.

Mobile v. Bolden, 446 U.S. 55 (1980)
[95, 124–125]
A three-person legislative, executive, administrative commission governed the city. In a class action suit, African Americans challenged the at-large elections as diluting minority votes and unconstitutional under the Fourteenth and Fifteenth Amendments. The Supreme Court reversed the lower court and upheld the constitutionality of the city commission.

Monongahela Bridge Co. v. United States, 216 U.S. 177 (1910)
[28]
The company built bridges over the river,

one bridge became an obstruction to navigation of the river. The company was ordered by the federal government to fix the bridge. The company refused and challenged the authority of the secretary of war to order it to make the changes. The Supreme Court upheld the federal order.

Monroe v. Pape,
365 U.S. 167 (1961)
[39]
Petitioners, African Americans, sued the police and the city for the police entering their house without a warrant, ransacking the premises, and subjecting one of them to interrogation, on open charges, for ten hours without legal counsel. The Supreme Court ruled that there could be legal action against the individual police officers, but there were no grounds to sue the city.

Moore v. East Cleveland,
431 U.S. 494 (1977)
[123]
Appellant lived with her son and two grandsons (who were first cousins) in a single-family dwelling. A city ordinance limited single-family dwellings to single families, the definition of which did not include the residents at the appellant's home. Appellant was convicted of violating the ordinance. The Supreme Court reversed the conviction.

Morgan v. United States,
298 U.S. 468 (1936)
[31]
The Secretary of Agriculture fixed the rates of buying and selling livestock at the Kansas City Stock Yards. The order

was challenged as a violation of the Due Process Clause of the Fifth Amendment. The Supreme Court reversed the decree and remanded the case.

Morissette v. United States,
342 U. S. 246 (1952)
[10, 200]
Morissette was convicted of stealing and selling government property—spent and apparently abandoned bomb casings on a federal practice-bombing range. He challenged asserting that there was no intent to commit a criminal act because he assumed the property was abandoned. The Supreme Court reversed the conviction.

Mormon Church v. United States,
136 U.S. 1 (1890)
[80]
Federal law prohibited polygamy in United States territories and allowed for the confiscation of property belonging to violators. This law, in effect, nullified the Church charter. The Church advocating the practice of polygamy challenged congressional authority to dissolve its charter. The Supreme Court upheld the federal law.

Morrison v. Olson,
487 U.S. 654 (1988)
[21, 97–98]
The case involves the constitutionality of the independent counsel provisions within the federal Ethics in Government Act. The Supreme Court upheld the law.

Mugler v. Kansas,
123 U.S. 623 (1887)
[26–27]
Pursuant to state law, Mugler was con-

TABLE OF CASES WITH CASE SUMMARIES   323

victed of manufacturing and selling intoxicating liquors. He challenged on the grounds that the law violated the Due Process Clause of the Fourteenth Amendment and the Kansas constitution. The Supreme Court upheld the conviction.

Muller v. Oregon,
208 U.S. 412 (1908)
[114]
State law limited the number of hours women could work per day. Curt Muller was convicted and fined for violating the law. He challenged on Fourteenth Amendment grounds (due process, equal protection, and privileges and immunities) and that it was an invalid use of state police power. The Supreme Court upheld the statute and Muller's conviction.

Munn v. Illinois,
94 U.S. 113 (1876)
[5, 169]
State law regulated warehouses and required grain inspections. Mandatory fees and licensing were also provided for in the statute. Munn was convicted of violating the law. He challenged on Fifth and Fourteenth Amendment grounds. The Supreme Court upheld the conviction.

Myers v. United States,
272 U.S. 52 (1926)
[17, 63]
Appellant was appointed by the President of the United States to be the Portland, Oregon, postmaster. The president subsequently demanded his resignation. Myers refused and the president removed him from office. Myers sued for his unpaid salary for the remainder of his term on the grounds that the president had no authority to remove him without the consent of the Senate, which was needed to appoint him. The Supreme Court affirmed the decision against Myers.

Nardone v. United States,
302 U.S. 379 (1938)
[192]
Petitioners were convicted of smuggling alcohol. Evidence used to convict was obtained by tapping telephone wires. No warrants were obtained. Petitioners challenged. The Supreme Court reversed the convictions.

National Endowment for the Arts
v. Finley,
524 U.S. 569 (1998)
[100]
Federal law allowed the petitioner to award financial grants to support the arts. Congress amended the statute to fund only art that conformed to general standards of decency. Consequently respondents were denied funding; they challenged on First Amendment grounds. The Supreme Court upheld the authority of the NEA to deny funding.

National Labor Relations Board v. Jones
& Laughlin Steel Corporation,
301 U.S. 1 (1937)
[31]
Respondent was ordered to cease and desist its unfair labor practices, as determined by the petitioner. The respondent failed to abide by the order, and the board sought judicial enforcement of its order. The lower court denied the request as

being outside of legitimate federal authority. The decision was challenged and the Supreme Court reversed, finding that the board had the constitutional authority to issue the order.

National League of Cities v. Usery, 426 U.S. 833 (1976)
[13, 107–108]
The minimum wage/maximum hour provision of the federal Fair Labor Standards Act was amended to include most state government employees. Appellants challenged the constitutionality of the amendments. The Supreme Court ruled for the appellants, finding the law as amended violated the Interstate Commerce Clause and that Congress could not intrude on the manner in which the states managed their own affairs.

Near v. Minnesota ex rel Olson, 283 U.S. 697 (1931)
[131]
State law authorized sanctions for obscene, lewd, malicious, scandalous, or defamatory newspapers, magazines, and periodicals. The newspaper published malicious material about the members of an impaneled grand jury. Actions were taken against Near, the publisher. He challenged on First and Fourteenth Amendment grounds. The Supreme Court found the statute to be unconstitutional.

Nebbia v. New York, 291 U.S. 502 (1934)
[105]
State law fixed the retail price of milk. Nebbia was convicted of violating the law. He challenged on due process and equal protection grounds. The Supreme Court affirmed the conviction and upheld the statute.

Neder v. United States, 119 S. Ct. 1827 (1999)
[223]
Petitioner was convicted of filing false federal income taxes, federal mail fraud, wire fraud, and bank fraud. The trial court ruled that certain facts of evidence were obvious without the need to send it to the jury for its decision. The challenge was whether the trial court's failure to submit the question to the jury was a harmless error or a reversible error. In fact, the Supreme Court ruled that there was no error.

New Jersey v. Portash, 440 U.S. 450 (1979)
[13]
Respondent, a municipal official, testified before a state grand jury under immunity established by state law that protected public employees from criminal prosecution for their grand jury testimony. He was then charged and convicted of misconduct and extortion, whose evidence was derived from his grand jury testimony. He challenged on Fifth and Fourteenth Amendment self-incrimination ground. The Supreme Court reversed the conviction.

New Jersey v. T.L.O., 469 U.S. 325 (1985)
[216–217]
Public-school teacher accused fourteen-year-old respondent student of smoking

in the public-school lavatory. The principal requested to inspect the student's purse. Upon conducting the unapproved search he found evidence of marijuana trafficking. The state brought juvenile delinquency charges against respondent. She challenged the admissibility of the evidence under the Fourth Amendment. The Supreme Court found no constitutional violation of the search-and-seizure guarantees.

New State Ice Co. v. Liebmann, 285 U.S. 262 (1932)

[105]

Pursuant to a state license, New State sold ice. They sought in federal court to enjoin Liebmann from doing the same without a license. The lower courts dismissed the bill of complaint for want of equity. The Supreme Court affirmed the decision to dismiss.

New York Times Co. v. Sullivan, 376 U.S. 254 (1964)

[136]

Respondent, a city official, sued petitioner for libel stemming from advertisements the newspaper printed. The trial court verdict was against the newspaper. The appeal was on First Amendment grounds. The Supreme Court reversed the verdict.

New York Times Co. v. United States, 403 U.S. 713 (1971)

[18–19, 90, 140–141, 232–233]

The United States sought to enjoin newspapers from publishing classified material (known as the Pentagon Papers). In a per curiam decision the Supreme Court found the government failed to meet the strict burden needed for the judiciary to authorize prior restraint.

New York Trust Co. v. Eisner, 256 U.S. 345 (1921)

[29]

Executors brought suit to recover estate taxes levied as allowed by federal law. The federal district court dismissed the suit and the Supreme Court affirmed.

New York v. United States, 326 U.S. 572 (1946)

[35, 105]

Federal law imposed a tax on the sale of mineral waters. New York failed to pay the tax and the United States sued. The State argued that they were engaged in a normal state function. The Supreme Court ruled that Congress could tax both public and private entities on the sales of mineral water and that the state was not immune from the tax.

New York v. United States, 505 U.S. 144 (1992)

[72, 110]

Federal law allowed for the creation of multistate regional compacts to dispose of low-grade radioactive waste. The statute established three incentives for the states to participate. Petitioner challenged the incentives as violating the Tenth Amendment and the Guarantee Clause (Art IV, 4). The lower court dismissed the suit. The Supreme Court ruled that two of the incentives were constitutional but the third failed to meet constitutional muster. They severed the third incentive and upheld the remaining statute.

Nixon v. Administrator of General Services,
433 U.S. 425 (1977)
[19–20, 44, 71, 244]
The President, following his resignation, made arrangements with appellee to warehouse his presidential materials. Under the agreement neither party could gain access to the materials for a prescribed period of time. Federal law was then enacted mandating the G.S.A. to take custody of all the materials and have them screened by archivists for historical value. The former president sued on several grounds. The Supreme Court affirmed the lower court's finding of no constitutional violations.

Nixon v. Fitzgerald,
457 U.S. 731 (1982)
[20, 96]
Respondent, while an employee of the Department of the Air Force during the Johnson administration, testified to a congressional subcommittee about cost overruns and technical difficulties of a new airplane. Two years later, with the switch to the Nixon administration, respondent was dismissed from his job as a result of departmental reorganization. He challenged, asserting that his dismissal was in retaliation for his congressional testimony. The Supreme Court found in favor of the president.

Northern Pipeline Construction Co. v. Marathon Pipe Line Co.,
458 U.S. 50 (1982)
[14, 47]
This case involved the constitutionality of the authority to create and delegate judicial authority to bankruptcy judges. The Supreme Court affirmed the constitutionality of non-Article III judges.

Northern Securities Company v. United States,
193 U.S. 197 (1904)
[27–28]
The United States brought suit against company accusing it of violating antitrust statutes. Company challenged the constitutionality of the relevant statutes. The Supreme Court affirmed the lower-court finding for the government.

Northwestern Band of Shoshone Indians v United States,
324 U.S. 335 (1945)
[230]
Petitioners sued for damages, allegedly caused by the respondent, pursuant to treaty. The Supreme Court found in favor of the government.

Norton v. Shelby County,
118 U.S. 425 (1886)
[61]
This case involved the constitutionality of bonds issued by the county, pursuant to state law. The Supreme Court affirmed the decision that the bonds were not valid.

O'Brien v. Brown,
409 U.S. 1 (1972)
[91]
On the recommendation of the states' Democratic Party, state party delegates were unseated. They challenged. The district court dismissed the suit. The Court of Appeals granted relief to the Califor-

nia delegates but denied it to Illinois's. The Supreme Court affirmed the Court of Appeals' decision ruling that a fuller review could not be instituted due to the time constraints of the controversy.

Ogden v. Saunders,
25 U.S. 213 (1827)
[4, 23, 57, 76]
New York State enacted a bankruptcy/insolvency law that allowed for the discharge of bankruptcies under contracts made within the state. In this case the statute's constitutionality was challenged under the Bankruptcy Clause (Art I, 8) and the Contract Clause (Art I, 10). The Supreme Court ruled that the state law was constitutional.

Olmstead v. United States,
277 U.S. 438 (1928)
[82, 190]
Petitioners were convicted of conspiracy to violate federal law by possessing, transporting, importing, and selling intoxicating liquors. Evidence used in their convictions came from private telephone conversations that were intercepted by wiretaps installed without a warrant. The petitioners challenged on Fourth and Fifth Amendment grounds. The Supreme Court, considering only the Fourth Amendment question, ruled there was no constitutional violation in the wiretap.

Olsen v. Nebraska ex rel Western Reference & Board Association,
313 U.S. 236 (1941)
[64]
State law required private employment agencies to fix the maximum compensa-tion they could collect from an applicant for employment. The law was challenged on due process grounds. The Supreme Court found no constitutional infirmities.

On Lee v. United States,
343 U.S. 747 (1952)
[200]
While wearing a hidden radio transmitter, a federal undercover agent engaged in conversations with the petitioner. The petitioner made several incriminating statements. The evidence was later used in petitioner's conviction on federal narcotics charges. The means of obtaining the evidence was challenged as a violation of the Fourth Amendment. The Supreme Court affirmed the conviction.

Oncale v. Sundowner Offshore Services, Inc.,
523 U.S. 75 (1998)
[247]
Petitioner, a male, sued respondent, his employer, for sexual harassment directed against him by male coworkers. The Supreme Court reversed the lower court and ruled that same-sex sexual harassment was actionable under federal law.

Opp Cotton Mills, Inc. v. Administrator of Wage and Hour Division,
312 U.S. 126 (1941)
[8–9]
This case involved (a) the constitutionality of the Fair Labor Standards Act, (b) whether the authority of the administrator prescribing a minimum wage is constitutional under the Fifth Amendment and (c) whether the administrator's findings were valid. The Supreme Court

found the Act, the administrator's duties, and the findings of the administrator constitutional.

Organization for a Better Austin v. Keefe, 402 U.S. 415 (1971)
[140]
Respondent was able to obtain an injunction against petitioner to cease distributing literature that was critical of his business practices. The Supreme Court reversed the injunction finding that the petitioner did not meet the burden required to have a prior restraint injunction imposed on a peaceful distribution of informational literature.

Orloff v. Willoughby, 345 U.S. 83 (1953)
[38]
Petitioner, a medical doctor, was conscripted into the military under the federal Doctor's Draft Law. He applied for a commission but because he refused to disclose information about his possible membership in the Communist Party, he was denied. He was assigned duties as a medical laboratory technician. He filed a writ of habeas corpus challenging whether he was required to stay in the military in light of the special circumstances to his induction. The Supreme Court ruled against petitioner.

Orr v. Orr, 440 U.S. 268 (1979)
[44–45]
Appellant husband was ordered to pay alimony to appellee wife. Two years later she filed a petition to find appellant in contempt for failing to maintain the pay-ments. He challenged the state law on the grounds that it required men—and not women—to pay alimony. The Supreme Court ruled that the gender discriminatory provisions of the statute did violate the Fourteenth Amendment.

Palko v. Connecticut, 302 U.S. 319 (1937)
[192]
Appellant was convicted of murder and sentenced to death. On appeal, the conviction was reversed. Subjected to a retrial, he challenged on the grounds that to be retried was tantamount to double jeopardy and would be a violation of the Fourteenth Amendment. The second trial again found him guilty and sentenced him to death. He challenged. The Supreme Court affirmed the conviction and sentence.

Palmore v. Sidoti, 466 U.S. 429 (1984)
[126]
Following her divorce from respondent, petitioner was awarded custody of their daughter. The following year respondent sought custody asserting a change in conditions, namely, the petitioner was cohabiting with an African American man. Custody was switched to the father and the mother challenged. The Supreme Court reversed the custody order.

Panama Refining Co. v. Ryan, 293 U.S. 388 (1935)
[7]
The president of the United States issued an executive order regarding the transportation of petroleum. The secretary of

the interior issued regulations carrying out the order. Panama sued to restrain federal officials from executing the regulations. The Supreme Court ruled in favor of the petroleum companies.

Panhandle Oil Co. v. Mississippi ex rel Knox,
277 U.S. 218 (1928)
[7]
State law placed an excise tax on the distribution of gasoline. Petitioner had a contract with the United States government to supply gasoline. The state sought to recover back taxes relative to the sale of gasoline to the federal government. Petitioner challenged the constitutionality of the state law. The Supreme Court, in finding for the petitioner, invalidated the statute.

Papachristou v. Jacksonville,
405 U.S. 156 (1972)
[210–211]
Petitioners were convicted of violating the city antivagrancy ordinance. They challenged. The Supreme Court reversed the convictions on the grounds that the ordinance was too vague for proper compliance and enforcement.

Parham v. J.R.,
442 U.S. 584 (1979)
[124]
Appellees, children in a state mental hospital, instituted a class action suit stating that the state procedures for the voluntary commitment of children violated the Due Process Clause. The Supreme Court found no constitutional irregularities.

Paris Adult Theatre I v. Slaton,
413 U.S. 49 (1973)
[142]
Respondents sought an injunction against petitioner for the showing of allegedly obscene movies. The Supreme Court vacated the lower-court ruling that the movies had no First Amendment protections.

Patterson v. McLean Credit Union,
491 U.S. 164 (1989)
[185, 245]
Petitioner, a black woman, was an employee of respondent for ten years. She challenged McLean's decision to lay her off. She asserted that she had been harassed, denied promotion, and discharged because of her race. The trial court prevented the jury from deciding the question of racial harassment. Second, it instructed the jury to find for the petitioner on the promotion-discrimination charge only if she had proven that she was more qualified for the promotion than the promoted white employee. The jury found for respondent on all three charges. On appeal, the Supreme Court affirmed the racial harassment finding and reversed on the jury instruction vis-à-vis the promotion-discrimination.

Paul v. Davis,
424 U.S. 693 (1976)
[180]
A photograph of respondent was included in a flyer of known active shoplifters following his arrest for shoplifting. He sued the police chief for distributing the flyer. The trial court granted

petitioner's motions to dismiss the complaint. The Supreme Court affirmed, finding no constitutional violation in the circulation of the information.

Payne v. Tennessee,
501 U.S. 808 (1991)
[220]
Petitioner was convicted of murder and intent to commit murder. During the sentencing phase the state sought the death penalty and had relatives of the deceased testify about the continuing effects of the crimes upon the victims' family. The jury sentenced petitioner to death. He challenged the validity of the victim impact statement. The Supreme Court affirmed the sentence.

Pearce v. Commissioner of Internal Revenue,
315 U.S. 543 (1942)
[33]
Petitioner and her husband separated in 1913. In 1916 an agreement was modified for him to pay a monthly alimony. An annuity was purchased to informally replace the alimony. The I.R.S. sought back taxes for the income derived from the annuity. The Supreme Court affirmed the finding that the annuity could be taxed.

Pennekamp v. Florida,
328 U.S. 331 (1946)
[133]
Newspaper and its editor were held in contempt for publishing editorials criticizing circuit court judges in the administration of criminal justice. The Supreme Court reversed the convictions, citing First Amendments reasons.

Perez v. Brownell,
356 U.S. 44 (1958)
[232]
In an action to deport Perez the United States denied that he was a citizen because he voted in a Mexican election and had fled the United States to avoid serving in the military during wartime. He challenged. The Supreme Court affirmed the deportation finding.

Perez v. United States,
402 U.S. 146 (1971)
[210]
Petitioner was convicted of loan-sharking, a violation of federal law. He challenged the authority of Congress to control local activity. The Supreme Court affirmed the conviction.

Personnel Administrator of Massachusetts v. Feeney,
442 U.S. 256 (1979)
[45, 123]
Appellee, a state employee, passed several state civil service examinations but was denied advancement because of the state's veteran's preference statutes. She challenged the statutes under the Equal Protection Clause. The Supreme Court upheld the state law.

Phalen v. Virginia,
49 U.S. 163 (1850)
[167]
Phalen was convicted of selling lottery tickets, an activity once approved but later prohibited under state law. He challenged under the Contract Clause. The Supreme Court upheld the amended state law.

Pierce v. Society of Sisters of the Holy Names of Jesus and Mary,
268 U.S. 510 (1925)
[171]
State law instituted compulsory public-school education. Appellee challenged the governing statute as a violation of the Religion Clause of the First Amendment. The Supreme Court affirmed the decrees enjoining the enforcement of the state law.

Pittsburgh Press Co. v. Pittsburgh Commission on Human Relations,
413 U.S. 376 (1973)
[43, 142–143]
Newspaper ran job classifieds under gender headings. Respondent ordered the newspaper to cease and desist in the practice. The paper challenged with free-press concerns. The Supreme Court upheld the commission's order.

Planned Parenthood of Missouri v. Danforth,
428 U.S. 52 (1976)
[243–244]
Two physicians challenged the state's abortion statute. The specific provisions challenged involved viability, written consent, spousal consent, parental consent, criminal sanctions against physicians, status of a surviving infant, time-factor procedural restrictions, and the mandate for record keeping. The Supreme Court affirmed the viability definition, written consent, and record-keeping requirement and reversed the provisions dealing with spousal consent, blanket parental consent, the time-factor procedural aspect, and criminal sanctions.

Planned Parenthood of Southeastern Pennsylvania v. Casey,
505 U.S. 833 (1992)
[72, 186]
This case challenged the following state abortion law provisions: informed consent, 24–hour waiting period, spousal consent, parental consent, and record-keeping requirements. The Supreme Court affirmed in part and reversed in part.

Plessy v. Ferguson,
163 U.S. 537 (1896)
[62, 113–114, 169–170]
Petitioner, a U.S. citizen of racially mixed descent (seven-eighths Caucasian, one-eighth African), paid for first-class passage on a railroad to travel intrastate. He took possession of a seat reserved for white passengers. Plessy was requested by the conductor to find a seat relegated to blacks. He refused and was arrested. He challenged on Thirteenth and Fourteenth Amendment grounds. The Supreme Court upheld the state law and the separate-but-equal doctrine.

Plyler v. Doe,
457 U.S. 202 (1982)
[47, 96]
State law denied funding to public schools for the education of school-age illegal aliens. In a class action suit the statute's constitutionality was challenged. The Supreme Court invalidated the statute, finding that it violated the Equal Protection Clause.

Poe v. Ullman,
366 U.S. 497 (1961)
[117–118]
Married women sought medical advice

for the protection of their health. In violation of the law, the physician recommended the use of contraceptive devices. The state convicted two women and the physician. They challenged the statute on Fourteenth Amendment grounds, asserting that the lives of the women would be denied without due process. The Supreme Court dismissed the appeals for lack of a present controversy.

Powell v. Alabama,
287 U.S. 45 (1932)
[191]
Petitioners, African Americans, were convicted of raping two white girls. They were sentenced to death. They challenged on Fourteenth Amendment grounds. The Supreme Court in reviewing only one aspect of the appeal (the denial of counsel to prepare an adequate defense) reversed the convictions.

Powell v. McCormack,
395 U.S. 486 (1969)
[42]
Petitioner was elected to serve in the House of Representatives. He was denied his seat by the adoption of a House resolution. Powell and voters challenged the resolution, asserting that it was unconstitutional. During the appeal, Powell was reelected and was allowed to take his seat in the next Congress. The Supreme Court affirmed in part and reversed in part.

Powell v. Pennsylvania,
127 U.S. 678 (1888)
[6]
State law regulated the manufacture and sale of oleomargarine. Powell was con-

victed of violating the law. He challenged the statute asserting Fourteenth Amendment protections. The Supreme Court affirmed the conviction.

Powell v. Texas,
392 U.S. 514 (1968)
[208]
Appellant was convicted, pursuant to state law, of public drunkenness. He challenged, arguing that he was a chronic alcoholic and as such was subject to a compulsion to drink. The Supreme Court affirmed the conviction.

Precision Instrument Manufacturing Co. v. Automotive Maintenance Machinery Co.,
324 U.S. 806 (1945)
[34–35]
This was a patent infringement case. The Supreme Court affirmed the district court's dismissal of the case, citing the unclean-hands doctrine.

Price v. Johnston,
334 U.S. 266 (1948)
[199]
Petitioner was convicted of bank robbery. He filed several writs of habeas corpus, all denied. The Supreme Court ruled that the lower court improperly dismissed the fourth writ.

Prince v. Massachusetts,
321 U.S. 158 (1944)
[237]
Prince, a Jehovah's Witness, was convicted of violating the state's child labor laws. She challenged the statute as a violation of her free religion rights. The Supreme Court affirmed the conviction.

Pruneyard Shopping Center v. Robins,
447 U.S. 74 (1980)
[71]
Appellees sought signatures for a petition at the shopping center. They sought to enjoin appellant from prohibiting their access to the shopping center for purposes of circulating the petition. The Supreme Court affirmed the lower court ruling that the appellant violated appellees' First Amendment rights.

Quaker City Cab Co. v. Pennsylvania,
277 U.S. 389 (1928)
[82]
Company was authorized to do business in the state as a foreign corporation. State taxes were levied on the cab company. They challenged under the Equal Protection Clause. The Supreme Court found for Quaker City.

R.A.V. v. St. Paul,
505 U.S. 377 (1992)
[149–150]
Petitioner was charged with burning a cross on a black family's lawn. Among other violations, he was charged with violating the city's bias-motivated crime ordinance. The Supreme Court agreed with the trial court that the ordinance was overly broad and invalid under the Fourteenth Amendment.

Radio Corp. v. United States,
341 U.S. 412 (1951)
[239]
The F.C.C. selected CBS's method of color television transmission. RCA challenged the decision by the commission not to reopen the hearings. The Supreme Court affirmed the F.C.C. procedural decision.

Railway Express Agency, Inc. v. New York,
336 U.S. 106 (1949)
[116]
Appellant sold advertising space on the sides of his express business trucks. It was convicted of violating the city's traffic regulations. Appellant challenged its conviction citing equal protection and due process grounds. The Supreme Court affirmed the conviction.

Rankin v. McPherson,
483 U.S. 378 (1987)
[50]
Respondent, an employee in the county police department, was discharged for making private remarks about the need to assassinate the president of the United States. She challenged the termination decision on free-speech grounds. The Supreme Court ruled in favor of the respondent.

Rathbun v. United States,
355 U.S. 107 (1957)
[175]
Petitioner was convicted of using interstate communications to threaten another's life. Police, at the urging of the potential victim, listened in on the threats. Petitioner challenged the conviction and the Supreme Court affirmed it.

Rawlings v. Kentucky,
448 U.S. 98 (1980)
[216]
Police, with an arrest warrant, searched the house of an acquaintance of petitioner, who was present at the time. Find-

ing limited evidence of marijuana use, the police obtained a search warrant. Executing the warrant, the police found more concrete evidence that was used in petitioner's conviction. He challenged under the Fourteenth Amendment. The Supreme Court affirmed the conviction.

Ray v. Blair,
343 U.S. 214 (1952)
[87]

The case involved the question of state authority in delegating to political parties the right to choose their nominees for presidential electors. The Supreme Court ruled that it was constitutional for parties to require the electors to pledge to support the parties' presidential and vice presidential nominees.

Rector, Church Wardens, and Vestrymen v. Philadelphia,
65 U.S. 300 (1860)
[77]

The state waived taxes to the Christ Church Hospital. The law was partially repealed eighteen years later. The hospital challenged, asserting that the initial waiver was perpetual and the act was a contract. The Supreme Court affirmed the constitutionality of the amended state law.

Regions Hospital v. Shalala,
522 U.S. 448 (1998)
[52]

Under the federal Medicare statute, hospitals can be reimbursed for educating interns and residents. Congress amended the act's reimbursement provision and respondent created a new re-audit rule,

which, when triggered, limited the amount of reimbursement due to the petitioner. The hospital challenged. The Supreme Court affirmed the lower court ruling in favor of the respondent's re-audit rule.

Reid v. Covert,
354 U.S. 1 (1957)
[201]

This consolidated case involved the authority of the military to court-martial and convict dependent civilians who accompany the armed services in foreign countries. The Supreme Court ruled that in capital cases during peacetime military tribunals had no authority to try civilians.

Reynolds v. Sims,
377 U.S. 533 (1964)
[106]

County voters challenged the state legislative reapportionment. They asserted that the result was discriminatory and disproportionate. The Supreme Court affirmed the district court finding that the state law violated the Equal Protection Clause.

Reynolds v. United States,
98 U.S. 145 (1878)
[5, 152]

Reynolds was convicted of bigamy, a violation of federal law. He challenged, asserting that the jury was improperly constituted, that the testimony was tainted, and that the federal government had no authority to create laws for the territories. The Supreme Court affirmed the conviction.

Richmond Newspapers, Inc. v. Virginia,
448 U.S. 555 (1980)
[46–47]
The state trial court granted a defense motion to close a murder trial to the public. Appellant challenged under free-press rights. The Supreme Court reversed the trial court's barring of the press and public from the public trial.

Richmond v. J. A. Croson, Co.,
488 U.S. 469 (1989)
[126–127]
Appellant city required city construction contractors to subcontract at least 30% of the contract revenue to minority business enterprises (MBE). Appellee lost a contract because of the MBE plan and challenged the constitutionality of the city rule. The Supreme Court affirmed the Court of Appeals' decision that the city plan was unconstitutional as created.

Riverside v. McLaughlin,
500 U.S. 44 (1991)
[72, 220]
Respondent was arrested without a warrant. He challenged the lack of probable cause proceedings, which, in the county, was combined with the arraignment procedure. He filed a class action suit challenging the constitutionality of the warrantless detention without a probable cause determination. The Supreme Court vacated the lower court's finding and remanded the case for further proceedings.

Robinson v. California,
370 U.S. 660 (1962)
[202]
Appellant was convicted of the chronic use of narcotics. State law penalized addiction to narcotics. He challenged the conviction as constituting cruel and unusual punishment (Eighth Amendment) and a violation of the Fourteenth Amendment. The Supreme Court reversed the conviction.

Robinson v. United States,
324 U.S. 282 (1945)
[195]
Petitioner was convicted of kidnapping and sentenced to death. He challenged the controlling statute's language ("liberated unharmed") as vague. The Supreme Court affirmed the conviction and sentence.

Rochin v. California,
342 U.S. 165 (1952)
[199–200]
Police learned that petitioner was selling narcotics. They forced their way into his house and bedroom where they discovered two capsules on a bedside table. Petitioner swallowed them in haste. He was taken to the hospital where he was induced to vomit. The tablets contained morphine. Petitioner was convicted of possession. He challenged on due-process grounds. The Supreme Court reversed the conviction.

Rock Island, A. & L.R. Co. v. United States,
254 U.S. 141 (1920)
[81]
Claimant owed internal revenue taxes. He challenged. The Supreme Court affirmed the Court of Claim's dismissal of claimant's petition.

Roe v. Wade,
410 U.S. 113 (1973)
[42–43]
This class action suit challenged the constitutionality of the state's criminal abortion laws. The Supreme Court ruled that appellant had standing to sue and provisions of the state law did violate due process.

Rome v. United States,
446 U.S. 156 (1980)
[94–95]
Appellant city made changes to its electoral system. The changes were challenged as denying or abridging the right to vote on account of race. The Supreme Court affirmed the lower-court findings of several constitutional violations.

Romer v. Evans,
517 U.S. 620 (1996)
[128, 186–187, 246–247]
Colorado voters amended the state constitution precluding any state governmental action specifically designed to protect the status of individuals due to their sexual orientation. Respondents challenged the amendment as violating the Equal Protection Clause. The Supreme Court struck down the amendment.

Rosales-Lopez v. United States,
451 U.S. 182 (1981)
[216]
Petitioner was convicted of smuggling Mexican aliens into the United States. At the trial, his motion to inquire into the possible prejudice toward Mexicans by potential jurors was denied. He chal-

lenged the conviction; the Supreme Court affirmed it.

Rosario v. Rockefeller,
410 U.S. 752 (1973)
[179]
Petitioner failed to enroll in a political party in a timely manner as required by state law as a condition of voting in a primary election. He challenged. The Supreme Court upheld the law.

Rosenbloom v. Metromedia, Inc.,
403 U.S. 29 (1971)
[43–44, 140]
Petitioner was acquitted of possessing obscene material. Respondent broadcast over its radio station facts related to his arrest. Petitioner sued for libel. The Supreme Court affirmed the Court of Appeals decision in favor of the respondent.

Ross v. Moffitt,
417 U.S. 600 (1974)
[43]
Indigent respondent was convicted of forgery. On the discretionary appeal he was denied the right to counsel. He challenged on due-process and equal-protection grounds. The Supreme Court reversed the Court of Appeals and ruled that the respondent was not entitled, as a matter of constitutional right, to counsel for a discretionary appeal.

Roth v. United States,
354 U.S. 476 (1957)
[240]
The case challenged the federal obscenity laws as a violation of the First, Ninth, Tenth, and Fourteenth Amendments. The

Supreme Court ruled that certain obscene materials do not have constitutional protections.

Rowan v. U.S. Post Office Department, 397 U.S. 728 (1970)
[139–140]
Appellants were publishers and distributors of direct mail. They challenged the federal law that allowed recipients of this kind of mail to have their names removed from a mailing list. The Supreme Court affirmed the constitutionality of the federal statute.

Rubin v. Coors Brewing Co., 514 U.S. 476 (1995)
[150–151]
Federal law prohibited beer labels from displaying alcohol content. Coors challenged the law on First Amendment grounds. The Supreme Court agreed that the law was unconstitutional.

Rummel v. Estelle, 445 U.S. 263 (1980)
[215–216]
Petitioner was convicted of his third nonviolent felony. As required by state law, his third conviction drew a mandatory life sentence. He challenged on Eighth and Fourteenth Amendment grounds. The Supreme Court affirmed the lower court decision validating the power of the state to enact recidivist laws.

Rust v. Sullivan, 500 U.S. 173 (1991)
[127–128]
Federal law prevented federal funds from being used to counsel the use of abortion as a method of family planning. Petitioners challenged the law as a violation of the First and Fifth Amendments. The Supreme Court affirmed the lower court and found no constitutional violations.

Rutkin v. United States, 343 U.S. 130 (1952)
[87]
Petitioner was convicted of failing to pay federal taxes on income derived from extortion. He challenged. The Supreme Court affirmed the conviction.

Sacher v. United States, 343 U.S. 1 (1952)
[37]
During a tumultuous criminal trial, the trial judge found petitioners (lawyers and defendants) guilty of criminal contempt. They challenged the judge's authority. The Supreme Court affirmed the convictions.

Saenz v. Roe, 526 U.S. ___ (1999)
[112, 187]
California enacted statutory requirements for state residents to receive welfare benefits. The law stated, in part, that recipients who have been residents of the state for less than twelve months would receive smaller benefits than other residents would. The law was challenged on equal-protection grounds. The Supreme Court ruled that the law was unconstitutional.

Saia v. New York, 334 U.S. 558 (1948)
[134]
Appellant, a Jehovah's Witness, obtained

permission to use sound amplification equipment for his religious lectures. He was denied a reissue of the permit. He went ahead with his loudspeaker-aided lectures and was arrested, tried, and convicted of violating the city ordinance. He challenged the ordinance as a violation of the First and Fourteenth Amendments. The Supreme Court reversed the conviction.

San Antonio Independent School District v. Rodriguez,
411 U.S. 1 (1973)
[91, 120]
A portion of the local funding to public schools in the state was derived from property tax. In this class action, appellees asserted that poorer communities have lower property taxes, which results in less aid going to the local schools. They argued that this violated the poor district's students' equal protection. The Supreme Court upheld the state's system of financing its public schools.

Santosky v. Kramer,
455 U.S. 745 (1982)
[96, 182]
State law allowed for the termination of parental rights if a finding by a preponderance of the evidence showed that the child was permanently neglected. Proceedings were initiated to terminate petitioners' parental rights. The Family Court found sufficiently evidence to terminate the rights and did so. Petitioners challenged on due process grounds. The Supreme Court found the preponderance standard unconstitutional and imposed

the more demanding, "clear and convincing" standard.

Schad v. Mount Ephraim,
452 U.S. 61 (1981)
[95–96, 147]
Appellants operated an adult bookstore, which included live nude dancing in violation of the commercial zoning ordinance. They challenged their conviction on First and Fourteenth Amendment grounds. The Supreme Court reversed the convictions.

Schall v. Martin,
467 U.S. 253 (1984)
[182]
State law allowed for the pretrial detention of an accused juvenile delinquent on the finding that the juvenile posed a serious risk of committing a crime. Detained appellees challenged the constitutionality of the statute. The Supreme Court found no due-process violations.

Schenck v. United States,
249 U.S. 47 (1919)
[129]
Schenck and others were convicted of conspiracy to violate the Espionage Act. They advocated and circulated information on military insubordination and obstruction of military recruitment. They challenged on First Amendment grounds. The Supreme Court affirmed their convictions.

Schlesinger v. Reservists Committee to Stop the War,
418 U.S. 208 (1974)
[69–70]
Respondents, an association, opposed the United States involvement in Viet-

nam. They challenged the status of members of Congress and executive branch officials who were members of the military reserve. They asserted that such dual responsibilities violated the Incompatibility Clause (Art I, 6, cl 12). The Supreme Court ruled that the respondents lacked standing to sue as taxpayers or citizens.

Schneider v. New Jersey,
308 U.S. 147 (1939)
[131–132]
Appellants were charged with violating various municipal ordinances prohibiting the distribution of handbills, picketing, and canvassing. Each challenged the ordinances on First Amendment grounds. The Supreme Court reversed the convictions.

Schware v. Board of Bar Examiners of New Mexico,
353 U.S. 232 (1957)
[201–240]
Bar examiners refused to allow petitioner to take the bar examination on the grounds that he did not demonstrate good moral character. This decision, in fact, denied petitioner admission to the state bar. He challenged asserting that his due-process rights were violated. The Supreme Court found for the petitioner.

Screws v United States,
325 U.S. 91 (1945)
[65, 85, 196–197]
Petitioners, law enforcement officers, arrested and beat to death Robert Hall, a black man. The petitioners were convicted of violating Hall's due-process rights. They

challenged. The Supreme Court reversed the convictions and remanded the case.

Scripps-Howard Radio v. Federal Communications Commission,
316 U.S. 4 (1942)
[65]
Appellant challenged the F.C.C.'s decision regarding a competitive radio station. They argued that because the F.C.C. made the decision without the benefit of a hearing, it was invalid. The question before the Supreme Court was whether the Court of Appeals has the power to stay the F.C.C. decision. The Court ruled that it could.

Shanks v. Dupont,
28 U.S. 242 (1830)
[167, 235]
The case involved the ownership of property, citizenship, and treaty law. The Supreme Court found for Shanks.

Shapiro v. Thompson,
394 U.S. 618 (1969)
[41–42]
Two states and the District of Columbia had laws that denied welfare assistance to appellees solely because they did not meet the residence-time requirements. Appellees challenged on the grounds that the statutes violated Fifth (District of Columbia) and Fourteenth Amendments (equal protection for the two state appellees). The Supreme Court struck down the statutes.

Sheppard v. Maxwell,
384 U.S. 333 (1966)
[137–138]
Petitioner was convicted of murdering

his wife. Extensive pretrial and trial publicity ran virtually unchecked by the trial judge. Petitioner challenged, filing a writ of habeas corpus. The Supreme Court ruled that the petitioner did not receive a fair trial under the Fourteenth Amendment, reversed the conviction, and remanded the case for further proceedings.

Simon & Schuster v. Crime Victims Board,
502 U.S. 105 (1991)
[149]

New York State law required that any entity contracting with an individual convicted of a crime in the state to write a book or other work describing the crime must give the state any proceeds earned from the work due the convicted individual. The money would be given to the victims of the crimes described. The publisher contracted with crime figure Henry Hill and was ordered to pay the proceeds. The publisher challenged the law on First Amendment grounds. The Supreme Court found the law unconstitutional.

Skinner v. Oklahoma ex rel Williamson,
316 U.S. 535 (1942)
[172–173]

State law allowed for the sterilization of habitual criminals convicted of two or more moral-turpitude felonies. The state initiated a jury trial proceeding to determine whether petitioner should be sterilized. The jury found that the procedure was in order. He challenged on several grounds (overly broad police power, due-process violations, sterilization was a cruel and unusual punishment, and

disputing whether he would have socially undesirable offspring). The Supreme Court reversed the sterilization order on equal-protection grounds.

Smith v. Allwright,
321 U.S. 649 (1944)
[34]

County officials denied petitioner, an African American, the right to vote in a primary election, solely on the grounds of his race. He challenged under the Fourteenth, Fifteenth, and Seventeenth Amendments. The Supreme Court decided for the petitioner.

Smith v. Goguen,
415 U.S. 566 (1974)
[91–93, 179]

Appellee was convicted of violating the state's flag-misuse statute (he had a small American flag sewn to the seat of his pants). He challenged the statute as being vague and overly broad. The Supreme Court affirmed the conviction.

Smith v. Texas,
311 U.S. 128 (1940)
[84]

Petitioner, an African American, was convicted of rape. He challenged the conviction on equal-protection grounds asserting that the state routinely denied blacks the right to serve on grand juries. The Supreme Court reversed the conviction.

Smith v. United States,
431 U.S. 291 (1977)
[145]

Petitioner was convicted of mailing obscene materials, a crime under federal law. He challenged, arguing that the state community standard was inappropriate. The Supreme Court affirmed the conviction.

Smythe v. Fiske,
90 U.S. 374 (1874)
[5]
Smythe, a duties collector, assessed import fees on Fiske's imported silk ties. Fiske challenged the federal law that authorized an allegedly excessive duty. The Supreme Court reversed the lower court and ruled for Smythe.

Snyder v. Massachusetts,
291 U.S. 97 (1934)
[63, 191]
Petitioners were convicted of murder and sentenced to death. During the trial the jury was brought to the scene of the crime. Petitioners were denied their motion to be present at the viewing. They challenged the denial as an abridgment of their due-process rights. The Supreme Court affirmed the conviction and sentence.

Sorrells v. United States,
287 U.S. 435 (1932)
[191]
Sorrells was convicted of possessing and selling whisky in violation of federal law. He argued that his actions were a consequence of entrapment. The Supreme Court reversed the conviction.

Sosna v. Iowa,
419 U.S. 393 (1975)
[107]
Appellant sought a divorce in the state. Her petition was denied because she failed the one-year residency requirement. She challenged on due-process and equal protection grounds. The Supreme

Court affirmed the state's right to impose the time requirement.

South Carolina v. Katzenbach,
383 U.S. 301 (1966)
[67–68]
The state challenged certain provisions of the federal Voting Rights Act of 1965. The Supreme Court dismissed the complaint and upheld the constitutionality of the act.

South Dakota v. Dole,
483 U.S. 203 (1987)
[15]
Federal law denied federal funds to states that failed to impose a twenty-one-year-old drinking age. The state challenged under Congress's spending powers (Art I, 8, cl 1) and the Twenty-First Amendment. The Supreme Court affirmed the federal spending power; they did not decide the Twenty-First Amendment question.

Southern Pacific v. Jensen,
244 U.S. 205 (1917)
[29]
Jensen was killed while on the job. Widow asserted rights under the state's Workmen's Compensation Act. Southern, engaged in interstate commerce, challenged the constitutionality of the Act. The Supreme Court found for Southern Pacific.

Southwestern Bell Telephone Co. v. Public Service Commission,
262 U.S. 276 (1923)
[237]
State commission reduced the telephone exchange service and installation rates. The company challenged. The Supreme Court found for the company.

Sparf v. United States,
156 U.S. 51 (1895)
[61]
Defendants were jointly tried and convicted of murder. They challenged the admissibility of a confession. The Supreme Court reversed only Sparf's conviction.

Spies v. United States,
317 U.S. 492 (1943)
[237]
Petitioner was convicted of attempting to evade paying his federal income tax. He challenged, asserting that the jury was improperly instructed with regards to intent and what constitutes a willful attempt. The Supreme Court reversed the conviction.

Stanley v. Georgia,
394 U.S. 557 (1969)
[139]
Appellant was convicted of possession of obscene films. He challenged the conviction asserting that the state obscenity law penalized private possession. The Supreme Court reversed the conviction.

Stanley v. Illinois,
405 U.S. 645 (1972)
[90]
Petitioner, an unwed father, was denied, without a hearing, custody of his children when the mother died. State law assumed that he was an unfit parent. He challenged. The Supreme Court found the lack of a hearing violated due-process of law and that the automatic assumption that unwed fathers were unfit parents (but not unwed mothers) violated the Equal Protection Clause.

Street v. New York,
394 U.S. 576 (1969)
[177]
Appellant was convicted of burning the American flag. He challenged on First Amendment grounds. The Supreme Court reversed the conviction.

Sturges v. Crowninshield,
17 U.S. 122 (1819)
[55]
The case involved the question of whether a state can enact a constitutional bankruptcy law. The Supreme Court ruled that the state does not have the authority to do so.

Sugarman v. Dougall,
413 U.S. 634 (1973)
[121]
State law permitted only United States citizens from holding prominent civil service positions. Appellees, registered resident aliens, were discharged from their civil service jobs. They challenged the constitutionality of the statute under the First and Fourteenth Amendments. The Supreme Court ruled that the statute did violate the Equal Protection Clause.

Sutton v. United Air Lines, Inc.,
527 U.S. ___ (1999)
[53]
Petitioners, myopic twins, applied to United for employment as commercial pilots. They were rejected because they failed United's uncorrected visual acuity requirement. Petitioners challenged the decision under the Americans with Disabilities Act. The Supreme Court ruled in favor of United.

Swann v. Charlotte-Mecklenburg Board of Education,
402 U.S. 1 (1971)
[119–120]
The school system had engaged in racial segregation. The court-approved plan for desegregating the system involved busing students and reassigning faculty. One component of the plan called for greater effort in the junior and senior high schools and less in the elementary schools. The Supreme Court affirmed the district court plan.

Swidler & Berlin v. United States,
524 U.S. 399 (1998)
[223]
White House counsel met with petitioner attorney at petitioner law firm to discuss legal matters. He later committed suicide and an independent counsel requested petitioner to testify as to communications it had with the White House counsel. Petitioner declined asserting attorney-client privilege. The Supreme Court ruled for the petitioner.

Tennessee v. Garner,
471 U.S. 1 (1985)
[217]
Police, responding to a prowler call, confronted suspect, identified him, and told him not to move. Garner began to flee, jumping over a nearby fence. Police officer shot and killed the suspect. Garner's father sued arguing that the shooting was a violation of his son's Fourth, Fifth, Sixth, Eighth, and Fourteenth Amendments. The Supreme Court found in favor of the police.

Tenney v. Brandhove,
341 U.S. 367 (1951)
[9–10]
Respondent sued petitioners for rights violation as part of his appearing in front of petitioner's state legislative committee in the process of conducting an investigation. The Supreme Court found for the petitioners.

Terminiello v. Chicago,
337 U.S. 1 (1949)
[135]
Petitioner gave a controversial lecture to an overflow audience. The crowd, protesting his presence, turned unruly. Petitioner criticized their behavior. He was arrested and convicted of disorderly conduct. He challenged on free-speech grounds. The Supreme Court reversed the conviction.

Terrett v. Taylor,
13 U.S. 43 (1815)
[54–55]
The case involved religious leaders challenging title to trust property. The Supreme Court found for Terrett.

Terry v. Adams,
345 U.S. 461 (1953)
[38]
Petitioners, African American voters, were denied the right to vote in an association election. Historically the association selected candidates to run in political primaries. The petitioners challenged. The Supreme Court found the association was part of the county political machinery and that they deprived blacks of the right to vote, contrary to the Fifteenth Amendment.

Terry v. Ohio,
392 U.S. 1 (1968)
[177, 207–208]
Police officer observed petitioner and others engaged in suspicious behavior. He confronted them and frisked them. He discovered concealed weapons on each of them. They were convicted; they asserted that the search was unconstitutional and as such the evidence was inadmissible. The Supreme Court affirmed the convictions.

Texas v. Johnson,
491 U.S. 397 (1989)
[98, 185]
Respondent burned an American flag during a political rally. He was convicted, pursuant to state law, of desecration of a venerated object. He challenged on First Amendment grounds. The Supreme Court affirmed the reversal of the conviction.

Texas v. White,
74 U.S. 700 (1868)
[102–103]
The state sold federal coupon bonds. With the outbreak of the Civil War, Texas withdrew from the Union. They used the unsold bonds to aid in the rebellion. The Confederacy lost the rebellion and the provisional state government sought to recover the bonds. Others asserted rightful ownership of the bonds. The Supreme Court ruled in favor of the state.

The Amistad,
40 U.S. 518 (1841)
[167]
African slaves "owned" by two Spaniards seized control of the ship transporting them across the Atlantic. Two members of the crew were killed. The ship was seized off the shores of New York, and the Africans were placed under arrest. The Spaniards claimed the Africans as their property, while others claimed the ship and the slaves as salvage property. The Supreme Court ruled that the Africans were free men and women, illegally taken from Africa and not liable for the deaths of the two crew members.

The Prize Cases,
67 U.S. 635 (1863)
[226]
Four cases were consolidated and commonly referred to as "The Prize Cases." Ships and cargoes were captured and claimed as prizes by the United States. The seized ships had formerly been aligned with the Confederacy during the Civil War. The questions before the Court involved the definition of war, whether a rebellion/insurrection was equivalent to a war, the authority of the president to seize "enemy" property, and the nature of sovereignty of United States citizens. The Supreme Court affirmed the seizure of some of the vessels and required the return of others.

Thiel v. Southern Pacific Co.,
328 U.S. 217 (1946)
[197]
Petitioner jumped out of a window of a moving train operated by respondent. He sued asserting that the respondent knew that he was out of his mind and it should not have let him board. Petitioner subsequently challenged the business-orientation of the

jury. His motion to strike the entire jury was denied. The Supreme Court reversed the denial of petitioner's motion.

Thomas v. Collins,
323 U.S. 516 (1945)
[237–238]

Appellant was a high union official. An attempt to unionize an oil and refinery company brought appellant to a rally to offer a speech. He was served with a restraining order preventing the speech. He addressed the rally and was arrested for contempt. He filed a writ of habeas corpus, which was denied by the state supreme court. The Supreme Court ruled in favor of the appellant.

Thornburgh v. American College of Obstetricians & Gynecologists,
476 U.S. 747 (1986)
[48–49, 71, 96–97, 109, 183–184]

Appellees challenged the state's abortion-control law. The Supreme Court affirmed the Court of Appeals' decision to enjoin enforcement of the entire state law.

Tilton v. Richardson,
403 U.S. 672 (1971)
[160]

Federal law provided grants to be used for the construction of college facilities. The law excluded the funding of secular school facilities used for religious purposes. Appellants challenged the funding of four church-related construction projects. The Supreme Court upheld the constitutionality of the federal funding.

Tinker v. Des Moines Independent School District,
393 U.S. 503 (1969)
[138, 139, 177, 241–242]

Petitioners, public school students, were expelled from school for wearing black armbands. Their intention was to conduct a peaceful protest of United States involvement in Vietnam. The Supreme Court found for the petitioners.

Tot v. United States,
319 U.S. 463 (1943)
[194]

Federal law prohibited individuals convicted of violent crimes from obtaining guns or ammunition by means of interstate commerce. Two separate individuals were convicted of violating the law. The Supreme Court invalidated the statute.

Townsend v. Yeomans,
301 U.S. 441 (1937)
[7]

State law regulated the handling, manufacture, and selling of tobacco by state tobacco businesses. The law was challenged as a violation of the Fourteenth Amendment. The Supreme Court upheld the state power.

Transamerica Mortgage Advisors, Inc. v. Lewis,
444 U.S. 11 (1979)
[13]

Respondent, a shareholder of petitioner, sued for fraud and breach of fiduciary duty, as governed by federal law. The Supreme Court affirmed in part and reversed in part.

Treasury Employees v. Von Raab,
489 U.S. 656 (1989)
[98, 184]
The United States Customs Service implemented a drug-screening program for employees who: (a) were involved in drug interdiction, (b) carried firearms, or (c) handled classified materials. The union challenged. The Supreme Court upheld the government authority on all but the classified-materials requirement.

Trimble v. Gordon,
430 U.S. 762 (1977)
[122–123]
State law allowed illegitimate children to inherit only from the mother (legitimate children could inherit from both parents). Appellants challenged on equal-protection grounds. The Supreme Court found the law's classification unconstitutional.

Trop v. Dulles,
356 U.S. 86 (1958)
[38–39]
Petitioner, a natural-born citizen and a private in the military, was convicted of desertion. He was sentenced to hard labor, forfeited his pay and allowances, and was given a dishonorable discharge. Years later he was denied a passport on the grounds that he was no longer a citizen because of his desertion conviction and dishonorable discharge. He challenged. The Supreme Court ruled in favor of the petitioner.

Truax v. Raich,
239 U.S. 33 (1915)
[170]
The state constitution set a minimum limit on the percentage of native-born citizens state businesses could employ (at least 80%). Appellee, a native-born Austrian, worked for appellant. Truax, in conformity to the law, dismissed appellee. Appellee challenged on Fourteenth Amendment grounds. Truax was also arrested for violating the law. The Supreme Court affirmed the order enjoining the enforcement of the law.

Trustees of Dartmouth College v. Woodward,
17 U.S. 518 (1819)
[22]
State law modified the college's charter. The college challenged on Contract Clause grounds. The Supreme Court ruled that the state law was unconstitutional.

Turner v. Bank of North America,
4 U.S. 8 (1799)
[3]
The case involved a promissory note payment intestate. The question before the Court was the scope of jurisdiction for the federal circuit courts. The Supreme Court found the lower court in error.

Turner v. United States,
396 U.S. 398 (1970)
[68]
Turner was convicted of violating federal narcotics laws. He challenged the statute's permission to infer guilt. The Supreme Court affirmed the heroin conviction and reversed the cocaine conviction.

Twining v. New Jersey,
211 U.S. 78 (1908)
[28]
Twining and others were convicted of intent to deceive. During the trial comments were made about the refusal of defendant to testify. The Supreme Court affirmed the conviction.

Tyson & Brothers-United Theatre Ticket Offices v. Banton,
273 U.S. 418 (1927)
[104]
Appellant, under state license, was in the business of reselling tickets of admission to theaters in New York City. It brought action to enjoin appellee from engaging in the same business since it violated a provision of the governing state law. Appellee challenged the constitutionality of the statute. On appeal, the Supreme Court reversed the decree instituting the injunction and found the statute in violation of the Fourteenth Amendment.

U.S. Term Limits, Inc. v. Thornton,
514 U.S. 779 (1995)
[72–73]
The case involved a challenge to an amendment of the Arkansas constitution imposing term limits on candidates for the U.S. House of Representatives and Senate. The Supreme Court ruled that the amendment violated the Qualifications Clause of the federal Constitution.

Ullman v. United States,
350 U.S. 422 (1956)
[66]
Petitioner appeared before a federal grand jury investigating national security/espionage matters. He refused to answer questions about his or others involvement with the Communist Party. He was granted immunity as allowed by federal law. He still refused to testify, and he was convicted of contempt. The Supreme Court affirmed the conviction.

United States v. Ballard,
322 U.S. 78 (1944)
[154–155]
Respondent was convicted of using the mails with the intent to defraud. Ballard challenged the admissibility of evidence relative to his religious beliefs. The Supreme Court reversed the conviction and remanded the case.

United States v. Ballin,
144 U.S. 1 (1892)
[6]
The case involved the constitutionality of a federal law—more specifically, whether a quorum of members of Congress were present to pass the legislation. The Supreme Court ruled that the legislation had been legally passed.

United States v. Balsys,
524 U.S. 666 (1998)
[234]
Respondent was subpoenaed to testify about his WWII activities and his immigration to the United States. Fearing his potential prosecution by a foreign nation, he asserted Fifth Amendment privileges. He challenged the order compelling his testimony. The Supreme Court ruled against the respondent.

United States v. Baltimore & Ohio Railroad Co.,
84 U.S. 322 (1872)
[103]
The case involved the constitutionality of municipal versus federal corporate income tax. The Supreme Court affirmed judgment for the railroad.

United States v. Bayer,
331 U.S. 532 (1947)
[198–199]
Defendants were convicted of bribing and receiving bribe money to alter military dispositions. Appeals related to confessions were asserted. The Supreme Court affirmed the convictions.

United States v. Belmont,
301 U.S. 324 (1937)
[17–18]
Russian business deposited money with Belmont, a private United States banker. The new Soviet government dissolved the corporation and appropriated all of its assets, including the deposited money. Respondents refused to pay the Soviet Union the money. The Supreme Court reversed the lower-court decision to dismiss the claim.

United States v. Bethlehem Steel Corporation,
315 U.S. 289 (1942)
[33]
The case involved contractual disputes between the federal government and Bethlehem for the construction of war ships during WWI. The Supreme Court affirmed the decision to dismis—a decision favorable to Bethlehem.

United States v. Borden Company,
308 U.S. 188 (1939)
[32]
The case involved milk producers and their allegedly trust-like practices. The Supreme Court dismissed one count and reversed the lower court's dismissal of three other counts. The Court remanded the case for further proceedings.

United States v. Brewster,
408 U.S. 501 (1972)
[12, 42]
Appellee, a former United States Senator, was charged with accepting bribes while a senator. The district court dismissed the indictment on Speech or Debate Clause grounds. The Supreme Court reversed the dismissal.

United States v. Butler,
297 U.S. 1 (1936)
[30, 31]
The predominant issue in this case involved a constitutional challenge to certain provisions of the federal Agricultural Adjustment Act. The Supreme Court ruled that the federal statute was constitutional.

United States v. Calandra,
414 U.S. 338 (1974)
[212–213]
Respondent's place of business was searched under a warrant. Federal agents seized evidence related to loan-sharking activity. Respondent was subpoenaed by a grand jury to testify about the activities. He refused citing Fifth Amendment protections. The district court granted his motion to suppress the evidence on the

grounds that the warrant was insufficient; it also decided that the respondent need not respond to any questions relative to the suppressed evidence. The government appealed; the Supreme Court reversed.

United States v. Carignan,
342 U.S. 36 (1951)
[199]
Respondent confessed to and was convicted of murder as a result of attempting to perpetrate a rape. The confession was the issue under appeal. The Supreme Court affirmed the reversal of the conviction.

United States v. Carolene Products Co.,
304 U.S. 144 (1938)
[7–8]
Federal law prohibited the interstate shipment of adulterated skim milk. Appellees were indicted for violating the law. They challenged the power of Congress to enact the law. The Supreme Court upheld the congressional authority.

United States v. Classic,
313 U.S. 299 (1941)
[64]
Appellees, commissioners of election, were indicted for violating voters' constitutional right to vote in federal elections. The Supreme Court reversed the district court's demurrer.

United States v. Columbia Steel Corp.,
334 U.S. 495 (1948)
[85]
This is a Sherman Act (federal antitrust statute) case. The Supreme Court affirmed

the district court verdict for appellee.

United States v. Cooper Corporation,
312 U.S. 600 (1941)
[84]
This case involved the question of whether under the Sherman Act the federal government is equivalent to a "person" as defined in the act. The Supreme Court affirmed the district court's dismissal of the complaint.

United States v. Curtiss-Wright Export Corporation,
299 U.S. 304 (1936)
[63]
Appellee was indicted for conspiracy to sell machine guns to Bolivia in violation to a Joint Resolution of Congress and a Presidential Proclamation. The Supreme Court reversed the district court's demurrer and remanded the case.

United States v. Darby,
312 U.S. 100 (1941)
[64]
The case involved violations of the federal Fair Labor Standards Act in the interstate shipment of lumber by employees paid below the minimum-wage requirements. The Supreme Court ruled in favor of the law and reversed the district court's demurrer.

United States v. Detroit Timber & Lumber Co.,
200 U.S. 321 (1906)
[236]
The case involved a property title dispute. The Supreme Court affirmed the lower-court finding for Detroit Timber.

United States v. Dionisio,
410 U.S. 1 (1973)
[212]
Individuals, including respondent, were subpoenaed by a grand jury to give voice exemplars. Respondent refused to comply on Fourth- and Fifth-Amendment grounds. The Supreme Court found no constitutional violations.

United States v. Doremus,
249 U.S. 86 (1919)
[170]
Doremus was indicted for violating a federal drug-revenue law. On demurrer the district court invalidated a provision of the law. The government appealed, and the Supreme Court reversed the lower court's invalidation.

United States v. E.C. Knight Co.,
156 U.S. 1 (1895)
[80–81]
Companies were indicted for violating antimonopoly federal laws. The circuit court dismissed the bills. The Supreme Court affirmed.

United States v. Fisher,
6 U.S. 358 (1805)
[3]
The case involved the question of whether the United States is entitled to be preferred to general creditors when the debtor becomes bankrupt. The Supreme Court ruled that the United States does deserve special considerations.

United States v. Fordice,
505 U.S. 717 (1992)
[128]
The state operated racially segregated public colleges. The district court found that the state had made some progress in desegregating and in disestablishing its *de jure* system. The Supreme Court vacated the findings. The Court provided new legal standards and remanded the case for further proceedings consistent with the new standards.

United States v. Harriss,
347 U.S. 612 (1954)
[87–88]
Appellees were charged with violating federal lobbying laws. The district court dismissed the case and found provisions of the law unconstitutional. The Supreme Court reversed the district court.

United States v. Hudson,
11 U.S. 32 (1812)
[3–4]
The question before the Court was whether the federal circuit courts could exercise common law jurisdiction in criminal cases. The Supreme Court answered in the negative.

United States v. Jin Fuey Moy,
241 U.S. 394 (1916)
[29]
The case involved a failure to pay a special tax on the dispensing of opium. The Supreme Court affirmed the district court judgment to quash the indictment of the defendant.

United States v. Kahriger,
345 U.S. 22 (1953)
[87]
Appellee was in the business of accepting wagers. He refused to pay an occupational tax. The district court dismissed the case, stating that the tax was unconstitutional. The Supreme Court reversed the dismissal.

United States v. Lee,
455 U.S. 252 (1982)
[161–162]
Appellee, a member of the Amish society, failed to withhold Social Security taxes from his employees' wages. The I.R.S. assessed him for the unpaid taxes. He challenged the tax law as a violation of his right to free exercise of religion. The Supreme Court reversed the lower court and ruled that the tax was constitutional.

United States v. Lopez,
514 U.S. 549 (1995)
[99, 246]
Respondent, a twelfth grade public-school student, was charged with carrying a concealed handgun to school in violation of federal law. The Supreme Court affirmed the Court of Appeals decision declaring that the federal law exceeded Congress's Commerce Clause authority.

United States v. Marion,
404 U.S. 307 (1971)
[210]
Appellees claimed that the government knew of their crimes for more than three years before indicting them. They asserted that the indictments were a violation of due-process (Fifth Amendment) and speedy-trial (Sixth Amendment) guarantees. The Supreme Court ruled against the appellees.

United States v. Monia,
317 U.S. 424 (1943)
[9]
The case involved grand jury testimony relative to federal-law violations. The testimony touched on an alleged offense by Monia, who was granted immunity (although he did not assert self-incrimination protections). He was convicted of the crimes. The Supreme Court affirmed the conviction.

United States v. Nixon,
418 U.S. 683 (1974)
[19]
White House aides and political operatives were indicted for criminal behavior. The government sought certain tape recordings, made by the President, to be used as evidence in the criminal trials. The president refused the subpoena and asserted a variety of executive branch privileges. The Supreme Court affirmed the lower-court order against the president.

United States v. Norris,
300 U.S. 564 (1937)
[192]
A Senate committee was investigating campaign expenditures. Respondent senator testified to the committee. Following the testimony of a subsequent witness, the senator asked to return to the committee and revise his contrary testimony. The senator was convicted for perjury. The Supreme Court affirmed the constitutionality of the conviction.

United States v. O'Brien,
391 U.S. 367 (1968)
[11]
O'Brien was convicted of burning his draft card as a political protest. He challenged on free speech grounds. The Supreme Court upheld the conviction.

United States v. Peters,
9 U.S. 115 (1809)
[3]
Individuals sought an order (mandamus) compelling Peters, a federal judge, to enforce a court order. The Supreme Court upheld the mandamus.

United States v. Price,
361 U.S. 304 (1960)
[11]
The case involved a requirement that the I.R.S. notify a taxpayer of an income-tax deficiency. The I.R.S. had taken action against respondent without the required ninety-day notification. He challenged. The Supreme Court affirmed the action.

United States v. Public Utilities Commission
of California,
345 U.S. 295 (1953)
[38]
Respondent-power company sold electricity to California, a Nevada county, and the Navy Department. The rates set by federal law were assessed on all the electricity on resale. The commission challenged on interstate commerce grounds. The Supreme Court upheld the federal rates law.

United States v. Rabinowitz,
339 U.S. 56 (1950)
[36–37, 174]
Respondent sold forged postage stamps to a government agent. The government then obtained an arrest warrant, and, while executing it, government agents searched the premises and seized additional material evidence, which was used as evidence in respondent's conviction. He challenged the search and the admissibility of the evidence seized without a warrant. The Supreme Court upheld the conviction.

United States v. Richardson,
418 U.S. 166 (1974)
[44, 69]
Respondent challenged the constitutionality of the existence of the C.I.A. because of how it accounts for its expenditures. The district court dismissed the case because the respondent-taxpayer did not have standing. The Supreme Court upheld the dismissal.

United States v. Rumely,
345 U.S. 41 (1953)
[174]
Respondent belonged to an organization that sold books of a political nature. Congress requested the names of customers who made bulk purchases. He refused and was convicted of refusal to furnish the requested information. The Supreme Court reversed the conviction stating that this specific congressional committee did not have the appropriate power to compel testimony.

United States v. Russell,
411 U.S. 423 (1973)
[212]
An undercover narcotics agent supplied respondent with a hard-to-obtain ingredient that could be used in the manufacture of an illegal drug. Respondent was convicted and appealed on an entrapment defense. The Supreme Court affirmed the conviction.

United States v. Salerno,
481 U.S. 739 (1987)
[49–50]
Respondents were arrested for RICO (racketeering) and a variety of other felony offenses. Pursuant to federal law allowing for the detention without bail of individuals standing trial, respondents were detained on the grounds that they posed a safety threat to individuals within the community. The respondents challenged the federal law on Fifth and Eighth Amendment grounds. The Supreme Court upheld the statute.

United States v. Seeger,
380 U.S. 163 (1965)
[158–159]
This consolidated case involved the conscientious objector exemption to the draft. The Supreme Court established guidelines to how the exemption was to be determined.

United States v. Spelar,
338 U.S. 217 (1949)
[9]
Spelar, a flight engineer, was killed in a take-off crash at a British airbase leased to the United States. The administratrix to Spelar's estate initiated action against the United States for negligence. The government asserted that the incident occurred in a foreign country and as such there were no grounds to sue the United States. The Supreme Court ruled for the United States.

United States v. Standard Oil Co.,
332 U.S. 301 (1947)
[65–66]
A Standard Oil truck driven by a Standard Oil employee injured an American soldier. The government sought to recover the costs of hospitalization and soldier's pay. The Supreme Court affirmed the Court of Appeals decision for Standard Oil.

United States v. United Mine Workers of America,
330 U.S. 258 (1947)
[35, 116]
The United States government owned and operated most of the nation's coal mines. The Union, advocating conditions favorable to its members, prepared for a strike. The government sought a temporary injunction, which was issued. The miners began a walkout in violation of the injunction. The Union was convicted of contempt and fined. The Supreme Court affirmed the convictions.

United States v. United States District Court,
407 U.S. 297 (1972)
[42, 178–179]
Three individuals were charged with conspiracy to destroy federal government property. A pretrial motion challenged the electronic surveillance evidence. The logs of the surveillance were sealed for national security reasons. The district court found the surveillance violated the Fourth Amendment and ordered the government to provide full disclosure. The government challenged. The Supreme Court affirmed the lower court's decisions.

United States v. Verdugo-Urquidez,
494 U.S. 259 (1990)
[233–234]
Respondent, a Mexican citizen, was en-

gaged in narcotics smuggling. He was apprehended by Mexican police and transported to the United States, where he was arrested. The Drug Enforcement Agency, working with Mexican authorities, searched respondent's Mexican residence without a warrant and seized evidence. The district court granted respondent's motion to suppress the warrantless seizure of evidence. The Supreme Court reversed.

United States v. Virginia, 518 U.S. 515 (1996)
[110–111]
The United States sued Virginia and the Virginia Military Institute for the latter's male-only admission policy as a violation of equal protection guarantees. As a remedy, Virginia founded Virginia Women's Institute for Leadership, a parallel program. The Supreme Court found that the state still violated the Fourteenth Amendment.

United States v. Wade, 388 U.S. 218 (1967)
[206]
Respondent was indicted for robbery. Several weeks later, without notice to his counsel, respondent was placed in a lineup. He was identified as the robber. He challenged on Fifth and Sixth Amendment grounds. The trial court denied his motions and he was convicted. The Supreme Court vacated the conviction and remanded the case.

United States v. White, 401 U.S. 745 (1971)
[209–210]
Respondent was convicted of narcot-ics violations. Evidence had been obtained from a warrantless electronic eavesdropping device worn by an informer. The informer could not be located for the trial and agents testified to the conversation they overheard. The Supreme Court upheld the conviction.

United States v. Willow River Power Co., 324 U.S. 499 (1945)
[115–116]
Willow River was compensated for impaired efficiency of its hydroelectric plant caused by the actions of the United States. The question before the Court was whether the damage to the plant was a result of a "taking" of private property, whose compensation is controlled under the Fifth Amendment. The Supreme Court ruled against Willow River.

United States v. Wiltberger, 18 U.S. 76 (1820)
[23]
Wiltberger was convicted of manslaughter that had taken place aboard an American ship off the coast of China. The Supreme Court ruled that American courts lacked the authority to hear the criminal case.

United States v. Wood, 299 U.S. 123 (1936)
[191]
Respondent was convicted of petit larceny in the police court in the District of Columbia. His jury was composed of government employees, as permitted by federal law. He challenged the impartiality of governmental employ-

ees in a government case. The Supreme Court upheld the conviction.

United States v. Wunderlich,
342 U.S. 98 (1951)
[174]
The case involved disputes about governmental contracts and who had the ultimate authority to make decisions resolving the disputes. The Supreme Court ruled for the United States.

United States v. X-Citement Video, Inc.,
513 U.S. 64 (1994)
[150]
Owner of a video rental store was convicted of selling pornographic videos, in violation of federal law. The law stated that a defendant must "knowingly" engage in commerce relative to the use of minors in the pornographic materials. The owner, stating that he did not know that the actress in the video was a minor, appealed the conviction on First Amendment grounds. The Supreme Court upheld the conviction.

University of California Regents v. Bakke,
438 U.S. 265 (1978)
[123]
Respondent, a white male, was twice denied admission to the university medical school. Racial minorities with lower test scores had admitted to the school. Asserting that the school's special admission policy was unconstitutional, he challenged on equal-protection grounds. The Supreme Court ruled that an admission policy based solely on race was unconstitutional. The Court found for Bakke.

Valley Forge Christian College v. Americans United,
454 U.S. 464 (1982)
[47]
Federal law allowed for the economical and efficient system of surplus federal government property, including surplus real property, for educational use. Property was "sold" to petitioner, a church-related college. Respondents challenged on Establishment Clause grounds. The Supreme Court ruled that respondents did not have standing.

Veazie Bank v. Fenno,
75 U.S. 533 (1869)
[26]
The state bank refused to pay federal taxes imposed on all banks, asserting that the law was unconstitutional. The Supreme Court found the law constitutional.

Vernonia School District 47J v. Acton,
515 U.S. 646 (1995)
[51–52]
School district instituted a random drug test of all student athletes. Acton was ineligible to participate in the football program because he refused to submit to the testing. He challenged on Fourth and Fourteenth Amendment grounds. The Supreme Court ruled in favor of the school district.

Viereck v. United States,
318 U.S. 236 (1943)
[193]
Petitioner was convicted of failing to supply required immigration registration materials to the secretary of state. He challenged the authority of the secretary. The Supreme Court reversed the conviction.

Village of Euclid, Ohio v. Ambler Reality Co.,
272 U.S. 365 (1926)

[237]

Appellee owned land in the village. The village adopted a comprehensive zoning ordinance. The ordinance would allegedly have deprived appellee of certain uses of its land. It challenged on due-process and equal-protection grounds. The Supreme Court found the ordinance constitutional.

Virginia Pharmacy Board v. Virginia Consumer Council,
425 U.S. 748 (1976)

[144–145]

Challenging the state statute prohibiting licensed pharmacists from advertising the prices of prescription drugs, appellees, consumers, sued the board. They asserted that the statute violated the First and Fourteenth Amendments. The Supreme Court affirmed the lower-court decision striking down the law.

Wallace v. Jaffree,
472 U.S. 38 (1985)

[71, 163–164]

Alabama laws required public schools to hold one-minute periods of silence for meditation and prayer and other, more active prayer sessions. Parent of three school-aged children challenged the laws. The Supreme Court found that the laws violated the Establishment Clause of the First Amendment and the Fourteenth Amendment.

Walz v. Tax Commission,
397 U.S. 664 (1970)

[159]

Appellant challenged commissioner's granting of property-tax exemptions to religious organizations for religious properties used solely for religious purposes. He asserted that such exemptions violated the Establishment Clause. The Supreme Court affirmed the lower-court decision for the appellee.

Ward v. Rock Against Racism,
491 U.S. 781 (1989)

[148]

City established guidelines for the use of parks for concerts aided with loudspeakers and amplifiers. The guidelines were challenged as a violation of the First Amendment. The Supreme Court upheld the guidelines.

Warden v. Hayden,
387 U.S. 294 (1967)

[176–177, 205]

Respondent was convicted of armed robbery. Prior to his arrest, respondent's wife allowed police to search their house. The police found respondent and evidence. He challenged. The Supreme Court upheld the warrantless arrest and warrantless seizure of evidence.

Ware v. Hylton,
3 U.S. 199 (1796)

[22]

State law allowed for the confiscation of property during the American Revolution. The law was contrary to a treaty. The Supreme Court invalidated the state law.

Warth v. Seldin,
422 U.S. 490 (1975)

[44]

Petitioners challenged the town's zoning ordinance, asserting that it prevented persons of low and moderate income from living in the town. The district court dismissed the case, ruling that the petitioners lacked standing. The Supreme Court affirmed.

Washington Market Co. v. Hoffman, 101 U.S. 112 (1879)
[26]
Hoffman and others owned business stalls in the market. Washington tried to sell the stalls. An injunction was sought. The Supreme Court ruled in favor of Washington Market.

Washington v. Davis, 426 U.S. 229 (1976)
[13]
Respondents, African Americans, applied for employment as police officers in the District of Columbia. They were denied employment. They challenged the recruiting procedures as racially discriminatory and, as such, in violation of the Fifth Amendment. The district court granted petitioners' motion for summary judgment. The Court of Appeals reversed and found for respondents. The Supreme Court reversed the Court of Appeals decision.

Washington v. Glucksberg, 117 S. Ct. 2258 and 117 S. Ct. 2293 (1997)
[99, 111, 187]
Respondents, physicians and gravely ill patients, challenged the state's statute banning assisted suicide. They argued that the law violated due-process protections. The Supreme Court upheld the statute criminalizing the assisting of suicide even for mentally competent, terminally ill adults.

Watkins v. United States, 354 U.S. 178 (1957)
[11]
Petitioner was summoned to testify before a congressional committee. He refused to answer questions relative to others' association with the Communist Party (although he answered about his own involvement). Refusal to answer was a misdemeanor violation of federal law. Petitioner was convicted. He challenged on due-process grounds. The Supreme Court reversed the conviction.

Watson v. Jones, 80 U.S. 679 (1871)
[152]
The case involved a dispute about which religious leadership owned the property on which the church was located. The Supreme Court affirmed the circuit-court decree for Jones.

Watts v. United States, 394 U.S. 705 (1969)
[139]
During a political rally, petitioner made an off-the-cuff remark that if he was drafted into the Army he would shoot the president. He was convicted of willfully threatening the president, a federal offense. He challenged. The Supreme Court reversed the conviction.

Wayte v. United States, 470 U. S. 598 (1985)
[217]
Petitioner refused to register with the Selective Service System as required by presidential proclamation. The federal government tried several times to encourage his compliance. With his contin-

ued refusal, he was indicted. The Court of Appeals reversed the dismissal of the case. The Supreme Court affirmed.

Weber v. Aetna Casualty & Surety Co., 406 U.S. 164 (1972)
[242–243]
Decedent died as a result of a mishap at work. Six minor children (two of whom were illegitimate) survived him. He lived with petitioner out of wedlock. The state's workmen's compensation law allowed benefits for the four legitimate children but denied any benefits for the two illegitimate children. In finding for the petitioner, the Supreme Court ruled that the state law violated the Equal Protection Clause.

Webster v. Reproductive Health Services, Inc., 492 U.S. 490 (1989)
[71–72]
Appellees challenged several provisions of the state's laws regulating abortions, including the following: (a) that life begins at conception, (b) that unborn children have protectable interests, (c) that medical tests were required to determine viability of the fetus when the mother reaches the twentieth week of pregnancy, (d) that public employees or facilities were prohibited from assisting in non-life-saving abortions, and (e) that the use of public funds to encourage mothers to seek abortions as a life-saving medical treatment was prohibited. The district court invalidated each controversial provision. The Supreme Court reversed.

Weeks v. United States, 232 U.S. 383 (1914)
[190]
Weeks was convicted of using the mails to transport lotteries and games of chance. He was arrested without a warrant, but his premises were searched and evidence was seized with a warrant. He sought to have his property returned. The Supreme Court ruled that some of the property must be returned.

Welsh v. United States, 398 U.S. 333 (1970)
[160]
Petitioner was convicted of failing to submit to his induction into the military. He asserted a conscientious-objector exemption. He challenged the religion-based criteria of the exemption. The Supreme Court reversed the conviction.

Wesberry v. Sanders, 376 U.S. 1 (1964)
[40, 67]
Appellants challenged the size of the population of their congressional district, which was significantly larger than other districts in the state. Their argument was that such disparities had the effect of reducing the equality of their votes with other votes cast in the state. The Supreme Court invalidated the state apportionment law and ruled in favor of the appellants.

West Coast Hotel Co. v. Parrish, 300 U.S. 379 (1937)
[31]
Appellee, an employee of appellant,

sued appellant for the differences between the wages paid to her and the minimum wage fixed by state law. The appellant challenged the law as a violation of the Due Process Clause. The Supreme Court affirmed the constitutionality of the state law.

West Virginia State Board of Education v. Barnette,
319 U.S. 624 (1943)
[34, 65, 133]
School regulations required all students and teachers to salute the American flag. Jehovah's Witnesses challenged on First and Fourteenth Amendment grounds. The Supreme Court invalidated the school rule.

Westfall v. United States,
274 U.S. 256 (1927)
[63]
Westfall was convicted of a conspiracy to misappropriate bank funds. He challenged the constitutionality of the controlling federal statute. The Supreme Court affirmed the conviction.

Whitney v. California,
274 U.S. 357 (1927)
[130–131]
Whitney was convicted of violating the state's criminal syndicalism laws. Asserting that the state law violated both the Due Process Clause and the Equal Protection Clause, she challenged the conviction The Supreme Court affirmed the conviction.

Wickard v. Filburn,
317 U.S. 111 (1942)
[18]
Federal agriculture law allowed for the establishment of market quotas for wheat, with a penalty for violation. Filburn, a farmer, sued Wickard, the secretary of agriculture, to enjoin enforcement of the penalty, arguing that free establishment of the quota and penalty were beyond congressional powers to regulate interstate commerce. The Court ruled against Filburn stating that Congress had the power to regulate homegrown wheat since it impacts wheat production and sales in interstate commerce.

Williams v. Illinois,
399 U.S. 235 (1970)
[68–69]
Williams was convicted of petty theft and sentenced to one year in prison and payment of a fine. State law mandated that if the fine was unpaid by the end of the prison term, the individual would have to work off the fine in prison. Williams did not pay the fine and argued that his indigence prevented him from paying it. He challenged on equal-protection grounds. The Supreme Court found in favor of Williams.

Williams v. North Carolina,
317 U.S. 287 (1942)
[34]
Petitioners were convicted of bigamy. The question before the Court involved a divorce decree in one state that was not recognized in another state. Petitioners challenged on constitutional grounds. The Supreme Court reversed the convictions and remanded the case for further proceedings.

Williams v. North Carolina,
325 U.S. 226 (1945)
[197, 238]
Man and woman, married to others, left North Carolina for Nevada. They obtained divorces and then married each other. They returned to North Carolina and were subsequently arrested and convicted of bigamy. The Supreme Court upheld the conviction.

Williams v. Rhodes,
393 U.S. 23 (1968)
[89]
State law established requirements for a new political party seeking a position on the ballot. Appellants challenged the election law as a violation of the Equal Protection Clause. The district court held the laws were unconstitutional and allowed the parties write-in space on the ballot. They appealed, wanting more than this level of relief. The Supreme Court granted relief to one appellant and denied it to the other.

Williamson v. Lee Optical of Oklahoma,
Inc.,
348 U.S. 483 (1955)
[117]
State law regulated the activities of licensed and unlicensed optometrists and ophthalmologists. The law was challenged as a violation of the Due Process and Equal Protection Clauses. The Supreme Court found no constitutional infirmities in the law.

Winters v. New York,
333 U.S. 507 (1948)
[134]
Appellant was convicted of possession with the intent to sell magazines with vio-

lent, graphic, and crime-related content. He challenged the state law as a violation of free speech and free press. The Supreme Court upheld the state law and conviction.

Wisconsin v. Constantineau,
400 U.S. 433 (1971)
[177]
Police chief had posted in the city's retail liquor stores notification that the sale or gift of alcohol to appellee, a resident of the city, was forbidden for one year. State law designed to protect citizens from excessive drinking problems authorized the posting. Appellee challenged on due-process grounds. The Supreme Court affirmed the lower-court ruling that the law was unconstitutional.

Wisconsin v. Mitchell,
508 U.S. 476 (1993)
[221]
Respondent was convicted of aggravated battery. His sentence was expanded, pursuant to state law, because he selected his victim on account of race. The state supreme court found the law a violation of the First Amendment. The Supreme Court reversed and upheld the enhanced sentence.

Wisconsin v. Yoder,
406 U.S. 205 (1972)
[160–161]
Respondents, observers of the Amish religion, were convicted of violating the state's compulsory school-attendance law. The law required children to attend school until age sixteen. Respondents removed their children from school after they completed the eighth grade. Respondents challenged on the Free Exer-

cise Clause of the First Amendment. The Supreme Court affirmed the decision for the respondents.

Witherspoon v. Illinois,
391 U.S. 510 (1968)
[207]
Petitioner was convicted of murder and sentenced to death. State law allowed for the dismissal of prospective jurors who expressed problems with the death penalty. Petitioner asserted that the resulting jury had a predisposition to impose the death penalty. The Supreme Court reversed the sentence.

Woods v. Cloyd W. Miller Co.,
333 U.S. 138 (1948)
[231]
The case involved the constitutionality of federal rent-control laws. The Supreme Court found no constitutional violations.

Wooley v. Maynard,
430 U.S. 705 (1977)
[161]
State law required noncommercial cars to bear the license plate embossed with the state motto "Live Free or Die." Appellees found the motto repugnant to their religious beliefs and covered it up. They were subsequently convicted of misdemeanors. The Supreme Court affirmed the convictions.

World-wide Volkswagen Corporation v. Woodson,
444 U.S. 286 (1980)
[244]
Respondents purchased a car in New York and were driving through Oklahoma when they were involved in an accident in which they sustained personal injuries. They sued the New York auto dealer and wholesaler in the Oklahoma state court. Petitioners challenged the jurisdiction of the state court, arguing on due-process grounds. The Supreme Court concluded that the state court did not have *in personam* jurisdiction over the petitioners.

Wright v. Rockefeller,
376 U.S. 52 (1964)
[88]
Appellants challenged the state's congressional-apportionment statute, arguing that its irregularly shaped districts were drawn for racial consideration. They asserted that such practices violated the Fourteenth Amendment (due process and equal protection) and the Fifteenth Amendment. The Supreme Court affirmed the lower-court finding that there were no constitutional violations.

Wright v. United States,
302 U.S. 583 (1938)
[32]
The question before the Court was whether a specific bill met the constitutional requirements (Presentment Clause and the pocket veto) that enabled it to become a law. The Supreme Court affirmed the lower-court opinion that the bill was not a law.

Yick Wo v. Hopkins,
118 U.S. 356 (1886)
[80]
Petitioner was convicted of violating the city's laundry-business ordinance. He challenged the law as arbitrary and dis-

criminatory. The Supreme Court ordered the release of the petitioner.

Young v. American Mini Theaters, Inc., 427 U.S. 50 (1976)
[145]
The city ordinance restricted the location of adult movie theaters. Respondents, operators of adult movie theaters, challenged the constitutionality of the ordinance. The Court of Appeals found the law constituted prior restraint and held it unconstitutional under the Equal Protection Clause. The Supreme Court reversed.

Young v. United States, 97 U.S. 39 (1877)
[226]
The case involved the seizure of ships involved in the running of a blockade during the Civil War. It also involved the presidential pardon of those giving aid and comfort to the enemies of the United States. The Supreme Court affirmed the decision against Young.

Youngstown Sheet & Tube Company v. Sawyer, 343 U.S. 579 (1952)
[66, 232]
The president issued an executive order directing the secretary of commerce to seize and operate most of the nation's steel mills. The secretary executed the order and the steel companies challenged the authority of the president. The Supreme Court invalidated the executive order as a violation of the presidential powers enumerated in Article II of the Constitution.

Zemel v. Rusk, 381 U.S. 1 (1965)
[136]
Appellant's application to travel to Cuba was denied. He challenged the authority of the secretary of state to deny him the right to travel. The Supreme Court affirmed the lower-court decision to grant appellee's motion for summary judgment.

Zobrest v. Catalina Foothills School District, 509 U.S. 1 (1993)
[165–166]
Petitioners, a deaf child and his parents, challenged the decision by respondent to deny a sign-language interpreter to accompany the child to his parochial high school. They argued that federal law and the Free Exercise Clause required Catalina to provide the interpreter. The district court granted respondent's motion for summary judgment. The Supreme Court reversed the lower court and decided that the Establishment Clause did not impose such restrictions.

Zorach v. Clauson, 343 U.S. 306 (1952)
[155–156]
State law allowed public schools to dismiss students early in order for them to attend religious centers for religious instruction or devotional exercises. Appellants challenged the "release time" as violating the Establishment Clause. The Supreme Court found no constitutional violations in the state law.

Appendix C

Table of Justices and Decisions by Justices

Appointed by President George Washington
1. James Wilson (Associate: 1789–1798. Died)
2. John Jay (Chief [1st]: 1789–1795. Resigned)
3. William Cushing (Associate: 1790–1810. Died)
4. John Rutledge (Associate: 1790–1791. Resigned)
5. John Blair (Associate: 1790–1795. Resigned)
6. James Iredell (Associate: 1790–1799. Died) [22, 54]
7. Thomas Johnson (Associate: 1792–1793. Resigned)
8. William Paterson (Associate: 1793–1806. Died)
9. John Rutledge (Chief [2nd]: 1795–1795. Unconfirmed)
10. Samuel Chase (Associate: 1796–1811. Died) [3, 10]
11. Oliver Ellsworth (Chief [3rd]: 1796–1800. Resigned)

Appointed by President John Adams
12. Bushrod Washington (Associate: 1799–1829. Died) [4, 23]
13. Alfred Moore (Associate: 1800–1804. Resigned)
14. John Marshall (Chief [4th]: 1801–1835. Died) [3, 4, 22, 23, 54, 55, 56, 57, 75, 76, 101, 224]

Appointed by President Thomas Jefferson
15. William Johnson (Associate: 1804–1834. Died) [3, 757, 76, 167, 235]
16. Henry Brockholst Livingston (Associate: 1807–1823. Died)
17. Thomas Todd (Associate: 1807–1826. Died)

Appointed by President James Madison
18. Gabriel Duvall (Associate: 1811–1835. Resigned)
19. Joseph Story (Associate: 1812–1845. Died) [17, 23, 54, 55, 167, 224]

Appointed by President James Monroe
20. Smith Thompson (Associate: 1823–1843. Died) [17]

Appointed by President John Quincy Adams
21. Robert Trimble (Associate: 1826–1828. Died)

Appointed by President Andrew Jackson
22. John McLean (Associate: 1830–1861. Died) [76]
23. Henry Baldwin (Associate: 1830–1844. Died) [23, 24, 57]
24. James Moore Wayne (Associate: 1835–1867. Died)
25. Roger Brooke Taney (Chief [5th]: 1836–1864. Died) [24, 25, 58, 76, 102, 225]
26. Philip Pendleton Barbour (Associate: 1836–1841. Died) [57]

Appointed by President Martin Van Buren
27. John Catron (Associate: 1837–1865. Died) [4]
28. John McKinley (Associate: 1838–1852. Died)
29. Peter Vivian Daniel (Associate: 1842–1860. Died) [25, 167]

Appointed by President John Tyler
30. Samuel Nelson (Associate: 1845–1872. Retired) [4, 226]

Appointed by President James K. Polk
31. Levi Woodbury (Associate: 1845–1851. Died) [25]
32. Robert Cooper Grier (Associate: 1846–1870. Retired) [167, 226]

Appointed by President Millard Fillmore
33. Benjamin Robbins Curtis (Associate: 1851–1857. Resigned) [58, 76, 102, 113]

Appointed by President Franklin Pierce
34. John Archibald Campbell (Associate: 1853–1861. Resigned) [77]

Appointed by President James Buchanan
35. Nathan Clifford (Associate: 1858–1881. Died) [26, 59]

Appointed by President Abraham Lincoln

36. Noah Haynes Swayne (Associate: 1862–1881. Retired) [5, 79]
37. Samuel Freeman Miller (Associate: 1862–1890. Died) [27, 79, 80, 152, 167, 226, 227, 235]
38. David Davis (Associate: 1862–1877. Resigned) [59, 77]
39. Stephen Johnson Field (Associate: 1863–1897. Retired) [5, 6, 27, 60, 61, 78, 103, 167, 168, 226, 236]
40. Salmon Portland Chase (Chief [6th]: 1864–1873. Died) [25, 26, 78, 102]

Appointed by President Ulysses S. Grant

41. William Strong (Associate: 1870–1880. Retired) [26, 77]
42. Joseph P. Bradley (Associate: 1870–1892. Died) [5, 60, 77, 78, 80, 168, 169]
43. Ward Hunt (Associate: 1873–1882. Disabled) [103]
44. Morrison Remick Waite (Chief [7th]: 1874–1888. Died) [5, 79, 152, 226]

Appointed by President Rutherford B. Hayes

45. John Marshall Harlan (Associate: 1877–1911. Died) [6, 26, 28, 62, 79, 80, 114]
46. William Burnham Woods (Associate: 1881–1887. Died)

Appointed by President James A. Garfield

47. Stanley Matthews (Associate: 1881–1889. Died) [80, 113]

Appointed by President Chester A. Arthur

48. Horace Gray (Associate: 1882–1902. Died) [61, 227, 236]
49. Samuel Blatchford (Associate: 1882–1893. Died)

Appointed by President Grover Cleveland

50. Lucius Quintus C. Lamar (Associate: 1888–1893. Died) [28]
51. Melville Weston Fuller (Chief [8th]: 1888–1910. Died)

Appointed by President Benjamin Harrison

52. David Josiah Brewer (Associate: 1890–1910. Died) [6, 61, 114, 236]
53. Henry Billings Brown (Associate: 1891–1906. Retired) [103, 113, 169]
54. George Shiras, Jr. (Associate: 1892–1903. Retired)
55. Howell Edmunds Jackson (Associate: 1893–1895 Died)

Appointed by President Grover Cleveland

56. Edward Douglass White[a] (Associate: 1894–1910. Elevated)
57. Rufus Wheeler Peckham (Associate: 1896–1909. Died) [81]

Appointed by President William McKinley

58. Joseph McKenna (Associate: 1898–1925. Retired)

Appointed by President Theodore Roosevelt

59. Oliver Wendell Holmes, Jr. (Associate: 1902–1932. Retired) [6, 7, 27, 28, 29, 30, 62, 63, 81, 104, 114, 115, 129, 130, 170, 171, 190, 236]
60. William Rufus Day (Associate: 1903–1922. Retired) [115, 170, 190]
61. William Henry Moody (Associate: 1906–1910. Disabled) [28]

Appointed by President William Howard Taft

62. Horace Harmon Lurton (Associate: 1910–1914. Died) [104]
63. Charles Evans Hughes (Associate: 1910–1916. Resigned) [170]
    [a]Edward Douglass White (Chief [9th]: 1910–1921. Died) [227]
64. Willis Van Devanter (Associate: 1911–1937. Retired) [6]
65. Joseph Rucker Lamar (Associate: 1911–1916. Died)
66. Mahlon Pitney (Associate: 1912–1922. Disabled) [114, 129]

Appointed by President Woodrow Wilson

67. James Clark McReynolds (Associate: 1914–1941. Retired) [170, 171]
68. Louis Dembritz Brandeis (Associate: 1916–1939. Retired) [30, 31, 63, 82, 105, 130, 131, 190, 237]
69. John Hessin Clarke (Associate: 1916–1922. Resigned)

Appointed by President Warren G. Harding

70. William Howard Taft (Chief [10th]: 1921–1930. Retired) [17, 29, 81]
71. George Sutherland (Associate: 1922–1938. Retired) [17, 30, 31, 63, 81, 104, 171, 172, 191, 192, 237]
72. Pierce Butler (Associate: 1923–1939. Died) [7]
73. Edward Terry Sanford (Associate: 1923–1930. Died)

Appointed by President Calvin Coolidge

74. Harlan Fiske Stone[b] (Associate: 1925–1941. Elevated) [7, 8, 31, 32, 64, 83, 172, 190]

Appointed by President Herbert Hoover

75. Charles Evans Hughes (Chief [11th]: 1930–1941. Retired) [7, 31, 32, 63, 82, 115, 131, 172, 191]
76. Owen Josepheus Roberts (Associate: 1930–1945. Resigned) [30, 34, 84, 105, 131, 132, 152, 153, 191, 192]
77. Benjamin Nathan Cardozo (Associate: 1932–1938. Died) [63, 82, 83, 105, 191, 192]

Appointed by President Franklin Delano Roosevelt

78. Hugo Lafayette Black (Associate: 1937–1971. Retired) [32, 33, 35, 36, 41, 67, 68, 83, 84, 87, 89, 119, 133, 155, 156, 159, 173, 174, 176, 192, 193, 194, 195, 197, 199, 201, 202, 204, 205. 228, 237, 238, 240, 241]
79. Stanley Forman Reed (Associate: 1938–1957. Retired) [33, 63, 132, 134, 173, 193, 232]
80. Felix Frankfurter (Associate: 1939–1962. Retired) [8, 9, 10, 32, 33, 34, 35, 36, 37, 38, 39, 64, 65, 66, 67, 88, 105, 116, 132, 134, 152, 173, 174, 175, 193, 194, 197, 198, 199, 200, 201, 229, 232, 238, 239, 240]
81. William Orville Douglas (Associate: 1939–1975. Retired) [39, 41, 44, 64, 69, 70, 85, 86, 88, 89, 90, 105, 117, 118, 133, 135, 137, 138, 142, 154, 155, 157, 172, 174, 176, 177, 178, 179, 196, 199, 201, 205, 208, 210, 228, 230, 232, 238, 241, 243]
   [b]Harlan Fiske Stone (Chief [12th]: 1941–1946. Died) [35, 65, 84, 85, 193, 228, 230]
82. Frank Murphy (Associate: 1940–1949. Died) [18, 34, 85, 133, 172, 173, 196, 227, 229, 230, 238]
83. James Francis Byrnes (Associate: 1941–1942. Resigned)
84. Robert Houghwout Jackson (Associate: 1941–1954. Died) [9, 10, 18, 34, 35, 37, 38, 66, 85, 87, 115, 116, 133, 153, 155, 156, 194, 195, 198, 199, 200, 229, 230, 231, 232, 237, 239]
85. Wiley Blount Rutledge (Associate: 1943–1949. Died) [35, 65, 116, 133, 195, 199, 228, 237]

Appointed by President Harry S Truman

86. Harold Hitz Burton (Associate: 1945–1958. Retired) [197]
87. Frederick Moore Vinson (Chief [13th]: 1946–1953. Died)
88. Thomas Campbell Clark (Associate: 1949–1967. Retired) [40, 66, 67, 137, 158, 200, 202]
89. Sherman Minton (Associate: 1949–1956. Retired) [89]

Appointed by President Dwight D. Eisenhower

90. Earl Warren (Chief [14th]: 1953–1969. Retired) [11, 38, 42, 66, 87, 116, 117, 136, 137, 156, 175, 203, 207, 232, 239]
91. John Marshall Harlan (Associate: 1955–1971. Retired)
92. William Joseph Brennan, Jr. (Associate: 1956–1990. Retired) [12, 13, 19, 42, 43, 44, 48, 50, 67, 90, 98, 99, 119, 122, 124, 125, 136, 140, 145, 146, 147, 148, 158, 159, 161, 162, 180, 181, 184, 185, 206, 208, 218, 240]
93. Charles Evans Whittaker (Associate: 1957–1962. Disabled)
94. Potter Stewart (Associate: 1959–1981. Retired) [13, 18, 41, 43, 88, 106, 107, 118, 119, 123, 134, 125, 142, 144, 145, 157, 178, 182, 202, 204, 205, 207, 210, 211, 212, 213, 214, 232, 233]

Appointed by President John F. Kennedy

95. Byron Raymond White (Associate: 1962–1993. Retired) [12, 14, 15, 47, 48, 49, 50, 69, 70, 71, 90, 91, 93, 96, 119, 122, 123, 126, 141, 143, 144, 147, 161, 179, 183, 203, 204, 206, 207, 209, 214, 215, 218, 242, 244]
96. Arthur Joseph Goldberg (Associate: 1962–1965. Resigned) [203]

Appointed by President Lyndon Baines Johnson

97. Abe Fortas (Associate: 1965–1969. Resigned) [89, 106, 138, 139, 177, 204]
98. Thurgood Marshall (Associate: 1967–1991. Retired) [42, 45,k 49, 71, 94, 95, 121, 123, 124, 139, 179, 182, 208, 213]

Appointed by President Richard M. Nixon

99. Warren Earl Burger (Chief [15th]: 1969–1986. Retired) [19, 20, 43, 44, 47, 68, 71, 90, 95, 96, 109, 119, 120, 124, 126, 139, 140, 142, 146, 147, 160, 161, 163, 180, 209, 210, 214, 216, 233, 242]
100. Harry A. Blackmun (Associate: 1970–1994. Retired) [42, 44, 46, 51, 71, 96, 123, 141, 143, 181, 182, 183, 186, 211, 216, 220, 222, 243, 244, 245]
101. Lewis Franklin Powell, Jr. (Associate: 1972–1987. Retired) [13, 20, 42, 46, 50, 69, 91, 94, 109, 120, 124, 126, 144, 145, 146, 164, 178, 179, 181, 211, 212, 215, 217, 242]
102. William Hubbs Rehnquist[c] (Associate: 1972–1986. Elevated) [13, 20, 43, 44, 45, 46, 47, 71, 92, 93, 95, 96, 107, 108, 121, 122, 125, 161, 164, 181, 182, 213, 215, 244]

103. John Paul Stevens (Associate: 1975) [13, 19, 45, 53, 70, 98, 109, 111, 112, 121, 146, 149, 150, 162, 183, 187, 215, 216, 217, 219, 234, 245]

Appointed by President Ronald W. Reagan

104. Sandra Day O'Connor (Associate: 1981–) [15, 16, 47, 48, 51, 72, 99, 108, 109, 110, 126, 163, 186, 217, 223, 233, 244]
     cWilliam Hubbs Rehnquist (Chief [15th]: 1986) [111, 127, 148, 165, 187, 220, 221, 233, 246]
105. Antonin Scalia (Associate: 1986–) [16, 21, 52, 72, 97, 98, 100, 110, 126, 127, 128, 150, 165, 186, 188, 218, 220, 221, 222, 223, 245, 246, 247]
106. Anthony Kennedy (Associate: 1988–) [50, 51, 52, 72, 73, 99, 110, 112, 148, 149, 151, 184, 185, 186, 219, 247]

Appointed by President George Bush

107. David H. Souter (Associate: 1990–) [74, 112, 149, 187]
108. Clarence Thomas (Associate: 1991–) [73, 189, 247]

Appointed by President William J. Clinton

109. Ruth Bader Ginsburg (Associate: 1993–) [111]
110. Stephen G. Breyer (Associate: 1994–) [118, 246]

Presidents without nominations to the United States Supreme Court

William Harrison, ninth president
Zachary Taylor, tenth president
Andrew Johnson, seventeenth president
Gerald R. Ford, thirty-eighth president
James E. Carter, thirty-ninth president

Appendix D
Keyword Index

abolition, 168–169
abortion, 43, 46, 48, 49, 97, 109, 182–183, 244
absolutist approach, 161
abuse of office, 20
abuse of power, 98, 102
access to dwellings, 242
accountability
  electoral accountability, 43
  moral accountability, 208
  political accountability, 116
accusation, 202, 210
  public accusation, 210
accusatorial function, 213
accused, 138, 191–193, 196–197, 199, 202–203, 210, 215–216
A.C.L.U., 108
acquaintances, 86
activities
  illegal activities, 210
  interstate activities, 105
  local activities, 105
  political activities, 132
  activity, 170
    economic activity, 246
    expressive activity, 149
    governmental activity, 157
    illegal activity, 213
A.D.A., 53
adjudication, 35–36, 47–48, 148, 213
  adjudicatory body, 14
  constitutional adjudication, 49–50, 63–64, 67, 69, 174
administration
  administration of justice, 104
  administration of law, 30
  government administration, 144
  judicial administration, 26
  prison administration, 45
  welfare administration, 104
administrative agency, 9
  administrative agencies, 15, 18, 70
  administrative discretion, 228

administrative agency (continued)
  administrative law, 53, 65
  administrative proceeding, 14
administrators, 18
  school administrators, 248
admission, 103–104
adolescence, 53
adults, 16, 106
adversary system, 206
advertising, 142–143, 145–146, 150, 181, 244
  false advertising, 150
  political advertising, 150
advisory opinions, 32
advocacy, 139, 150
affirmation, 198
agencies, 89
agnostic, 156
alcohol abuse, 186
alien, 181
allegations, 193
alleged criminal transactions, 216
alleged offense, 201
allegiance, 232
almighty, 156
ambition, 77
amending process, 32, 66, 104, 106
amendment
  Civil War amendments, 181
  Eighth Amendment, 198, 202, 214–216, 218, 221–222
  Fifteenth Amendment, 68, 88, 95
  Fifth Amendment, 94, 208
  First Amendment, 16, 41, 43, 89, 93–94, 106–107, 111, 129–130, 133, 135–139, 141–151, 154–157, 160–163, 173, 177, 221, 233
    First Amendment limitations, 136
  Fourteenth Amendment, 6, 40, 41, 114–115, 117, 135, 171, 184–185, 196, 202
  Fourth Amendment, 111, 172, 179, 198, 204–205, 207, 208, 216–217, 220
  Nineteenth Amendment, 88

amendment *(continued)*
  Ninth Amendment, 210
  Seventeenth Amendment, 88
  Sixth Amendment, 193, 204
  Tenth Amendment, 64, 110, 210
  Thirteenth Amendment, 227
American experiment, 229
American flag, 98
American interests, 234
amplifiers, 135
amusement, 145
anarchy, 59, 82, 211
ancestry, 228
anonymity, 140, 150
antireligious, 156
antisocial deeds, 10, 208
appellate
  appellate judges, 53
  appellate process, 35, 40, 43
  appellate review, 43, 175
  appellate tribunals, 138
appointive power, 103
appointments, 70
apportionment, 67, 75
appropriations, 15
arbitrary action, 116
arbitrary and capricious, 180
arbitrary control, 6
arbitrary imposition, 118
arbitrary power, 63
arbitrary restraint, 170
armed forces, 234
arrest, 198, 201–202, 204, 207–208, 210
  arrestee, 220
  arrest warrant, 198
art, 145
Articles of Confederation, 92
Article I, 69
  Article I courts, 39
  Article I judges, 14
Article III, 45, 47
  Article III courts, 14, 47
  Article III judges, 39
assimilation, 161, 228
associations, 93, 160, 176
  free association, 135
  political association, 161
atheism, 161
  atheist, 13, 156
  atheistic, 156
attitudes, 142
attorney, 193, 236

attorney *(continued)*
  attorney–client confidentiality, 223
audience, 135, 144, 157
aural aggression, 134
authority, 201
  congressional authority, 4, 5, 7, 9, 10, 13, 21,
    38, 92, 103–104, 226
  constitutional authority, 12–13, 26, 29, 32,
    38–39, 42–44, 49, 70, 72–73, 81–82, 86,
    101, 103–104, 108, 110, 121, 123, 235, 244
  elective authority, 103
  executive authority, 232
  federal authority, 64
  governmental authority, 67, 81–83
  judicial authority, 3, 4, 6, 11–13, 22–23, 26–29,
    32–34, 36–40, 43–45, 47, 49, 50–51, 54–55,
    61, 65–67, 69, 86, 88, 90, 95–97, 99–100,
    103, 105–107, 118–119, 121–122, 127, 164,
    184–186, 210, 226, 231, 242
  legislative authority, 3–4, 6–7, 9–10, 23, 26–
    27, 61, 101, 186
  local authority, 50, 197
    local authorities 197
  presidential authority, 18, 21, 226
  public authority, 113, 204
    public authorities, 124
  scope of authority, 173
  sentencing authority, 219–220
  state authority, 102
  statutory authority, 32
  military authorities, 228
autocracy, 63
automobiles, 200, 244
autonomy, 71, 139
  personal autonomy, 111
  state autonomy, 27

badge of infamy, 180
bail, 50
ballot position, 89
ballots, 94, 103
banishment, 61
bankruptcy, 14, 47, 77
  bankruptcy courts, 14, 47
barbaric, 180
barbarism, 80
baseball, 243
behavior, 241
  suspicious behavior, 207, 219
  workplace behavior, 247
beliefs, 107, 130, 142, 155, 159, 161–162, 164,
  190

beliefs *(continued)*
  religious beliefs, 152, 233, 238
belligerence, 242
  belligerent, 230
    belligerent rights, 226
  belligerents, 226
benedictions, 165
benefits, 128
biases, 126
bible, 164
  bible reading, 48
bicameral, 6
bigamy, 152
Bill of Rights, 11, 39, 65, 68, 90, 119, 122, 132,
    150, 157, 164, 174, 176–177, 180, 184, 198,
    201, 234
birth, 241, 243
birth control, 183
black codes, 119
blameworthiness, 218
body politic, 96
boundaries, 225
breach of discipline, 214–215
broadcaster, 146
broadcasting, 137, 147
brutalities, 230
budget, 162
burden of proof, 195, 197, 209, 211
bureaucracy, 90
bureaucrat, 174
business, 108, 140, 222, 237, 243

cabinet officer, 18
Caesar, 156
campaign, 94, 144–145
  campaign contributions, 93
  campaign financing, 94
  campaign pledge, 52
candidacy, 143
candidates, 93, 94, 179
capacity, 84, 106
capital, 82
capital cases, 196
capital defendant, 218
capital punishment, 198, 207, 211, 213, 218,
    222
capital sentencing, 218
capture, 226
careers, 169
case law, 20, 90–91
case load, 35, 39, 40
case record, 36

cases, 28, 45
  capital cases, 196
  noncapital cases, 218
cases and controversies, 39, 47
caste, 62, 114
caveat emptor, 237
centripetal forces, 105
censorship, 131, 134–137, 139, 148, 151
census, 89
certiorari, 29
chain of events, 215
change, 83
chaplain, 162
  chaplains, 157
character, 17, 196, 199
  moral character, 191, 240
  political character, 172
chastity, 125
checkpoints, 219
checks and balances, 55, 63, 69, 71
chief executive, 17, 139, 224
chief magistrate, 17
children, 51, 89, 106, 124, 171, 182, 186, 204,
    216, 237, 240, 243, 248
  child abuse, 150
  childbearing, 183
  childbirth, 49
  child neglect, 186
  child rearing, 186
  minors, 144
  schoolchildren, 165
choice, 106, 182–183
Christianity, 80
Christmas, 163
church, 156
church–related colleges, 160
circumstantial evidence, 202
cities, 244
citizen, 77, 152, 171, 210, 232, 245
  citizenry 93, 140, 143
  citizens, 3, 47, 70, 74, 78–79, 82, 94, 96, 100,
    102, 104, 106, 108, 112, 114, 146, 220
  citizenship, 11, 58, 62, 76, 79, 113, 176, 181,
    187, 225, 232, 240
    second–class citizenship, 138
  dangerous citizens, 50
  native-born citizens, 168
  naturalized citizens, 168
  noncitizens, 181
civics, 94
civil government, 152
civil law, 118

civil liberties, 108, 172
  civil liberty, 172
civil life, 169
civil litigation, 194
civil rights, 55, 103, 114–115, 167, 173, 178, 247
civil society, 25
civil trials, 205
Civil War, 60, 226
  Civil War amendments, 181
civilian, 38, 43
civilization, 164, 181, 229, 236, 239
  ancient civilizations, 238
civilized behavior, 184
civilized nations, 224
civilized state, 201
class division, 62
classification, 63, 243
  classifications, 117
classifieds, 142
classroom, 53
  classrooms, 87
clear and present danger, 129, 131, 135
coercion, 83, 89, 124
college, 128, 160
  college students, 160
  colleges, 128
    church–related colleges, 160
color, 118
colored persons, 115
commander–in–chief, 38, 226, 231–232
commerce, 36, 78, 150, 243
  Commerce Clause, 13, 36, 85–86, 174
  commercial, 133
    commercial expression, 145
    commercial speech, 146, 150–151
    commercial transactions, 7
    commercial vendors 181
  commerciality, 96
  interstate commerce, 92, 246
common law, 21, 51, 55, 66, 171, 208, 220, 242, 245
common sense, 66–67, 247
common tribunal, 225
communication, 91, 132, 135, 140, 233
  communicative elements, 186
  congressional communication, 12
  peaceful communication, 146
  political communication, 93–94, 144
  presidential communications, 19, 20
  private communications, 19, 244
communities, 96
  community, 80, 84, 111, 120, 170, 214, 243

communities (continued)
    colonial community, 35, 225
    community interests, 170
  political communities, 226
  social community, 71
compact, 77, 101
  compacts, 104
comparative law, 215
comparative legal systems, 29
comparative religion, 164
compelling interest, 184
compelling needs, 143
compensation, 116, 244
compensatory damages, 112
competition, 83, 237
  market competition, 130
complex conditions, 7
compulsory–attendance, 161
compulsory exclusion, 228
compulsory school attendance, 240
compulsory treatment, 202
concepts
  novel concepts, 245
conduct, 16, 35, 38, 71, 73, 79, 83–84, 100, 118, 125, 133, 142, 145, 156, 175, 179, 187, 193, 197, 206, 247
  official conduct, 136
  prohibited conduct, 73
confession, 195, 199
  contessions, 199
confessor, 195, 199
confidence
  governmental confidence, 77, 82, 91, 147
  public confidence, 69
confidentiality, 19, 233
confinement, 124, 202
confiscation, 51
conformity, 126, 185
Congress, 3–6, 8–10, 12–14, 16–17, 30, 32, 42, 45, 47, 52, 74–75, 85, 88, 91, 98, 108–109, 113, 157, 159, 164, 176, 232
  congressional action, 8, 85
  congressional acts, 32
  congressional authority, 4–5, 7, 9–10, 13, 21, 38, 68, 92, 103–104, 108, 226
  congressional committees, 11
  congressional communication, 12
  congressional decision–making, 11
  congressional districts, 67, 89
  congressional expression, 10
  congressional intent, 7–11, 13, 18, 24, 26, 33, 38, 44–45, 47, 53, 81, 179–180, 228, 232

Congress *(continued)*
  congressional language, 160
  congressional limitations, 108, 129–130
  congressional motives, 11
  congressional objectives, 13
  congressional orders, 103
  congressional oversight, 20, 227
  congressional power, 5–6, 12–13, 20, 65–66,
      74, 92, 112, 185, 210
    congressional powers, 105, 129, 228
  congressional process, 12
  congressional record, 11
  congressional responsibilities, 232
  congressional silence, 33
  congressional will, 10, 33, 59
  member of Congress, 11, 12
conjecture, 148
conscience, 31, 34, 171, 238
consequences, 239
constituency, 6, 162
constitution, 3, 5, 9, 23–24, 31, 55–62, 64–69,
      71, 76, 79, 83, 108, 141
  color–blind constitution, 114, 125
  constitutional actions, 84
  constitutional adjudication, 43, 49–50, 63–64,
      67, 69, 174
  constitutional admissibility, 195
  constitutional ambiguity, 11
  constitutional analysis, 99
  constitutional authority, 12–13, 26, 29, 32,
      38–39, 42–44, 49, 70, 72–73, 81–82, 86,
      101, 104, 108, 110, 121, 123, 235, 244
  constitutional balance, 198
    constitutional balances, 105
  constitutional balancing, 43
  constitutional bans, 147
  constitutional boundaries, 68
  constitutional change, 61, 66
  constitutional command, 120
  constitutional confines, 23
  constitutional conflict, 8, 55, 57–58, 66
  constitutional construction, 4, 57–61, 172
  constitutional convention, 68
    state constitutional conventions, 60
  constitutional debate, 60, 66
  constitutional deficiencies, 222
  constitutional democracy, 51, 208
  constitutional design, 112
  constitutional development, 40
  constitutional deviations, 61
  constitutional discourse, 128
  constitutional doctrine, 66

constitution *(continued)*
  constitutional entitlement, 111, 182
  constitutional errors, 142, 204
  constitutional evolution, 61, 70
  constitutional expectations, 35
  constitutional freedoms, 34, 52
  constitutional government, 131
  constitutional growth, 66
  constitutional guarantee, 127
    constitutional guarantees, 6, 66, 70, 104,
        147, 204, 208, 214, 229
  constitutional history, 65, 71, 92, 102, 196,
      208
  constitutional imperatives, 245
  constitutional intent, 54, 64, 73
  constitutional interpretation, 25, 28, 30, 32,
      40, 42–43, 55–64, 66–67, 69, 71, 135, 141,
      159, 172, 219
  constitutional jurisprudence, 71, 221
  constitutional language, 57–58, 60, 64, 68, 90,
      123, 224
  constitutional law, 63, 65, 69, 109, 220
  constitutional legislation, 236
  constitutional legitimacy, 71, 99, 242
  constitutional limitations, 26, 28, 34, 40, 73,
      107, 109, 131–132, 148, 217, 222–223, 231,
      242
  constitutional mandate, 223
  constitutional manipulation, 221
  constitutional method, 191
  constitutional mission, 212
  constitutional obedience, 60
  constitutional organization, 84
  constitutional permission, 63
  constitutional philosophy, 118
  constitutional power, 24, 66, 117
    constitutional powers, 57, 60
  constitutional principle, 121, 127
    constitutional principles, 30, 40, 49, 66, 69,
        71, 184
    unconstitutional principles, 229
  constitutional processes, 113
  constitutional prohibitions, 73, 86, 221
  constitutional protection, 187, 193, 204, 240
    constitutional protections, 132, 135, 145,
        215
  constitutional provisions, 62, 64, 67, 112
  constitutional question, 82
    constitutional questions, 30, 43, 61, 63, 112
  constitutional regime, 187
  constitutional requirements, 36
  constitutional restraint, 106, 113

constitution *(continued)*
    constitutional restraints, 72, 95, 105
    constitutional restrictions, 59, 64, 75, 105
    constitutional right, 204
       constitutional rights, 11, 40, 43, 45, 65, 79,
          84, 97, 100, 104, 106, 111, 123, 127–129,
          137, 139–140, 173, 176–177, 179, 187–
          189, 192, 196, 202–203, 229
    constitutional rules, 70
    constitutional safeguards, 90, 107, 117
    constitutional self–preservation, 56
    constitutional silence, 85, 127
    constitutional speculation, 60
    constitutional spirit, 4
    constitutional stability, 87
    constitutional status, 112
    constitutional support, 77
    constitutional system, 41, 193
    constitutional theory, 6, 16, 54, 63, 71, 130, 242
    constitutional threats, 52
    constitutional value, 57, 72
       constitutional values, 107
    constitutional violation, 120–121
    constitutional uniformity, 56
    constitutionality, 7, 29–33, 35, 49, 54, 61, 63,
       65, 89, 104, 121, 126, 128, 159, 165
    constitutions, 170
       state constitutions, 76, 106, 168
consumer, 86
  consumers, 239
contempt, 13, 37, 77
  contempt of law, 82
contraception, 181
contract, 28, 171
  contracts, 77, 84, 114, 170, 178, 236, 245
  freedom of contract, 170
contributions, 180
controversy, 29
conventional thought, 87
conventions
  constitutional conventions, 68
  political conventions, 91
  state constitutional conventions, 60
conviction, 175, 191, 200–201, 204, 206
  convictions, 31, 22
  criminal convictions, 126
copyright, 93, 129
corporal punishment, 122, 214
corporations, 82
corruption, 80, 87
counsel, 20, 37, 44, 175, 191, 196, 202–203, 206,
  211

counsel *(continued)*
  defense counsel, 138, 203, 206
  independent counsel, 98
  legal counsel, 202
  right to counsel, 192, 203, 211
counter–majoritarianism, 111
courage, 50, 241
court, 25, 158
  court appearance, 203
  court of justice, 3, 11
  court of law, 210
  court practice, 35
  court proceedings, 134
  court staff, 138
  courtroom, 134, 137
    courtroom television, 203
  juvenile court system, 209
  courts, 5, 6, 24, 46
    Article I courts, 39
    Article III courts, 14, 47
    bankruptcy courts, 14, 47
    courts of justice, 56, 219
    criminal courts, 202
    family courts, 89
    federal courts, 3, 41, 48, 53, 91, 99, 112
    juvenile courts, 89, 204
    state courts, 48, 66, 112, 195
    trial courts, 138
credibility, 195
creed, 88, 118, 196
crime, 4, 42, 61, 68, 137, 191–194, 197–200,
  204–205, 207, 210, 212, 214, 216
  crime detection, 200
  crimes, 206, 231, 236
    intrastate crimes, 210
    sex crimes, 216
  elements of crime, 194, 221
  unrecognized crime, 230
  violent crime, 199
criminal, 149, 191, 199
  criminal case, 213
    criminal cases, 193
  criminal commission, 211
  criminal conviction, 126
  criminal courts, 202
  criminal defendants, 221
  criminal degree, 192
  criminal evidence, 220
  criminal guilt, 223
  criminal justice, 37, 136–137, 147, 211
  criminal law, 11, 195, 204, 208–209, 214,
    220, 223

criminal *(continued)*
  criminal laws, 141
  criminal offender, 211
  criminal offense, 107, 199, 202, 209
  criminal penalties, 193
  criminal procedure, 195–197, 229
  criminal proceeding, 217, 230, 232
  criminal prosecution, 190, 223
  criminal sanctions, 199
  criminal speech, 139
  criminal trial, 37, 134, 138, 203, 206, 213, 219
    criminal trials, 205
  criminals, 207, 215, 219, 234
criminality, 118, 145, 155, 161, 177, 180, 208, 211
criminology, 195
crisis, 52
critics, 136
criticism, 39, 44, 46, 49, 140, 147, 165
  judicial criticism, 33, 41
cross examination, 192–193, 206
cruel and unusual punishment, 198, 202, 215, 221
culpable, 215
  culpable defendant, 213
cults, 160
cultural institution, 238
culture, 121, 229, 247
  contemporary culture, 239
currency, 78, 161
current affairs, 133
curriculum, 41, 94, 107
custody, 78, 161
custom, 77, 106
  customs, 29, 86

damages, 122
  compensatory damages, 112
  monetary damages, 112
dance, 16, 186
  dancing, 148
    performance dancing, 149
danger, 177, 228–229, 239
  imminent danger, 131
death, 99, 187, 215
  death penalty, 187, 195, 198, 207, 211, 214, 216, 218, 222
  random death, 215
  right to die, 187
debate, 14, 90, 136
  public debate, 149
debt, 77

debt *(continued)*
  debt of gratitude, 235
  debtors, 77
decency, 96, 230
deception, 237
Declaration of Independence, 88
defamation, 180
defamatory, 149
defendant, 13, 137, 147, 191, 194, 196, 209–210, 213, 216, 218–219
  capital defendant, 218
  culpable defendant, 213
  defendants, 202
    criminal defendants, 221
defense, 191, 193, 196, 202
  defense counsel, 138, 203, 206
  defense tactic, 211
  legal defense, 213
definitions, 58, 237, 247
  legal definitions, 9
degenerate offspring, 171
deliberative process, 131, 134
delinquency, 205
delegated powers, 59
delegation, 7, 11–12, 61, 66, 68, 70, 80
democracy, 6, 36, 54, 69, 84, 90, 94, 96, 128, 131, 134, 162, 176, 186, 194
  constitutional democracy, 51, 208
  laboratories of democracy, 105
  representative democracy, 43, 80, 99
democratic
  democratic experimentation, 75
  democratic institutions, 91, 132
  democratic majority, 127
  democratic principles, 128
  democratic process, 99, 219
  democratic republic, 181
  democratic society, 173, 222, 240
  democratic system, 31, 100
dependency, 241
deportation, 229–230, 232
deprivation, 178
  deprivations, 123
desecration, 92–93, 98, 179, 185
desegregation, 51, 119–120, 128
despot, 174, 199
  despotism, 59, 61, 173, 194
    judicial despotism, 26
detained, 208
detention, 228–229
deterrence, 125, 200, 217, 222
Dickens, (Charles), 89

dictatorship, 130, 193
dignity, 37, 140, 180, 185, 194
  human dignity, 173, 204
diplomacy, 20, 227, 233–234
  diplomatic, 19
disapproval, 224
discipline, 146
discourse
  national discourse, 148
  political discourse, 148
  social discourse, 145, 148
discretion, 174, 240
discrimination, 62, 84, 95, 102, 115–116, 118–
    121, 123–128, 181, 185, 243
  historical discrimination, 124
  invidious discrimination, 118
  private discrimination, 185
  racial discrimination, 119, 229
  statutory discrimination, 117
discriminatory intent, 123
discussion, 238
  political discussion, 131
disease, 202
disobedience, 146
dispute resolution, 53
disputes, 135
dissension, 146
dissent, 150, 242
  political dissent, 179
distribution, 140
districting, 65
diversity, 121, 124, 126, 156, 161
divine ordinance, 169
divinity of Christ, 155
divorce, 107, 178, 238
doctors, 109
doctrine, 27
  doctrines, 33
    judicial doctrines, 33
    religious doctrines, 155
documents, 141
  religious documents, 165
dogma, 152
  dogmatism, 87
domestic peace, 177
domestic relations, 80, 96, 107, 167
domestic security, 42, 178
domicile, 107
double jeopardy, 201
dress codes, 233
driving, 200
drug, 212

drug (continued)
  drug testing, 98, 184
  drug use, 98
  drugs, 186
    illegal drugs, 184
    war on drugs, 98
due process, 38–40, 42, 68, 90, 98, 105, 113–114,
    116–119, 123–124, 126–127, 138, 180, 182,
    184, 187, 229
  Due Process Clause, 49, 122–123, 174
  procedural due process, 122
  substantive due process, 123
duties, 86
  duty, 11, 98, 207
    political duty, 131

eavesdroppers, 206
economic
  economic activity, 246
  economic conditions, 118
  economic disadvantage, 156
  economic ill, 242
  economic interest, 116
  economic impediment, 170
  economic objectives, 107
  economic policies, 105
  economic self–reliance, 112
  economic struggle, 232
  economic system, 86
  economic theory, 28
  economic welfare, 83
economy, 77–78
education, 41, 46, 51, 87, 94, 99, 107,
    111, 120–121, 124, 126, 128, 138, 159,
    161, 163–164, 166, 203, 217, 240–242,
    246
  higher education, 111, 126, 138, 160
  legal education, 115
  parochial education, 160
  postgraduate education, 160
  primary education, 160
  public education, 158
  secondary education, 160
  secular education, 160
educational experience, 203
educational tool, 203
Eighth Amendment, 198, 202, 214–216, 218,
    221, 222
election, 20
  elective authority, 103
  elective power, 103
  electoral accountability, 43

election *(continued)*
  electoral process, 31, 52, 80, 88–91, 93–95, 106, 118–119, 179–180
  electoral system, 87
  presidential elections, 87
electorate, 91
electric chair, 198
electrocution, 218
emanations, 176
emancipation, 102
embargoes, 86
emblem, 185
emergency, 228, 231
  emergency power, 75, 82
emotional impact, 148
emotionalism, 196
emotions, 135, 190
  retributive emotions, 230
empiricism, 116
employees, 86
  public employees, 98
employers, 186
employment, 86, 169, 239, 247
  employment law, 247
ends/means, 15, 51, 63–64, 75, 92, 99, 110, 236, 245, 248
enemy, 230
  enemy nation, 230
enforcement, 11
  enforcement priorities, 217
English, 243
entertainment, 134, 203
entrapped, 212
enumerated rights, 184, 187
equal opportunity, 51
equal protection, 42, 44, 94, 111, 118–128, 211, 243
  Equal Protection Clause, 106, 128
equal representation, 67
equal rights, 114–115, 170
equality, 62, 79, 88, 98, 114, 123, 240
  gender equality, 114, 126, 169
  political equality, 88
  racial equality, 114
  social equality, 114, 170
equity, 238
error
  constitutional errors, 142, 204
  grammatical errors, 149
  human error, 214
  judicial errors, 37
  legal error, 192

error *(continued)*
  police error, 210
  procedural errors, 193
espionage, 190
establishment, 152
  Establishment Clause, 157–166
ethical, 238
ethics, 155, 164, 241
ethnic groups, 243
evidence, 142, 186, 191, 193–194, 196–198, 200–201, 205–206, 210, 214–215, 217–218, 220–221, 223
  circumstantial evidence, 202
  criminal evidence, 220
  exculpatory evidence, 206
  mitigating evidence, 218
  physical evidence, 212
  rules of evidence, 246
  victim impact evidence, 220
evidentiary restrictions, 213
evil, 85
  ancient evils, 174
  human evils, 174
evolution, 159
exclusionary rule, 213, 215, 220
executive, 231
  chief executive, 17, 139
  executive authority, 232
  executive branch, 12, 17–19, 52, 70, 79, 84, 141, 227, 230
    executive branch officials, 17
  executive clemency, 5
  executive confidences, 231
  executive decisions, 231
  executive department, 12, 17
  executive discretion, 224
  executive limitations, 70, 232
  executive officials, 20
  executive order, 84
  executive power, 21
  executive privilege, 19, 20
  state executive, 214
exigencies, 59, 62
exile, 232
exoneration, 210
expenditures, 144
experience, 30, 36, 57, 62, 79, 96, 116, 167, 228
  human experience, 219
  life experiences, 211
experimental technique, 122
experimentation, 105, 239
expression, 93, 143, 146–149, 172

expression *(continued)*
  commercial expression, 145
  expression of opinion, 130
  free expression, 93, 138, 140
  freedom of expression, 130
  political expression, 94
expressive activity, 149
external affairs, 18
extortion, 87

facts, 133
factfinder, 209
fact–finding, 9, 197
factual assertions, 136
fair
  fair play, 196
  fair trial, 191, 202, 230
  fair warning, 191
fairness, 31, 90, 123–124, 180, 222, 238
  standards of fairness, 230
fair and impartial jury, 138
faith, 34, 130, 156, 162–163, 196
  faiths, 165
faithful discharge, 224
falsehoods, 131, 149, 192–193, 237
false advertising, 150
false speech 129, 136
families, 167
  family, 50, 80, 171, 178, 186, 232, 236, 243
    family courts, 89
    family law, 96, 107, 169
    family organization, 169
fates, 244
favoritism, 144
fear, 131, 174
federal
  federal authority, 64
  federal balance, 53
  federal courts, 3, 41, 48, 53, 91, 98, 112
  federal government, 70, 79, 103
  federal law, 110
  federal offense, 11
  federal power, 8, 16, 248
  federal rights, 53
  federal system, 105–106, 173, 220, 244
federalism, 5–6, 8, 15–16, 23, 27, 42, 50, 57, 66,
    68, 73–74, 80, 90, 95–96, 98, 101–103, 106,
    109–110, 117, 128, 161, 188, 197, 220, 246,
    248
fetus, 109, 244
fiduciary responsibility, 240
Fifteenth Amendment, 68, 88, 95

Fifth Amendment, 94, 208
fighting words, 150, 153
film viewing, 139
financial integrity, 112
financial resources, 182
financial system, 78
financial wherewithal, 175
firearms, 99, 184, 246
First Amendment, 16, 41, 43, 89, 93–94, 106–
    107, 111, 129–130, 132–133, 135–139, 141–
    151, 154–157, 160–163, 173, 177, 221, 233
  First Amendment limitations, 136
flag, 92–93, 179, 185
  American flag, 98
  flag burning, 177, 185
force
  excessive use of force, 221
  national force, 232
foreign affairs, 18–20, 141, 230–231, 234
foreign governments, 225
foreign powers, 225
foreseeability, 239
fortunes, 167
forum, 35
founders, 67, 86, 131
founding fathers, 164
Fourteenth Amendment, 6, 40–41, 107, 114–
    115, 117, 135, 171, 184–185, 196, 202
Fourth Amendment, 111, 172, 179, 198, 204–
    205, 207–208, 216 217, 220
framers, 22, 36 54, 56–58, 60–61, 64, 67–69, 71,
    73–74, 78, 88, 92, 95, 123, 129, 134, 158,
    177, 184, 223
fraud, 237
free access, 86
free assembly, 131, 138
free association, 135
free competition, 86
free exercise, 152
  Free Exercise Clause, 163
free expression, 93, 138–140
free government, 77, 231
free people, 28, 219, 227
free press, 41, 131–133, 141–143, 149, 173, 240
free religion, 133, 161
free society, 124, 209
free speech, 33, 41, 93, 107, 129–136, 138–139,
    148–149, 151, 177, 240
freedom, 74, 97, 100, 118, 122, 131, 152–153,
    167, 169, 171–172, 174–177, 179–180, 182,
    185, 189, 230
  freedom of contract, 170

freedom *(continued)*
  freedom of expression, 130
  freedom of movement, 189
  freedom of religion, 153, 155–156
  freedom of thought, 174
  freedoms, 90, 145, 229
    religious freedoms, 155
  personal freedom, 170
  religious freedom, 157
freeman, 169
freemen, 171
frisked, 208
frustration, 51
fundamental law, 78, 190
fundamental liberties, 184
  fundamental liberty, 182
fundamental principles, 3, 28
fundamental rights, 6, 123, 138
future, 56–57
  future generations, 72

gambling, 167
gangs, 192
  street gangs, 189
gang members, 100
gender, 111
  gender equality, 114, 126, 169
  gender rights, 125
generations, 61
Gettysburg Address, 88
God, 156–159, 164
gold, 77
good name, 177
gospel, 155
governance, 181
governing, 66
government, 30, 75, 109, 143, 163, 167, 193, 202
  civil government, 152
  constitutional government, 131
  dissolving government, 55
  federal government, 70, 79, 103
  free government, 77, 231
  government activities, 83
  government administration, 144
  government charter, 9
  government expansion, 83
  government instruments, 65
  government intrusion, 167, 183
  government officials, 82
  government operations, 144
  government proceedings, 144
  government services, 98

government *(continued)*
  limited government, 59
  local government, 95, 240
  moral government, 235
  national government, 18, 23, 64, 73–74, 81,
    93, 108, 110
  oppressive government, 223
  popular government, 131
  representative government, 12–13, 84, 100,
    147
  republican government, 74, 101
  self–government, 49, 59, 70, 76, 80, 87–88, 90,
    102, 208, 222
  state government, 108 240
governmental
  governmental action, 11, 124, 229
  governmental activity, 157
  governmental authority, 67, 82–83
  governmental awareness, 94
  governmental complexity, 88
  governmental confidence, 77, 82, 91, 147
  governmental costs, 154
  governmental decisionmaking, 188
  governmental ends, 148
  governmental entities, 181
  governmental function, 33
    governmental functions, 84
  governmental immunity, 74
  governmental institutions, 80, 228–229
  governmental intrusion, 81, 177–178, 180
  governmental lawlessness, 82
  governmental legitimacy, 67, 82
  governmental limitations, 26, 79, 133
  governmental mischief, 33
  governmental objective, 175
  governmental officials, 90
  governmental operations, 71
  governmental organization, 56
  governmental philosophy, 118
  governmental power, 18, 75, 79, 119, 223
    governmental powers, 56, 63
  governmental process, 52, 81, 87, 131
    governmental processes, 131
  governmental prohibitions, 154
  governmental regulations, 93, 139, 174
  governmental restraints, 140, 245
  governmental searches, 222
  governmental services, 91
  governmental stability, 87
  governmental theory, 79–80
graduations, 165
grammatical errors, 149

grand jury, 212–213
grievances, 44, 47, 96, 131
group bias, 216
group identity, 160, 181
group marriage, 238
groups, 176
guardians, 124
guidance counselor, 166
guilt, 190–191, 193, 197, 201–202, 206, 209,
    213–215, 219–220, 228, 236
  criminal guilt, 223
  moral guilt, 219
gun violence, 246

habeas corpus, 132
habits, 61, 167
happiness, 54, 70, 75
  pursuit of happiness, 171, 180
hardships, 229
harm, 218–220
  imminent harm, 149
hate, 131
hazards, 239
headnotes, 236
health, 83, 99, 111, 182, 236
health, and welfare, 186, 202
hearers, 238
hearing, 124
heresy, 152
heroes, 98
heritage, 139, 156, 158, 164–165, 187
highway, 200
  highways, 244
historical context, 67
historical discrimination, 124
historical events, 129
historical interest, 244
historical practice, 185
history, 19, 24–25, 29–30, 34, 36–37, 39, 44, 51,
    58, 60–64, 69, 72–73, 76, 80, 83, 93, 96, 98,
    106, 111, 113, 115, 118, 120, 132, 135,157–
    158, 164–165, 171, 173–174, 179, 181, 199,
    202, 208, 216, 222, 228, 230, 235, 238, 240,
    243
  constitutional history, 65, 71, 92, 102, 196,
      208
  judicial history, 90, 94, 103
  legal history, 113
  legislative history, 11, 38
  political history, 196
  statutory history, 125
Holmes (Oliver Wendell), 96

homosexuality, 187, 247
honesty, 147, 237
honor, 177, 240
hostile forces, 229
hostile resistance, 226
hostile workplace, 247
hostilities, 224
  hostility, 157
    racial hostility, 125
household, 139
  households, 238
housing, 242
House of Representatives, 67, 158
human affairs, 92
human body, 245
human dignity, 173, 204
human error, 214
human gestation, 43
human institutions, 56
human interaction, 245
human interest, 240
human life, 109–110, 187, 215
human motivations, 181
human rights, 173
human sacrifice, 152
human suffering, 219
human will, 200
humanity, 127, 218, 228
humility, 37
hunting, 123
husband, 236, 244

ideas, 10, 130, 135–136, 144–145, 150
  novel ideas, 105
ideology, 108
illegal activities, 210
  illegal activity, 213
illegal drugs, 184
illegitimacy, 241, 243
imbecility, 171
immigration, 133, 232
imminent, 139
  imminent danger, 131
  imminent harm, 149
immunity, 20–21, 112, 154, 170
  state immunity, 83
  tax immunity, 83
impartial, 191
impeach, 206
impeachment, 20
implied powers, 90, 106, 176
imprisonment, 199

in camera, 231
incarceration, 199
incitement, 129–131, 135, 139, 149, 153
income tax, 87, 162
Incompatibility Clause, 70
incompetence, 171
incorporation, 119, 184
independence, 27
independent agencies, 15
Indian race, 225–226
Indian tribes, 228
indictment, 191, 210
indigence, 46, 175
  indigency, 40, 213
  indigents, 211
indignities, 230
indignity, 201
individual, 188
  individual liberties, 228
  individual restraints, 245
  individual rights, 40, 221, 225
  individual security, 190
  private individual, 140
inducements, 89
industrial power, 85
industry, 243
infants, 243
inferences, 238
in forma pauperis, 40
information, 9, 14, 20, 91, 151
  information gathering, 136
  political information, 147
informers, 210
informing the public, 134
infringement, 171
inhumane, 215
injunction, 140
injury, 44
injustice, 77, 127, 138
inmates, 216
innocence, 191, 197, 201–202, 206, 212–213, 215
innocent, 219–220
  innocent bystander, 215
insurrection, 226
integration, 121, 124, 128
integrity, 4, 86, 177
intellectual abstraction, 172
intelligence, 231, 233
intent, 57, 221, 238, 247
interest groups, 88
internal affairs, 18
internal order, 216

internal security, 19, 42
international affairs, 176, 233
international controversy, 225
international law, 226, 230
international relations, 19
interpreter, 166
interrogation, 171, 201
interstate activities, 105
interstate commerce, 6, 92, 246
interstate revenues, 243
intolerance, 150, 156
instrumentalities, 7
intrusive act, 172
inventions, 239
investigations, 98, 212, 219
investigative function, 213
invocations, 164–165
involuntary servitude, 169, 227

jail, 199
  jail sentence, 211
Jeffersonian philosophy, 142
Jehovah's Witnesses, 153–154
journalism, 133, 149
journalists, 143
judge, 31, 134, 203
  judge–made law, 49
  judges, 6, 13–14, 21, 25, 27, 29, 33, 36–37, 47,
    54, 59, 66, 137, 173, 246
    appellate judges, 53
    Article I judges, 14
    Article III judges, 39
  judging, 31, 45
judgment, 24, 31, 167
  moral judgment, 211
judicial
  judicial abuse, 37
  judicial action, 124
  judicial activism, 36, 45–47, 96
  judicial adherence, 69
  judicial administration, 26, 35, 137
  judicial analysis, 109, 217
  judicial approval, 200
  judicial authority, 3–4, 6, 11–13, 22–23, 27–29,
    32–34, 36–40, 43–45, 47, 49–51, 54–55, 61,
    65–67, 69, 86, 88, 90, 95–97, 99–100, 103,
    105–107, 118–119, 121–122, 127, 164, 184–
    186, 210, 226, 231, 242
  judicial caseload, 44
  judicial cognizance, 227
  judicial competence, 30, 43
  judicial consciousness, 31

judicial *(continued)*
  judicial construction, 8, 52, 193, 229
  judicial corrections, 48
  judicial credibility, 94
  judicial criticism, 33, 41, 111
  judicial declarations, 33
  judicial decision making, 34, 37, 128
  judicial decisions, 236
  judicial decrees, 219
  judicial despotism, 26
  judicial discretion, 50, 51
  judicial doctrines, 33
  judicial duty, 22, 27
  judicial errors, 37
  judicial evaluation, 42
  judicial footnote, 66
  judicial forbearance, 41
  judicial formalism, 209
  judicial formula, 38, 118
    judicial formulas, 33, 89, 117, 120
  judicial forum, 44
  judicial function, 30, 32, 33, 34, 35, 36, 37, 39,
    40, 42, 44, 47
  judicial guidance, 198
  judicial history, 90, 94, 103
  judicial independence, 33, 36, 37, 50
  judicial insight, 45
  judicial interference, 42
  judicial intent, 53
  judicial interpretation, 45, 59, 118, 185
  judicial intervention, 40
  judicial history, 51
  judicial judgment, 100, 116, 145
    judicial judgments, 28
  judicial legislating, 38
  judicial legislation, 29, 86
  judicial legitimacy, 34, 36, 42, 44, 47, 49–51,
    62, 65, 67, 69, 72, 88, 95–96, 99, 105, 108–
    109, 118, 122–123, 127, 184, 220, 241
  judicial limitations, 18, 45, 68, 70, 105, 217,
    225–226, 230, 242
  judicial logic, 122
  judicial mind, 10
  judicial oath, 24, 39
  judicial officers, 214
  judicial opinions, 22, 29, 46, 66
  judicial order, 120
  judicial outcomes, 37
  judicial overreaching, 29
  judicial power, 23, 26–29, 31–32, 39, 41, 47,
    54, 70, 79, 86, 124
  judicial prayer, 164

judicial *(continued)*
  judicial predilection, 119
  judicial proceedings, 113
  judicial process, 24, 26–27, 30–38, 43, 45, 49,
    68, 83, 109, 137, 141, 197, 222
  judicial protection, 27
  judicial psychoanalyzing, 38
  judicial rationalization, 229
  judicial relief, 40
  judicial remedies, 46, 50–51, 65, 67, 71, 88, 96,
    107, 120, 128, 138, 242
    judicial remedy, 38, 40
  judicial responsibilities, 37, 42–43, 60
    judicial responsibility, 34, 69
  judicial restraint, 33, 36, 38, 44–45, 47, 69,
    105–107, 118
  judicial review, 4–5, 7–9, 12–13, 16, 22, 25–26,
    28, 30–31, 33, 36, 39, 42, 44–45, 47, 49–50,
    54–56, 64–65, 67–68, 71–72, 96, 104, 109,
    111, 117, 123, 125, 132, 159, 165, 217, 231–
    232, 236, 242
  judicial role, 23–24, 28–29
  judicial romanticism, 243
  judicial solutions, 238
  judicial standards, 120
  judicial supervision, 217
  judicial test, 38
    judicial tests, 195
  judicial trust, 223
  judicial will, 19, 184
  judicial wisdom, 41, 45, 119, 242
judiciary, 3, 11, 18, 29–31, 33, 42, 44, 55–56,
    122–123, 178, 191
  overburdened judiciary, 53
juries, 198, 214
jurisdiction, 3–4, 23, 26, 81
jurisprudence, 27, 47, 58, 81, 186, 201, 244
  constitutional jurisprudence, 71, 221
juristic person, 84
juror, 197, 203
  jurors, 138, 147, 218
jury, 84, 134, 137, 142, 148, 155, 190, 196, 207,
    210, 221, 223
  fair and impartial jury, 138
  jury duty, 35, 116
  right to jury, 132
justice, 22, 30, 44, 47, 50, 67–68, 78, 85, 104,
    113, 168, 191, 196–198, 206, 216, 219, 222,
    233
  administration of justice, 104
  courts of justice, 56, 219
  criminal justice, 37, 136–137, 147, 211

justice *(continued)*
  essential justice, 212
  injustice, 77, 127, 138
  juvenile justice, 205
  miscarriage of justice, 137
  natural justice, 28, 54
  obstruction of justice, 192
  public justice, 84
  vigilante justice, 211
justiciable case or controversy, 159
juvenile courts, 89, 204
juvenile court system, 209
juvenile legal system, 204
juvenile justice, 89, 205
juvenile proceedings, 216

knowledge, 87, 171
  legislative knowledge, 8

labor, 82, 169
laboratories of democracy, 105
laboratory, 246
laissez–faire, 112
landlord–tenant relationship, 242
language, 22, 24, 42, 58, 62–64, 243
  congressional language, 160
  constitutional language, 57–58, 60, 64, 68, 90,
    123, 224
  statutory language, 191
  treaty language, 227
law, 13, 24, 62, 170, 175, 189, 197
  administration of law, 30
  administrative law, 53, 65
  case law, 20, 90–91
  civil law, 118
  color of law, 196
  common law, 21, 51, 55, 66, 171, 208, 220,
    242, 245
  comparative law, 215
  constitutional law, 63, 65, 69, 109, 220
  controlling law, 86
  court of law, 210
  criminal law, 11, 195, 204, 208–209, 214, 220,
    223
  employment law, 247
  family law, 96, 107, 169
  federal law, 110
  fundamental law, 78, 190
  general law, 27, 31
  international law, 226, 230
  judge–made law, 49
  lawlessness, 79, 177, 208

law *(continued)*
  law of nations, 224
  laws, 77, 115
    criminal laws, 141
    state laws, 68, 111, 117, 122
    traffic laws, 200
    unconstitutional laws, 61
    unwise laws, 31
  martial law, 229
  municipal law, 6
  natural law, 74
  positive law, 71, 101
  reach of law, 126
  rule of law, 44, 67, 74, 82, 152, 168, 176, 211
  science of law, 191
  state law, 35, 118
  supreme law, 104
  tort law, 71
law enforcement, 42, 99, 192, 194, 198, 200,
    203, 206–208, 211, 217, 220, 223
  law enforcement officers, 138, 214, 217
lawmakers, 183
law schools, 247
law students, 115
lawyer, 194, 202–203, 213, 235
  lawyers, 108, 202, 244, 247
  zealous lawyers, 37
leaders, 76, 98
  leadership, 77
learning, 10
leaflets, 140
legal
  legal advice, 202
  legal assistance, 213
  legal bar, 194
  legal burdens, 243
  legal consistency, 34
  legal construction, 235
  legal counsel, 202
  legal defense, 213
  legal definitions, 9
  legal development, 245
  legal doctrines, 35
  legal education, 115
  legal error, 192
  legal essays, 32
  legal expenses, 213
  legal fees, 213
  legal fiction, 30
  legal flexibility, 43
  legal guidelines, 41
  legal history, 113

legal *(continued)*
  legal limitations, 33
  legal obligations, 178
  legal practice, 155
  legal precedents, 34
  legal principles, 28, 33, 35
  legal procedure, 209
    legal procedures, 61
  legal proceedings, 113
  legal process, 30
  legal profession, 235–236, 240–241
  legal purposes, 237
  legal reality, 70
  legal recognition, 236
  legal recourse, 50
  legal reform, 89
  legal reporter, 236
  legal responsibilities, 240
  legal rights, 192
  legal rules, 36
  legal status, 239
  legal system, 39, 73
    comparative legal system, 29
    juvenile legal system, 204
  legal tender, 77–78
  legal terminology, 237
  legal tradition, 10
  legal training, 202
legislation, 4, 7–9, 11, 30, 36, 44–45, 54, 58, 64,
    85, 97, 114, 156, 161, 170, 173, 176, 234, 245
  constitutional legislation, 236
  regulatory legislation, 8
  state legislation, 6, 104
legislative, 234
  legislative abuse, 5, 101
  legislative adherence, 69
  legislative authority, 3–4, 6–7, 9–10, 23, 26–
    27, 61, 101, 186
  legislative body, 6
  legislative branch, 70, 84, 195
  legislative conduct, 10
  legislative confidence, 10
  legislative courage, 10
  legislative decisions, 215
  legislative deliberation, 231
  legislative discretion, 7, 81
  legislative drafters, 16
  legislative duties, 10
  legislative experience, 7–8
  legislative flexibility, 16
  legislative function, 9, 242
  legislative good faith, 125
  legislative halls, 156–157

legislative history, 11, 13, 26, 38
legislative immunity, 10, 13
legislative information, 6
legislative intent, 3, 5–6, 8–9, 13–14, 16, 19,
    22–23, 27, 49, 52, 63–64, 95, 115, 117, 125,
    176
legislative investigations, 11
legislative judgment, 8–9, 143
legislative knowledge, 8
legislative legitimacy, 10
legislative limitations, 70
legislative policy, 9, 30, 206
legislative power, 5–7, 26, 39, 63, 67, 79, 86,
    88, 113, 125, 152, 162, 164
legislative practice, 63
legislative privilege, 12
legislative preferences, 132
legislative process, 6, 11–15, 42, 88, 90, 105
legislative purpose, 16, 118
legislative record, 13, 38
legislative representatives, 88
legislative responsibilities, 26
legislative review, 3
legislative self–management, 12
legislative structure, 106
legislative supervision, 170
legislative tasks, 12
legislative veto, 15, 68
legislative wisdom, 65
legislator, 13
  legislators, 10, 12, 16, 91, 97, 165, 222
legislature, 4, 6–7, 14–15, 89
  legislature motivation, 162
  legislatures, 3, 5, 26, 46, 51, 90, 245
  state legislature, 54
    state legislatures, 54, 65, 68, 86, 92, 101–
    102, 106, 128, 164
  super legislature, 86
lethal injection, 222
letter, 55
liability, 71
liberal construction, 25
liberation, 189
libertarian views, 34
liberties, 97–98, 101–102, 167, 172, 179
  civil liberties, 108, 172
  fundamental liberties, 184
  individual liberties, 228
  liberty, 23, 25–26, 28, 35, 50, 68, 71–73, 77, 82,
    90, 98, 113–114, 118, 122–123, 126, 131,
    137, 163, 169–175, 177, 179–183, 184–186,
    188, 194, 199, 201, 219, 229–230
    civil liberty, 172

liberty *(continued)*
    fundamental liberty, 182
  personal liberties, 178
license plates, 161
lies, 129
life, 71, 99, 111, 175
  civil life, 169
  human life, 109–110, 187, 215
  life experiences, 211
  potential life, 109, 182
  reverence for life, 211
lifetime tenure, 36
life sentence, 216
limited government, 59
Lincoln, (Abraham), 77, 88
line item veto, 52
liquor traffic, 239
listener, 146
literacy, 199
literature, 140
litigants, 108
litigation, 35, 39, 43, 116, 136
litigating, 194
littering, 132
loan sharking, 210
lobbying, 88
local activities, 105
local authorities, 197
  local authority, 50
local exhibition, 243
local government, 95, 240
local interests, 35
localities, 29
  locality, 58
Lochner, 112
logic, 29, 96
loitering, 189
lotteries, 167
loyalty, 60, 86–87, 228, 233, 235
lying, 195
lynch law, 211

magistrate, 201, 208
  magistrate's judgment, 198
mail, 139–140
majorities, 131
  majority, 6, 116, 119, 150
    majority power, 90, 105
    majority rights, 121
    majority rule, 41
malice, 149
malpractice, 109
man, 169

market competition, 130
marketplace, 145
markets, 86
marriage, 34, 80, 106–107, 171, 173, 178, 181,
    236, 238, 243–244
  group marriage, 238
  marital relationship, 178, 244
  remarriage, 178
martial law, 229
mass production, 239
mass society, 144
masters, 102
material falsification, 192
maxims, 24
  ancient maxims, 174
meaning, 238
media, 147
  news media, 144
Medicaid, 182
medical alternatives, 109
medical procedure, 109
  medical procedures, 182
medically necessary, 182
member of Congress, 11, 12
memories, 212
men, 125
  young men, 125
mental illness, 171
mental institutions, 124
mental state, 195
mentally competent, 99
mentally ill, 202
mercy, 213, 219
merits, 29
message, 185
miles per gallon, 244
military, 19, 38, 43, 146, 227,
    233
  military authorities, 228
  military commander, 233
  military discipline, 233
  military discretion, 229
  military emergency, 229
  military necessity, 229
  military officials, 233
  military order, 229
mind, 72
  state of mind, 191
minor offenses, 211
minor victims, 216
minorities, 95
  minority, 46
    minority group, 95

minorities *(continued)*
    minority interests, 125
    minority power, 90
    minority rights, 121
    persecuted minorities, 34
minors, 144, 181, 186, 216
miracles, 155
miscarriage of justice, 137
misconduct, 199, 201
  gross police misconduct, 214
misleading, 146
modern life, 172
monarchy, 55
monetary damages, 112
money, 144, 182
monogamy, 238
monuments, 92
moot issue, 43
moral, 46
  moral accountability, 208
  moral character, 191, 240
  moral choices, 126
  moral depravity, 215
  moral government, 235
  moral guilt, 219
  moral judgment, 211
  moral obligation, 118, 230
  morality, 33, 97, 107, 126, 155, 187,
     200, 236, 238, 241, 243, 245
  morals, 76, 167
morale, 146
  troop morale, 233
motion pictures, 41
motivation, 200
motive, 221
motor home, 218
municipal law, 6
municipalities, 133
murder, 213–215
  murderer, 214, 218
music, 148

national
  National Anthem, 158
  national defense, 19, 227–228,
    233
  national discourse, 148
  national emergencies, 132
    national emergency, 32
  national force, 232
  national government, 18, 23, 64,
    73–74, 81, 83, 108, 110

national *(continued)*
  national interest, 233
  national power, 85, 112
  national property, 92
  national safety, 141
  national security, 19
  national solidarity, 83
  national well–being, 83
nationhood, 93
nation–building, 62
nation–states, 84
Native Americans, 227, 230
naturalization, 133
natural law, 74
nature of man, 208, 211
necessary and proper, 92
  Necessary and Proper Clause, 4
neighborhoods, 115
neutrality, 155
neutral principles, 121
news, 129, 141
  news coverage, 147
  news media, 144
  newspaper, 142–143
    newspapers, 133, 141, 154
New Testament, 155
Nineteenth Amendment, 88
Ninth Amendment, 210
nonjusticiability, 67
nontheistic, 160
notoriety, 140
nudity, 16, 96, 144, 149, 186
nuisance, 135, 237

oath, 31, 192, 198, 236
  judicial oath, 24, 39
  oath of allegiance, 181
  oaths, 5, 156, 168
obedience, 77
obligation
  legal obligations, 178
obscene, 149, 153
  nonobscene speech, 150
obscenity, 41, 142, 144, 150, 240
obstruction of justice, 192
occupations, 170–171
offenders, 216
offense, 215
  offenses, 215
offensive, 146
  offensive speech, 145
officeholders, 161

officer, 17
  judicial officers, 214
  law enforcement officers, 138
  superior officers, 194
  police officer, 205
officials, 196, 198
  executive officials, 20
    executive branch officials, 17
  government officials, 82
    governmental officials, 90
  public official, 6, 84
    public officials, 17, 95, 116, 122
  school officials, 124, 138
  state officials, 122
  subordinate official, 84
official act, 180
official conduct, 136
oligarchy, 25, 36
openness, 90
opera, 46
opinion, 5, 44, 46, 51, 52
  expression of opinion, 130
  public opinion, 41, 52, 80, 88, 121
  opinions, 48, 81, 130
opportunities, 240
oppression, 4, 18, 98
order
  preservation of order, 214
  public order, 5
ordinance, 132
  ordinances, 155
organic institutions, 62
organism, 62
original intent, 25, 71
organizations, 176
orthodoxy, 241
outcasts, 210
outlaws, 168, 206
out-of-court conversations, 203
oversight, 43, 98, 144
  congressional oversight, 20, 227
overt act, 231
ownership, 173, 216, 226, 245

pamphleteer, 144
pamphleteering, 150
pamphlets, 140
pardon, 19
  pardons, 5
parens patriae, 124, 182
parent, 241
  parents, 124, 182, 186, 237, 242, 248

parents (continued)
  parental failure, 186
parole, 215
parties, 29
party primaries, 93
passion
  passions, 145
  undue passion, 196
patients, 109
patriotism, 4, 60, 172, 231, 241
peaceful communication, 146
peaceful world, 230
pedestrian, 173
penal code, 11, 23
penalties, 81, 209
  penalty, 219, 230
    death penalty, 187, 195, 198, 207, 211, 214,
      216, 218, 222
penumbra of uncertainty, 105
penumbras, 176, 184
people, 4–5, 7, 54, 73
peremptory challenges, 221
performance, 186
periodicals, 154
perjury, 192, 196, 199
perpetual, 57
  perpetual union, 103
personality, 46
personal activities, 132
personal freedom, 170
personal liberties, 178
personal rights, 48
personal security, 207
personal views, 28
persons, 24
philosophical convictions, 211
philosophy, 81, 85, 117, 119, 122, 186
  governmental philosophy, 118
  Jeffersonian philosophy, 142
  political philosophy, 83, 128
phrases, 62
physical evidence, 212
physical restraint, 169
plain duty, 31
plain meaning, 55, 60, 62, 71
plea, 206, 209
pleading, 193
Pledge of Allegiance, 158
police, 99, 137, 177, 189, 196, 199, 201–202, 204,
    206–208, 210–211, 213, 219–220
  gross police misconduct, 214
  police error, 210

police *(continued)*
  policeman, 205
  police methods, 198
  police officer, 205
  police surveillance, 177
  police testimony, 198
  state police, 199
police power, 6, 16, 81, 99, 114, 131–132,
    142, 150–151, 177, 179, 200
  police powers, 129
police state, 87
policies, 91
  policy, 58, 185
    legislative policy, 9, 30, 206
    policy goals, 128
    public policy, 8, 15, 26, 85, 87, 95,
        99, 105, 107, 128, 195, 228, 241, 246
    school policy, 53
  state policies, 106
political, 59, 80
  minor political parties, 94
  political abuse, 67
  political accountability, 116
  political activism, 165
  political advertising, 150
  political association, 161
  political attitudes, 94
  political beliefs, 108, 179–180
  political body, 103
  political branches, 43, 70, 234
  political character, 172
  political communications, 93–94, 144
  political communities, 226
  political consensus, 99
  political controversies, 25
  political conventions, 91
  political criticism, 93
  political debate, 93
  political decision, 95
    political decision making, 128
  political departments, 225–226, 231
  political dialogue, 142
  political discourse, 148
  political discussion, 131
  political dissent, 179
  political duties, 17
    political duty, 131
  political equality, 88
  political expression, 94
  political history, 196
  political ideas, 94
  political information, 147

political *(continued)*
  political institutions, 77
  political mischief, 88
  political participation, 93
  political parties, 89, 94, 180
    minor political parties, 94
  political philosophy, 12, 83, 128
  political preferences, 180
  political prejudice, 85
  political pressure, 87
    political pressures, 37
  political process, 32, 36, 40, 94, 96–97, 100,
    105, 109, 111, 165
  political propaganda, 144
  political questions, 97
  political reality, 70
  political recourse, 5
  political reform, 40
  political responsibilities, 152–153
    political responsibility, 19, 110
  political rights, 103, 167
  political society, 25, 153
  political speech, 128, 150
  political stability, 87
  political status, 102
  political subdivisions, 110
  political success, 109
  political support, 93
  political symbolism, 93
  political system, 22, 91, 140
  political theory, 6
  political truth, 3
    political truths, 131
politicians, 144
politics, 10, 46, 96, 98, 173
polity, 140, 181
polyandry, 238
polygamy, 80, 152, 238
polygyny, 238
polls, 5
poor women, 182
pornography, 41, 96, 137, 150
possession, 216
potential life, 109, 182
poverty, 44, 46, 118
power, 4, 7, 25, 64, 76–77, 80, 85, 174, 199, 201
  abuse of power, 98
  appointive power, 103
  arbitrary power, 63
  congressional power, 5–6, 12, 20, 65–66, 74,
    92, 112, 185, 210
  constitutional power, 23, 66, 117

power *(continued)*
  decentralized power, 85
  defined power, 79
  elective power, 103
  emergency power, 78, 82
  executive power, 21
  federal power, 8, 16, 248
  governmental power, 18, 75, 79, 119, 223
  industrial power, 85
  judicial power, 23, 26–29, 31–32, 39, 41, 47,
    54, 70, 79, 86, 124
  legislative power, 5–7, 26, 39, 63, 67, 79, 86,
    88, 113, 125, 152, 162, 164
  limited power, 79
  majority power, 90, 105
  minority power, 90
  national power, 85, 112
  political power, 85
  powers, 57, 61
    congressional powers, 105, 129, 228
    constitutional powers, 57, 60
    delegated powers, 59
    express powers, 90, 106
    governmental powers, 56, 63
    implied powers, 90, 106, 176
    reserved powers, 82
    state powers, 57, 104, 108
  presidential power, 66
  reserved power, 64, 73
  scope of power, 81
  state power, 8, 85, 104
  war power, 29, 231
practical rights, 170
practicality, 200
pray, 163
prayer, 48, 155–158, 162, 164
  judicial prayer, 164
  school prayer, 164
  voluntary prayer, 164
preaching, 154
precedent, 48, 66, 69, 71, 115, 123
  precedents, 39, 245
preferences, 125
  legislative preferences, 132
  racial preferences, 127
  social preferences, 111
pregnancy, 43, 109, 125, 182–183, 244
  teenage pregnancy, 125
prejudice, 114, 126, 193
  political prejudices, 85
  social prejudices, 170
presidency, 19, 20, 98

president, 17–18, 20, 168, 226, 231–232
presidential
  presidential advisors, 20
  presidential aides, 20, 21, 98
  presidential archives, 19
  presidential authority, 18, 21, 226
  presidential communications, 19, 20
  presidential competence, 18
  presidential elections, 87
  presidential limitations, 226
  presidential misconduct, 20
  presidential politics, 94
  presidential power, 66
  presidential resignation, 19
press, 20, 129–130, 137–138, 141, 143–145, 154,
  216
  free press, 41, 131–133, 141–143, 149, 173, 240
  responsible press, 141
pretrial publicity, 147
principle, 43, 56, 73, 238
  principled, 241
  principles, 22, 24, 29, 31, 43–44, 51, 54–55, 57,
    63, 71, 75, 78, 101–102, 104, 116, 190
    constitutional principles, 30, 40, 49, 66, 69,
      71, 184
    democratic principles, 128
    fundamental principles, 3, 28
    legal principles, 28, 33, 35
    neutral principles, 121
    principle of disproportionality, 216
    unconstitutional principles, 229
prior restraint, 131
prison, 169, 221
  prison administration, 45
prisoner, 196, 214, 216
privacy, 19–20, 71, 134, 139–140, 153, 167, 172–
  181, 184, 200, 205, 207, 216, 218
  invasion of privacy, 180
private activity, 181
private affair, 194
  private affairs, 171
private communications, 19, 244
private discrimination, 185
private enterprise, 213
private individual, 140
private interests, 93
private rights, 6, 130
private sector, 179, 183
private suit, 74
  private suits, 112
privileged class, 83
privileges, 79, 102, 104, 115, 122, 169, 171, 229

privileges and immunities, 123
  Privileges and Immunities Clause, 187
probable cause, 42, 184, 198, 201, 204–205,
    207–208, 217
probative value, 201
procedural errors, 193
procedural restrictions, 213
procedural rights, 116
procedural rules, 222
procedure, 35, 107, 173
  criminal procedure, 195–197, 229
  legal procedures, 61
  medical procedure, 109
    medical procedures, 182
process, 212
procreation, 171, 173
product, 145
profession, 155
progress, 54
promiscuity, 238
proof, 191, 206
  burden of proof, 195, 197, 209, 211
  standard of proof, 209
propaganda, 134
  political propaganda, 144
property, 24–25, 28, 51, 55, 71, 93, 101, 173–
    174, 216, 226, 244–245
  property rights, 84, 114–116, 119, 122, 178
  property tax, 91
  real property, 242
prosecuted, 212
prosecution, 11, 44, 191, 194, 197–198, 202, 206,
    209, 211–213, 219, 236
  public prosecution, 200
  prosecutions, 168
prosecutor, 203
prosecutorial decisions, 217
prosecutorial discretion, 197
prosecutorial effectiveness, 217
prosecutors, 137, 206
proselyte, 153
prosperity, 83
protection, 204
  state protection, 125
protest, 177
  protests, 138
proximity, 129
prurient interest, 240
public, 203
  informing the public, 134
  public accusation, 210
  public attention, 147

public (continued)
  public authorities, 124
    public authority, 113, 204
  public benefit, 173
  public buildings, 144
  public comprehension, 52
  public concern, 82, 240
  public confidence, 69
  public convenience, 132
  public debate, 149
  public discussion, 131, 140
  public education, 158
  public employees, 98
  public excitement, 193
  public expectations, 44, 104
  public finance, 82, 91, 119, 158
    public financing, 15, 93, 109, 120, 128
  public function, 173
  public funding, 107, 164, 240
  public funds, 69
  public good, 63, 97, 113
  public institution, 47
  public interest, 29, 65, 133, 140, 179–180, 184,
      203, 236
  public issues, 90, 136
  public justice, 84
  public official, 84
    public officials, 6, 17, 95, 116, 122, 163
  public opinion, 10, 24–25, 27, 33, 41, 52, 80,
      88, 121
  public order, 5, 172
  public parks, 119
  public places, 186
  public policies, 7
    public policy, 8, 14–15, 26, 85, 87, 95, 99,
        105, 107, 128, 195, 228, 241, 246
  public pressure, 148
  public prosecution, 200
  public relations, 98–99
  public responsibilities, 240
  public revenue, 87
  public rituals, 156
  public school, 164–165, 215
    public schools, 41, 48, 94, 121, 157, 165
  public school teacher, 157
    public school teachers, 171
  public sentiment, 25, 235
  public trial, 134
  public use, 244
  public welfare, 81, 84, 86, 104–105, 107, 135,
      171, 173
  public's interest, 202

publication, 141, 145
publicity, 135
  pretrial publicity, 147
publisher, 134, 143
  publishers, 154
publishing, 130
pursuit of happiness, 171, 180
punishment, 4–5, 11, 37, 61, 81, 103, 118, 125–
    126, 159, 167, 190, 193, 198, 201, 205, 211,
    213–215, 218, 226, 232
  corporal punishment, 122, 214
  cruel and unusual punishment, 198, 202,
    215, 221
purse, 78

qualifications, 168
  voter qualifications, 119
quarantine, 202
quasi–judicial, 18, 39
quasi–legislative, 39
questioning, 208

race, 25, 60–62, 76, 79, 84, 88, 102, 114–115,
    118–119, 121, 123, 125, 127, 168, 170, 173,
    179, 186, 196, 216, 228, 236
  Indian race, 225–226
  race relations, 221
  white race, 226
racial
  racial composition, 120
  racial discrimination, 119, 229
  racial equality, 114
  racial hostility, 125
  racial indifference, 125
  racial instincts, 114
  racial preferences, 127
  racial segregation, 120
racism, 123
rape, 215
  statutory rape, 125
rational basis, 8, 100, 128
rational process, 118
reach of law, 126
reading, 139
reason, 132
reasonable doubt, 197, 209, 220, 231
reasonable persons, 99
reasoning, 24
rebate, 83
rebellion, 60, 232
recordmaking, 14
redress, 6

reformation, 200
regulation, 7–8, 51, 81, 117, 124, 132, 148
  governmental regulations, 93, 139, 174
  regulations, 6, 9, 15, 86, 108, 110, 152, 170,
    179, 222
    state regulations, 155
  regulatory legislation, 8
  regulatory tax, 170
  state regulation, 173
religion, 13, 34, 48, 88, 152, 154–165, 173
  comparative religion, 164
  free religion, 133, 161
  freedom of religion, 153, 155–156
  religions, 159
religious, 238
  religious adherent, 162
  religious beliefs, 152, 233, 238
  religious believers, 155
  religious convictions, 153, 155
  religious differences, 153
  religious diversity, 158
  religious doctrines, 155
  religious documents, 165
  religious freedom, 157
    religious freedoms, 155
  religious indoctrination, 160
  religious organizations, 159
  religious persecution, 156
  religious practice, 233
  religious teachings, 155
  religious training, 159
  religious worship, 128
remand, 36
remedy
  judicial remedies, 46, 50–51, 65, 67, 71, 88, 96,
    107, 120, 128, 138, 242
    judicial remedy, 38, 40
  statutory remedies, 26
removal, 17
reporter, 141
  reporters, 149
reporting, 129, 133
representation, 105
representative body, 227
representative branches, 69
representative democracy, 43, 80, 99
representative government, 12–13, 84, 100, 147
representatives, 10, 12, 75–76, 90
  legislative representatives, 88
repression, 131
republic, 25, 59, 77, 131, 227
republican government, 74, 101

reputation, 86, 143, 149, 177, 199
research, 239
resources, 44, 102
responsibilities, 229
restraint
  arbitrary restraint, 170
  bodily restraint, 171, 175
  physical restraint, 169
  prior restraint, 131
restrictions, 186
retaliation, 200
retribution, 211
revenue, 81, 133
  public revenue, 87
reversal, 204
revolution, 103
right, 176, 178–180, 183, 189, 207
  basic right, 232
  constitutional right, 204
  right of dominion, 226
  right to a speedy trial, 210
  right to be heard, 191
  right to counsel, 192, 203, 211
  right to die, 99, 111, 127, 187
  right to jury, 132
  right to know, 141
  right to speak, 136
  right to travel, 187
  right to work, 170, 175
rights, 3, 96, 102, 132
  absolute rights, 135
  basic rights, 140
  belligerent rights, 226
  cardinal rights, 171
  citizens' rights, 6
  civil rights, 55, 103, 114–115
  constitutional rights, 11, 40, 43, 45, 65, 79, 84,
      97, 100, 104, 106, 111, 123, 127–129, 137,
      139–140, 173, 176–177, 179, 187–189, 192,
      196, 202–203, 229
  enumerated rights, 184, 187
  equal rights, 114–115, 170
  federal rights, 53
  fundamental rights, 6, 123, 138
  gender rights, 125
  human rights, 173
  individual rights, 40, 221, 225
  infringement, 171
  legal rights, 192
  majority rights, 121
  minority rights, 121
  personal rights, 48

rights (continued)
  political rights, 103, 167
  practical rights, 170
  private rights, 6, 130
  procedural rights, 116
  protected rights, 128
  property rights, 84, 114–116, 119, 122, 178
  social rights, 79
  societal rights, 126
  state rights, 155
    states' rights, 15, 51, 64, 103, 111, 246
  statutory rights, 173
  substantial rights, 170
  unalienable rights, 122
  unremunerated rights, 187
  victims' rights, 219
  voting rights, 95
rights and privileges, 58, 226
rights of man, 230
riot, 202
ripeness, 36
risks, 207
risk of harm, 100
Roe, 49, 109, 183
roundup, 211
rule, 22
  exclusionary rule, 213, 215, 220
  rule of law, 30, 39, 44, 67, 74, 82, 152, 168,
      176, 211
rules, 119
  constitutional rules, 70
  procedural rules, 222
  rules of evidence, 246
  subordinate rules, 7
  substantive rules, 222
  technical rules, 28

sacrilegious, 157
safeguards, 170
safety, 75, 139, 189, 200, 239
  national safety, 141
sanctions, 13
school, 86, 124, 163, 243
  public school, 164–165, 215
    public schools, 41, 48, 94, 121
  public school teacher, 157
    public school teachers, 171
  school administrators, 248
  school boards, 121
  school officials, 124
  school policy, 53
  school prayer, 164

school *(continued)*
  schoolchild, 214
  schoolchildren, 165
  schools, 99, 107, 120, 241–212, 246, 248
    law schools, 247
    public schools, 41, 48, 157, 165
    sectarian schools, 166
science, 9, 114, 127, 159, 190, 200, 206, 245–246
search, 98, 198, 207–208
  search and seizure, 200
  search warrant, 198, 207–208
searches, 176
  governmental searches, 222
second-class citizenship, 138
secrecy, 19–20, 180, 231, 233
sect, 152
sectarian, 160, 165
  sectarian schools, 166
secular, 163
security, 20, 70, 77, 82, 232
  domestic security, 42, 178
  individual security, 190
  institutional security, 216
  personal security, 207
segregation, 115, 118, 121
  racial segregation, 120
seizure, 198, 208
  seizures, 176, 219
self-interest, 196
self-restraint, 31
Senate, 17, 158
sentencer, 218
sentencing, 216, 220
  mandatory sentencing, 216
  sentencing authority, 219–220
  sentencing decisions, 219
  sentencing options, 211
separation of powers, 6, 8–9, 12–15, 20, 26, 31, 40–42, 50, 57, 63, 65–67, 69–73, 96, 98, 230, 232
sequestration, 202
serious injury, 215
service, 145
servitude, 169
  involuntary servitude, 169, 227
Seventeenth Amendment, 88
severability, 7
sex, 240
  same sex, 247
  sex crimes, 216
  sexual harassment, 247
  sexual intercourse, 125

sex *(continued)*
  sexual relations, 178
  sexual violence, 137
  sexual embrace, 142
  sexuality, 248
  sexually abused, 216
  sexually explicit speech, 150
shocks the conscience, 200
sign-language teacher, 166
silence, 134
sin, 162
Sixth Amendment, 193, 204
slavery, 5, 24–25, 102, 119, 167–169, 179, 245
  involuntary servitude, 169, 227
  servitude, 169
slippery slope, 35, 242
slogans, 65
sobriety, 219
social
  social community, 71
  social connections, 226
  social discourse, 145, 148
  social duties, 5
  social engineering, 165
  social equality, 114, 170
  social ill, 242
    social ills, 186
  social impact, 247
  social issues, 91
  social mores, 238
  social objectives, 107
  social order, 184
  social preferences, 111
  social prejudices, 170
  social reform, 89
  social relations, 79
  social rights, 79
  social services, 98
  social standards, 9
  social status, 239
society, 44, 46, 76–77, 86, 90, 94, 96, 139, 144, 171, 184–185, 197, 210–213, 216, 221, 236, 239–240, 244
  civil society, 25
  complex society, 9
  democratic society, 173, 222, 240
  free society, 124, 209
  mass society, 144
  multiracial society, 186
  ordered society, 122
  orderly society, 202

society *(continued)*
  organized society, 172, 211, 214
  political society, 25, 153
societal
  societal concerns, 37
  societal interests, 36, 181
  societal issues, 42, 126
  societal needs, 118
  societal norms, 220
  societal problems, 44
  societal rights, 126
sociology, 9, 114, 122
soldier, 194
soul, 183
sovereign
  sovereignty, 18–19, 24–25, 27, 55, 61, 64, 70,
      72–74, 77–78, 80–81, 84, 92, 102, 104–105,
      108, 110, 112
    state sovereignty, 83, 122
speaker, 136
  speakers, 135
speech, 134–136, 139–140, 144–146, 148–149,
      153–154, 161, 221
  commercial speech, 146, 150–151
  criminal speech, 139
  false speech, 41, 129
  free speech, 33, 41, 93, 107, 129–136, 138–139,
      148–149, 151, 177, 240
  nonobscene speech, 150
  offensive speech, 145
  political speech, 128, 150
  proscriable speech, 150
  sexually explicit speech, 150
Speech and Debate Clause, 10, 12, 13
Spencer, (Herbert), 114
spirit 55, 172
spiritualism, 97
spousal relations, 107
spouse, 244
standards, 7
  standards of fairness, 230
  standards of proof, 209
standing, 47
stare decisis, 30, 34, 49, 72
state, 98, 114, 127, 142, 171, 178, 187, 202
  state action, 215
  state authority, 102
  state autonomy, 27
  state constitutional conventions, 60
  state constitutions, 76, 106, 168
  state courts, 48, 66, 112, 195
  state executive, 214
  state government, 108, 240

state *(continued)*
  state immunity, 83
  state independence, 220
  state interest, 48, 52, 99, 109, 181, 243
    state interests, 110–111
  state law, 35, 118
    state laws, 68, 112, 117, 122
  state legislation, 6, 104
  state legislature, 54
    state legislatures, 65, 68, 86, 92, 101–102,
        106, 128, 164
  state objectives, 117
  state officers, 103
  state officials, 122, 196, 198
  state police, 199
  state policies, 106
  state power, 8, 85, 104
    state powers, 57, 104, 108
  state protection, 125
  state regulation, 107, 173
    state regulations, 155
  state resources, 211
  state responsibility, 197
  state rights, 155
    states' rights, 15, 51, 64, 103, 111
  state sovereignty, 83, 122
  state statutes, 48
  states, 3–6, 18, 24, 26, 28, 41, 44–45, 55–56, 58,
      73–74, 76–77, 79–80, 83–84, 86, 89–90,
      93–94, 96, 99, 102–110, 112, 115, 117–119,
      121–122, 126, 138–139, 161–162, 173, 175,
      177, 179, 181–182, 184, 187, 200, 226, 237,
      239, 244–245, 248
statehood, 103–104
state-sponsored torture, 221
statistical technique, 122
statistics, 186
statute, 8, 9, 11
  statutes, 9, 30, 31, 32, 45
statutory
  statutory ambiguity, 197
  statutory authority, 32
  statutory command, 9
  statutory construction, 9, 13, 23, 26, 31, 32,
      45, 237
  statutory discrimination, 117
  statutory history, 125
  statutory implementation, 23, 82
  statutory intent, 8–9, 12, 16, 45, 63, 97, 125,
      139, 197
  statutory interpretation, 5, 8–9, 16, 26, 29,
      31–33, 35, 38, 44–45, 49, 52, 81, 97, 160,
      195

statutory *(continued)*
  statutory language, 11, 26, 191
  statutory legitimacy, 108
  statutory limitations, 111
  statutory overreaching, 27
  statutory purpose, 38
  statutory remedies, 26
  statutory requirements, 45
  statutory rights, 173
  statutory significance, 9
stealing, 141
stereotypes, 186
sterilization, 173
strict construction, 56, 71
strict interpretation, 59
students, 53, 138, 164, 217, 241–242, 246
  law students, 115
style, 140
subject matter, 146
subordinate official, 84
subordinate rules, 7
subpoena, 18
  subpoenas, 11
subsidies, 128
subversive, 5
suffrage, 76, 80
suicide, 99, 111
superior officers, 194
suppression, 150, 194
  suppression hearings, 213
supreme being, 159
supreme law, 104
surveillance, 42, 87, 179, 192, 216
  electronic surveillance, 205
  police surveillance, 177
suspect, 204
swearing, 140
sword, 78
symbolism, 92–93, 98, 110

taking doctrine, 51
takings, 244
talents, 167
taste, 140
  tastes, 142
tax, 83
  income tax, 87, 162
  property tax, 91
  regulatory tax, 170
  taxation, 7, 50, 75, 79, 81–83, 87, 91, 102–103, 120, 133, 154, 156, 162
  taxpayers, 69, 82, 87
  tax compliance, 87

tax *(continued)*
  tax exemptions, 159
  tax immunity, 83
  tax liability, 87
teacher, 86
  teachers, 53, 87, 94, 107, 164, 217, 242, 248
    public school teacher, 157
      public school teachers, 171
teaching, 154, 248
technology, 134, 137, 217, 239
teenage pregnancy, 125
telephone, 175
television, 136–137, 203
  courtroom television, 203
temptation, 123
Tenth Amendment, 64, 110, 210
terminally ill, 99
territories, 75, 226
  territory, 64, 81, 84
terror, 89
testify, 11, 219
testimony, 13, 192–193, 197–198
textbooks, 159
textual problems, 52
Thanksgiving, 164
theology, 162
theories, 28
Thirteenth Amendment, 227
thought, 34, 149
  freedom of thought, 174
  thoughts, 87, 107, 142, 190
threats, 89, 139
tort law, 71
torture, 198
  state-sponsored torture, 221
totalitarian, 208
  totalitarianism, 96, 138
trade, 243
tradename, 146
tradition, 50, 69, 111, 115
  legal tradition, 10
  traditions, 29
traffic laws, 200
traitors, 224
tranquility, 115
transcript, 134
trash, 184
travel, 191, 244
  right to travel, 187
treason, 196, 226, 231, 235
treasury notes, 77–78
treaties, 227–228, 234
treaty, 227

treaty *(continued)*
  treaty language, 227
trial, 191, 193–194, 196–197, 203, 211
  criminal trial, 37, 134, 138, 203, 206, 213, 219
    criminal trials, 205
  fair trial, 191, 202, 230
  pretrial publicity, 147
  public trial, 134
  retrial, 192, 212
  right to a speedy trial, 210
  trial arena, 203
  trial courts, 138
  trial process, 203
  trials, 136–137, 147, 192
tribunal, 192, 197
  common tribunal, 225
troop morale, 233
trust, 85, 199, 233
truth, 25, 136, 145, 192, 197, 206, 240
  political truth, 3
tyrannies, 131
  tyranny, 63, 68, 76, 79, 150, 193

unconstitutional laws, 61
unconstitutional principles, 229
undesirables, 211
uniformity, 58–59, 119, 142, 233
union, 3, 58, 103, 226
  perpetual union, 103
United States, 84, 103
unity, 83
unrestrained abuses, 172
untruths, 129
utterance, 132
  utterances, 134, 136

vagrancy, 211
value, 77–78, 145, 237
  probative value, 201
  values, 71, 90, 94, 147, 175, 183
vengeance, 200
veniremen, 207
verdict, 194
vicarious liability, 247
vice president, 168
vices, 239
victim, 214–215
  victim impact evidence, 220
  victm impact statement, 218
  victim's family, 218
  victims' rights, 219

victims, 168, 193, 202, 204, 207
  minor victims, 216
viewpoints, 128, 146
vigilante justice, 211
violence, 80, 132, 139, 207
  gun violence, 246
  sexual violence, 137
violent crime, 199
violent self–help, 204
virtue, 241
  virtues, 94, 239
voter qualifications, 119
voters, 93
voting, 88–90, 106
  voting rights, 95
vulgarity, 140

waiver, 223
war, 77–78, 162, 194, 224, 226–229
  declaration of war, 226
  warfare, 224
  war–making branches, 228
  war power, 229, 231
warrant, 198
  arrest warrant, 198
  search warrant, 198, 205, 217
  warrants, 205
Washington, (George), 77, 164
wealth, 119
weapons, 207
welfare, 123
  economic welfare, 83
  general welfare, 92, 108
  public welfare, 81, 84, 86, 104–105, 107, 135,
    171, 173
  welfare administration, 107
western world, 80
white persons, 115
white race, 226
wife, 236, 244
willful, 237
will of the people, 131
wired, 210
wiretap, 190
  wiretapping, 141
wisdom, 4, 6, 19, 36, 39, 76, 99, 106, 116
  judicial wisdom, 119, 242
  legislative wisdom, 65
witness, 13, 192, 195, 203, 211–212
  witnesses, 11, 38, 137–138, 168, 197, 206, 213,
    219

woman, 182
  womanhood, 169
women, 111, 186, 239
  poor women, 182
  young women, 125
words, 10, 42, 55, 62
  fighting words, 150, 153
work environment, 117
workplace
  hostile workplace, 247
  workplace behavior, 247

worship, 152, 162,
  171
  religious worship,
  128
writ of assistance, 198
writers, 149
wrongdoing, 214

xenophobia, 232

youths, 144

About the Author

Christopher A. Anzalone is the former editor of a legal studies publishing program at an educational publishing house. He lives in upstate New York with his wife and three children.